# confronting al qaeda

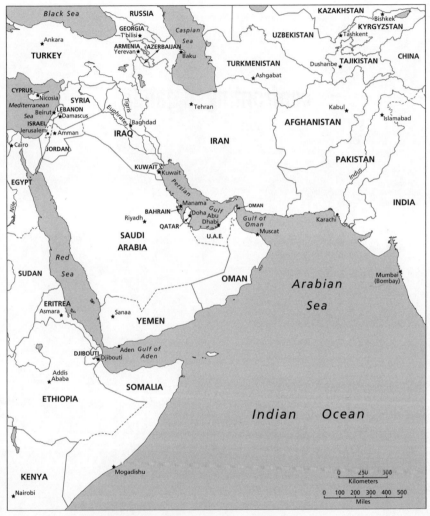

*Core Zone of U.S.-Al Qaeda Conflict*

# confronting al qaeda

## New Strategies to Combat Terrorism

KEVIN McGRATH

NAVAL INSTITUTE PRESS
*Annapolis, Maryland*

Naval Institute Press
291 Wood Road
Annapolis, MD 21402

Library of Congress Cataloging-in-Publication Data

McGrath, Kevin
 Confronting Al Qaeda : new strategies to combat terrorism / Kevin McGrath.
   p. cm.
 Includes bibliographical references and index.
 ISBN 978-1-59114-503-5 (hbk.)
 1. Qaida (Organization) 2. War on Terrorism, 2001-2009. 3. Terrorism   Prevention.
 4. United States—Foreign relations—21st century. 5. United States—History, Military—
21st century.—I. Title.
 HV6432.5.Q2M42 2011
 363.325'160973—dc22

                                                    2011005305

Printed in the United States of America.

19 18 17 16 15 14 13 12 11     9 8 7 6 5 4 3 2 1
First printing

This book is dedicated to all, both civilian and military,
who choose to commit to and give of themselves
to the fight against Al Qaeda.

# Contents

# Abbreviations

| | |
|---|---|
| AFP | Agence France-Presse |
| ALP | Afghan Local Police |
| AMISOM | African Union Mission in Somalia |
| ANA | Afghan National Army |
| ANP | Afghan National Police |
| AQAP | Al Qaeda in the Arabian Peninsula |
| AQI | Al Qaeda in Iraq |
| ATA | Afghanistan Transitional Authority |
| CBO | Congressional Budget Office |
| CIA | Central Intelligence Agency |
| CTIC | Counterterrorist Intelligence Center |
| DNI | Director of National Intelligence |
| DoD | Department of Defense |
| EFP | explosively formed projectile |
| EU | European Union |
| FATA | Federally Administered Tribal Areas (Pakistan) |
| FATF | Financial Action Task Force |
| GAO | Government Accountability Office |
| GDP | gross domestic product |
| GIA | Armed Islamic Group (Algeria) |
| GSPC | Salafist Group for Preaching and Combat (Algeria) |
| HiG | Hezb-e-Islami/Gulbuddin (Afghanistan) |
| HVT | high-value target |
| IAEA | International Atomic Energy Agency |
| ICBM | intercontinental ballistic missile |
| IED | improvised explosive device |
| IRA | Irish Republican Army |
| IRGC | Iranian Revolutionary Guard Corps |
| IRI | International Republican Institute |
| ISAF | International Security Assistance Force (NATO) |
| ISI | Inter-Services Intelligence Directorate (Pakistan) |
| JSOC | Joint Special Operations Command |
| KP | Khyber Pakhtunkhwa (formerly NWFP) |
| NATO | North Atlantic Treaty Organization |
| NGO | nongovernmental organization |
| NIE | National Intelligence Estimate |

| | |
|---|---|
| NPT | Nuclear Non-Proliferation Treaty |
| NSA | National Security Agency |
| NSC | National Security Council |
| NWFP | North-West Frontier Province (Pakistan), now known as Khyber Pakhtunkhwa |
| PRT | Provincial Reconstruction Team (Afghanistan) |
| PTDT | Partnership to Defeat Terrorism |
| SOF | Special Operations Forces |
| START | Study of Terrorism and Responses to Terrorism (University of Maryland consortium) |
| STRATCOM | United States Strategic Command |
| TFT | Terror Free Tomorrow |
| TTP | Tehrik-e-Taliban Pakistan (Pakistani Taliban) |
| UAE | United Arab Emirates |
| UN | United Nations |
| UNSC | United Nations Security Council |
| UPI | United Press International |
| USAID | U.S. Agency for International Development |
| USA PATRIOT | Uniting and Strengthening America by Providing Appropriate Tools Required to Intercept and Obstruct Terrorism |
| WMD | weapons of mass destruction |

# Acknowledgments

This book is the result of a collaborative effort of supporting people, without whom nothing of any real value would have been accomplished. I would particularly like to thank my dissertation committee, whose commentary transformed spirited blathering into a coherent argument and formed the basis of this work. I would also like to thank some truly elite colleagues—Paul, Ollie, Kevin, Lantz, Travis, KB, Big H, Little H, MOAM, KC, Lisa, Maximum Leader, Admiral Turner, Russ, Will, Jose, George, and Mike, among others. I have learned a tremendous amount, both professional and personal, from these colleagues, friends, and mentors. Their influence is present throughout this work, and I owe them a tremendous debt, both professional and personal. I would also like to thank the family and friends who kept me sane during this long project. Lastly, I would also like to thank the Naval Institute Press, without whose indulgences this project never would have come into being.

# Introduction

*When people are entering upon a war they do things the wrong way round. Action comes first, and it is only when they have already suffered that they begin to think.*

—Thucydides

Upon returning from my third trip to Afghanistan, a friend posed an expected question. "How are things going over there? Is Al Qaeda almost done?" He received an unexpected answer: "America is still in the first phase of its 9/11 response. The United States' fight with Al Qaeda, and developing a long-term U.S. strategy to win it, still has a long way to go."

As noted by the 9/11 Commission: "The United States did not, before 9/11, adopt as a clear strategic objective the elimination of Al Qaeda." Unhindered by U.S. efforts, Al Qaeda became steadily more potent during the 1990s as U.S. attention focused on Cold War detritus—Yugoslavia's breakup, dual containment in the Gulf, securing the Soviet nuclear arsenal, debating the role of NATO, and Balkan peacekeeping missions to establish new international norms. From September 11 until the present, however, U. S. domestic and foreign policy remains unswervingly confronted by a critical question: How does the United States defeat Al Qaeda, a non-state transnational terrorist entity espousing militant political Islam, without losing its democratic character?

Despite the absence of any major attacks on U.S. soil since 9/11, this question cannot be ignored. Al Qaeda is the leading embodiment and organizer of a global jihadist movement comprised of the over one hundred militant political Islamist movements to emerge since the 1980s. The Al Qaeda–published "Wills of the Washington and New York Battle Martyrs" states that the 9/11 attacks were but the start. Though Al Qaeda has not yet achieved another 9/11-scale success against the United States, the post-9/11 annual increase in Al Qaeda–connected terrorist attacks against the United States and its allies shows no signs of abating.[1]

The U.S. and international response to Al Qaeda will be crucial to determining the trajectory of both existing and emerging groups. If Al Qaeda is discredited and destroyed, it will signal to other would-be terrorists the consequences of executing mass casualty attacks. If Al Qaeda thrives, more groups are likely to emulate it.

This book's central contention is that the failure to quickly subdue Al Qaeda in the U.S.-led international effort following 9/11 is a result of the U.S. government's failure to place sufficient emphasis on the rival and conflicting political agendas of the United States and Al Qaeda. In other words, the heavy emphasis on force and coercion-oriented hard-power efforts to the near exclusion of politically-oriented soft-power ones weakened the United States' ability to effectively counter Al Qaeda. Instead of comprehensively addressing the Al Qaeda phenomenon by both neutering the group's hard-power capabilities and blunting its political appeal by engaging it in a manner consistent with traditional U.S. political values and foreign policy emphases—most notably the rule of law, a participatory political system emphasizing international institutions, and democratic values, such as human rights—the Bush administration approach, which the Obama administration has yet to fundamentally alter as of 2011, has only partially weakened Al Qaeda's organizational capacity while fanning Al Qaeda's political appeal at unbounded and ever-increasing military, economic, and political cost to the United States.

Al Qaeda's continued menace a decade after 9/11 strongly indicates that hard power is necessary. Al Qaeda and its allies have successfully attacked U.S. allies throughout Europe. Al Qaeda and its allies have attempted multiple terrorist attacks against the U.S. homeland. Only efforts to capture or kill terrorist perpetrators by the United States and allied governments have prevented even worse violence.

Yet hard power, while necessary, is not a sufficient approach. The underlying political conflict of the U.S.-Al Qaeda struggle is Al Qaeda's jugular. This political conflict alone is the primary inspiration for Al Qaeda to increase its membership, the primary link to sustain its cohesiveness within an international polyglot membership, the primary guide for its actions, and the fundamental means for it to appeal to nonmembers for assistance.

Continuing the original post 9/11 U.S. strategy can, at best, only achieve a holding action. The United States must simultaneously manipulate the struggle's political factors as it presses Al Qaeda organizationally through force. This will enable the United States to not only blunt Al Qaeda's hard-power efforts against it, but it will also enable the United States to go on the strategic offensive to subdue the Al Qaeda threat and manage it at acceptable cost while keeping it in perspective with competing U.S. interests.

## BACKGROUND

Support for the United States swelled from both foreign governments and foreign publics in the wake of the September 11 attacks. Not only did traditional allies rally to the U.S. cause, but "even countries with which the United States has had tense and often confrontational relationships, such as Iran, which remains on the State Department's list of 'terrorist states,' expressed unusual sympathy with the United States' pain. Iran's president at the time, Mohammad Khatami, immediately issued a condemnation of 'the terrorist attacks' and expressed 'deep sorrow and sympathy' for the victims. Syria's young President Bashar al-Assad sent a letter of condolence to President George W. Bush strongly condemning the terror attacks."[2] The United States had moral and political authority as a victim. The world's states and their publics overwhelmingly stood behind the United States on the cusp of its 9/11 response to destroy Al Qaeda, which at that time was effectively unbloodied and at its peak.

Four key Bush administration decisions governed the U.S. 9/11 response:[3]

First, President Bush drew a distinction between Al Qaeda and Islam writ large. He emphasized that bin Laden's "extremism . . . has been rejected by Muslim scholars." Ideologically, President Bush isolated and stigmatized Al Qaeda.

Second, President Bush specified America's post-9/11 opposition by declaring the enemy to be "a radical network of terrorists, and every government that supports them." For the first time, Al Qaeda's terrorism included nation-states. No foreign entity, most notably Afghanistan under the Taliban's regime, was off-limits to a U.S. response. Organizationally, President Bush isolated and stigmatized Al Qaeda and denied it neutral ground in which to hide by declaring that, from the U.S. perspective, "either you are with us, or you are with the terrorists."

Third, President Bush ruled out politically engaging Al Qaeda's agenda. President Bush elaborated that "America was targeted for attack because we're the brightest beacon of freedom . . . in the world. . . . The terrorists who attacked our country on September 11, 2001, were not protesting our policies. They were protesting our existence."[4] This stance placed the onus for any political change upon Al Qaeda. Amid Al Qaeda's unswerving efforts to kill innocent Americans as a tool to redressing the political grievances for which it held the United States responsible, all U.S. effort would be devoted to killing, capturing, and otherwise disrupting Al Qaeda's membership and their activities. The U.S.-Al Qaeda struggle would be a martial contest.

Fourth, President Bush linked Al Qaeda's terrorism to other U.S. interests and security challenges, most notably weapons of mass destruction by proclaiming Iran, Iraq, and North Korea an "axis of evil." The 9/11 attacks proved Al Qaeda and its associates were focused U.S. enemies. If the "axis of evil" members obtained weapons of mass destruction, these states, all U.S. enemies, would have the ability to give them to Al Qaeda terrorists. Following the logic of "the enemy of my enemy is my friend," there was no reason not to conclude that governments opposed to the United States and possessing the worst weapons would not collude with terrorists harboring the worst of intentions toward the United States.

These four decisions had profound implications:

Philosophically, the United States adopted a preemptive focus. For the first time since World War II, the United States would espouse a foreign policy doctrine of proactively employing force as it saw fit to prevent potential threats from ever materializing. Instead of either using force as a last resort in the face of a clear and present danger or, in an effort to less confrontationally pursue peace through strength, rely upon the threat of an overwhelming and destructive U.S. response to deter aggressors, the United States announced it now considered itself bound only by its own judgment.

Politically, the United States tarred Iraq, Iran, and North Korea with the stigma of Al Qaeda. Despite a lack of any substantive connections, these "axis of evil" adversaries were now directly linked to a U.S. foe that had just committed the most devastating terrorist attack in U.S. history. Their political vulnerability, both internationally and domestically with the U.S. public, rose dramatically.

Strategically, the United States unified some of its leading and most potent antagonists. The combination of a new U.S. foreign policy doctrine calling for the proactive use of military power, a clearly delineated target set of U.S. enemies associated with terrorists who had just struck the U.S. homeland, and a willingness by the American public to support military action abroad following 9/11 made vulnerable not just Al Qaeda, but any entity the United States associated with it. Iraq, Iran, and North Korea, disparate entities which previously had little in common apart from a general U.S. antipathy, now had incentives not only to collaborate, either directly or indirectly, but also to actively stymie U.S. interests where vulnerable.

The Bush administration initiated four main post-9/11 U.S. actions under this framework. Contrary to post–Cold War norms, the United States unilaterally deposed Afghanistan's Taliban regime that provided Al Qaeda sanctuary by only cursorily involving the United Nations and key allies. Contravening international law, and in spite of outright allied opposition, the United States sidestepped UN approval and unilaterally invaded Iraq in the name of combating Al Qaeda to deny it potential access to weapons of mass destruction (WMD). Beyond the rule of U.S. law, the United States partnered with select allies around the world to set up a secretive prison and detainment system publicly acknowledged to have violated human rights,[5] a step interwoven with a unilateral practice of secretly detaining and spiriting prisoners away to these jails and to allied states with checkered human rights records to submit suspects to interrogations not permissible under U.S. law. Lastly, the United States took an increasingly hostile posture toward Iran, citing Iran's nuclear efforts, its involvement in Iraq, and Iran's potential to aid terrorists if it acquired WMD.

In the eyes of both other states and the world's publics, traditional U.S. political values and foreign policy emphases—the rule of law, a participatory political system emphasizing the importance of international institutions, and democratic values, such as human rights—provide legitimacy to U.S. political leadership. Al Qaeda is directly challenging U.S. legitimacy by attempting to lead a global militant Islamist insurgency against the U.S.-led world system.[6] Increasing U.S. legitimacy is thus crucial to combating and defeating Al Qaeda.

Global public perception, however, is that the U.S. response to 9/11 significantly violated traditional pillars of U.S. foreign policy, and U.S. world standing fell dramatically. Even setting aside the negative spike stemming from the 2003 U.S. invasion of Iraq, international public support has yet to meaningfully rebound. The United States is no longer generally perceived as a force for good in the world despite its highly publicized campaign to combat Al Qaeda, whose violence and political goals garner low international public support.[7]

The Obama administration, for better and for worse, inherited this starting point. The Obama administration is now obliged to forge a new path magnifying past successes and redressing past weaknesses. It must do so, however, with increasingly scarce political, economic, and military resources.

## THE APPROACH

Devising a new, post–George W. Bush strategy pitting U.S. strengths against Al Qaeda's weaknesses to stymie Al Qaeda's success—its ability to survive as a coherent entity and execute terrorist attacks to further its political agenda—requires assessing Osama bin Laden's Al Qaeda against the four main requirements that make any terrorist entity viable.

First, any terrorist entity must have an ideology manifested in a political agenda designed to redress its grievances. Al Qaeda employs a clear religio-political doctrine to justify and guide its actions as well as recruit and sustain itself. Chapter One delineates Al Qaeda's ideology and agenda as well as the operational dynamics it creates for the U.S.-Al Qaeda struggle.

Second, any terrorist entity must have a strategy consistent with its ideology to enact its political agenda against the state, who is seeking to squelch it. Al Qaeda has a clear strategic plan to implement its religio-political doctrine. After outlining Al Qaeda's strategy in Chapter One, Chapter Two goes on to review not only the post-9/11 U.S. response to Al Qaeda, but also the evolution of both U.S. and Al Qaeda strategies resulting from their respective thrusts and counter-thrusts throughout the Bush administration.

Third, any terrorist entity must have an organizational structure able to survive state efforts to eradicate it. Al Qaeda's command and control arrangements as well as its tactics, techniques, and procedures have allowed it to execute terrorist acts despite a global effort to destroy it. Chapter Three describes Al Qaeda's organizational capacity and modus operandi following the post-9/11 U.S. response.

Fourth, any terrorist organization must have resources, which, in practical terms, means cash. Al Qaeda acquires, transfers, and expends money to finance its terrorist activities. Chapter Three also explicates this issue.

Looking toward the future, Chapter Four addresses the U.S.-Al Qaeda struggle's underlying political conflict that U.S. policy makers have heretofore neglected. The gap between the two actors' competing political agendas, as well as how they pursue them, is highlighted. Going one step further, this chapter explores how these disconnects translate into operational advantages and disadvantages for both the United States and Al Qaeda.

With this political and operational baseline, the remainder of this book outlines and assesses the chief pivot points the Obama administration's anti–Al Qaeda efforts will confront. In Chapters Five through Eight, which address Iraq, Iran, Pakistan, and Afghanistan respectively, the results of the Bush administration's actions and the Obama administration's initial steps are reviewed. Impending decision points are then identified and assessed.

The conclusion provides macro-level recommendations. This chapter not only speaks to specific choices identified in each of the Obama administration's chief decision points against Al Qaeda, but it also submits general policy guidelines. Placing Al Qaeda in context with competing U.S. security policy policies, and larger U.S. foreign policy, is addressed.

## CONCLUSION

The Bush administration's immediate response to 9/11 has severely damaged Al Qaeda. Al Qaeda's state sanctuary has been destroyed. Al Qaeda's training camps, through which in the 1990s as many as 20,000 fighters may have passed, no longer operate unhindered. Its funding streams have been severely hampered. Thousands of operatives have been killed or detained, and public estimates cite as few as four hundred hard-core followers remaining under Osama bin Laden's immediate purview. Most significantly, Al Qaeda has been unable to successfully execute large-scale terrorist attacks.[8]

Al Qaeda, however, has not been vanquished. Multiple new Al Qaeda franchises have opened in Europe, North Africa, and the Middle East. A steady stream of volunteers continues to replenish Al Qaeda's personnel losses. Significant attacks have been launched, such as the Madrid train bombing that caused Spain to withdraw from Iraq, and major new assaults, such as a foiled attempt by Al Qaeda to simultaneously down ten airplanes, continue to be planned.

The United States cannot escape Al Qaeda's ire. So long as the United States remains a key player on the world stage, it will be a target. So long as the United States remains an open and free society, it will always be vulnerable.

Al Qaeda alone possesses both the will and the ability to strike the U.S. homeland in order to influence U.S. politics domestically and impact U.S. interests abroad through violence. Its stated goals to reshape the international system remain unmet, and they will almost certainly never be achieved. Nonetheless, Al Qaeda has vowed to continue attacking until it succeeds.

The challenge now before the United States is how to transition from a force-oriented, resource-intensive push designed to inflict short-term damage and alleviate an immediate danger to a more viable long-term strategy that stays within the United States' military and economic capacity while still pursuing other important U.S. interests. The immediate post-9/11 U.S. response—two major wars with no clear end in sight, costing thousands of U.S. lives and over $1 trillion—is not sustainable. Having been reduced, the threat posed by Al Qaeda must now be managed.

This book suggests the answer to successfully managing the Al Qaeda threat over time is found in correctly calibrating the balance between manipulating the politics surrounding the U.S.-Al Qaeda struggle (soft power) and the continued selective application of force and coercion (hard power). Traditional U.S. political values and foreign policy emphases and approaches, previously minimized by the Bush administration, must take a stronger role in both U.S. strategic decision-making calculations as well as their execution. Such an approach defends the U.S. political system from terrorism's subversion, and it furthers U.S. national advantage by undercutting Al Qaeda and magnifying the impact of U.S. hard-power efforts.

# Chapter 1

# The Framework of the U.S.-Al Qaeda Struggle

*If theory without policy is for academics, then policy without theory is only for gamblers.*

—J. Mayone Stycos

Neither terrorism in general, nor Al Qaeda in particular, constitutes irrational violence. Al Qaeda, the lead decision-making authority of the greater jihadist movement, opts for terrorism over alternative options as a tactic to influence its political engagement with the United States in pursuit of its agenda.[1] Such a consistent internal logic means systematic scrutiny of Al Qaeda, its actions, and the greater U.S.-Al Qaeda conflict can forge a deeper understanding.

The Bush approach, though sufficient for the initial U.S. counterattack, is highly unlikely to yield further substantial gains. The heavy post-9/11 U.S. emphasis on hard power—the coercive military, intelligence, and legal means of the state—has reduced Al Qaeda's organizational capacity for violence. The near-exclusion of soft power, however—the political values, interests, and nature of the actors—has neglected the U.S.-Al Qaeda conflict's inherent political dimension that motivates and governs these political actors. Al Qaeda thus survives as a potent threat.

Reviewing the four key aspects of any terrorism conflict in the U.S.-Al Qaeda context to determine which are fungible yields an analytic framework. This will identify not only Al Qaeda's strengths and vulnerabilities but also those of the United States. This understanding can then form a cornerstone to devise a strategy pitting U.S. strengths against Al Qaeda's weaknesses while simultaneously defending U.S. vulnerabilities.

## WHO ARE THE PARTICIPANTS?

Two main antagonists are in the fight. The United States, backed by a loose coalition of similar allied states, is engaged against Al Qaeda, which is backed by a loose coalition of similar allied non-state terrorist groups.[2] These antagonists have markedly differing structures, means of cohesion, and political traditions— all of which provide the United States and Al Qaeda with very incongruent strengths and vulnerabilities.

The twenty-first century United States is an established, self-perpetuating nation. This entity is a polyarchy of power administering itself via representative democracy. Universally recognized territorial sovereignty and integrity are its tangible, enabling foundation.

Al Qaeda, on the other hand, is a relatively recently created transnational terrorist group, composed of members from every Muslim society, and dependent upon external recruitment for survival. It is structured as a network—multiple decentralized nodes (Osama bin Laden's Al Qaeda central in Pakistan, Al Qaeda in the Arabian Peninsula [AQAP], etc.)—linked together primarily by loose horizontal ties, not vertical integration, wherein authority is heavily delegated and all work in concert toward the same common purpose.[3] Al Qaeda has no universally recognized territorial sovereignty or integrity.

Directly disrupting U.S. internal structure is very difficult. It is uniquely threatened only by another entity compromising U.S. territorial sovereignty and integrity. As of the twenty-first century, no credible threat exists or is ever likely.

It is also exceptionally difficult to disrupt Al Qaeda's structure. It is uniquely threatened only by another entity capturing or killing all of its members. Al Qaeda's network structure, however, makes it very hard to eradicate it in its entirety even if one part of it is destroyed.

With both parties safely ensconced within durable structures, their respective purposes dovetail into conflict. The United States seeks to be self-governing and live according to its desired political character, which includes personal liberties, private economic activity, and limited government, in pursuit of its self-defined interests. The U.S. political character, however, because it is a reflection of popular will in a free society, is open to change, and this provides a window of vulnerability.

The practical alternative for U.S. rivals unable to threaten the U.S. structure is to pursue indirect efforts to manipulate the U.S. public to force political change. Al Qaeda's self-selected purpose capitalizes on this vulnerability in that it seeks to exploit its opponents' structures to induce political change in other actors in pursuit of its political agenda, which it is unable to implement on its own. Political stimulus via terrorism is virtually guaranteed to induce at least some change in Al Qaeda's opponents, though that change may not be what Al Qaeda had planned. The combination of Al Qaeda furthering its agenda by relatively easily executed political violence, whose impact can easily be spread by mass media, and using religious and cultural factors to justify its agenda only makes it even more dangerous and difficult to subdue.

Paradoxically, the United States' continued cohesiveness and viability as a coherent political entity is not especially threatened despite its inherent and systemic vulnerability. The United States, as a modern nation-state, has multiple, mutually reinforcing social, political, and economic bonds. The U.S. polyarchy of power makes the United States more resilient as the impact of a terrorist attack is compartmented because the various dimensions of U.S. unity and strength are segregated and dispersed.

The main risk is that the American people, or their government, will renounce the U.S. political essence and choose to abandon uniquely U.S. political processes, and the political values with which those processes are imbued and which they reflect. Because of the magnitude and nature of such a decision, it is not only unlikely to be taken lightly, but it will also be difficult to execute in a meaningful and sustained fashion, though lesser short-term digressions are certainly possible. Internal unity supporting a particular political agenda, as compared to the political system, is not required for the United States to remain a cohesive and viable political entity.

By contrast, Al Qaeda's cohesiveness and continued viability as a coherent political entity is not particularly vulnerable, but it is deeply at risk if endangered. An artificial creation congealed for a particular political purpose from other natural entities, Al Qaeda's political agenda serves as the entity's chief means of both unity and identity as the agenda, not any formal governing process reflective of the participants' wills, governs execution. While this lack of debate ensures focus, such required political purity keeps active membership low as competing, unmet needs and interests are subordinated. When dissent arises, the combination of Al Qaeda's dependence upon its political agenda for unity and identity with the fragmentary, nonhierarchical nature of its network structure means the entity can easily fall apart, which only becomes more likely if it experiences success and circumstance born of weakness no longer dictates choices.

Underlying and flavoring all of these differences are largely mutually exclusive political traditions. Each tradition not only sees itself as the ultimate ideological solution, albeit for different reasons, but each is also a proactive, proselytizing school of thought. The result is perpetual ideological conflict, which enables real-world conflict when married to conflicting interests and disparities in power.

The U.S. political system's ideological origin and guiding framework is Western Europe's Enlightenment. Critical reasoning, science, and humanism trump religious dogma as a guide to life. Representative democracy is the essentially unquestioned expression of governance for these sentiments. Ideologically, the U.S. system's firmly rooted niche in the political spectrum is that of classical liberalism—most notably featuring the rule of law, the individual as the primary unit of the social order, and the individual acquisition and ownership of property.

Al Qaeda's ostensible guiding framework is a line of Islamic jurisprudence stemming from thirteenth-century jurist, intellectual, and political activist Taqi al-Din Ahmad Ibn Taymiyya. He called for a literal interpretation and rigorous implementation of the original sources of sacred guidance. The early Muslim community founded at Medina was held up as the model for an Islamic state. The Quran, the revelation of God, and the Sunnah of the Prophet were to be taken at face value. By purifying Islam's practice to renew and reform society, reformers would be able to regain lost power and glory, which, he assessed, resulted from human error in straying from the identified path of God.

Ibn Taymiyya's vision melded thought with action. He saw an inseparable tie between religion and the state so that the purpose of the state was to rule by religious tenets. He drew distinctions between religion and culture, and religious practice trumped all other concerns. Conflict with anyone not copacetic in the eyes of the adjudicating religious authority—regardless of their ethnic, religious, cultural, familial, or national background—was legitimated.

The stage was set for enduring discord. A sharp divide existed between true believers and all others. Those outside of the circle, either non-Muslims or excommunicated Muslims, were legitimated as possible objects of violence. Crucially, no adjudicating religious authority was specified. When translated to the modern era, the combination of Islam's lack of an official secular-religious divide and its comprehensive and detailed code of conduct emphasizing action, as opposed to the Christian emphasis on belief, positions reformers so motivated for social, political, and economic conflict with a modern international system not dominated by either Islam or its adherents.

In the early twentieth century, Hassan al-Banna, the founder of Egypt's Muslim Brotherhood, and Mawlana Maududi, the founder of Pakistan's Jamaat-e-Islami, took Ibn Taymiyya as their inspiration as they faced the question of how to cope with the challenge of modernity and its impact upon traditional Islamic society. Modern nationalism, which emphasizes a sense of identity based upon factors such as language, tribe, and ethnicity, was challenging the universal, pan-Islamic ideal of the equality and solidarity of all Muslims. In the politico-military realm, which saw European domination throughout the Middle East, Islam appeared to be falling victim to Western imperialism.

These two reformers saw Islam as the alternative to the failures and limits of both Marxism and Western-style capitalism. In their view, Islam is a total, all-encompassing way of life that guides the individual and the community on both a personal and political level. Islam was thus competing not as a means of political, social, and economic organization belonging to a particular faction as a means to gain advantage, but rather as a comprehensive alternative capable of reshaping the world and achieving a just and equitable social order for all. The Quran, the Sunnah of the Prophet, and the early Muslim community are the foundations of Islam and are a guide for daily life. Sharia, Islamic law, is the ideal for a modern Muslim society, and it is independent of Western models. Straying from Islam, and by default relying on the West, is the cause of Muslim decline, and so, conversely, returning to the true path can restore greatness. In this vein, science and technology were to be harnessed, but in an Islamic context that filters out the impact of Western culture to avoid an infection of Westernization and secularization.

Jihad, which differs from war, which is fought for selfish or material reasons, was to be the means to this noble end. Jihad—a momentous and sacred moral struggle to achieve good against a preponderant evil on a personal level, the greater jihad, or in a politico-military manner, the lesser jihad—both individually and collectively, in both ideas and in action, was to Islamize both society and the world. It was to be simultaneously offensive, by attacking opposing subversive alternative principles and ideology, though not the opponents' land, and defensive, for Muslims needed to regain their power to implement their views.

Maududi and al-Banna sought to work within the existing secular world system to achieve evolutionary change. Though initially resistant, both leaders accepted nationalism and democracy, albeit with qualifications consistent with furthering their religio-political principles. In the end, they created the prototypes of contemporary Islamist political parties.

Egyptian theologian and member of the Muslim Brotherhood Sayyid Qutb, who is generally acknowledged to be the godfather of Al Qaeda–style terrorism, radicalized this body of thought. Qutb saw implementing an Islamic government not as an option for which to strive, but as a divine commandment to be realized. Qutb assessed this could only be achieved through violent, revolutionary change. The differences between Islam's tenets and the world system, as perpetuated by powerful vested interests, negated any chance of working within the system.

Qutb did not allow for middle ground. As with Ibn Taymiyya, Qutb divided the world into a camp of the good, that of Islam, and a camp of the bad, which consisted of all others. The West was perceived as a political, economic, and religio-cultural threat. Going one step further, he declared secularized, Westernized Muslim elites atheists and thus subject to obligatory holy war.

Akin to Ibn Taymiyya, Qutb combined thought with action. Drawing upon Maududi, Qutb emphasized the need to create a special vanguard group of true believers. It was to be their privilege and duty to serve as a lighthouse in a sea of non-Islamic ignorance to awaken and lead all true Muslims to the way of God. It was then the duty of all true Muslims to participate in the struggle against injustice and evil.[4]

Politically, even though Al Qaeda's interpretation of Islam has been decisively rejected everywhere, with the possible exception of the Taliban's Afghanistan, it exists as an enduring and vibrant minority view in virtually all Muslim societies. Unfortunately, a combination of Al Qaeda's notoriety from its violence and observers' ignorance has at least partially colored peaceful Islamic political activism with Al Qaeda's image. Al Qaeda, in turn, can and does usurp the image, if not actual resources and political support, of these nonmilitant Islamic political activists to artificially inflate its strength.

Operationally, Al Qaeda engages a U.S.-led world order as the leader of a global militant Islamic insurgency. An insurgency is herein defined as "a struggle between a non-ruling group and the ruling authorities in which the non-ruling group consciously uses political resources (e.g., organizational expertise, propaganda, and demonstrations) and violence to destroy, reformulate or sustain the basis of legitimacy of one or more aspects of politics."[5] As bin Laden stated just after 9/11, "I must say that my duty is just to awaken Muslims to tell them as to what is good for them and what is not." As such, Al Qaeda will never surrender to U.S. "crimes and vices," and so the U.S.-Al Qaeda conflict is a fight to the finish.[6]

Unlike in offensive jihad, which is meant to bring new lands under Muslim control as well as convert new adherents to Islam, Al Qaeda claims not without some justification that Muslims as a people, Muslim lands, and Islam as a faith have all been besieged by non-Muslims led by the United States and its allies.[7] Bin Laden calls upon the world's Muslims to recognize this fact and respond. Osama bin Laden is "inciting others to join, not because he orders them to, but because God has ordered them to do so in what He revealed in the Koran."[8]

Unlike in an offensive jihad, a defensive jihad does not require a universally acknowledged leader to declare it. No approving authority is necessary, and any secular or clerical authority that hinders a response against external aggression is in the wrong. Despite not being an educated Islamic scholar, bin Laden is not doctrinally precluded.

"The historical model for such action is the medieval hero Saladin who, though only a regional commander, organized and led a successful defense against the armies of the second Crusade." Osama bin Laden, a noted leader in the successful anti-Soviet jihad, is of the same mold. His high personal standing permits him to speak to the Muslim, particularly the Arab, world. His words are not drenched in hypocrisy, and they are taken as genuine. To those positively disposed, that bin Laden is so actively hunted by the United States not only proves his potency at unsettling an immoral world order, but it also vindicates the righteousness of his cause and the likelihood of his ultimate triumph.[9]

Unlike in offensive jihad, defensive jihad is a personal responsibility, and so every Muslim must contribute to the fight as best they are able once Islam—in terms of its people, its land, and the faith—has been attacked. This obligation, at least in theory, cannot be avoided under the rubric of a defensive jihad. Such an individualistic orientation to this mode of religio-political action enables

Al Qaeda to issue a call for defensive jihad and allow self-selecting Muslims to join it with religious justification.

Al Qaeda's agenda and an all-permeating religion are mutually reinforcing. "Each individual faces a fateful decision, one that will decide where he or she spends eternity. If bin Laden's argument is accepted, he or she must take up arms or otherwise support the mujahideen, or face eternal damnation for not performing a duty mandated by God."[10]

The real-world manifestation of Al Qaeda's intellectual pedigree has not been seriously challenged. Secular Muslim governments, particularly in the Middle East, have increasingly persecuted politically active Islamists. These governmental authorities have drawn a distinction, however, between individuals committing unlawful acts threatening the state and the unquestioned moral authority of Islam. The practical result has been to vilify individual regime opponents without vilifying their inspiring cause.

The most likely net result for the United States is a long and enduring conflict. Al Qaeda's religio-political tradition is not only well established, but it will also likely endure even if Al Qaeda is defeated. The United States is an outsider entity that is vilified by Al Qaeda and to which Al Qaeda presents itself as an alternative, and so the United States cannot speak directly in a credible manner to Al Qaeda's members and supporters. At best, the United States can only hope to serve as an illicit enticement to seduce Al Qaeda's actual or potential advocates who are sufficiently uncommitted. A long-term U.S. strategy to manage the problem, not eliminate it, is necessary.

## WHAT ARE THE ACTORS' INTERESTS?

Al Qaeda, not even a legitimate member of the nation-state system, is the political and operational leadership node and symbolic standard-bearer for a current of religio-political thought that seeks to undermine the United States, the international system's military, economic, and political leader who is seeking to preserve existing arrangements. Such mutually exclusive core interests make conflict unavoidable. That conflict's nature and intensity, however, is malleable.

In Al Qaeda's view, the West, as led by the United States, subjects Muslims to "an ocean of oppression, injustice, slaughter, and plunder" on a global scale. As noted by bin Laden,

"For God's sake, what are the documents that incriminate the Palestinian people that warrant the massacres against them, which have been going on for more than five decades at the hands of the Crusaders and the Jews. . . . What documents incriminated the Muslims of Bosnia-Herzegovina and warranted the Western Crusaders, with the United States at their head, to unleash their Serb ally to annihilate and displace the Muslim people in the region under UN cover?

. . . There are many other countless issues." The West, especially the United States, victimizes Muslim peoples primarily because of their adherence to Islam. Conflicting national interests are simply not a significant factor. "All Muslims that the international Crusader-Zionist machine is annihilating," declared Bin Laden, "have not committed any crime other than to say Allah is our God."[11]

Al Qaeda's singular worldly mission, therefore, is to restore the fallen position of the Muslim peoples in world affairs. To do so, Al Qaeda wishes to wipe away current international boundaries, which it perceives as artificial Western-imposed demarcations that divide rather than unite Islam, and reestablish the caliphate, which will then rule a multinational, unified Islamic empire. Al Qaeda also seeks the withdrawal of all U.S. and allied forces from Islamic countries. Lastly Al Qaeda seeks to establish sharia, for only by closely adhering to all facets of Islam, which Al Qaeda views as God's instructions and so by definition are supreme and correct, can victory be achieved.

Bin Laden's Al Qaeda has been unwavering in its goals. Its intermediary objectives to achieve those goals, however, have evolved over time in relation to current events and organizational needs. As of 2011, bin Laden, via jihad, seeks to redress six specific worldly political grievances.[12]

First, bin Laden routinely cites the Palestinians' plight. The vast majority of Muslims in general and Arabs in particular find Israeli abuses utterly contemptible. The United States becomes a target because the Israelis are perceived to operate with unfettered U.S. backing.

Second, U.S. and Western troops are present on the Arabian Peninsula, the holy cradle of Islam. This is defamation in the militants' eyes. Further, the presence of such troops only goes to show the weakness and apostate character of local pro-U.S. regimes.

Third, Al Qaeda claims that the United States supports corrupt, tyrannical Muslim governments that repress their own peoples to curry U.S. favor. These governments are sell-outs who could not exist without U.S. succor. Worse than Western governments allied with the United States, these governments are apostates, and so they must be eliminated.

Fourth, the United States supports governments that repress or are engaged in counterinsurgency efforts against their Muslim minorities. Russia, India, and China are leading examples. Al Qaeda charges that what the United States cannot do directly, it is doing indirectly via other world powers.

Fifth, the United States economically exploits Muslims. The United States pressures oil suppliers, especially Arab ones, to keep prices low for U.S. benefit. This comes at the expense of potential wealth that the Muslim masses could accumulate to better their lives.

Sixth, the United States has directly occupied Muslim lands. Most notably, allied and U.S. forces are in Afghanistan, which holds a special place in Islamic lore due to the anti-Soviet jihad. The U.S. occupation of Iraq also directly subjugates Arabs in a religiously significant area.

Four broader themes can be distilled:

First, Al Qaeda is not attempting to conquer new lands. Per defensive jihad, it is responding to aggression. All of the issues annotated apply to political objectives that derive from either Islamic history or existing Muslim communities. As Al Qaeda has noted, "The American imposes himself on everyone. . . . Why are we fighting and opposing you? The answer is very simple: Because you attacked us and continue to attack us."[13]

Second, these political objectives are defensive and not invasive or transformative in nature. Osama bin Laden is not attempting to either destroy or convert the United States and its allies to Islam, though he has offered to aid this process, a necessary condition in Islamic just-war theory before attacking a non-Muslim foe. He is not trying to excise U.S. immorality. He simply does not wish it impressed upon Muslims.

As bin Laden explains: "We are defending ourselves against the United States. This is why I used to say that if [Muslims] do not have security, the Americans also will not have it. This is a very simple formula. . . . This is the formula of live and let live."[14]

These sentiments stand in direct contrast to former U.S. ambassador to Iraq Paul Bremmer's statement summarizing President Bush's oft-asserted idea that "there is no point in addressing the so-called root causes of [bin Laden's] terrorism. We are the root cause of his terrorism. He doesn't like America. He doesn't like our society. He doesn't like what we stand for. He doesn't like our values."[15]

While no fan of many U.S. social and cultural practices, Al Qaeda takes issue with specific U.S. policy actions that directly impact both it and its interests. As explained by bin Laden, "The United States, which has become the uncontested sole superpower, is . . . taking a direct approach to secure its interests in the world without regard to the interest of others, because it considers itself the sole power in the world and the world should adapt to what it wants."[16]

Third, Al Qaeda is replying in kind to the treatment that it perceives Muslims to be receiving. As bin Laden explained when speaking to the U.S. people, "Just as you kill, you are killed. Just as you bombard, you are bombarded."[17]

Fourth, bin Laden places the blame for the current U.S.-Al Qaeda struggle in U.S. hands. As the world's dominant power, the United States has shaped the world to its liking. Al Qaeda is simply seeking to redress grievances on behalf of the Muslim peoples, whom Al Qaeda sees as victims of a situation created by the United States and its allies. "The cause of the reaction must be sought and the act that triggered this reaction must be eliminated. The reaction came as a result of the aggressive U.S. policy toward the entire Muslim world."[18]

Osama bin Laden states Al Qaeda will not go away until the United States changes its actions. "So the case is easy: America will not be able to leave this ordeal unless it leaves the Arabian Peninsula, and stops its involvement in Palestine, and in all the Islamic world. If we give this equation to any child in an American school, he will easily solve it within a second. But, according to [President] Bush's actions the equation won't be solved until the swords fall on their heads, with the permission of Allah."[19]

In an attempt to yoke democracy to his cause and circumvent the U.S. government, Osama bin Laden has even directly beseeched the U.S. public to use its democratic system to alter its government's actions. In a mid-November 2001 interview, bin Laden asked "the American people to check the anti-Muslim policies of their government. They had described their government's policy against Vietnam as wrong. The American people should prevent the killing of Muslims at the hands of their government."[20]

Al Qaeda has outlined the path to peace. The state of the world reflects "an unfair division. The time has come for us to be equal. . . . The road to safety [for the United States] begins by [the United States] lifting oppression."[21] In bin Laden's eyes, neither the U.S. government nor the American people can claim ignorance.

The United States has three broad compelling interests in the U.S.-Al Qaeda struggle. Internally, the United States seeks to ensure its political character. Externally, the United States seeks to ensure its security, and, more broadly, to preserve the international order from which it derives sustenance and sustains its dominant world position.

The still-open question of how to secure these external interests, which the Bush administration interpreted as ensuring the pre–September 11 international status quo, is now before the Obama administration. It inherits certain root interests driven by the U.S. world position in direct conflict with Al Qaeda that, if not inherently unchangeable, will not be alterable in anything but the very long term. The nuances in choosing, defining, and implementing some of the more fungible aspects of U.S. aims atop a cornerstone of conflict form the Obama administration's starting point.

Critically, Al Qaeda's grievance against U.S. exploitation of Middle East oil is unlikely to be resolved soon or easily. A key pillar of U.S. strength is its economic might, upon which U.S. military might is based. The United States has the largest, most innovative, and nearly the most independent economy in the world.[22] The premise, and thus chief vulnerability, for post-industrial, information-age U.S. economic might is securely meeting U.S. energy needs. In practical terms, the United States must have a stable, reliable, source of affordable oil for both itself and its allies. The Middle East, notably the Persian Gulf, is fundamental to this need.

Critics argue that relying upon oil from the Middle East, Al Qaeda's heartland, creates unnecessary friction. Other sources of supply—Mexico, Venezuela, Russia, Nigeria, and the Caspian Basin—exist. Disengaging from the Middle East's oil would redress a key Al Qaeda grievance. It would also create U.S. leverage over key Al Qaeda–related states, such as Saudi Arabia, that is currently lacking because of oil dependence.

The world's energy situation, however, belies this approach. "The oil market is seamless: no matter where the United States buys its oil, any reduction in the supply will result in price increases everywhere and will affect the entire global economy. The question is not where one buys oil so much as it is who has the capacity to supply oil and affect the market." Although it currently produces only a quarter of world oil supplies, the Middle East holds between two-thirds and three-quarters of all known oil reserves. Although natural gas and other energy sources have reduced the relative weight of oil in the global energy market, oil still accounts for 40 percent of the world's energy consumption and is not projected to drop below this level for the next twenty years. The United States and the West will have to continue to define the region as vitally important.

Simultaneously, other countries are likely to increase their need for Middle East oil and compete with the West for these resources. China, for example, now imports 60 percent of its oil from the Persian Gulf, and forecasts for the next two decades show a possible increase of up to 90 percent. In fact, China has already begun investing in energy exploration in Iran, and Iran is now China's main supplier.

Though the Gulf's share of the world oil market has dropped since the 1970s as local production levels have slowed and other states' exports have increased, alternative states not only lack sufficient production, but their political reliability is also not assured. Venezuela, a promising new source of oil in the 1990s, for example, is now run by a dictator who cites oil as a potential anti-U.S. weapon. Mexico and Nigeria's capacities are a shadow of the Gulf. Caspian Basin development, whose lure is ever present, has been stymied since the Cold War's end by regional political instabilities, which also prevent a guarantee of reliable delivery. Lastly, the United States has no desire to depend upon a re-assertive, Caspian-dominating Russia, which has only 5 percent of global reserves and will deplete them by 2040 at current extraction rates.

Only the Gulf monarchies, who share a mutual political and economic dependency with the United States, are at least relatively reliable. In particular, no other state has the current impact on and the potential for future importance to the oil market as Saudi Arabia. While no other country commands such a capacity, its trump card remains its spare production capacity, which allows it to affect the market significantly by withholding or increasing supply.[23] Al Qaeda's complaint against U.S. support for Middle East monarchical and authoritarian regimes, therefore, is also unlikely to be resolved soon or easily.

These regimes also facilitate other U.S. interests. Most immediately, they combat Al Qaeda. Given low U.S. public standing in the world at large and the Middle East in particular, it is not safe to say that other regimes would be as cooperative. These regimes, particularly Saudi Arabia, are also vital to countering Iran. Lastly, these regimes surround Israel, a cultural and strategic U.S. regional ally, and different regimes might take a more hostile position toward it.

As such, Al Qaeda's criticism against the presence of U.S. forces on the Arabian Peninsula and in the Persian Gulf supporting these governments is also unlikely to be resolved soon or easily. The United States is wedded to the region. Regional animosities, such as the U.S.-Iran rivalry, can deny the United States guaranteed access to its resources. From the U.S. perspective, American regional involvement in the Middle East is necessary to secure U.S. interests.

Beyond the Middle East, Al Qaeda's objection against U.S. validation and acknowledgment of other regimes that oppress Muslims, such as China and Russia, is also unlikely to be resolved soon or easily. Russia suppresses a Chechen Islamic insurgency. China oppresses the Uighurs, a restive Muslim minority in western China. While the United States has registered objections to these acts, the United States has multiple economic, security, and political interests interwoven in complex relationships with these other world powers. While a key factor in Al Qaeda's worldview, it is not reasonable to expect that the issue of other states repressing their Muslim citizens will trump all other U.S. interests and thus cause the United States either to sever ties with these world powers or make this topic a fulcrum issue for U.S. foreign relations.

While some U.S.-Al Qaeda issues may be open to amelioration, these are not. Short of one side surrendering or altering its interests to the point of wholesale reinventing itself, the U.S.-Al Qaeda conflict is an enduring one. A long-term view is necessary.

## HOW ARE THE ANTAGONISTS WORKING TO SECURE THEIR INTERESTS?

The United States and Al Qaeda have each undertaken both operational and political efforts to further their interests. Each side has met with mixed success. In contrast to Al Qaeda, however, the United States has emphasized operational activity, thus leaving Al Qaeda to shape the political context and the political impact of U.S. actions.

### Al Qaeda's Chosen Path to Victory

Al Qaeda seeks to persuade through the political advertising technique of terrorism, herein defined as an illegitimate act of violence against a symbolic, innocent victim intended to induce a state of terror in a target group beyond the immediate victims in the process of challenging authority in order to coerce political change.[24] "Indifference [following terrorist acts] is impossible. Those who originally did not even ask themselves what 'those lunatics' were after are forced to take notice of them, to discuss their ideas, and to take a stand for or against. Through deeds which attract general attention, the new idea [promulgated by the terrorists] insinuates itself into peoples' heads. . . . Such an act does more propagandizing in a few days than do thousands of pamphlets." Unable to impose their agenda through established political processes or outright war, the terrorists, who are very difficult to defeat purely through arms, force the polity they attack to react predominantly politically, not militarily.[25]

Though it uses violence, terrorism differs significantly from war:

Unlike war, terrorism does not allow for engendering massive amounts of human and material destruction. Potential destruction resulting from acts of terrorism is simply not on a scale comparable with the organized political violence found in either guerilla or conventional war. Even a mass casualty attack, such as a conventional 9/11-style assault or possible use of a crude weapon of mass destruction, pales in comparison to what an organized military force can accomplish through the sustained and systematic professional application of violence, particularly if backed by the resources of a state.[26]

Also unlike war, terrorism cannot yield a conclusive military victory. The target set differs. Terrorists focus on "counter-value," innocent, noncombatant, and symbolic victims. War, by contrast, focuses primarily on "counterforce," combatant objectives that enable the writ of the state. There is no chance, therefore, to implement a political agenda in a militarily created political vacuum. A terrorist attack serves an entirely different purpose compared to war—political agitation.

Lastly, in contrast to war, which has a direct, and essentially two-sided, nature, terrorism is a multisided equation. It involves an interlocking series of direct and indirect relationships. These links interact as part of a process that occurs in a specific, sequential, four-step order.

First, the terrorists choose a specific target set. The targets must be symbolically relevant to the terrorists' agenda to ensure the impending violence is flavored with politics. They must also be morally innocent to ensure an attention-getting reaction. The 9/11 attacks on the World Trade Center met these criteria, since it was populated by noncombatant civilians engaged in peaceable commercial activity. The victims defined moral innocence as they were neither directly nor indirectly engaged in inflicting military harm upon anyone. Because it was a hub of U.S.-based global commerce, Al Qaeda deemed it the symbolic flagship and operational nerve center of U.S. economic oppression of Muslim lands.

Second, the terrorists challenge the existing authority by publicly and brutally killing their intended victims. The victims' apparently random selection combined with their innocence magnifies the resulting tragic, victimizing, and fear-inducing feelings since the general public—the real political target of the attack—now feels endangered. This sociopolitical disorientation is intended to loosen the targeted public's tie to the status quo, which operates counter to the terrorists' political agenda, and shake the target public from political complacency, thus opening it to the possibility of new ideas. With 9/11, Al Qaeda attacked a symbolic target and killed more than three thousand innocent civilians in an innovative way. Surveys showed fears of another attack. Social and political complacency had been shattered as people groped for explanations.

Third, the attack manifests and relays the terrorists' political message through the deaths of the victims, whose defining traits correspond to specific terrorist political grievances. Hitherto ignored contentious issues become highlighted. Al Qaeda communicated its 9/11 message in two ways. First, the symbolism of hitting an iconic U.S. economic entity radiated. Second, to ensure that there was no misinterpretation, Al Qaeda released videos directly explaining the attacks and their purpose to both the U.S. government and the U.S. public. These actions not only raised awareness of Al Qaeda, but also of its motivating political grievances.

Fourth, the targeted public's role switches. The terrorists' hope is that their "propaganda by the deed" will cause the general public to internalize the terrorists' message, reevaluate the status quo, and find it unacceptable.[27] Ideally, the targeted public then pressures its government for political change in line with the terrorists' political agenda, thus offering it respite from continued violence and horror. With 9/11, Al Qaeda sought to induce the U.S. public to pressure the U.S. government for changes to U.S. foreign policy concerning economic and security issues relative to the world's Muslim peoples. Al Qaeda did not, however, successfully execute stage four. Al Qaeda's violence deafened its U.S. target audience to its political grievances.

Looking outward from the terrorists' point of view, Al Qaeda's 9/11 terrorist violence largely backfired. Al Qaeda did shake the U.S. public from its complacency. Counterproductively, however, the U.S. public combined its newfound awareness of Al Qaeda with a desire for revenge and the defense of its perceived interests defined largely in pre-9/11 terms.

Looking inward from the terrorists' point of view, however, 9/11 was largely successful in achieving terrorism's three secondary goals—provocation, morale/unity building, and eliminating opposing forces. The attacks clearly provoked the United States, thus keeping Al Qaeda in the public eye, a crucial step not only for advertising its cause to its enemies but also an important action for future recruiting efforts. Al Qaeda's stunning 9/11 victory, its most ambitious undertaking to date, certainly buoyed the organization's morale and empowered its leadership, thereby increasing team unity. Al Qaeda also weakened its foremost opponent by dealing a blow to a U.S. economy in recession and simultaneously forcing major new government expenditures as the United States responded to the attacks.

From 9/11 through 2011, Al Qaeda has pursued parallel efforts. Operationally, Al Qaeda has opted to employ terrorism and, to a lesser extent, guerilla war to stymie U.S. efforts in Iraq and Afghanistan, while lessening its emphasis on the U.S. homeland. Because bin Laden deputy Ayman al-Zawahiri acknowledges "that however far our [Al Qaeda's] capabilities reach, they will never be equal to one-thousandth of the capabilities of the kingdom of Satan [the United States] that is waging war on us," Al Qaeda has also attempted to amplify, manipulate, and exploit the political dimension to magnify the political impact of its operational efforts. As al-Zawahiri has articulated, "more than half of this battle is taking place in the battlefield of the media." Al Qaeda "can kill the captives by bullet . . . [but] that would achieve that which is sought after without exposing ourselves to the questions and answering to doubts."[28]

### The United States' Chosen Path to Victory

Operationally, the Bush administration defended the homeland, and, by extension, U.S. interests, through a strong offense. After an initial and cursory focus on Afghanistan, the Bush administration concentrated primarily on Iraq with a secondary focus on Afghanistan while supporting capture/kill efforts for the rest of the world on the premise that countering Al Qaeda abroad made the United States safer at home.[29] Both domestically and internationally, it cast Al Qaeda as a national security threat and employed coercive means—such as the military, law enforcement, and intelligence—to locate and detain Al Qaeda's members to disrupt its activities.

Politically, the Bush administration attempted to blunt Al Qaeda by refusing to politically engage Al Qaeda's agenda. Domestically, it denied Al Qaeda's arguments entry into the U.S. public sphere and tried to hermetically seal the U.S. public from Al Qaeda's message by discouraging the broadcasting of its messages.[30] Internationally, Bush attempted to isolate, discredit, and ignore both Al Qaeda and its political agenda.

The Obama administration's actions have yet to significantly deviate. Operationally, Iraq and Afghanistan remain the primary focus, though President Obama has emphasized Afghanistan over Iraq. The remainder of the world's Al Qaeda hot spots, such as Yemen and Somalia, continue to be a second-tier priority as the Obama administration employs coercive national security tools— military, law enforcement, and intelligence—to detain Al Qaeda members and disrupt their activities. Politically, the Obama administration has continued to deny both Al Qaeda and its grievances access into the U.S. public debate while disavowing Al Qaeda's political nature.

President Obama has, however, positioned himself to possibly deviate from the Bush administration's approach. Operationally, the Obama administration has made clear that it is seeking a final exit from Iraq, thereby making Afghanistan the primary emphasis and allowing for increased attention and resources to other global hotspots. Politically, the Obama administration has, at its outset, seriously engaged Israel about a viable two-state solution to redress the plight of the Palestinians, a fundamental Al Qaeda grievance.

## WHAT ARE THE STRENGTHS AND WEAKNESSES OF THE U.S. AND AL QAEDA APPROACHES?

Though hard-power efforts by both Al Qaeda and the United States are highly visible, and utterly necessary to achieve their goals, their complementary political efforts will be the ultimate arbiter. The political level not only creates micro-level problems for the hard-power aspect that stunts U.S. effectiveness, but, on the macro level, it also determines the struggle's duration. Until U.S. strategy is substantively altered, the conflict's dynamics favor Al Qaeda.

### The U.S. Perspective

The U.S. approach is not without merit. Operationally, the business end of Al Qaeda's terrorism is killing, and coercive U.S. national security tools—the military, law enforcement, and intelligence—save lives by weakening Al Qaeda's capacity for violence, which would otherwise go unabated. Politically, shutting out Al Qaeda's agenda to U.S. society will somewhat mitigate the effects of the terrorism process. There are, however, fundamental shortcomings that, if not redressed, could hollow key U.S. pillars of strength and endanger the U.S. political character.

Time is a crucial factor. The U.S. role as the economic, military, and political leader of the international system is premised upon U.S. hard-power capacity, but the United States cannot remain on a war footing indefinitely without significantly and detrimentally impacting not only its economic and military power, but also the numerous, diverse, and competing political interests that must be secured to maintain U.S. standing. In contrast to war, where political change happens at the end when one side can no longer fight it off, terrorism forces political change by perpetuating the conflict. The intimate, extreme, and violent nature of terrorist action within a society provokes an extreme, out-of-character political response because the pain caused is so deep and wounding it cannot be permitted to be repeated. The longer the struggle, the more attacks are launched, and the more numerous and intense the reactions of the terrorists' target are likely to be. The unique U.S. political character is increasingly endangered.

With no clear, objective military yardsticks, there is no inherently obvious and recognizable end point within U.S. control. Rather, the conflict's duration will largely be based upon the terrorists' desire to continue toward their political goals relative to their achievements, compared against their losses, and as weighed against inspiration. As with guerilla war, the path to political victory through a violent global insurgency is paved with willpower.

Al Qaeda's inspiration is the idea that it is doing God's work by fighting against unbelievers, who now dominate an unjust world. The massive U.S.-Al Qaeda power disparity means an operative can only truly expect to advance the cause rather than defeat the enemy. Realistically, an operative can expect to die in its service rather than see the fruits of victory.

This paradigm cannot be falsified. An Al Qaeda win directly validates the ideology. An Al Qaeda loss only validates the premises for which the cause is fought and meets the expectations of its adherents.

Operationally, a hard-power dominated approach puts the United States at a systemic disadvantage. By definition, Al Qaeda has tactical advantage—its members are unknown, its membership self-selects from a global population, and it chooses the place, time, and means of attack on a global scale. Al Qaeda's attacks against civilians do not challenge the state, thus speaking past U.S. war power created and organized in defense of the state. The U.S. military may capture and kill some of Al Qaeda's members. Given Al Qaeda's tactical advantages, the United States is highly unlikely to either solve the problem by wholly obliterating Al Qaeda as an organization or to credibly threaten to inflict damage severe enough to employ deterrence.

First, the concept of deterrence requires data. When dealing with terrorism, an inherently secretive phenomenon, precise and reliable data are critically missing. Organizational numbers, identities, locations, plans, intentions, and so forth, on the part of both the terrorists and U.S. antiterrorist forces are all unknown.

Second, these data must be communicated between the antagonists. In the U.S.-Al Qaeda struggle, the identities of all relevant actors are not known. No formal link between the United States and Al Qaeda exists. No reliable intermediary exists. No credible threat can be effectively conveyed.

Third, the antagonists must make comparative loss-to-gain judgments based upon this missing information. In the absence of reliable data and a means of communicating it, such decisions cannot be made. The terrorists' political ideology becomes the default setting for this conclusion. Al Qaeda makes its decisions per a vision that cannot be falsified, and Al Qaeda operatives are ready and willing to accept death as both a means and as an end.

Fourth, both sides must be able to guarantee the ability to inflict certain retaliation upon each other in response to a particular course of action to ensure a prohibitive risk-versus-gain conclusion. Terrorism, by definition, pits a vast minority who acknowledges its utter power inferiority against an opponent that the minority openly acknowledges could destroy it. Not only do Al Qaeda terrorists accept this going in, but the fact that they challenge the state indirectly by attacking innocents who can't defend themselves means state power is only a secondary risk. In contrast to traditional state-based deterrence, which is premised upon a desire for survival and forces a clear choice between surviving and executing a particular policy action, political ideology (which does not need to force a choice between survival and policy goals), not raw military power calculations, drives the train.

Al Qaeda spokesman Abu Ubayd al-Qurashi, using the logic above, issued a statement mocking U.S. hard power efforts to cow it. "Deterrence: This principle is based on the assumption that there are two sides that seek to survive and defend their interests—but it is completely eliminated when dealing with people who don't care about living but thirst for martyrdom. While the principle works well [in warfare] between countries, it does not work at all for an organization with no permanent bases and with no capital in Western banks, that does not rely on aid from particular countries. As a result, it is completely independent in its decisions, and it seeks conflict from the outset. How can such people, who strive for death more than anything else, be deterred?"[31]

The political dimension in charting U.S. strategy thus has a twofold role. Looking inward, the United States must fundamentally adhere to its vulnerability-inducing traditional political values despite Al Qaeda's terrorist attacks. To do otherwise allows the U.S. political system to be subverted by terrorism through a self-inflicted, intrinsic loss stemming from abandoning the political principles that define the U.S. political character, which is under Al Qaeda's direct assault as it attempts to manipulate the U.S. public and government. Looking externally, the political dimension plays a key role because of the inherently long-term nature of the U.S. hard-power approach. Altering the political context of the struggle is the one malleable factor that can enhance U.S. efforts against Al Qaeda's hard-power capabilities, found in its organizational and financial dimensions, while sapping the potency of Al Qaeda's political grievances that fuel it. The conflict's timeline can then potentially be altered in U.S. favor.

The U.S. political effort must be twofold. Directly, U.S. efforts must capitalize on vulnerabilities in Al Qaeda's nature to exploit internal political tensions in order to reduce its organizational coherence and effectiveness. Indirectly, U.S. efforts must focus upon both the general populace from which Al Qaeda derives its strategic viability and the state structures that govern these foreign populations, in order to reduce Al Qaeda's organizational resources, such as manpower, support, and political, and thus operational, maneuvering room. With political efforts aimed at these two audiences to address bones of contention between the United States and Al Qaeda in the background, the effectiveness and impact of U.S. hard-power actions in the foreground can be significantly magnified.

Engaging the U.S.-Al Qaeda struggle's political dimension—the antagonists' root political and ideological conflict—is not, however, without risk. Engaging the political dimension gives Al Qaeda a measure of de facto recognition, and thus validation. Al Qaeda's political agenda is introduced into the political debate with the force of fear and violence behind it, and the U.S. national interest could be harmed. Closing the U.S. political sphere to Al Qaeda helps blunt the terrorism process from gaining traction. The gains in engaging the U.S.-Al Qaeda struggle's political dimension, however, far outweigh the risks.

The terrorism process is not actually blunted. Precluding Al Qaeda's contentions from the U.S. public sphere by banning their public statements from mainstream U.S. media in an age of mass communications does not prevent Al Qaeda's operatives from communicating.[32] Instead, alternative agendas fill this political vacuum at the expense of a more genuine and constructive political debate of, by, and for the American people reflecting the public will relative to Al Qaeda while decisions are made and actions are taken by government in secret nonetheless. In doing so, the United States effectively subverts its own political character, which is fundamentally at issue in a struggle with terrorists.

Crucially, the United States effectively cedes the strategic initiative. Disavowing terrorism's political dimension and, by extension, Al Qaeda, which is by nature a political actor, restricts U.S. policy to hard-power means. Proactively moving toward a political resolution to diffuse the conflict is effectively precluded. At best, the United States is forced to play an effective defense.

The United States is faced with a conscious trade-off that goes to the heart of its position as leader of the international system. On the one hand, there is total freedom of action through the unilateral, power-based pursuit of U.S. interests rooted in actual or potential coercion. On the other hand, there is a somewhat restricted U.S. freedom of action that takes into account the political interests and sensitivities of other actors relevant to the fight, particularly relative to both states and the world publics, particularly Muslim ones, where Al Qaeda is present.

This potentially somewhat limiting course of action, however, offers the perception of increased legitimacy for the United States' world position, its actions, and its interests in the eyes of international organizations, states, and foreign publics. As will be more fully articulated in Chapter Four, traditional U.S. political values and foreign policy emphases are largely embraced by each of these key actors. Political decisions and their implementation within these guidelines are likely to generate public support, which will generate the political capital necessary for the United States to engage these actors to isolate, undermine, and destroy Al Qaeda.

The United States is at a decision point. External to the United States, the Obama administration has the benefit of being a "new face" with a differing domestic constituency that enables new policy choices. Internal to the United States, domestic critics of U.S. post-9/11 terrorism policy, of which there are many, will now be forced to parse between domestic partisan tendencies and true national-level policy analysis due to the White House shift.

### Al Qaeda's Perspective

Al Qaeda is not unhindered. Al Qaeda must always work to avoid the United States' long arm, which is manifest in both unilateral efforts and alliances with various Muslim and non-Muslim states throughout the world. Furthermore, the lesser development of the societies from which Al Qaeda springs also presents a resource challenge.

The U.S.-Al Qaeda struggle's dynamics as of 2011, however, present Al Qaeda with a crucial long-run advantage—Al Qaeda's unaddressed political grievances are an exploitable source of political angst for actual and potential supporters. Al Qaeda thus has an un-countered opportunity to rally susceptible Muslims both for recruitment and for operational support. Al Qaeda will very likely be able to recover from any short-term tactical losses inflicted by superior U.S. hard-power capabilities, and Al Qaeda's operational potency will very likely continue to increase in the long term as the cumulative effect of politically inciting U.S. hard-power actions becomes manifest.

Most significantly, Al Qaeda has adroitly exploited the ever-increasing international anti-U.S. political angst by adding a media arm, as-Sahab (The Cloud), that is "perhaps the most effective propaganda machine ever assembled by a terrorist or insurgent network," to reach new heights in recruiting and fundraising.[33] This media arm now produces hundreds of missives per year for Internet distribution. By March 2009, for example, Osama bin Laden had released his twenty-ninth tape since 9/11 castigating the United States and its allies while providing strategic encouragement and advice to his followers.[34]

"Many U.S., Pakistani, and European intelligence officials now agree that Al Qaeda's ability to launch operations around the globe didn't diminish after the invasion of Afghanistan as much as previously thought. Al Qaeda's leadership, with bin Laden's direct blessing, made the decision to activate sleeper cells in Saudi Arabia in 2003, prompting a wave of car bombings and assassination attempts. . . . From hideouts in Pakistan, according to court testimony and interviews, bin Laden's deputies ordered attacks on a Tunisian synagogue in 2002, a

British consulate and bank in Istanbul in 2003, and the London transit system in 2005. U.S. intelligence officials also blame the Al Qaeda brain trust for orchestrating dozens of other failed plots, including a plan to blow up transatlantic flights from Britain in August 2006." In fact, by the close of the Bush administration, according to then CIA director Michael V. Hayden, Al Qaeda was still as powerful as it was six years prior, "still capable of training people from around the world . . . and then sending them off around the world to stage attacks."[35]

## CONCLUSION

Peaceful political discourse cannot bridge the gap of the largely mutually exclusive U.S. and Al Qaeda agendas. Al Qaeda has opted to employ terrorism to gain an outsized effect to further an agenda it could not achieve through political means alone. The conflict, therefore, will play out on both political and hard-power levels.

As the world's economic, military, and political leader, the United States can effectively do as it chooses. Operationally, the Bush administration worked from the premise that "the experience, charisma, and organizational skills of Al Qaeda's top men would be difficult or impossible to replace." It pursued a "kill or capture" strategy to decapitate Al Qaeda's leadership akin to taking down an organized crime family almost exclusively via hard power—the military, law enforcement, and intelligence—wherein traditional U.S. foreign policy political norms and values that have historically governed U.S. decisions to use force— the rule of law, a participatory form of governance executed via an embrace of international institutions, and democratic values such as human rights—held little sway.[36] Politically, the Bush administration partnered this coercive approach with general non-engagement toward both Al Qaeda and its agenda. As of 2011, the Obama administration has not yet significantly deviated from this approach.

After roughly a decade of concerted effort, however, the United States, the most powerful state in the international system, has been unable to neuter Al Qaeda—a numerically small, resource-poor, transnational terrorist group hunted by every state. Not only is Al Qaeda surviving, but it remains an influential and threatening force. Given the intense military, economic, and political costs of the U.S. effort, time is not on the U.S. side.

Crucially, the United States has sustained intrinsic political harm. "It is not the people Al Qaeda might kill that is [sic] the threat. *Our* [emphasis in original] reaction is what can cause the damage. It's Al Qaeda plus our response that creates [sic] the existential danger."[37] The character of the U.S. political response is critical. Through 2011, however, the terrorists have induced the United States to subvert its political values and processes domestically by engaging in torturous interrogations, extralegal detention, and so forth, and externally by undertaking unilateral, offensive invasions of other countries, actively aiding repressive governments, and so forth.

Consequently, U.S. national advantage has also been harmed. Massive quantities of finite and tangible U.S. economic, military, and political resources have been expended and continue to be paired against infinite and intangible political grievance and anger drawn from the world's disenfranchised, angry, and otherwise disaffected Muslim population. These costs, which have no foreseeable end, have been so significant that key U.S. pillars of strength that secure U.S. world standing—economic might, upon which U.S. military strength is based, and global U.S. political legitimacy—are being undermined.

Though conflicting political agendas shape the conduct of the fight, U.S. efforts to win the U.S.-Al Qaeda terrorism struggle, a political contest, are structured as if the United States were trying to beat an opponent in war, a military contest. At best, this tack is a holding action that hopes to exhaust the enemy, which in this case has grandiose secular political goals, has recorded significant achievements, and possesses a deep will rooted in a religio-political vision that is not falsifiable. At worst, this approach puts the United States in a defensive crouch, strategically undermines U.S. strengths, and cedes Al Qaeda the strategic initiative.

The main prize still at stake, which will largely determine the outcome of the U.S.-Al Qaeda struggle, is, per the triangular nature of terrorism in the context of a global insurgency, the political support of the uncommitted masses of coreligionists whom Al Qaeda seeks to usurp. As al-Zawahiri explained in his 2005 letter, Al Qaeda's goals "will not be accomplished by the *mujahed* movement while it is cut off from public support, even if the jihadist movement pursues the method of sudden overthrow. This is because such an overthrow would not take place without some minimum of popular support and some condition of public discontent which offers the *mujahed* movement what it needs in terms of capabilities in the quickest fashion. Additionally, if the jihadist movement were obliged to pursue other methods, such as a popular war of jihad or a popular intifada, then popular support would be a decisive factor between victory and defeat."[38]

The Obama administration must engage Al Qaeda's political agenda, which the United States can impact, to undercut Al Qaeda's religio-political vision, which the United States cannot impact. Because the prize demographic of the uncommitted masses of coreligionists Al Qaeda seeks to usurp largely embraces traditional U.S. political values and foreign policy emphases, there is an incipient potential for U.S. success. The United States can use these principles to guide both U.S. decision-making and policy implementation to dissipate Al Qaeda's political and security threat and manage its residue at a long-term sustainable cost.

The next chapter outlines the initial efforts, and results, by both Al Qaeda and the Bush administration against one another. Encapsulating the initial seven years of dedicated U.S. efforts when Al Qaeda's destruction became a national priority, it serves as the springboard from which Obama administration efforts must launch. Only by thoroughly understanding this past effort can any future effort, particularly one in line with an analytic framework emphasizing political cognizance, be successfully undertaken.

Chapter 2

# A Game of Twister: Al Qaeda Strategy versus Bush Administration Strategy

*If you wish to conduct offensive war you must know the men employed by the enemy. Are they wise or stupid, clever or clumsy? Having assessed their qualities, you prepare appropriate measures.*
—Sun Tzu

After fruitlessly attacking U.S.-supported authoritarian regimes germane to Al Qaeda's membership, Al Qaeda consolidated its efforts against the United States, a tack that culminated in 9/11. Unawakened to the Al Qaeda threat prior to 9/11, the Bush administration responded with a consistently offensive posture. Its initial salvos consisted of invading Afghanistan and Iraq, attacking Al Qaeda's diffuse global presence, dispatching U.S. forces to aid governments in subduing their local Al Qaeda allies, and launching a charm campaign to improve U.S. public standing. These were followed up with an increasingly hostile focus on Iran in an attempt to secure U.S. efforts in Iraq, as a part of securing broader U.S. regional interests, while initiating limited unilateral U.S. efforts against Osama bin Laden's Al Qaeda central in Pakistan.

Both U.S. and Al Qaeda strategies inflicted hard-power damage. Al Qaeda, however, manipulated the politics of the U.S.-Al Qaeda conflict much more adeptly. Though bloodied, it was fundamentally unshaken, and it remained potent at the Bush administration's close.

Post-9/11 underlying political, economic, and military trends favor Al Qaeda. The Bush administration's approach manifested both hard- and soft-power weaknesses that, if left unaddressed, will likely yield Al Qaeda several medium- to long-term power-based and political victories. With time on Al Qaeda's side, the resulting challenges before the Obama administration will be steep, and the political, economic, and military resources to meet them will be limited.

## PART I: INITIAL BLOWS
### Al Qaeda's Pre-9/11 Strategy

Al Qaeda initially took a comprehensive, simultaneous, system-wide approach to altering the U.S.-led international system. Guerilla and terrorist campaigns against Muslim regimes oppressing their people in cooperation with the United States, as well as U.S. forces throughout the Middle East, were the prime targets. International backers immediately absent the region received only secondary emphasis at best.

Al Qaeda's hard-power capacity necessitated this approach. No uniting force existed after the Red Army's defeat in Afghanistan, and there was no pan-Islamic leader to alter the national orientation of the many Islamic resistance groups. The anti-Soviet jihad was an aberration reflecting a unique confluence of political and social trends at the time.[1] The constituent parts were far more powerful than the center. The best manner for the center to act upon its mission and rally support was to assist others, who were more nationally oriented.

Underlying soft-power factors dovetailed. The Prophet Mohammed, when fighting his enemies, had commanded that the "near" enemy be dealt with first before attacking the "far" enemy, an injunction that, in contemporary times, correlated with pursuing national-level Islamic resistance movements first before addressing any international support they might receive. More recently, nineteenth-century European colonialism had instilled a nascent sense of nationalism, and so Islamic resistance movements focused first on their own indigenous problems.

Very little headway was achieved. Country-per-country, "the jihadists were overmatched by the security apparatus of the states."[2] Limited jihadist resources were being squandered.

To fight battles on a country by country basis was to combat the symptoms, U.S. proxies in a U.S.-dominated system, versus the root disease, U.S. power and influence. The United States, the cornerstone of the unjust international system, was the real problem. If it could be taken down, the rest of the system would collapse on its own or be easily defeated.

By the late 1990s, bin Laden was working to focus the global jihad and Al Qaeda, its vanguard, against the United States.[3] Apart from having greater economy and efficiency against the enemy, this United States–first tack allowed Al Qaeda to rise to prominence. By keeping the hatred of Al Qaeda members focused on the United States, a deeply unpopular country, Osama bin Laden subsumed internal rivalries to a higher cause while harnessing a powerful inspiration to draw recruits.

Attacks continued against the United States and its interests during the 1990s under this strategic rubric. Al Qaeda–inspired jihadists attacked the Central Intelligence Agency (CIA) and the World Trade Center in 1993. Al Qaeda itself bombed American embassies in Kenya and Tanzania in 1998. Al Qaeda nearly sank the USS *Cole*, a U.S. naval frigate, in Yemen in 2000. Finally, in 2001, Al Qaeda's efforts culminated with the 9/11 attacks.

## Bush Administration 9/11 Strategic Response

The Bush administration defined Al Qaeda as a national security threat. It rationally applied all of the hard-power resources it could muster. Though the caveat of soft power was acknowledged, it was given a distinctly secondary emphasis. This perspective, which was to remain constant through both of the administration's terms, initially manifested itself in four simultaneously executed, interlocking steps.

Step I, large-scale offensive military action, initially consisted of the 2001 U.S. invasion of Afghanistan to deprive Al Qaeda of its pre-9/11 sanctuary.[4] Not only did U.S. forces give chase to Al Qaeda and depose its Taliban protectors, but the United States also installed the Afghanistan Transitional Authority (ATA) under Pashtun tribal leader Hamid Karzai, who was backed by U.S. military personnel, to hold national elections and create a democracy as a bulwark against terrorist domination.[5] In fall 2004, in what was widely viewed as a free and fair election, Hamid Karzai became Afghanistan's first democratically elected president. The national legislature came into being in spring 2005 in what also was widely viewed as a free and fair election.[6]

U.S. desires for security, however, did not materialize. U.S. and allied forces initially beat back the Taliban and Al Qaeda. Al Qaeda–backed Taliban and other indigenous militant allies never fully retreated, however, and they resurged in 2006 to seriously contest the south and east of the country while launching terrorist attacks in the capital.[7] With the possibility of meaningful additional U.S. forces out of the question leading up to and following the 2003 U.S. invasion of Iraq, Karzai's writ never effectively extended beyond Kabul's gates.

After consciously excluding other nations to keep unilateral control during the initial invasion, the Bush administration called for foreign augmentation to the U.S. force structure, and roughly 20,000 foreign troops from nearly thirty countries ultimately arrived. Only four countries—Canada, the Netherlands, the United Kingdom, and France—took on meaningful and substantive combat roles, however, and most nations provided only a political token contribution without genuine military importance. Numerous "national exceptions," such as Germany's prohibition on its using forces in combat, further restricted their utility.

The Bush administration turned to building up Afghanistan's security forces to fill the security vacuum and authorized a 75,000-man army complemented by a 200,000-man national police force. The army, however, was both understrength and incapable of concerted action without direct U.S. support.

The police, while presenting a wide and diffuse presence, were broadly regarded as corrupt and ineffective.

To compensate, the Bush administration attempted to yoke Pakistan as a regional proxy. The United States would avoid significant commitments of U.S. forces already dedicated to Iraq while enlisting Pakistani manpower backed by U.S. aid to bear the military and political costs of pursuing Al Qaeda and its indigenous allies. With Pakistan as a U.S. ally there was, in theory, no place to hide from the 2001 U.S. juggernaut as Al Qaeda, the Taliban, and other indigenous militants fled Afghanistan to Pakistan's semi-autonomous Federally Administered Tribal Areas (FATA).

However, Pervez Musharraf, Pakistan's then-president, initially balked. He cited not only a lack of domestic political support but also inadequate military capability. He refused to deploy into the FATA.

When his refusal coincided with the public unmasking of Pakistani nuclear scientist Abdul Qadeer Khan's global black market nuclear activities that purportedly gave Libya, Iran, and North Korea nuclear weapons potential, however, Musharraf finally relented to U.S. pressure and dispatched 70,000 troops from Pakistan's Frontier Corps, a paramilitary auxiliary, into the FATA in the winter of 2003–2004, despite increased regional anti-U.S. sentiment and no discernable increase in Pakistani military capability.[8] Meanwhile, Abdul Qadeer took sole responsibility for any illicit proliferation activity emanating from Pakistan. He apologized on television in English, which the average Pakistani does not understand. He was placed under house arrest, though he was still allowed to retain the wealth he gained from his purportedly illicit activities. The U.S. initiated no actions against Abdul Qadeer, the government of Pakistan, or any of its members in an international diplomatic, political, legal, economic, or military manner.[9] While negotiations over this incident between Musharraf and then–Secretary of State Colin Powell were, and remain, secret, so a deal cannot be proven, there is, nonetheless, a strong correlation between Pakistan better serving U.S. counterterrorism interests and the potentially massive flap over WMD proliferation to two members of the "axis of evil" emanating from a purported U.S. ally.[10]

Pakistani pressure on the militants, however, eased markedly in fall 2006. Responding to domestic political pressure and rising tensions with India, Islamabad signed the Waziristan Accord with regional tribal and militant leaders. Pakistan offered a ceasefire, which meant that Islamabad would pay reparations to the Taliban, return their weapons, refrain from attacking the Taliban, and pull its troops back from the region. The militants and tribal leaders agreed to refrain from setting up camps, to not set up a parallel government, to eject foreign fighters from the region, and to cease cross-border attacks into Afghanistan. A clause of this self-policed deal stipulated that Pakistani forces would return if the indigenous tribal potentates failed in their obligations.[11]

The tribes, however, were either unwilling or unable to control their territory, the very condition that had made federal troops necessary in the first place.
Cross-border attacks into Afghanistan tripled after the deal was inked. Further,
the Taliban and associated militants began systematically killing tribal leaders
seen as helping Islamabad.[12] The Taliban and Al Qaeda have a measure of popularity in FATA, the birthplace of the modern global jihadist movement, whose
midwife and de facto guardian was Pakistan, which had employed these same
Islamic guerillas as regional foreign-policy implements since the 1979 Soviet
invasion of Afghanistan.[13]

Islamabad had no desire to return to the FATA. In the wake of federal
authorities storming the Red Mosque, a Taliban-connected Islamic militant center, an insurgent tribal spokesman pronounced the treaty dead, and Taliban and
Al Qaeda elements retaliated by killing scores of federal troops. Nonetheless, and
in spite of rising violence, Islamabad pronounced the treaty a success in February
2007, advocated more autonomous zones, and actively withdrew its forces.[14]

Bush administration policy toward Pakistan at this time was akin to U.S.
policy toward Russia when Boris Yeltsin was in power. Both sets of policies were
formed in a highly fluid post–Cold War environment in response to a crisis. Both
times—at the individual, the state, and the international levels—few options
appeared available. The result, in both cases, was temporary progress on immediate goals without developing an enduring foundation for sustainable policy.

At the individual level, each set of U.S. policies depended on a strongman.
During the 1990s, the United States staked its Russia policy on Yeltsin, a cre-
dentialed former senior Communist who was seen as a workable interlocutor
capable of negotiating a political system in chaos and at odds with U.S. interests.
During the Bush administration, the United States staked its counterterrorism
policy on Musharraf, a general seen as a secular bulwark against rising Islamic
militancy in a nuclear-armed country.

At the state level, the United States gave de facto blessing to a change in
regime. In supporting Yeltsin, the United States effectively blessed his assumption to a newly emerging democratic Russia. Implicitly, the United States blessed
Musharraf's earlier coup against Pakistan's democracy to get Pakistani assistance
against Al Qaeda.

At the international level, the United States viewed each man as insurance
against potentially even worse threats. Even if Yeltsin did not reform Russia's
socioeconomic and political systems, he would at least secure Russia's nuclear arsenal. Even if Musharraf was not helpful against Al Qaeda, he would at least secure
Pakistan's nuclear arsenal.

The utility of this approach breaks down, however, when accounting for
differing U.S. interests in the two countries and acknowledging Pakistan's
unique domestic and international context. Unlike Russia, Pakistan is not a

major power. It is not inwardly focused. And it is not surrounded with weak and benign neighbors. The long term would be very different.

Pakistan has a hostile neighborhood with numerous overlapping and tense political, economic, and security issues. To its east and south, Pakistan immediately confronts India, which has massive geographic, population, economic, and military advantages, while the Kashmir issue keeps tensions simmering and burgeoning U.S. ties to India, such as the U.S.-Indian nuclear deal, stoke Pakistani fears. To the north, Pakistan must engage China, a historic supporter who is manipulating it against India, with whom China is in regional competition, and Russia, a former Cold War adversary still supportive of its former client state India. To its west, Pakistan must engage Iran, which has extensive influence over Afghanistan as it conflicts with the United States, Pakistan's primary backer, over Afghanistan, Pakistan's adjacent neighbor.

In contrast to Moscow's defensive, internal orientation, Pakistan's perennial fear of encirclement by hostile, more powerful neighbors forces an outward orientation. With actual or potential problems on all sides, Pakistan has always sought strategic depth in Afghanistan, which provides a buffer to enemies and their proxies who are otherwise cheek to cheek. Influential through strong ethnic, political, and economic ties, Pakistan has always ensured a placating client state in Kabul or, conversely, fostered adequate chaos so that Afghanistan would be sufficiently weak, and thus neither exploitable by hostile neighbors, particularly India, nor a threat in itself. Equally significant, a strong and self-sufficient Afghanistan would force Pakistan to confront its own indigenous militants, whom it had created over decades, vice exporting and exploiting them for regional gain.

Musharraf's dictatorial political system was basically a continuation of a previous political and socioeconomic system instituted under former dictator Mohammed Zia-ul-Haq that had been interrupted by a brief era of democratic governance. As such, Musharraf's dictatorial system was intertwined with and dependent upon the very forces of Islamic militancy that the United States was seeking to combat.[15] Intensively combating these forces would undermine Musharraf's own position domestically with the state institutions and political parties upon which he depended. Because the United States wanted to see a strong and stable Afghanistan, Musharraf had to walk a fine line placating Bush to ensure continued aid while securing Pakistani interests, and he did so by splitting the difference between Al Qaeda and the Taliban.

The Taliban were, by far, the easier target. The Taliban had a far larger membership, had once been a public organization, and had previously had formal diplomatic ties to Pakistan.[16] Yet, in spite of routine public U.S. and Afghan claims that the Taliban and its leadership had taken refuge in Pakistan, Al Qaeda suffered far more at Pakistani hands.

Al Qaeda was not only more threatening, but it was also more politically palatable to address. Unlike Afghanistan's Taliban, Al Qaeda had made attempts on Musharraf's life and attacked the Pakistani state.[17] While Osama bin Laden and Ayman al-Zawahiri were popular figureheads whose arrest might cause a political backlash, rank-and-file members could be detained without local political trouble because they were foreigners devoid of strong social, economic, and political roots in Pakistan.

Musharraf's interests significantly advanced. External to Pakistan, a policy of splitting the difference and preserving and controlling the deposed Taliban, a force capable of significantly affecting Afghanistan's future, could advance Pakistani national interests by keeping the United States, upon which Musharraf was uncomfortably dependent, both occupied and Pakistan-dependent in securing Afghanistan. Internal to Pakistan, Musharraf could simultaneously harm Al Qaeda as an organization and maintain internal political balances with domestic militants and ethnic minorities, such as the Pashtuns, who have overwhelmingly provided Taliban manpower. Either way, the threat of Islamic militancy was kept simmering to ensure continued U.S. aid and political blessing, both of which could be withdrawn at any time, and longer-term political reform that might have advanced Pakistani democracy was forestalled.

While Musharraf the man was part of the problem, Musharraf's supporting political system was the larger issue, and U.S. foreign policy elites were cognizant of that. A 2007 poll of Council on Foreign Relations members found that while 11 percent thought that Musharraf was making significant headway against terrorism and 23 percent thought that Musharraf was being unhelpful in the struggle against terrorism, the vast majority, 66 percent, thought that while Musharraf could perhaps have been more helpful, it was unlikely that another general would have been significantly more so.[18] Nonetheless, several unredressed flaws in the Bush administration's Pakistan policy enabled this dynamic and perpetuated U.S. vulnerability.

Most significantly, the Bush administration consistently appeared to act on the premise that Musharraf's government was not only the sole meaningful regional barrier between the United States and unchecked Islamic militancy, but that the Pakistani state was also perpetually in danger of succumbing to the Islamists. The Pakistani Islamists, however, lacked broad public support. "Islamic parties have never garnered more than 13 percent in any free parliamentary elections in Pakistan."[19] In Pakistan's last major election in 2002, religious political parties received just 11 percent of the vote. Capitalizing on surging anti-American sentiment after the U.S. invasion of Afghanistan in 2001, this election was likely the Islamist high-water mark. By contrast more than 28 percent was won by the secular party led by Benazir Bhutto, the former prime minister.

As evidenced by how he played both sides of the coin, Musharraf was not afraid of either the political Islamists or the Islamic militants. On the one hand, Musharraf's status as a personal target of Al Qaeda won him a reputation in the West as a terrorist fighter. He routinely spoke ominously about the Islamists' rising power, and the U.S. foreign policy establishment widely perceived him as a voice of moderation. On the other hand, he regularly brokered agreements with the Islamists in the provinces as a way to gain allies amid the growing national support for his civilian challengers like Nawaz Sharif and Benazir Bhutto. Ironically, these secular leaders were Musharraf's natural allies against the Taliban, Al Qaeda, and their political backers.[20] If Musharraf was able to negotiate with his smaller Islamist political enemies to contain more serious secular political enemies, then he almost certainly did not fear the possibility of the political Islamists and their militant wings taking power.

Fearful of losing its regional proxy, the Bush administration lavished aid upon Pakistan with few to no strings attached. To ensure Pakistan's solvency after 9/11, the Bush administration arranged for an extension on $13.5 billion in Pakistan's foreign debt, an amount that would have crushed Pakistan's economy if it were ever called in. Militarily, the Bush administration went on to expend roughly $11.2 billion during its tenure to root out terrorists in Pakistani tribal areas. Of this, $7.5 billion consisted of direct cash subsidies to Pakistan's armed forces, which used this money for India-centric weapons to double its inventory of heavy artillery, self-propelled howitzers, and combat helicopters while increasing its antitank missile stockpile from 200 to 5,250. By 2007, Musharraf was "the fifth-largest recipient of U.S. aid—the Bush administration proposed $785 million [for Pakistan] in its budget."[21]

The money and military hardware from the United States was crucial for Pakistan's armed forces to keep pace with India, Pakistan's self-perceived greatest threat. "To the extent that Mr. Musharraf's government feels real pressure, it is from those within the Pakistani military who worry most about alienating Washington and jeopardizing the flow of military aid to Pakistan."[22] It is a very reasonable supposition that tying this military aid to action against Al Qaeda, as opposed to using it as a bribe for action on multiple U.S. interests, would have likely spurred new Pakistani military activity in FATA.

Underwriting all of this was an internal conflict in U.S. policy. On the one hand, 2007 U.S. counter-proliferation policy viewed it as necessary to support Musharraf. He was a force for stability in a semi-stable country with nuclear weapons. On the other hand, this aspect of U.S. policy, when combined with the nature of the Pakistani political system, gave Musharraf leverage over the United States and curtailed U.S. counterterrorism efforts in line with Musharraf's interests, which demanded that he rebuff U.S. calls to thoroughly root out Pakistani-based Islamic militancy, incorporate the FATA into the state structure, or restructure Pakistan's domestic political balances.

By the close of 2006, U.S. efforts to destroy Al Qaeda in Pakistan were at a standstill. Al Qaeda was ensconced in the tribal areas, and no significant public Pakistani effort existed to pursue it. Burdened by these internal flaws, existing U.S. policy had reached its limits.

Meanwhile, after U.S. forces kept the Taliban's spring 2002 offensive in check, a post-9/11 hyper-empowered President Bush, less than one year after 9/11, began making the argument in summer 2002 that Iraq's Saddam Hussein was a clear and present danger by asserting that Saddam maintained viable links to Al Qaed—a claim that the 9/11 Commission would later debunk while also dispelling any notions that Al Qaeda had maintained an independent presence inside Iraq prior to the 2003 U.S. invasion.[23] President Bush repeatedly alluded to Saddam in the context of 9/11, and this persuasion via innuendo proved so effective that, during the summer and fall of 2002, roughly 20 to 25 percent of Americans believed that Saddam Hussein had been directly involved in 9/11. About 48 percent thought that even if he was not involved, Saddam Hussein still retained strong links to Al Qaeda.[24]

Compounding the threat, President Bush claimed Saddam Hussein was seeking weapons of mass destruction, which, if Iraq did not use them to attack the United States directly, could be given to Al Qaeda.[25] Critics presented no firm evidence to conclusively prove otherwise. In a public psyche still traumatized by 9/11, President Bush's arguments gained traction, particularly after Colin Powell's presentation at the United Nations, and Pew polling showed public support for unilateral action rising.[26]

The Bush administration also presented Iraq as a soft-power opportunity with hard-power benefits. As explained by Douglas Feith in 2004, Iraq could serve as the first step to "transform the Middle East and the broader world of Islam generally,"[27] by creating a liberal democracy that could then be replicated throughout the region. U.S. ideological and, by extension, geopolitical, preeminence would be projected into a region populated by millions of Arab Muslims, and a swamp of potential Al Qaeda support would be drained to U.S. strategic advantage.[28]

Despite a lack of UN approval, a U.S.-led "coalition of the willing" attacked the 400,000-strong Iraqi armed forces in March 2003 and took the country within one month at a loss of only 137 dead.[29] This smashing victory, however, was counterproductive in combating Al Qaeda. Reinforcing political and hard-power dynamics rapidly spiraled counter to U.S. interests.

Internationally, the U.S. invasion of Iraq appeared wanton and unjust, and it violated not only traditional U.S. political values, but also the generally accepted political norms and values of both developed and developing states and their publics, particularly Muslim ones from which Al Qaeda draws its support. The United States, which had the world's sympathy post-9/11, became increasingly isolated, and U.S. credibility, legitimacy, and moral authority suffered.[30]

Al Qaeda cast itself as defending against this broadly unpopular U.S. action, and its overall popularity rose, which strengthened its hard-power capacity through increased recruitment, territory, and finances from the general populace. Al Qaeda in Iraq not only came into existence, but it became the most active Al Qaeda franchise, and its violence significantly shaped the tenor of Iraq's political evolution. More broadly, the declining capacity of U.S.-allied authoritarian Muslim states, whose range of action is reduced by pro–Al Qaeda and anti-American public opinion, also reduced overall U.S. efficacy and strategic depth.

Domestically, the U.S. public became increasingly divided. By blending Saddam Hussein with Osama bin Laden, two very different people who are viewed very differently throughout the world, the potency and integrity of the term "terrorism" depreciated. Continued bandying about of the counterterrorism banner on subjective topics other than Osama bin Laden's Al Qaeda and its purported Pakistani safe havens produced domestic political fragmentation and turmoil, and this limited the U.S. government's freedom of action.

Step II, deploying U.S. troops around the world against major known Al Qaeda allies, was intended to help governments threatened by Al Qaeda–associated terrorists reclaim their sovereignty. U.S. actions primarily involved sending U.S. Special Forces and intelligence operatives to either engage in direct pursuit efforts or assist local forces. U.S. efforts against Abu Sayyaf in the Philippines most prominently exemplified this.[31]

Step III, efforts to capture, detain, and interrogate Al Qaeda's leadership and membership, attacked Al Qaeda's diffuse global presence. Al Qaeda is a network, which by design is akin to a balloon. Pressure on one point will only cause the network to dissipate at the contact area and expand elsewhere. Pressure must be applied holistically throughout to shrink the balloon. The Bush administration was confronted with the fact that Al Qaeda had "cells [operating] in about sixty countries, and Islamic insurgencies [existing] in nearly twenty."[32] While Afghanistan and, later, Iraq were at the forefront, a global solution was required to avoid the mistake of employing "a two-country solution to a sixty-country problem."[33]

The Bush administration quickly signed an executive order after 9/11 authorizing the CIA to capture or kill Al Qaeda militants globally.[34] The CIA established Counterterrorist Intelligence Centers (CTICs) in more than two dozen countries in the Middle East, Europe, and Asia. Foreign and U.S. intelligence officers worked side by side to track and capture suspected terrorists and to destroy or penetrate their networks. The U.S. officers and their counterparts at these centers made daily decisions on when and how to apprehend suspects, where and how to interrogate and detain them, and how to disrupt Al Qaeda's logistical and financial support. No matter where the information originates, the CTIC assesses it and coordinates with the local service for action.[35]

This network of centers co-opting foreign security services leverages host-nation strengths of access to and understanding of their society, to U.S. weaknesses of knowledge and access to foreign publics, while allowing the United States to apply its chief strengths—political, economic, and military resources. It remains the essence of the CIA's strategy. Virtually every capture or killing of three thousand suspected terrorists external to Iraq since 9/11 during the Bush administration resulted from this bilateral cooperation.[36]

With such a tightly focused and mutually beneficial agenda of precluding being attacked by Al Qaeda or its allies, this bilateral cooperation has largely persisted despite other political tensions stemming from competing and conflicting priorities elsewhere in the course of normal diplomatic relations. In Indonesia, for example, the State Department doled out tiny amounts of assistance to the Indonesian military only when it made progress on corruption and human rights, but the CIA poured money into Jakarta and developed intelligence ties there after years of tension. In Paris, as U.S.-French acrimony peaked over the Iraq invasion in 2003, the U.S. and French intelligence services were creating the CIA's only multinational operations center and executing worldwide sting operations.[37]

Starting in spring 2004, then–Secretary of Defense Donald Rumsfeld signed an executive order authorizing Special Operations forces to attack Al Qaeda anywhere in the world. It was a sweeping mandate to conduct operations in approximately fifteen to twenty countries not at war with the United States. Locales where Al Qaeda militants were believed to be operating or had sought sanctuary—such as Yemen, Saudi Arabia, Pakistan, and Syria—were the primary focus. The authorities, decision-making arrangements, and contingency plans were put in place on the shelf to take advantage of fleeting opportunities that would have otherwise been missed due to a disconnect between operational realities and the timelines of bureaucratic decision-making. The order's authorities were ultimately invoked to execute missions roughly one dozen times.[38]

Secretary of Defense Robert Gates subsequently honed the effort. He signed a follow-on order that specifically directed the DoD (Department of Defense) to plan a series of operations against Al Qaeda and its associated allies in Pakistan. Increasing interagency collaboration, he also directed formerly independent DoD efforts to be coordinated with the CIA in both planning and execution against tribal area targets.[39]

The Bush administration also reinvigorated the U.S. rendition program. This process of U.S. authorities unilaterally seizing non–U.S. citizens abroad without the permission of either the target suspect's government or the government of the country where they are seized was used throughout the 1990s to bring terrorists such as CIA shooter Mir Aimal Kansi before U.S. courts. The Bush administration, however, altered this practice by sending suspects to allied countries with bad human rights records, such as Egypt and Uzbekistan, to conduct interrogation not permissible under U.S. law.[40] The Bush administration denied this practice was "outsourcing torture," but the *Washington Post*'s Dana Priest, who has broken many stories about this practice since late 2002, quoted a CIA official engaged in renditions that assurances torture would not happen were "a farce."[41] Additionally, the CIA established a series of secret prisons in allied states, known as "black sites,"[42] where Al Qaeda prisoners were tortured for information using water-boarding and other "enhanced interrogation" techniques.[43] Meanwhile, the Department of Defense created a separate system to detain, interrogate, and eventually adjudicate prisoners at Guantánamo Bay that was initially beyond the reach of U.S. law.

The Bush administration also attacked Al Qaeda's communications, the sinews of a diffuse network. Most notably, the Internet's anonymity presents a double-edged sword. If these communications can be either interdicted or exploited, counterterrorism efforts can run sting operations, gather information, and plant disinformation to fragment the network.

The United States and its allies have leveraged their world position to co-opt the technological edge upon which the world's communications, transportation, and information technology industries are, and will continue to be, dependent. The Defense Department's Partnership to Defeat Terrorism (PTDT), a collection of "more than one thousand executives of Fortune 500 companies and experts in academia have become part of what until now has been an informal PTDT network, according to a STRATCOM [United States Strategic Command] briefing paper. That group has been tapped more than two dozen times for assistance, the paper says."[44] Such public-private partnerships against Al Qaeda have allowed the state to effectively form its own network in the private sphere to counter the network of this non-state enemy.

The combined results of the intelligence liaison and communications initiatives have netted thousands of suspected terrorist operatives. Though still very valid, their effectiveness has likely plateaued. The most crucial countries are already involved, and Al Qaeda has had time to adapt.

Striking the financial dimension, President Bush apparently caught Al Qaeda off guard when he publicly signed Executive Order 1324 directed against "Al Qaeda, bin Laden, and associated terrorist groups, freezing any assets belonging to the listed terrorists or their supporters and blocking any economic transactions with them."[45] The Office of Foreign Assets Control replaced its previous counter-narcotics focus with a host of new terrorist front, cover, and other sympathetic organizations to its existing list and, at 12:01 AM on September 24,

2001, the freezes began. Within one month, U.S. and foreign financial institutions froze nearly $100 million in terrorist assets. The U.S. Office of Foreign Assets Control then released the names of 2,500 companies and individuals whose assets were to be blocked. The U.S. government publicly issued additional lists of designated terrorist supporters into the winter of 2002. "The goal was to try to deprive the terrorists of money, but this approach also served to assure the general public that action was being taken in the area of terrorist financing and to keep the intelligence and world communities focused on identifying terrorist financiers."[46]

Congress enacted numerous financial regulations that had been largely rejected prior to 9/11 under the USA PATRIOT (Uniting and Strengthening America by Providing Appropriate Tools Required to Intercept and Obstruct Terrorism) Act. The secretary of the treasury now had the power to name countries, institutions, or transactions found to be of primary money-laundering or terrorist-financing concern, and to implement new requirements that U.S. banks more closely scrutinize their relationships with foreign persons and banks. A multitude of financial industries—insurance companies, money-service businesses, broker dealers, and credit card companies—were potentially subject to a host of new requirements, including reporting suspicious financial activity on the part of their customers to the Treasury Department. Federal Reserve examiners were now tasked with inspecting banks for compliance with antiterrorism directives.[47]

Nonetheless, the larger problem was still unaddressed. "The United States is not, and has not been, a substantial source of Al Qaeda funding."[48] Not connected to U.S. banking entities, much of Al Qaeda's money simply fell outside the scope of unilateral U.S. government efforts.

The Financial Action Task Force (FATF), a group of more than thirty countries and nongovernmental organizations at the heart of the modern financial world that seeks to tighten controls on monetary and financial transfers to prevent criminal abuse, became the engine of multilateral U.S. efforts. In the months after 9/11, the FATF expanded its remit beyond setting standards for the detection and prosecution of money laundering to include setting standards for preventing terrorist financing. It made eight recommendations, the most prominent of which included creating the ability to freeze terrorist assets, licensing informal money remitters, and regulating nongovernmental organizations (NGOs).[49]

With the United States as a driving force, the United Nations Security Council codified these recommendations into mandatory international law. On September 28, 2001, resolution 1373 mandated that member nations had to formulate laws to designate individuals and entities as supporters of terrorism, which could preclude Al Qaeda from raising the money necessary to create an

Afghan-style refuge or from accruing the sums necessary to buy weapons of mass destruction, and freeze their assets, which forces them into slower, more expensive, and less reliable methods of moving and storing money. Shortly thereafter, more than one hundred nations drafted and passed laws addressing terrorist financing or money laundering. As of 2004, approximately 170 nations had created the legal ability to freeze terrorist assets.[50] Numerous additional supporting UN resolutions were also passed, most notably establishing sanctions and travel bans against Al Qaeda, the Taliban, and other affiliates and splinter groups. New UN committees were set up to implement the resolutions. Wary of being publicly named and losing their assets, Al Qaeda sympathizers may have become more reluctant to provide overt support.[51]

Though symbolically and politically significant, this effort did not yield overwhelmingly tangible results. "Al Qaeda can apparently still draw on hardcore donors who knowingly fund it and sympathizers who divert charitable donations to it."[52] Most terrorist attacks are remarkably inexpensive to execute, and there are multiple, complex, informal venues for moving money.

Apart from conceptual weaknesses, implementation was also flawed. Financial industry efforts to create financial profiles of terrorist cells and terrorist fund-raisers proved unsuccessful, and self-policing efforts are limited at best. The U.S. government could not resolve the innate conflicts between evidence-based, court-driven law enforcement and U.S. intelligence, which never before had to be not only quick and actionable but also able to survive a court challenge against such a complex problem set. Initial terrorist designations of suspect individuals and activities were undertaken with limited evidence, some of which reflected more suspicion than fact.[53] Numerous legal challenges resulted, and the United States and the UN were forced to "unfreeze" assets.

Weaknesses in seizing or freezing terrorism monies gave way to a sustained effort to "follow the money," which does not show a suspected NGO or individual actually funds terrorist groups.[54] Rather, certain fund-raising groups or individuals are "linked" to terrorist groups via common acquaintances, group affiliations, historic relationships, phone communications, or other such contacts. This identifying and associative information can then be combined with other data on known or suspected individuals, and independent intelligence and law enforcement investigations against likely terrorists and their supporters can be pursued. Over time, a holistic picture can be painted of the terrorist financing web, which is filled with both witting guilty people and the culpable but innocent unwitting. Since no irreversible decisions are forced and sources of information are preserved for future exploitation because they do not need to be revealed in court, an entire network can be taken down through simultaneous pressure on all nodes at once rather than selectively attacking identified nodes that can then be replaced.

Despite this technique's advantages, the Bush administration's subsequent interdisciplinary "follow the money" approach did not prove to be a panacea either. New laws and terrorism-financing controls have made it easier to investigate cells under surveillance, or after an attack, and this can produce new leads. As summarized by former chief money-laundering investigator for Scotland Yard Cliff Knuckley, however, detecting potential terrorist plots simply by monitoring bank transfers or cash flows—the basis of most current antiterrorism financing laws—is exceedingly difficult because of their ostensibly legitimate or low-level criminal nature. When funds are seized after an attack, accounts have often already been depleted, or the amounts are minuscule. When seized before an attack, such certitude is necessary—particularly regarding intent—that intelligence gathering and the legal realm continue to have difficulty meshing.[55]

Strong words and highly visible initial steps were simply not followed up with sustained and meaningful action. UN member states froze the assets of roughly three hundred Al Qaeda and Taliban members following 9/11. By early 2004, 112 countries had signed on in some form to assist in suppressing terrorist financing. Yet, within the last few years of the Bush administration, few assets were being frozen, and many countries still had not put in place the legal framework necessary to take action. Arms embargoes and travel bans were not being enforced. By 2009, the Bush administration's efforts were on the cusp of coming apart.

Coordination problems mounted as disagreement continued to arise on exactly who was a terrorist, who should be targeted, and who was guilty or innocent. Blacklists from the U.S. Treasury, the United Nations, and the European Union were not concentric. The procedures by which they compiled, explained, and managed the lists were not uniform. In fact, critics leveled that it was clear in several cases that politics had overshadowed legitimate security concerns. In January 2009 the forty-seven-nation Council of Europe stated that the UN and EU blacklists were "totally arbitrary and have no credibility whatsoever."[56]

Early mistakes and disagreements sapped the enthusiasm of other countries to either freeze assets at all or to act simply because the United States made a request. Multilateral freezing mechanisms now have waiting periods before money can be frozen, which means that virtually no new money is actually frozen since the element of surprise is gone. Even if it is frozen, this step is often circumvented within weeks by simple methods due to lax enforcement.[57]

Deeper philosophical and legal differences have also risen to the fore as 9/11-induced urgency faded, and cooperation began to falter. Britain and France, for example, raised concerns about their ability to enforce UN sanctions based on evidence kept secret by the UN that is not made privy to the defendant. The European Court of Justice declared that such secret lists violate the "fundamental rights" of those targeted.

The United States complemented this initial flurry of voluntary, multilateral, financial-system-centric activity with bilateral approaches, most notably with Saudi Arabia and the Gulf states. While problematic at first, this effort ultimately proved moderately successful. Assigning credit to U.S. persuasion efforts, however, would be dubious.

The U.S. intelligence community has identified Saudi Arabia as Al Qaeda's primary source of money both before and since 9/11. Fund-raisers and facilitators from throughout Saudi Arabia and the Gulf raise money for Al Qaeda from witting and unwitting donors and divert funds from Islamic charities and mosques. While no evidence surfaced that the Saudi government itself or any individual senior officials had knowingly assisted Al Qaeda, the 9/11 Commission found rife de facto passive assistance stemming from a lack of awareness of the problem combined with a failure to conduct effective oversight.

Saudi Arabia's cooperation did not meaningfully improve until Al Qaeda proved a political threat to the kingdom. Initial hurdles—lack of a U.S. strategy to counter Saudi terrorist financing, the failure to present U.S. requests through a single high-level interlocutor, and U.S. unwillingness to obtain and release actionable intelligence to the Saudis—were corrected, but cooperation was still ambivalent and selective. Al Qaeda operations in May and November 2003 within the kingdom, however, focused the Saudi government's attention on its terrorist-financing problem, and U.S.-Saudi cooperation dramatically improved.

Despite somewhat improved cooperation from Saudi Arabia after 2003, the Bush administration's complementing step of bilateral outreach efforts was largely met with only symbolic cooperation. By the Bush administration's close, the U.S. Department of State analogizes Kuwait, a key U.S. ally, to assisting in the manner Saudi Arabia did prior to when it became a victim of a series of Al Qaeda attacks in 2003. The United Arab Emirates, the primary financial center of the Middle East, had only two analysts assigned to terrorist financing by 2009.

Regardless of the approach, the U.S.-Al Qaeda struggle's political dimension was given short shrift. The long-ago neutralization of whatever few acknowledged wealthy backroom financiers and secret bank accounts that did exist, when contrasted against Al Qaeda's enduring presence and potency, shows that rather than a crime family, which can be deconstructed through countering a limited membership, Al Qaeda is the embodiment of a political current. Al Qaeda's ability to raise and move money acts as a barometer of its political support. Any future solutions must recognize this political nature, which in practical terms means a) an emphasis on a large volume of small-sized donations, b) unofficial channels, c) a multidisciplinary approach blending intelligence and law enforcement emphasizing intelligence, and d) as with the U.S. narcotics problem, addressing both the incentive to give (demand) at least as much if not more so than the money arriving (supply).

At first blush, Steps I–III paid real dividends. Discounting battlefield detainees in Iraq and Afghanistan, roughly four thousand people were detained worldwide from 9/11 until summer 2005, with Pakistan alone transferring over seven hundred Al Qaeda operatives. No major terrorist attacks occurred against the U.S. homeland or its interests, and several major plots were disrupted, the most significant being an attempt to hijack ten airliners out of Heathrow.[58]

Step IV, the Department of State's "Shared Values" campaign, tried to address the political aspect of countering Al Qaeda by improving U.S. public standing. "The effort was designed by a talented Madison Avenue advertising executive; she described the task as 'almost as though we have to redefine what America is. This is the most sophisticated brand assignment I have ever had.' It was to feature public-service ads televised in Muslim countries, as well as CD-ROMs, pamphlets, and a splashy magazine for young Muslims."[59]

The U.S. soft-power effort, however, was drastically less successful than the hard-power effort, and the campaign ended in early 2003. Conceptually, the Shared Values campaign was "apparently . . . flawed, with the films showing how well Muslims lived and were treated in America, rather than explaining or defending U.S. policies. Worse, the countries asked to run the films—Egypt, Jordan, and Lebanon—refused, saying they would not 'run messages on behalf of other governments.'"[60]

The United States was also not a credible interlocutor. As of the twenty-first century, the United States is perceived as a "hated and feared advocate of a new imperial order, one that has much the same characteristics as nineteenth-century European imperialism: military garrisons; economic penetration and control; support for leaders, no matter how brutal and undemocratic, as long as they obey the imperial power; and the exploitation and depletion of natural resources. Because Muslims have seen this before, America is no longer the nation of Franklin Roosevelt, who destroyed fascism and forced Churchill to begin dismantling the British Empire, nor of Dwight Eisenhower, who stopped the brazen, racist Anglo-French-Israeli land grab at Suez, nor even of Ronald Reagan, who defied the atheistic Soviets, armed the mujahideen, and freed Eastern Europe. It is, moreover, no longer the nation to which Muslims will give the benefit of the doubt in situations where America claims to be an even-handed, honest broker in dealing with them relative to Israel or other matters. . . . Rather, America is now regarded as a nation that supports and protects Arab tyrants from Rabat to Riyadh, that has abandoned multiple generations of Palestinians to cradle-to-grave life in refugee camps, and that blindly supports Israel, arming and funding her anti-Muslim violence and preventing Muslims from arming sufficiently to defend themselves."[61]

As explained by Shibley Telhami in the *Middle East Journal*, "We in the West, in the United States, cannot wage that war of ideas. For one thing, we would not be trusted. I do not think that the U.S. policy right now can be oriented at 'winning [the] hearts and minds' of the Middle East in the short term. That is not going to happen. The U.S. has a legacy of decades that is based in part on our policy and in part on impression; it is not going to be able to change the paradigm overnight simply by a charm campaign. . . . People are not going to trust the message if they don't trust the messenger."[62] Only U.S. actions in sync with touted U.S. values, not words alone, will be able to credibly engage the grievances, priorities, and interests of the public upon whom Al Qaeda depends and seeks to co-opt.

### Al Qaeda's Response to Initial Bush Administration Post-9/11 Strategy

Losing Mullah Mohammed Omar's Afghanistan, which possessed the potential to provide a strategic sanctuary, was an undeniable setback. It hindered a core tenet of Al Qaeda's strategy—"that radical Islamists must gain control of a nation . . . [as] a prelude to knocking over the dominoes of the world's secular Muslim regimes."[63] Al Qaeda responded by fleeing to Pakistan's tribal areas from where it continued the fight by interlacing itself with indigenous militant groups, who were positioned to take advantage of the extensive regional infrastructure that had existed since the Soviet era. Pakistani sovereignty, meanwhile, protected Al Qaeda and its militant allies against direct U.S. attacks of any serious magnitude or substance.

Al Qaeda, however, took the long view. As explained by bin Laden, "The one who prolonged us with one of His helping hands and stabilized us to defeat the Soviet Empire is capable of prolonging us again to defeat America on the same land, and with the same sayings, and that is the Grace of God." Akin to the early Islamic victories of Badr and the Battle of the Trench, where Prophet Mohammed won against superior forces, the stage was now set for a Soviet-era, mujahideen-style victory over U.S. and allied forces.[64]

By contrast, the U.S. taking of Iraq, a situation born of offensive U.S. action, was a gift to the jihadist movement, and Osama bin Laden's Al Qaeda quickly co-opted emerging Iraqi-based anti-U.S. Islamic militant forces. As compared to Afghanistan, where Al Qaeda drew the United States into a trap, this was a fight of U.S. choosing on turf of U.S. choosing, and the Bush administration publicly avowed the fight's importance.[65] Not only would an Al Qaeda victory in Iraq possibly create a chink in the international system in the heart of the Middle East, but it would have tremendous political cachet. In the interim, the massive consumption of U.S. political, economic, and military resources necessary to sustain Iraq's barely existent, U.S.-backed government burdened the United States, and thus indirectly aided Al Qaeda efforts in Afghanistan and elsewhere, while Al Qaeda exploited anti-U.S. sentiment to increase its operational capacity.

Facilitating these two victories became Al Qaeda's primary objective. Yet, whether intentionally or not, Al Qaeda had picked a fight with the Western world, and its immediate need was to adjust the strategic balance. Not forgetting its main enemy, Al Qaeda temporarily loosened its U.S.-only focus to strike the United States indirectly via its allies, especially the Europeans, to reduce the number of combatants. Framed within an increasingly anti-U.S. post-9/11 political climate where the United States and other major world powers, particularly Europe, had been drifting apart, especially since the 2003 invasion of Iraq, Al Qaeda began to launch attacks in late spring 2002, after Afghanistan stabilized. "Of the twenty nations Al Qaeda threatened, eighteen [were] attacked, a 90 percent correlation" by 2004.[66]

These attacks struck a balance between conveying the ability to inflict enough pain at will and striking allied countries on a 9/11 scale that might provoke retribution. The 2004 Madrid train bombing, which immediately preceded a national election, was emblematic. After this attack killing hundreds, which Al Qaeda explained as both a warning and retribution for Spanish policy, an antiwar president was elected. Spain quickly withdrew from Iraq.

"Its allies wept with America after September 11 and then swiftly concluded that only America was under attack. The idea that Western civilization had been the target was not convincing. While America and its allies stood shoulder to shoulder when they faced a common Soviet foe, Islamic terrorism seemed to have America alone in its sights. Why cozy up to a primary target, America's allies asked themselves, when it will only make you a secondary one?"[67]

## PART II. SECURING GAINS AND PREPARING FOR THE LONG RUN
### U.S. Efforts

With the fall 2006 release of the Iraq Study Group's report establishing common terms of debate and the Democratic takeover of Congress forcing the issues it raised, the Bush administration was forced to review its policy in Iraq, which it touted as the central front against Al Qaeda to preclude giving Al Qaeda a Middle East base from which to attack the United States.[68] The administration opted to secure Iraq, and U.S. interests generally, through confronting Iran, whom it saw as a regional fulcrum aiding Iraqi insurgents, Afghan insurgents, and pursuing nuclear weapons that Iran could give to terrorists while menacing other U.S. interests—notably Israeli security and a stable U.S. oil supply, among others—by implementing a series of four interlocking understandings with the Israelis, Saudis, and Jordanians, allies who also saw an Iranian threat. The ultimate result, however, was to make combating Islamic militancy a function of competing U.S. interests to Al Qaeda's strategic benefit.[69]

At the core of this approach, the Bush administration sought to ensure Israeli security. Protecting Israel's citizenry and territorial integrity from both external attack as well as internal subversion was a necessary precursor to regional stability given the potential political and military fallout from a serious threat. Given Israel's close ties to the United States, this U.S. priority also created a U.S.-disposed regional power balance.

In response to Arab concerns, the Bush administration made the Israeli-Palestinian issue a focus, but it did so in line with the views of Israel's conservatives. Israel's ceding of Gaza effectively killed President Bush's "Road Map" to Palestinian statehood and, with no diplomatic headway since Hamas's 2006 parliamentary election, intra-Palestinian violence rose.[70] The region widely viewed the United States as having shifted from the role of honest broker to openly favoring Israel with a conservative bent. A respected Arab interlocutor was needed, and so the Saudis vowed to urge the Palestinians to work together and in earnest with Israel.[71]

Achieving an Israeli-Palestinian peace agreement would likely have directly increased U.S. strategic leverage in the region. With the Palestinians, the political space that Iran could have exploited would have likely decreased as they, especially Hamas, would then not have desperately needed foreign backing against a U.S.-backed Israeli Goliath.[72] With Israel, increased peace and stability inside Israel would have likely improved Israel's range of political maneuver—a factor rich with potential to be exploited to U.S. benefit.

The United States would also likely have gained indirect political, and thus strategic, benefit from improving the Palestinians' plight. In the eyes of much of the rest of the world, particularly among Muslims, the United States is seen as allowing the suffering of the Palestinians to continue. A U.S.-credited just and enduring peace ending indefinite hostilities could only improve U.S. standing with the world's Muslim publics, the masses from which Al Qaeda draws support.[73]

To this end, then–Secretary of State Condoleezza Rice held the widely attended 2008 Annapolis Israeli-Palestinian conference.[74] Reflecting the administration's formal view, the conference called for a Palestinian state before President Bush left office. Worse than if the Bush administration had not tried, however, little U.S. action followed, and U.S. standing suffered after raising the issue's prominence and participants' hopes.

Viewing any Shiite gains as benefitting Iran—despite the role of competing interests of the region's Shia (who exist under a wide variety of political, economic, and security circumstances throughout the region), the role of nationalism, which has been driven into the region since colonization, and the role of ethnicity with the Persian/Arab distinction—the United States and its allies were also to work against Shiite ascendance in the Middle East. Virtually all of the Sunni regimes upon whom the United States depends have Shia minorities. It was perceived that empowering Sunni regimes against their Shia minorities made these U.S.-allied states more internally unified, and thus better able to counter Iranian influence.[75]

In Lebanon, where the Bush administration's calculus placed Hezbollah in particular and its Shiite followers in general under Iranian sway,[76] the Bush administration, and the Saudis at its behest, gave vast political and financial aid to Sunni Prime Minister Fouad Siniora for his political struggle with Hezbollah's Sheikh Hassan Nasrallah. "American, European, and Arab officials [stated] that the Siniora government and its allies had allowed some aid to end up in the hands of emerging Sunni radical groups in northern Lebanon, the Bekaa Valley, and around Palestinian refugee camps in the south. These groups, though small, were seen as a buffer to Hezbollah; at the same time, their ideological ties were with Al Qaeda."[77]

It is not at all a given that Hezbollah, a domestic Arab Lebanese political entity with stature and its own agenda, would blindly follow and sacrifice itself for Persian Iran and its interests. At one point when Hezbollah was weaker and overly dependent upon foreign aid, it may have been at the mercy of and done the bidding of Iran, perhaps even if counter to its own short-term interests, but Hezbollah has evolved beyond this window of vulnerability.[78] Within Lebanon, Nasrallah had become the nominal leader of the largely sectarian political protests against the Siniora government. While acknowledging its violent capabilities, Hezbollah is viewed by most Lebanese as "a political force of some note, with a role to play inside Lebanon."[79]

While akin to when the United States and its Saudi proxy yoked Sunni jihadist strength to fight the Soviets in Afghanistan, the crucial difference now was that the U.S.-Saudi alliance was attempting to manipulate Al Qaeda–style jihadists against Iran, a Middle Eastern Muslim, albeit Persian and Shiite, country. The underlying premise that Sunni jihadists would see Shiite Muslims as a bigger enemy than the United States, a non-Muslim country generally held by jihadists to be responsible for Muslim suffering throughout the world, however, is simply not an ideologically safe bet. Iconic militant al-Zawahiri explicitly forbidding attacks upon Shia in favor of attacks on the United States, the common enemy, in a 2005 letter letter to Abu Musab al-Zarqawi, the then-leader of Al Qaeda in Iraq, attests to the dubiousness of this premise.[80]

At best, the United States will have manufactured more of the very radical Sunni jihadists who constitute Al Qaeda while playing one U.S. enemy against another so that U.S. aims are achieved at the militants' expense.[81] The militants will execute the goals that the U.S.-Saudi alliance intends for them. They will also be destroyed or sufficiently weakened in the process.

At worst, and cognizant that it only took nineteen operatives to execute the 9/11 attacks, the United States will have increased the pool of potential enemy recruits. The militants will not execute the goals that the United States intends for them. They will also turn on their regional benefactors upon becoming self-sufficient.

As evidenced by Al Qaeda, there is no guarantee that this movement can be controlled once it is stoked. Though accepting help from secular regimes, they are rejectionists of the modern nation-state system. They have their own goals, objectives, and desires. Once they are made capable and self-sufficient, state leverage over them decreases. The summer/fall 2007 fighting in Beirut at the Nahr al-Bared Palestinian refugee camp against Fatah al-Islam exemplified this.[82]

Lastly, the Saudis, as a U.S. proxy, were to weaken Syrian president Bashar al-Assad's regime through engaging al-Assad's political opposition. The Bush administration accused Syria of being a major conduit of fighters, money, and weapons for the Iraqi insurgency, which also threatened the Saudis. The Bush administration further accused Syria of being a conduit for Hezbollah, thereby enabling a de facto alliance with its Iranian backers while enabling it to pressure the United States in Lebanon. Underlying everything, the Syrians were still at odds with Israel over the Golan Heights.[83] By pressuring Syria, the Bush administration sought movement on one or more of these fronts.

Refusing an engagement policy but also lacking leverage to pursue meaningful containment or compel substantial policy changes, the administration opted to try to undermine Syria's dictatorship by secretly assisting its internal opposition, which meant engaging Syria's Muslim Brotherhood. Despite their common goal of deposing Bashar al-Assad, the Muslim Brotherhood's core ideological identity prevented it from directly engaging the United States. Once again, the Saudis served as the United States' proxy interlocutor.

As in Lebanon, this tack flirted with the very Sunni jihadists the United States is trying to defeat. Even in the Syrian context where there is a secular component to the Syrian opposition, there is no guarantee that the secular component has or will maintain the upper hand, or that it could substantively impact the outcome. The same strengths and weaknesses found in the administration's approach to Lebanon again applied.

With this plan in place, the Bush administration ratcheted up the political and military tension between the United States and Iran. Starting in August 2006, the U.S. military began detaining and interrogating hundreds of Iranians in Iraq. "'The word went out . . . for the military to snatch as many Iranians in Iraq as they can,' a former senior intelligence official said. 'We're working these guys and getting information from them. The White House goal is to build a case that the Iranians have been fomenting the insurgency and they've been doing it all along—that Iran is, in fact, supporting the killing of Americans.'"[84]

On January 10, 2007, President Bush stated in a televised speech that Iran and Syria were "allowing terrorists and insurgents to use their territory to move in and out of Iraq. Iran is providing material support for attacks on American troops. We will disrupt the attacks on our forces. We'll interrupt the flow of support from Iran and Syria. And we will seek out and destroy the networks providing advanced weaponry and training to our enemies in Iraq."[85] On January 14, 2007, Vice President Dick Cheney warned of "a nuclear-armed Iran, astride the world's supply of oil, able to affect adversely the global economy, prepared to use terrorist organizations and/or their nuclear weapons to threaten their neighbors and others around the world."[86] In winter 2007, the U.S. baseline naval force in the Gulf was indefinitely increased from one carrier strike group to two. Vice President Cheney publicly emphasized this was a warning to Iran and should not be misconstrued as being related to Iraq. When new groups rotated in, virtually all of Iran would be at risk to U.S. forces.[87] These heightened tensions became a permanent facet of U.S.-Iranian relations, and speculation abounded as to whether or not the Bush administration would launch a parting attack in its closing months before it ceded power.

The intended results in Iraq, however, did not materialize. At the Bush administration's close, the United States' political fate in Iraq was hitched to Iraq's Shia leaders in an electoral democracy where the Shia formed roughly half to two-thirds of the population, but the Shiite and American visions for Iraq were at odds. The United States wanted a unified, federal-style Iraq where the three main religio-ethnic confessions shared power, and the United States used its political, economic, and military aid to pressure the Iraqi government to meet the majority of the U.S.-established governance, economic, and security benchmarks—necessary milestones for political reconciliation and economic development such as determining political boundaries, sharing oil revenue, and so forth—that would enable the development of an inclusive government and a U.S. withdrawal.[88] In the immediate wake of decades of repression, however, it was highly unlikely that the Shia would peacefully surrender power in any significant way to a Sunni minority,[89] and the Shia leadership, with Iranian support, sought to dominate the country to the exclusion of other religio-ethnic groups. Not a unified lot, the Iraqi government's Shia leadership was also potently pressured by rival Shiite militia leaders, upon whom the government was dependent for survival because of Sunni resistance and de facto Kurdish independence.

Moqtada al-Sadr personified this conundrum. He pressured the Iraqi national government to strongly pursue sectarian interests. He and the United States clashed militarily. At the same time, he was effectively sustaining the Iraqi national government, a vehicle for Shiite national dominance. The United States was simultaneously dependent upon and in conflict with Iraq's emerging power structure.

From the perspective of the United States, these Shiite militia leaders could not be allowed to dominate Iraq. At best, they were an unwitting extension of Iranian influence. At worst, they acted at Iran's behest.[90]

The U.S.-dependent national government's Shia leadership, upon whom the United States depends, was becoming increasingly isolated and weakened as it failed to capitalize on the 2007 U.S. troop surge to make headway on the Bush administration benchmarks to significantly broaden its base of appeal.[91] The Kurds refused to cede Kirkuk to the central government, and they intimated war if their autonomy was reduced. The patience of the Sunnis, who ended their insurgency in the expectation of inclusion into the emerging power structure, was wearing thin as the Shiite-led government failed to keep its promises of jobs and political power, and they also intimated violence.[92]

The Bush administration was caught in a catch-22 situation. If the United States squeezed Iran, Iran squeezed the Shia militias, who could attack U.S. troops and pose as stumbling blocks in Iraq's national political process, upon which the United States depended. If Iran wished to squeeze the United States, it ensured that the United States would stay bogged down by energizing the militias. A continued U.S. presence supporting the Iraqi national government permitted the existing situation to continue. Pressing for meaningful change toward U.S. goals, however, only destabilized the Iraqi national government and risked unraveling it completely.

Invading Iraq to "fight them there so that we don't have to fight them here" made no sense when the war started as Iraq had no real connection to Osama bin Laden's Al Qaeda.[93] Now, however, Al Qaeda is now almost certain to benefit regardless of the outcome. If Iraq succeeds, Al Qaeda, in the eyes of its potential followers, will claim credit for anything short of a capable government in a pacified country completely absent U.S. forces. Unwittingly playing into Al Qaeda's hands, President Bush stated prior to departing office that manageable violence, as opposed to peace, was acceptable, and senior U.S. military officers questioned the Iraqi state's viability absent a continued U.S. presence.[94] If Iraq ultimately descends into chaos, Al Qaeda will be able to claim and receive credit for having defeated the leader of the international system in the eyes of its potential followers by virtue of being the last one on the battlefield. Al Qaeda's perceived potency will increase its standing within the greater jihadist community, and Al Qaeda will gain more influence to convert to operational muscle.

A regional proxy war will likely result in Iraq should the U.S.-backed national government fail. Iraq's Sunni neighbors, particularly the Saudis, will likely back Iraq's Sunni confession.[95] The Iranians will very likely continue to back the Shia. The Kurds will likely either be left by the wayside, invaded by Turkey, or harassed from all sides in an effort to tamp down stirrings of Kurdish independence within Iraq while squelching any international influence that might rile up restive Kurdish populations among Iraq's neighbors, particularly Turkey and Iran.

The Bush administration's fear that Al Qaeda will obtain a new base from which to attack the United States, however, is unlikely to happen. Al Qaeda is not popular in Iraq.[96] Iraq's Sunnis embraced Al Qaeda because they fought common enemies—the U.S., Kurd, and Shia forces. Future inter-confessional war will provide AQI (Al Qaeda in Iraq) a sectarian niche. AQI's actions, however, will be limited to the interests and sensitivities of its besieged Sunni hosts. To the extent intercommunal peace develops, Al Qaeda's window for existence will almost certainly progressively weaken.

With U.S. political, economic, and military resources substantively focused on Iraq, the Bush administration continued to rely upon Pakistan, whose efforts were minimal at best, as a proxy force despite Afghanistan's rapidly deteriorating political, economic, and military situation. Publicly, the administration kept the issue low profile, and only readied a small troop dispatch, which fell to the Obama administration to execute. Privately, however, the Bush administration went on the offensive in the Al Qaeda heartland in an attempt to score operational victories without altering its greater strategy and policy framework.

The Bush administration introduced unmanned drone missile strikes. Throughout 2006 and 2007, the United States sought permission for each launch, which totaled only ten. By summer 2008, however, a series of terrorist plots in Europe were disrupted that all traced back to Pakistan. The Bush administration promptly reversed its policy of seeking Pakistani permission, and the volume of attacks rose dramatically. From August 31, 2008, to late March 2009, the U.S. government carried out at least thirty-eight drone strikes in northwest Pakistan.[97]

U.S. officials stated that this effort had achieved the most serious disruption against Al Qaeda since 2001 with nine senior Al Qaeda leaders killed out of a list of twenty, as well as dozens of lower-level operatives. Even more significantly, distrust grew in Al Qaeda circles. Per one U.S. official, "people are showing up dead or disappearing." The militants "started hunting down people who they think are responsible" for security breaches. Al Qaeda was "losing a bunch of their better leaders. But more importantly, they're wondering who's next."[98]

Pakistan embraced the effort. Not only was it consistent with Musharraf's plan to split the difference between Al Qaeda and the Taliban, but it also burdened the United States with the vast majority of the political fallout. Meanwhile, Musharraf's Al Qaeda enemies were dealt substantive losses.

Publicly, the Pakistani government protested these missile attacks. The Pakistanis stated these strikes were violations of its sovereignty. They further claimed the attacks were eroding trust between the allies.

Privately, however, the Pakistanis actively assisted. They permitted use of their bases at Shamsi, Jacobabad, Pasni, and Dalbandin. These locations put virtually all of the insurgent staging points and infiltration routes into Afghanistan within U.S. range.[99]

U.S. and British special operations troops also began conducting missions inside Pakistan starting in March 2008, following a January 2008 agreement with Musharraf. Intended as surreptitious reconnaissance, not ground combat, these missions were designed to gather intelligence on enemy leadership, which could then be attacked by unmanned drones. In July 2008, however, without informing the British, a classified national security presidential directive authorized "'kinetic' operations against targets on the HVT [high value target] list."

While this approach increased U.S. security by not relying upon a Pakistani state suspected of warning targets of impending U.S. attack, these efforts had "not killed or captured any prominent Al Qaeda leader" by fall 2008. Hundreds of deaths in collateral damage resulted. When these unilateral strikes began and the pace subsequently increased, Pakistani military cooperation decreased and U.S.-Pakistani political tensions increased.

At the state level, Pakistan reacted vociferously. In September 2008, Pakistan threatened to cut off U.S. access to Karachi, the port through which 85 percent of U.S. supplies bound for Afghanistan flowed. Pakistan also appealed to Britain to stop the U.S. practice, thus threatening to cause friction in the U.S.-British alliance. These attacks even united Pakistan's fractious civilian and military leaders, who vowed to defend sovereignty "at all costs."[100]

At the public level, there was widespread revulsion to U.S. efforts. Pakistani public opinion against the United States rose markedly, thus constraining the Pakistani state. The intense collateral damage handed the militants a major propaganda victory. It also drove the general public and the militants closer together through collective victimization, which increased the militants' political support and operational capacity. This was the direct opposite of what a counterinsurgency effort is supposed to accomplish—driving a wedge between the insurgents and the general public and isolating the militants.

### Al Qaeda's Efforts

While Iraq and Afghanistan were important foci, they were not viable operational bases for Al Qaeda, and so Al Qaeda sought to exploit ungoverned areas nominally controlled by weak state structures, failed states with no functioning government, or states with internal insurgencies. Such areas are typically awash with weapons. They often lack a strong U.S. presence, either directly or through proxy. If existent, host-nation governments are either too weak to harm Al Qaeda, can be co-opted, or are supportive of Al Qaeda, out of genuine belief, national interest, or fear. Often there is a local militant group with whom Al Qaeda can ally itself operationally and upon whom it can piggyback politically to further enhance its position. Ideally, these areas also strike a balance between isolation, which affords sanctuary to enable rear-area functions and organizational development, and access to the front.

Somalia exemplified Al Qaeda capitalizing on a failed state.[101] Lacking a functioning, sovereign central government since the end of the Cold War, Somalia had devolved into a series of fiefdoms under warlord or tribal control in a long-running, low-grade civil war, in which the United States briefly engaged under President Bill Clinton, whose efforts ended with the "Blackhawk down" incident. After the Kenyans ended their Bush administration-backed 2006–2008 occupation meant to squelch an Islamist-leaning government, the weak tribal-based Somali transitional government became dominated by the Islamists, who have historically never had a foothold in Somali society.

In a move reminiscent of the Taliban, who rose to power as a force for law and order amid chaos and against weak opposition, citing noble motives based in religious justifications, Somalia's Al Qaeda-linked al-Shabab militia reduced the weak internationally recognized government to a few square city blocks of sovereignty. Only a combination of roughly seven thousand troops from the largely U.S.-funded African Union Mission in Somalia (AMISOM) and U.S. weapons shipments to Somalia's internationally backed government, actions which are much more of a stop-gap measure than reflective of a genuine policy, precluded another Taliban-style state. Al Qaeda, however, has gained de facto national political cover in this increasingly hospitable political and operational environment.[102]

Yemen also became important. The tribal structure, not the national government, dominates in the more remote and distant regions from the capital. Lack of physical infrastructure and economic development combined with very limited state capacity provide both physical and political isolation, all of which collectively yield a kind of semiautonomy throughout much of the country. An Al Qaeda presence estimated in the hundreds has slid into pre-existing crevices of internal domestic unrest and political instability. It has fallen to the Obama administration to engage Yemen with a blend of security, economic, and political assistance to enlist the Yemeni state as an indigenous surrogate against an increasingly multinational jihadist presence.[103]

Meanwhile, embracing the Clausewitzian dictum of attacking an enemy's center of gravity, Al Qaeda leveraged time to threaten the U.S. public with "economic bankruptcy" through targeting "key sectors of your economy until you stop your injustice and aggression." As bin Laden noted in 2004, "America is a superpower, with enormous military strength and vast economic power, but all of this is built on foundations of straw. So it is possible to target those foundations and focus on their weakest points, which even if you strike only one-tenth of them, then the whole edifice will totter and sway."[104] Unfortunately, the economic facts since 9/11 support Al Qaeda's view that "aborting the American economy is not an unattainable dream."[105]

Al Qaeda's operations are relatively cheap. The 9/11 attacks, Al Qaeda's largest operation that took approximately one year to execute, only cost roughly $500,000. The March 2004 Madrid train bombings only took approximately $80,000. The July 7, 2005, London subway bombings needed only $15,000, and this included airfare to travel to Pakistan to consult with Al Qaeda planners. In a 2009 London trial of men accused of planning to blow up airplanes bound for the United States in 2007, it has been explained in open court how ingredients were purchased at local drugstores to build bombs that would have cost approximately fifteen dollars apiece.[106]

Reflecting the asymmetric nature of the struggle, Al Qaeda has made headway toward its goal of being able to "rip . . . [its enemies] . . . apart economically, as well."[107] Al Qaeda's efforts to sustain itself at U.S. expense by raising money inside the United States and allied economies include systematic criminal enterprises that have proven very successful. Credit card fraud, theft, reselling stolen goods, and purposely obtaining loans for ostensibly legitimate reasons with the intent to default on them are commonplace.

By contrast, Bush administration hard-power efforts have proved costly, and they do not come at Al Qaeda's expense. In 2008, the Bush administration's last full year, one year worth of post-9/11 war effort cost approximately $238 billion on top of a baseline defense budget of $482 billion, for a total of $720 billion in defense spending, a 62 percent baseline increase from 2001, which does not include classified CIA spending, the FBI budget, and the costs associated with other national security agencies.[108] In 2010, cumulative post-9/11 war spending exceeded $1 trillion. Upon inheriting two open-ended wars, the Obama administration's Office of Management and Budget forecast in 2009 the costs of another decade of fighting at roughly $889 billion.[109] Only World War II, which deployed seventy-five times as many forces in a national mobilization for roughly four years, has been more expensive.

Despite these new outlays, President Bush chose to limit the public impact of the war by not asking for wartime economic sacrifices and keeping domestic political priorities largely unchanged. Not only did the administration pass significant tax cuts, thereby reducing revenue, but it also launched the Medicare prescription drug plan, the most significant new entitlement program in decades whose long-term costs will only grow, without also submitting a way to pay for it. President Bush ultimately presided over seven straight years of deficits.[110]

The net cost of Bush administration policies, when accounting for both government spending as well as the war's broader impact on the U.S. economy, has been broadly assessed at $3 trillion. A certain amount of this was clearly unavoidable in pursuing Al Qaeda after 9/11. Much of the economic burden incurred, however, was by choice, as with Iraq, and its impact has been power-fully negative.[111]

The cost of the U.S. war in Afghanistan has almost certainly been dramati-cally increased. The United States devoted at least four times as much money to its war effort in Iraq in 2004, 2005, and 2006 as it did in Afghanistan. Rather than devoting U.S. economic and military resources in 2003 to Afghanistan instead of Iraq before the Taliban and the warlords reasserted control—a move that would likely have proven to be both an effective and efficient follow-up to the stunning 2001–2002 U.S. victory—the Taliban now have the upper hand and the war has become open-ended. The Obama administration's 2010–2011 surge will almost certainly be more expensive than it had to be.

Prior to the U.S. war in Iraq, oil cost less than $25 per barrel, and futures markets predicted that it would hold around that level. With the onset of the war, oil shot up to $140 by 2008. Not only did the war create regional instability that dampened investment in the Middle East, but such dramatically increased prices wreak havoc on the U.S. economy while simultaneously empowering oil-dependent U.S. adversaries, such as Iran.

The U.S. debt soared from $6 trillion in 2001 to just short of $10 tril-lion by 2008. For the first time in American history, the entire war effort was financed by borrowing, and taxes were cut despite the onslaught of major expenditures. All economic pain was simply pushed forward to the future, which will now almost inevitably see a period of significant infla-tion at some point. At the same time, the war-related debt is likely to grow even further as veteran health care, disability payments, and other yet-to-be incurred expenses come to fruition, items which could total up to another half-trillion dollars. When coupled with the Bush administration's failure to even submit plans to meaningfully enlarge the armed forces until near the end of Bush's second term, despite critical troop shortages in both theaters, the wars will almost certainly drag on longer than necessary.[112]

These war-related financial imbalances almost certainly impacted the U.S. government's ability to respond to the 2008 financial crisis. Such massive war-related debt gave the government far less room to maneuver than it would have had otherwise, which constrained the size of the Obama administration's stimu-lus package and any further government efforts, such as follow-on spending to address high unemployment. Consequently, the recession will be longer, unem-ployment will be and remain higher, and deficits will be larger than they would have been without such massive war-related spending. To the extent that the war helped create the conditions for or encouraged loose monetary policy and lax regulations leading up to the housing/financial crisis because of the extensive U.S. capital flow abroad for oil, foreign contractors, and so on, instead of stimu-lating the U.S. economy with domestic spending, the Iraq war and the Bush administration's economic and political policies indirectly helped contribute to the intensity of the post-crash Great Recession and, by extension, brought on the first contraction in the global economy in sixty years.

The United States is on the cusp of facing guns-or-butter political choices. Though the Bush administration's 2007 budget as a percentage of gross domestic product (GDP) was 20 percent with 18.8 percent financed by revenues and 1.2 percent by deficit—which is in line with federal spending averages over the last sixty years of 19.5 percent of GDP financed by 17.9 percent revenues and 1.6 percent deficit spending, with a close GDP balance between defense and entitlement spending at 6.4 percent and 5.1 percent—new contextual factors make it unsustainable. Beneath this veneer of stability, spending on 1960s Great Society entitlement programs, such as Medicare and Medicaid, rose to fill the gap between U.S. spending and increasing U.S. economic capacity to maintain overall spending levels while defense spending as a percentage of GDP steadily fell from its World War II peak. This silent defense cut enabling entitlements avoided consciously forcing political prioritization and the forging of a domestic consensus. As shown by the post-9/11 era, however, indefinite reductions in defense spending as a percentage of GDP due to relatively sustained and significant economic growth coupled with an ever-declining credible security threat, either real or perceived, is not a safe assumption.

Particularly when played out against changing demographics that show an ever-shrinking workforce supporting an increasingly aging population, raw U.S. economic capacity and contemporary taxing and spending priorities are incapable of supporting the United States' current social, political, and economic choices during a long-term, hard-power-dominated U.S.-Al Qaeda struggle. "With declining defense spending gone and Baby Boomer retirements beginning in 2011, America confronts unmitigated and unleashed entitlement spending. According to the Congressional Budget Office (CBO), the three largest entitlement programs—Social Security, Medicare, and Medicaid—alone will increase from 8.4 percent of GDP to 25 percent in 2082."[113] This assessment presumes a) Medicare and Medicaid expenses will moderate, b) high revenues streaming from a repeal of the Bush tax cuts and strong economic output in 2011, and c) unmitigated revenue generation by the Alternative Minimum Tax—none of which has proven to be a safe assumption, much less a likely one. On these current, somewhat rosy budgetary premises, the CBO projects U.S. government revenues will barely cover just these three entitlement programs, much less the rest of the federal budget.

The Bush administration's decoupling of political agendas and their inherent economic burdens has proved strategically hobbling. In the short run, this approach skewed the public debate and set the United States off onto a war in Iraq that was counterproductive to combating Al Qaeda while consuming massive political, economic, and military resources. In the long run, but no less important, this approach has created a new political status quo with artificially low, and unrealistic, expectations regarding the human and political costs of war and peace, as well as their inherent economic obligations. Future administrations will be forced to do exactly what the Bush administration avoided—building enduring domestic consensuses and taking a leadership role to set and balance domestic and foreign priorities to pit the U.S. public's willpower against that of Al Qaeda. Unfortunately, future decisions requiring more of the general public will likely be that much more difficult, and the freedom of action of future administrations will likely be constrained.

Meanwhile, from Al Qaeda's point of view, regardless of whether or not it is correct, the United States is on the economic ropes, and U.S. allies are hurting. In the long run, its strategy of prolonging the fight has been validated. In the short run, Al Qaeda may well assess that the time to attack is in the midst of U.S. economic suffering, particularly in light of the prolonged period since a major strike against the U.S. homeland and an untested president in office, so that U.S. efforts against it might be forced into remission.[114]

## CONCLUSION

Al Qaeda initially attacked U.S.-supported dictatorships throughout the Middle East, the homelands of Al Qaeda's membership, but it was overwhelmed by local security forces. Al Qaeda then took an indirect, U.S.-centric approach and attempted to induce global change by attacking the international system's leader and central support column. After several smaller attacks, this strategy culminated with 9/11.

The Bush administration launched a simultaneously executed four-step response. First, it launched major military initiatives that quickly deposed Al Qaeda's Taliban enablers to deprive Al Qaeda of its Afghan base and, citing a link or the possibility thereof between it and Al Qaeda in the context of weapons of mass destruction post-9/11, the Bush administration successfully deposed Saddam Hussein's regime. Second, the Bush administration attacked Al Qaeda's diffuse global presence. It yoked host-government intelligence capacities and attacked Al Qaeda's communications in the course of setting up a global dragnet with extra-legal detention arrangements. Third, the Bush administration dispatched U.S. troops to aid local governments in battling key Al Qaeda allies, such as the Abu Sayyaf group in the Philippines. Fourth, the Bush administration launched a hearts-and-minds charm campaign to increase U.S. political appeal among the Muslim masses.

Al Qaeda adapted. It prioritized Iraq and Afghanistan. With most of the world arrayed against it, Al Qaeda loosened its U.S.-only focus and began to attack U.S. allies to alter the strategic balance.

Despite some notable successes, such as detaining thousands of Al Qaeda operatives worldwide and successfully helping some governments to subdue their Al Qaeda affiliates, the Bush administration's hard-power net results were mixed. It failed to decisively defeat Al Qaeda and its Taliban enablers in the Afghanistan-Pakistan theater or establish a stable state in Afghanistan. It also failed to create a self-sustaining and viable allied regime in Iraq. Collectively, these actions consumed U.S. political, economic, and military resources, and the U.S. ability at the Bush administration's close to respond to new threats or to reinforce threatened gains was slim to nonexistent.[115]

Crucially, U.S. soft-power efforts failed horribly. Rather than addressing the political grievances that mobilized Al Qaeda to attack the United States in the first place or that induce Al Qaeda's actual or potential followers to provide financial and operational support, the administration's charm campaign talked past the problem of explaining contentious U.S. policies by touting U.S. virtues and cultural openness. Select U.S. hard-power actions, most notably the U.S. invasion of Iraq, continued to inflame public opinion throughout the developing world, particularly among Muslim countries that are Al Qaeda's primary support, and U.S. hard-power actions became a jihadist recruiting engine. With the Bush administration's efforts fundamentally ignoring the conflict's political dimension, Al Qaeda survived the hard-power onslaught bloodied but fundamentally unshaken.

To consolidate its gains, the Bush administration expanded the fight to Iran. While providing for Israel's security, the United States pressured the Shia in Iraq, sought to deny Iran political leverage in Palestine, and funneled jihad-ists against Iranian ally Syria and perceived Iranian proxy Hezbollah. This tack not only stoked jihadist capacity, but it also blurred the U.S. strategic focus by addressing Al Qaeda as a function of countering Iran, with which Al Qaeda was not, and is not, inherently bound. Only unilateral U.S. missile strikes from unmanned drones in Pakistan, which increased in frequency as the administration's end neared, and some largely unsuccessful U.S. commando raids directly attacked the Osama Bin Laden Al Qaeda problem set.

Al Qaeda, on the other hand, settled in for the long haul. While continuing its efforts in Iraq and Afghanistan, Al Qaeda established new forward pres-ences in Yemen and Somalia—both of which were largely devoid of effective state control, had culturally conducive societies, were awash in weapons, were permeated by domestic conflict into which Al Qaeda could insinuate itself, and afforded easy access to nearby battlefields. More indirectly at the strategic level, Al Qaeda leveraged time, which exploits the U.S.-Al Qaeda struggle's economics to Al Qaeda's benefit. It also pits popular U.S. political sentiment, which wavers significantly and can be expected to falter as the wars in Iraq and Afghanistan drag on, against Al Qaeda's political will, which has remained steadfast and focused since its inception.

By the Bush administration's end, the fight had temporarily stabilized. Stability, however, does not equate to stalemate. Underlying political, economic, and military trends favored Al Qaeda.

The United States is likely to suffer strategic hard-power losses when this tenuous stability exhausts itself. Al Qaeda's political power, and thus its operational capacity, will likely increase. Using the international political context to frame and guide its application of force, Al Qaeda was successfully, albeit incrementally, achieving its political goals. Unlike the Bush administration, Al Qaeda had embraced and manipulated the political dimension—and it was gaining.

Chapter 3

# Herding Cats: Al Qaeda
# Post-9/11 Modus Operandi

*The enemy, as the military is fond of saying, is both thinking and adaptable.*
—U.S. government official

The business end of terrorism is killing. To effect this on a sustained basis for political purposes requires the ability to securely 1) plan, support, and execute missions, and 2) recruit, train, and support operatives. All the while, the terrorists must communicate their political message amid state efforts to eradicate them.

Al Qaeda has this capacity because it has constantly adapted to its changing environment. Existing U.S. approaches have caused significant damage and, as of 2011, Al Qaeda is organizationally and financially pressed. Existing U.S. approaches, however, have also largely exhausted their potential, while Al Qaeda's never-ending evolution keeps it a viable, potent threat.

## POST-9/11 MASS, STRUCTURE, AND OPERATIONS
### Mass

Estimates vary widely about Al Qaeda's overall post-9/11 bench strength. The London International Institute of Strategic Studies' Strategic 2003–2004 Survey cited 18,000 Al Qaeda militants worldwide. By contrast, a Saudi official, speaking on background, told United Press International he estimated there were no more than 5,000 Al Qaeda activists and supporters. The CIA, in turn, claims Al Qaeda can draw upon the worldwide support of roughly 6–7 million radical Muslims, 120,000 of whom the CIA estimates are willing to take up arms.[1]

Regardless of the estimate, Al Qaeda has a troublesome manpower reservoir. By comparison, the Irish Republican Army (IRA) had no more than 500 militants, of which maybe 150 were truly hard-core during its 1970s heyday. The West German Baader-Meinhof gang had even fewer, with some estimates going as low as 50 hard-core activists, yet both groups wreaked havoc for years.[2]

## Structure

Prior to 9/11, Al Qaeda had four vertically integrated main entities in descending order in a formal chain of command led by Osama bin Laden.[3] This center projected itself throughout the world by maintaining authority, power, and influence over all subordinate elements. Al Qaeda, however, was not a strict top-down hierarchy. There were loose lateral ties within each main entity, and the whole entity functioned more like a decentralized network with delegated authority as orders flowed from the top down, with initiative also flowing from the bottom up.[4]

The first main entity, the heart of the organization, was a command and control node located in Afghanistan that consisted of three layers. At the top was the overall emir of the entire organization, Osama bin Laden, who did not have a deputy but did have informal advisors. The next layer was a consultative council appointed by bin Laden consisting of very senior, experienced, and trusted members. These men were prominent personalities and trusted followers to ensure legitimacy and loyalty. Merit was relevant, but family, friendship, and nationality also mattered. The last layer, which was decimated after 9/11, consisted of four operational committees, each of which was headed by an emir who was in turn supported by a deputy emir, to handle day-to-day affairs. The military committee executed terrorist operations supported by a finance committee to fund them, a religious studies committee to justify them, and a media/publicity committee to advertise them.[5]

Despite a post-9/11 pummeling, the central command node appears to remain vibrant. The top two layers—Osama bin Laden and key aides, such as Ayman al-Zawahiri—are publicly purported to be in Pakistan's tribal areas, from where they continue to broadcast Internet messages and dispatch instructions. In fact, this command node, which retains centralized control over a reduced organizational core, appears to be expanding its general political guidance and influence over other like-minded, yet independent, militants, such that it is now leading an emboldened movement as much as it is an organization. At the committee level, Al Qaeda appears to be functioning as a systemic organization, not a uniquely contrived amalgam of irreplaceable personalities, with troop losses being regenerated and replacement leaders appointed.[6]

Al Qaeda's second entity, the 055 Brigade—which, prior to 9/11, consisted of approximately two thousand fighters mostly from the Middle East, Central Asia, South Asia, and the Asia-Pacific region who served as shock troops for the Taliban army—has become a shadow of its former self as it lost roughly 25 percent of its strength fighting alongside the Taliban in the 2001 U.S. invasion. As defeat became inevitable, Osama bin Laden ordered this Al Qaeda strategic reserve, which had its most experienced and motivated fighters, to retreat into Pakistan's semiautonomous tribal regions. The 055 Brigade has since taken the moniker of the Shadow Army, and it is now the core of a future force to fight U.S. and Pakistani government efforts in the region and conduct terrorism overseas.[7]

Al Qaeda's third main entity, which was often drawn from the 055 farm team, consists of a global terrorist network of Al Qaeda members posted around the world to conduct attacks or, as exemplified by the 9/11-associated Hamburg Cell, to provide logistical support as a subordinate offshoot of the command node, and it too appears to have been severely weakened. Al Qaeda's displacement from Afghanistan destroyed the centralized headquarters, support, and planning functions. This low-hanging fruit of known and suspected operatives not seized prior to 9/11 were quickly taken down once the political winds shifted, and the U.S. Department of State puts the number of suspects detained since 9/11 at roughly four thousand.[8]

The September 2006 Waziristan Accord nonaggression pacts between FATA tribes, militants, and Islamabad, and other similar agreements, however, hold the seeds of rejuvenation for Al Qaeda's third main entity. New Al Qaeda camps dovetail with allied local militants, many of whom Pakistani intelligence has traditionally assisted as a foreign policy tool to compensate for political weakness or conventional military inferiority when dealing with its neighbors, particularly India. With Al Qaeda interweaving itself into internal Pakistani politics, both Pakistan's choice to combat Al Qaeda and the means to do so requires balancing competing priorities, which may or may not coincide with U.S. interests. Prior to 9/11, the United States viewed these arrangements as a local affair and never pressed the issue. Post-9/11, however, Al Qaeda has found comfortable safe haven in areas under tribal and militant suzerainty, and so local insurgencies and regional political issues have now taken on global implications.[9]

Al Qaeda is reported to have established several camps in North Waziristan, and there is apparently "no shortage of recruits or arms." Now emphasizing the training of "white Muslims" who carry Western passports, there is no standard jihadist profile for authorities to detect. Per the July 2007 National Intelligence Estimate (NIE), the backbone of the jihadist infrastructure not only has not been dismantled, but it is regenerating, and the United States now faces a "heightened threat environment."[10]

Al Qaeda's fourth main entity consists of a loose global network of affiliated and associated transnational groups and sympathetic individuals. Al Qaeda has historically co-opted local groups, which had narrow, country-specific agendas. By aligning itself with local militant groups, vice subsuming them into the organization, Al Qaeda was able to develop roots in the militants' countries without assuming ownership of their struggle. By themselves, these local militant cells were too small and weak to make a political impact. Those who pledged a measure of loyalty and allegiance to Al Qaeda, however, benefited from Al Qaeda's intelligence, money, equipment, training, and recruitment efforts—all force multipliers—and these local militants used the Al Qaeda network to coordinate their activities, which, in turn, increased Al Qaeda's sway.[11]

This main entity has dramatically expanded and risen to the fore as Al Qaeda's most capable and active element. Prior to 9/11, this workhorse consisted of roughly twenty-four groups in sixty countries, totaling roughly five thousand to twelve thousand men, with an Afghan-based core of only thirty key officials. Post-9/11, U.S. actions in Iraq and Afghanistan have only increased militant political angst and increased Al Qaeda's ranks.[12] Not under Al Qaeda central's direct control, these fourth main entity members, who are primarily linked to Al Qaeda's command node by the Internet, have varying degrees of closeness and supplication.

Most often, regional Islamic militant groups functioning independently of Al Qaeda enter into mutual alliances for specific operations or campaigns and then slowly become affiliates.[13] The 2006 morphing into Al Qaeda Organization of the Islamic Maghreb by Algeria's Salafist Group for Preaching and Combat (GSPC), an offshoot/successor of the GIA's (Armed Islamic Group) fight, embodies the story of a self-developed group pledging fealty. Despite an antagonistic history stemming from GIA's slaughtering thousands of innocent civilians in trying to replace Algeria's secular, military-backed government with a fundamentalist Islamic state, post-9/11 Al Qaeda leadership needed safe havens. In a move that erased the Algerians' pariah status in militant Islamic circles and that simultaneously gave Al Qaeda a local affiliate and an operational foothold in North Africa, Osama bin Laden anointed GSPC.[14] The Algerian network, with Al Qaeda's assistance, has since rapidly transformed itself from a local group devoted solely to seizing power at home into a global threat with cells and operations across North Africa, Europe, and the Middle East. It now sponsors training camps in the Sahara and the Sahel, and it supplies fighters to Iraq and Chechnya. The network has also planted deep roots in Europe, where authorities have broken up cells since 2006 in France, Germany, Italy, Spain, and Switzerland.[15]

While Al Qaeda's affiliates have historically focused on issues indigenous to their geographic niche, or, if they looked abroad, it was toward the U.S.-led wars in Iraq and Afghanistan, this dynamic appears to be in flux as of winter 2009–spring 2010. For the first time, an Al Qaeda affiliate, Al Qaeda in the Arabian Peninsula (AQAP), moved beyond attacking U.S. interests and allies abroad to directly attacking the U.S. homeland with its attempted bombing of a U.S. airliner on December 25, 2009, by Umar Farouk Abdul Mutallab. April 2010 witnessed a failed car bombing attempt by an operative of the Pakistani Taliban to bomb New York City's Times Square. Fall 2010 witnessed a Lockerbie-style attempt by AQAP to down multiple planes in mid-air through mail bombs.

While it is still too early to call definitively as of 2010, it appears that Al Qae-da's method of attack also appears to be changing from less frequent, cataclysmic 9/11-style attacks, to low-intensity urban warfare, as embodied in the 2005 London subway bombings. Britain's Sky News foreign affairs editor Tim Marshall reported in late September 2010, for example, that Western intelligence agencies uncovered terrorist plans to simultaneously launch commando raids in cities in Germany, France, and Britain similar to what happened in 2008 in Mumbai, which witnessed the killing of 173 innocent civilians mostly with nothing more than AK-47s, some rudimentary training, and a willingness to die fighting. Al Qaeda's increasing emphasis on recruiting Westerners, notably American and European members of the Muslim diaspora or converts to Islam and others not from Middle Eastern and South Asian countries traditionally associated with Al Qaeda, only increases the odds of success for such an approach.[16]

This strategy, a historical favorite of twentieth-century terrorists and whose value was recognized by late Saudi Arabian Al Qaeda leader Abd al-Aziz al-Muqrin in his combat manual *The War Against Cities*, provides Al Qaeda re-alistic interim steps toward reaching its still unwavering grand objectives at a time when it is increasingly pressed in Pakistan and its spectacular event attack cycle appears broken, even if Al Qaeda has not fully relinquished these 9/11-style aspirations. Not only does this strategy pose lower material demands—standard small arms, such as assault rifles and rocket-propelled grenades, and standard terrorist weapons, such as improvised explosive devices, are all that is neces-sary—but the personnel, training, and planning requirements, as well as execu-tion, are also easier.[17] Far from lacking potency, a direct, ongoing, long-running, low-intensity conflict with Western security forces in urban areas, similar to the Irish Republican Army's bombing campaigns in Belfast and England in the 1980s, has the potential to induce a steady flow of casualties. Both governments and the general public will be forced to confront Al Qaeda–connected violence on a more recurring and immediate basis. When this traditional terrorist tactic is married with its global network, Al Qaeda is positioned to panic and disrupt the U.S. and allied Western societies in a coordinated fashion on a global scale.[18]

This approach is also likely to yield a more closely integrated and power-ful network. As noted by Michael Leiter, director of the National Counterter-rorism Center, "Regional affiliates and allies can compensate for the potentially decreased willingness of Al Qaeda in Pakistan—the deadliest supplier of such training and guidance—to accept and train new recruits." Because such at-tacks permit the perpetrators to identify individual targets, such as when the Mumbai attacks focused in on Jews and Hindus, Al Qaeda will be able to blunt the criticism that it induces Muslim casualties, thereby strengthening its appeal among potential supporters.[19]

The potential combination of more diverse and numerous combatants directly arrayed against the United States markedly raises the U.S. hard-power threat. Crucially, the increasing radicalization of American citizens, and their relatively easy access to Al Qaeda affiliates such as Somalia's al-Shabab, Pakistan's Taliban, and Al Qaeda in the Arabian Peninsula makes it increasingly easy for Al Qaeda to strike inside the United States.[20] New measures will be needed.

The increasing scope of these emerging threats will also most likely force new political choices among competing priorities, both within and between domestic and foreign affairs, to reallocate limited and already strained U.S. economic, political, and military resources. Such a deadly and increasingly present terrorism menace, however, could very easily wear down and shake public confidence as much if not more so than a horrific but exceedingly rare 9/11-style attack. The likely domestic U.S. and allied response—increased paranoia accompanied by more voluminous and more rigid security measures—will likely make domestic politics more fractious and contentious, politicize counter-terrorism efforts, and further isolate Muslim communities from the rest of the larger societies. Such politically distorting pressure from Al Qaeda will only make it even more difficult for the United States to retain the freedoms organic to its political character and to govern in its best interests.[21]

Al Qaeda's associated groups, which are more numerous among developing countries in the Middle East, Asia, and Africa, are also rising in number and lethality. In contrast to affiliated groups, Al Qaeda's command and control node does not maintain direct connections with associated groups. Though these groups share an ideological affinity with Al Qaeda and their very existence is often Al Qaeda–inspired, they operate independently, though in line with Al Qaeda's general philosophy. The Army of Islam, a Palestinian group which claims to have played a key role in the capture of Israeli Corporal Gilad Shalit, for whose return the 2006 Israeli-Lebanese war was ostensibly fought, exemplifies this newfound phenomenon.[22]

It is the individuals who self-actualize into becoming Islamic militants and self-originating cells, however, that have risen to the fore. "'Europe is a field of jihad, and it evolved from a logistical base for the operations of a centralized Al Qaeda to a battlefield itself,' Steve Simon, a former counterterrorism official in the Clinton White House and a senior analyst at the government-funded RAND Corporation, said. 'The foot soldiers . . . recruited themselves right in their own slums. The alienation and the anger behind these attacks [have] been incubating in Europe for more than a decade. The war in Iraq has intensified the resentment, even fury, of these people.'" Though they can exist anywhere, they are most successful and most prevalent in European and other liberal democracies, which, in contrast to Middle Eastern dictatorships that do not afford legal and political freedoms, have asylum and civil liberties laws that the jihadists manipulate to secure their persons and continue their activities. "The British capital, described by some terrorism specialists as 'Londonistan,' has a long history of Islamic militancy."[23]

Mustafa Setmariam Nasar, the foremost author in "*jihadi* strategic studies" whose 1,604-page tome entitled *The Call for a Global Islamic Resistance* analyzes and determines the "best practices" and lessons of twentieth-century Islamic insurgencies, advocates decentralized personal contact. Centralized secret groups are vulnerable if one member is arrested. Open combat fritters away jihadist energy against superior U.S. firepower instead of directing it to the Islamic awakening.[24]

By contrast, the "jihad of individualized terror" employs centrally dispatched singleton trainers in the post-9/11 high-threat environment. Armed with general guidance by ranking command nodes, they link up with local, self-sufficient militants to execute terrorism behind enemy lines with extensive operational autonomy. Though operational control, efficacy, and targeting precision are potentially sacrificed, this approach directly focuses on inspiring an Islamist political awakening while avoiding superior enemy firepower and penetrating centralized Western command and logistics lines. Lower-level attacks like the 2004 Madrid train bombings, technically unsophisticated and inexpensive yet still effective, embody this approach.[25]

### Operations

Al Qaeda, a consummate technology user, has so harnessed the Internet that terrorist activities are effectively now "Web-directed phenomena." Twelve terrorist-related Web sites prior to 9/11 have since grown to more than 4,500. "The Internet is the ideal medium for terrorism today: anonymous but pervasive." [26] It is "a bargain-basement, redundant system for distributing information . . . [that] can't [be] shut . . . down anymore."[27] "As the Taliban collapsed and Al Qaeda lost its Afghan sanctuary, Osama bin Laden biographer Hamid Mir watched 'every second Al Qaeda member carrying a laptop computer along with a Kalashnikov' as they prepared to scatter into hiding and exile. On the screens were photographs of September 11th hijacker Mohamed Atta."[28]

Al Qaeda has found the Web to be an excellent recruitment tool. Compared to their Afghan jihad predecessors, the newest generation of Al Qaeda members is far more technologically sophisticated. The Web's anonymity masks ancient prejudices and offers a "'virtual sanctuary' on a global scale" to propagandize.[29]

Al Qaeda also uses the Web for training. "If you want to conduct an attack, you will find what you need on the Internet." Again, this virtual sanctuary permits a safe classroom in a hostile post-9/11 operating environment.

The Internet has also been used to execute terrorist activities. In the cyber realm, Al Qaeda has facilitated computer hacking against government authorities. In the real world, operatives have used the Internet's anonymity, pervasiveness, and reliability to communicate information and increase operational security.[30]

The Internet and associated media have, however, proved to be double-edged swords. Dramatic political change is occurring in the Middle East, and the Sunni jihadist movement is now global in scope with its own momentum.[31] Al Qaeda's traditional leadership—Osama bin Laden, Ayman al-Zawahiri, and a coterie of key aides who previously played a dual role as both intellectual and operational leaders—have great cachet but are losing their immediacy. As other elements score operational victories—the political coin of the realm—and other religio-political leaders access the media, particularly the Internet, with greater regularity than bin Laden, whose visibility is requisitely lower while on the run, Al Qaeda central must struggle to ensure that it remains paramount to direct the front lines in the ever-evolving jihadist movement.

Osama bin Laden's new challenge is to avoid becoming a revered, yet detached, iconic figurehead over the jihadist movement for which he has sought to be an operational and political vanguard leader. The Department of Defense has found that a series of Saudi and Jordanian clerics are becoming more theologically, and thus politically, influential than high-profile standard-bearers such as Osama bin Laden and Ayman al-Zawahiri. Osama bin Laden's political agenda and religious justifications are well known. It is the deeper, more tailored arguments, however, that are recruiting new people. It is these young, educated, capable, easily accessible, Internet-based clerics who are making the more resilient arguments.[32]

## AL QAEDA'S FINANCIAL DIMENSION

Since 9/11, the United States has systematically worked to dismantle Al Qaeda's financial capabilities. Reviewing how Al Qaeda generates, handles, moves, and spends its money begs several questions: Where does Al Qaeda get its financial support? How has Al Qaeda's financial structure and health changed due to U.S.-led efforts to squeeze it dry? What are its financial prospects? Though the United States achieved significant initial success and has continued to rate its own efforts as effective, U.S. progress has slowly stagnated.[33]

### Generating Income

Al-Zawahiri bemoaned to al-Zarqawi in 2005 that "many of the lines have been cut off." U.S.-led efforts, however, are largely failing. "Notwithstanding the successes . . . groups associated or affiliated with Al Qaeda still appear to be able to carry out an attack, as and when they feel so inclined. Either they had the money already when they needed it, or they have no problem getting it."[34]

Osama bin Laden's fabled wealth has never played a significant role.[35] The wealth of Osama bin Laden's family has been greatly exaggerated. From about

1970 until 1993 or 1994, bin Laden received roughly $1 million per year from his family. In 1994, the Saudi government forced bin Laden's family to find a buyer for his share of the family construction business and placed the proceeds into a frozen account. This effectively divested bin Laden of what would otherwise have been the $300 million fortune commonly ascribed to him.[36] Osama bin Laden's Sudanese assets, purportedly totaling thirty-five companies when he lived there from 1992 to 1996, were more successful in gaining him influence with the Sudanese government than in producing revenue. When he left Sudan in 1996, Sudan's government expropriated bin Laden's assets, some of whose ownership was disputed, and seized his accounts so that, by 1996, bin Laden had almost nothing left. Al Qaeda has had to externally generate revenue.[37]

State funding has also never played a key role. The end of the Cold War, the approximate time of Al Qaeda's birth, eliminated the need for states to fund proxy groups, though significant aid already disbursed during the 1980s remained viable long into the next decade. During the 1990s, the overall political tolerance for terrorism, and the possibility that it could be justified, also significantly declined. Either directly, as has been alleged relative to Sudan, or through proxies such as the Taliban, state funding progressively declined as a meaningful option for Al Qaeda after the Soviet jihad. The last vestiges evaporated post-9/11 with the defeat of the Taliban and other local militant groups, Al Qaeda's cut-out to Pakistan, and U.S. pressure.[38]

Legitimate, openly made financial investments played a minor role in Al Qaeda's early days. Most prominently, in pre-9/11 Sudan, bin Laden helped to capitalize Sudan's leading bank while opening multiple other companies, such as construction firms in his own name. The post-9/11 regulatory environment, however, has made Al Qaeda a pariah, frozen any known investments, and effectively prohibited any future direct investments in any meaningful way.

A sizable network of front companies played a more significant role in Al Qaeda's infancy. Designed not just to facilitate operational activity, these operations were, at a minimum, self-sustaining if not producing a profit. "For instance, [Al Qaeda] owned boats and had a fishing business in Mombasa; in Sweden it invested in the hospital equipment industry; in Denmark in dairy products; and in Norway in paper mills." The post-9/11 regulatory, legal, and intelligence environment, however, has effectively eliminated this possibility in any meaningful way.[39]

Charities and nongovernmental organizations played a key role prior to 9/11. Not only did such organizations raise funds, but their very nature effectively launders the money. By the mid-1990s, the CIA estimated that fifty Islamic charities "support[ed] terrorist groups, or employ[ed] individuals who [were] suspected of having terrorist connections."[40]

In some cases, Al Qaeda thoroughly co-opted existing charities. The organizations' employees, or, at a minimum, their leadership, knew that their purpose was to funnel money to Al Qaeda. "In those cases, Al Qaeda operatives had control over the entire organization, including access to bank accounts," as with the Wafa Charitable Foundation.[41]

More commonly, however, Al Qaeda specifically targeted and penetrated specific foreign branches of large and well-recognized international charities, such as the KindHearts association of Toledo, Ohio, to exploit cracks in the philanthropy system writ large, and the actual organization in question was not significant in itself. Weaknesses in oversight and organizational structure in these nonprofit institutions, when combined with the time taken up by global transactions to remote parts of the world, presented an easily exploitable situation. If not at the headquarters, exploitation was easy enough to do in a remote corner of the world at the field level.[42]

The political impact of the 9/11 attacks, however, was dramatic. Pre-existing political and financial interests that had previously staved off government oversight were overridden. New laws and regulations at both the national and international level not only empowered governments around the world to take direct action, but also required them to do so.

While writ large this venue is far less lucrative post-9/11, it has not been eliminated. Most organizations Al Qaeda would seek to usurp, however, are located outside of the United States, where enforcement is most effective. The United States is thus dependent upon political winds—reference the United States, Al Qaeda, and local interests where the charity is located—for government enforcement abroad or the willingness of charities to be co-opted.

Most significantly, cultural factors preserve this venue's potential utility. *Zakat*, Islam's mandatory religious obligation to give alms, differs from Western society's secular charitable donations. There is no conceptual civic-religious divide in Muslim societies, as shown by Saudi Arabia's proclamation of the Quran as its constitution. The giving of alms, therefore, not only has charitable implications but civic ones as well, and *zakat* "functions as a form of income tax, educational assistance, foreign aid, and political influence."[43]

In particular, Saudi-connected entities to disseminate and employ donations are an established source of humanitarian relief in the developing Islamic world. In fact, Saudi Wahhabi schools are sometimes the only providers of education in poor areas. (Wahhabism is a literal interpretation of the Quran emphasizing historic practices for governing all aspects of life and society.) Sometimes they are the only Islamic schools available, even in affluent countries. Most notably, they have funded mosques and schools in Pakistan, Central Asia, Europe, and even the United States. Because no civic-religious divide exists, a major goal of Saudi charities is to spread Wahhabi beliefs, which are germane to Al Qaeda's religio-political vision, throughout the world. While it is highly unlikely that these institutions are blatantly programming terrorists, Western critics have lambasted Saudi charities for fostering a hostile political and religious environment conducive to terrorism.

Crime has remained a consistently viable and enduring wellspring both pre- and post-9/11. Financial crimes, particularly credit card fraud, have been heavily used and, as evidenced by captured manuals providing detailed instructions, Al Qaeda even established a special Afghan training camp. Al Qaeda's European network, which is dominated by Algerians, once raised nearly $1 million per month via this work.

Common crime—as shown by Al Qaeda operatives in Jordan who sustained themselves preparing for the millennium attacks by committing bank robberies, burglaries, and forging checks—has also sufficed.[44] These local criminal activities bypass the U.S.- and EU-created global financial dragnet, which has already frayed considerably due to its largely informal and voluntary nature as competing political issues and tensions have risen. Investigations into several plots in Europe have shown that Al Qaeda operatives were often flush with cash through drug dealing and credit card fraud, and that they often raised far more money than necessary. The cell responsible for the 2004 Madrid train bombing, for example, spent approximately $80,000, but it had access to more than $2.3 million worth of illegal drugs it could have sold to raise money. "That's the cleverness of these schemes—to keep it under the radar," said Stephen Swain, former head of Scotland Yard's international counterterrorism unit. "By doing this, they can raise significant amounts of money fairly quickly, and there's no real way to detect it."[45]

Amid the reduction of so many previous options, one new revenue stream has opened up: named franchises. Al Qaeda in Iraq, which is assisted by Al Qaeda in the Maghreb, directly confronts the U.S. effort in Iraq via highly visible attacks. Their highly publicized work enabled them to raise funds more successfully than the more isolated, lower-visibility Al Qaeda central. As with Al Qaeda in Iraq, these franchise groups are remitting money to the center instead of vice versa.[46]

The evolution of the Internet, a stateless medium largely beyond the reach of government authorities, has opened up yet another venue for Al Qaeda's efforts. Al Qaeda is now using gambling websites to launder money.[47] The possible permutations of users (both witting and unwitting), locations, and amounts are myriad.

Ultimately, however, wealthy and generous individual Arab benefactors, particularly Saudis, have taken the lead and, as prior to 9/11, they remain Al Qaeda's mainstay. The jihadist cause writ large, and Al Qaeda in particular, has had the requisite popularity throughout the Middle East. With the donors knowing that they were in some way supporting the families of fighters, much of their money, directly or indirectly, has ultimately made its way to Al Qaeda or its subsidiaries.

To place their role in perspective: donations from the Persian Gulf in 2009 outpaced the Taliban's estimated revenue derived from Afghanistan's Helmand province, the heart of the Taliban's drug-supply money, which is estimated in the hundreds of millions of dollars. This revenue stream helps to finance the entire Taliban government in exile seeking to retake Afghanistan through a full-time, multiyear, nationwide insurgency. Meanwhile, Al Qaeda's terrorism, which is far less intense, costs far less and is ably sustained by wealthy individual benefactors. As with charities, the United States is thus dependent upon political winds—reference the United States, Al Qaeda, and local interests where an individual is located—for government interdiction as well as the willingness of individuals to lend financial support.

### Handling and Moving Money

Designated Al Qaeda financial officers are charged with collecting funds. Rather than being centrally selected, trained, and dispatched, financial officers were kept indigenous to their areas of responsibility. This provides them a strong sense of the local financial and political communities, which enables operatives to manipulate and blend witting and unwitting sources.

Regional financial officers, who lead professional support cells, which raise funds, enable frontline operational cells, which expend the funds. The professional support cells are neither collocated with operational cells nor geographically overlapping with their operational areas. This not only compartmentalizes both personnel and information, thus limiting potential network damage should any particular officer be detained, but it also reduces the likelihood of negative political blowback by conducting attacks in an area separate from where the funds for it are derived.

Several key financial security principles guide these financial officers. Monies are divided between operational funds, which are to be expended in pursuit of operational objectives, and support money, which is to be invested for financial return to grow more operational resources for the future. Operational funds are not stored in just one place. Access to the money is restricted, and only a necessary few have knowledge of the operational funds. Security precautions are taken when transporting large amounts of money. When not in use, money is held by sympathetic nonmembers to lessen the chance of compromise. Money is only spent when necessary.[48]

The separation of operational and support cells necessitates constantly transferring money around the world within the organization, and financial officers developed multiple mechanisms. Despite playing a significant fund-raising role, charitable and nongovernmental organizations played only a minor role in transferring money. Banks, *hawala* dealers, and couriers took the lead, with Al Qaeda usually using a mix of these while blending witting and unwitting participants. Though significantly modified post-9/11, Al Qaeda's financial machinery remains viable.

Banks were a leading tool prior to 9/11 for Al Qaeda fund-raisers to store and move money. Al Qaeda's bank account network had support accounts, which were registered in the names of Al Qaeda–controlled charities and companies, and operational accounts, which were registered in the names of either reliable sympathizers or the names of Al Qaeda members who were not publicly suspected. Subject to less regulatory and intelligence scrutiny, Al Qaeda often made highly respected Western banks into unwitting co-conspirators. At the same time, Al Qaeda also used Islamic banks, whose top one hundred institutions possessed a multibillion-dollar global capitalization in 2000 with an annual turnover of approximately $100 billion.

Al Qaeda usually transferred money from support accounts to the operational accounts through several bank accounts in order to disguise their true purpose. While the vast majority of banks were most certainly unwitting collaborators, several individual banks did act as witting facilitators. Among the customer base, charitable and nongovernmental organizations assisted Al Qaeda, often unwittingly, by moving money for terrorists through their accounts.[49]

The official banking system, however, no longer plays a meaningful role post-9/11. Instead, there is a newfound sense of urgency to the transfers. "The money seems to be distributed as quickly as it is raised, and [the United States government has] found no evidence that there is a central 'bank' or 'war chest' [to and] from which al Qaeda [reposes and] draws funds."[50]

Al Qaeda relied heavily upon the *hawala* system prior to 9/11. Through a *hawala* dealer, a customer is able to transfer money at small commission to friends, family, business associates, and so forth. A customer requests to transfer money, which is usually paid up front but may be paid at a later time at the *hawala* dealer's discretion. The dealer of whom a request is made calls another dealer physically close to the intended recipient who provides the "transferred amount." The *hawala* dealers involved later square accounts, either in cash or through subsequent business deals. For a single transaction, *hawala* dealers will often use both fellow *hawala* dealers and either the formal banking system or money remitters.

Though informal, the *hawala* system can handle volume. Roughly one thousand Pakistani *hawala* dealers processed roughly three times the exchange volume handled by the nation's official banking system in the year 2000. Some of this was done in transactions as large as $10 million. In 2001, it was estimated $2–5 billion would pass through Pakistan's *hawala* system alone.[51]

Such a system is ripe for terrorist exploitation. As the literacy rate in *hawala* societies is usually low, few, if any, records or receipts are kept, and any actual records have no consistency in quantity or quality of notation. Government regulation is weak to nonexistent. At the same time, operatives are able to take advantage of the formal banking system one degree removed without having to actually formally register for an account, which might draw scrutiny.[52]

Because the Taliban's banking system was so antiquated and undependable, Al Qaeda had no choice after it moved to Afghanistan in 1996 but to heavily use the *hawala* system. Once Al Qaeda's profile rose after the August 1998 East Africa bombings and government scrutiny of the formal worldwide financial system increased around the globe, *hawalas* again rose in importance. "Al Qaeda used about a dozen trusted *hawaladars* [*hawala* dealers], who almost certainly knew of the source and purpose of the money. Al Qaeda also used both unwitting *hawaladars* and *hawaladars* who probably strongly suspected that they were dealing with Al Qaeda but were nevertheless willing to deal with anyone."

*Hawala* networks, while still existent, now play a lesser role. "The *hawala* network that existed prior to 9/11 seems to have been largely destroyed. Several of the main *hawaladars* who were moving money for Al Qaeda before 9/11 have been detained, and the identities of others have been revealed in seized records. Al Qaeda may have developed relationships with other *hawaladars*, however, and it most likely uses them to move some of its money."[53]

Lastly, couriers were a primary pre-9/11 means of secure conveyance. Given the trust required, couriers were typically recruited from within Al Qaeda with traits that could help a traveler keep a low profile. Language skills, ethnicity, and documentation received key consideration. Practicing operational security, Al Qaeda's couriers carried the money without knowing its intended purpose. To further blur any traceable pattern, Al Qaeda occasionally blended *hawala* and courier segments into a single transaction. According to one source, "al Qaeda reportedly used a Pakistani-based money changer to move $1 million from the UAE [United Arab Emirates] to Pakistan, at which point the money was couriered across the border into Afghanistan" and distributed throughout the organizational network.

Al Qaeda and its affiliates have relied increasingly upon couriers to haul money post-9/11. Moving funds by courier requires planning, coordination, and communication, and these things take time. Further, the limited supply of trusted couriers has caused significant delays, especially to Al Qaeda operatives in distant locations. As of mid-2006, however, "it is a trend that has accelerated."[54]

## Spending Income

Prior to 9/11, Al Qaeda's expenditures were estimated at roughly $30–35 million per annum. Post-9/11, the U.S. government assesses Al Qaeda's overall annual budget to be roughly $3–5 million per year.[55] Though an order of magnitude lower, Al Qaeda's reduced annual budget is not dramatically disproportionate to its reduced expenses.

Al Qaeda no longer pays roughly $10–20 million annually in rent to stay in the good graces of the Taliban, who were notoriously strapped for cash and increasingly relied upon Al Qaeda for military needs, including arms and vehicles, as well as social projects. Instead, Al Qaeda is now most likely giving money to Pakistani tribal chiefs, which almost certainly costs less than when Al Qaeda supported the Afghan state. Apart from the lesser need for money and a less developed economy in which to actually spend it, which only magnifies its effect, Al Qaeda has strong popular support throughout Southwest Asia. When combined with Al Qaeda's propensity for violence, it is highly unlikely that Al Qaeda's senior leadership would be extorted.

Organizational infrastructure and start-up expenses—jihadist salaries, propaganda, weapons, technology, physical infrastructure, transportation, housing, offices, and so forth, estimated to have totaled roughly $50 million over several years—have also decreased. Al Qaeda's industrial-scale training infrastructure in Afghanistan, which is now in U.S. hands, cannot be rebuilt to a similar level while members remain in hiding, and Pakistani facilities readied during the Soviet jihad still remain. Heavy personnel losses mean that there are simply far fewer fighters and their families to support, though Al Qaeda still supports those remaining.

The demand for strategically and selectively established alliances, by funding other Islamic militant groups and their operations to harness their members, contacts, and facilities, in lieu of its norm of providing logistical and other operational support to build alliances, has also waned. Following 9/11, Al Qaeda became an established player and Osama bin Laden is now revered. It no longer needs to purchase friends as many lesser groups perceive Al Qaeda to be the jihadist gold standard and voluntarily seek association with it.

Among the smallest and least frequent of its expenses, Al Qaeda continues to directly expend money on specific terrorist attacks. The 1998 U.S. embassy bombings in East Africa (approximately $10,000), the 9/11 attacks (roughly $400,000–500,000), the October 18, 2002, Bali bombings (around $20,000), and potential maritime operations against oil tankers in the Strait of Hormuz (about $130,000) were all Al Qaeda–funded. These operational funds were generally frugal one-time payments limited to operational expenses vice a sustained cash flow, however, and daily living and other associated bills were the responsibilities of the operatives themselves.[56]

Al Qaeda has always made these decisions akin to a research foundation. Certain projects were driven, and thus funded, by the main organization. Most projects, however, were submitted from outside the organization for review accompanied by a request for funds, with a few projects selected and most rejected. Post-9/11, however, "Al Qaeda has become decentralized and it is unlikely that the Finance Committee still exists. The direction and financing of operations are now based more on personal relationships with operatives than on a management structure."[57]

Al Qaeda is simply less active with centrally directed and funded operations than prior to 9/11. The eighteen- to twenty-four-month major attack cycle has been broken. Increasing reliance post-9/11 upon local cells to run low-cost yet effective operations has minimized financial needs. "Law enforcement officials in London said Al Qaeda cells are trained to plot and live on the cheap. Operatives lead ascetic lives, often keeping their day jobs or depending on their families to cover expenses. Above all, they are taught to build bombs that are lethal but crude and inexpensive. Almost every terrorist plot in Europe in recent years has followed a simple formula: homemade explosives stuffed into backpacks, shoes, suitcases, or car trunks."[58]

## CONCLUSION

Operationally, Al Qaeda has been forced to decentralize since the Taliban's fall. The rump command node, hunkered in Pakistan and protected by the vestiges of the 055 Brigade and indigenous militants, is directing a decimated but regenerating global terrorist network. The post-9/11 emphasis on offshoot entities has ceded the initiative to Al Qaeda's loosely organized like-minded groups and individuals who live and operate within the world's publics at the expense of the world's states. Al Qaeda now leads an emboldened movement as much as it does a coherent organization.

Financially, Al Qaeda's need for external fund-raising because it is not backed by a multimillionaire Osama bin Laden creates a crucial vulnerability. Post-9/11 U.S. efforts have hemmed the pre-9/11 unbridled money flows, and Al Qaeda, though remaining financially viable, is now pressed. The 9/11 attacks, Al Qaeda's most expensive and most significant, however, cost only $500,000 to plan and execute, and Al Qaeda's slew of attacks since then have largely cost one-tenth as much, if not less. Such inexpensive plotting strongly suggests that the assumption that Al Qaeda's finances could be defeated by hunting for a network of wealthy financiers and freezing bank accounts was a fundamental miscalculation. Informal means beyond the legitimate financial world and state control—crime and donors to raise money, and couriers and *hawala* dealers to move money—now sustain Al Qaeda.

Both operationally and financially, Al Qaeda has been forced to dwell and operate among the world's publics beyond U.S. shores. Other states, therefore, are the key to victory. No foreign government knows another country's public better, much less its private sphere activity, than does that public's government.

No foreign government is in a position to pursue private-sphere elements of another society that are hostile to it better than that society's own government. This forces the United States to endure two mutually complementary disadvantages.

First, the United States is at the mercy of the capacity of foreign states. Al Qaeda's support overwhelmingly comes from the developing world. The United States is at a systemic disadvantage in having to rely upon the weak governing authorities of the very developing countries from which Al Qaeda derives its strongest support.

Second, the United States is at the mercy of local politics. It is the politics of the developing world that sustain Al Qaeda to begin with and enable it to strike its developed-world targets—the United States and Europe. Hostile politics only further weaken the political will of local governments to apply whatever actual state capacity exists.

No government, no matter how powerful and totalitarian in nature, can totally dominate the private sphere from which Al Qaeda derives its sustenance. Whether via multilateral or bilateral means, attempting to starve Al Qaeda of money—a technical process to seize or trace funds—and detaining operatives—a result of blending intelligence, military, and law enforcement capabilities—ultimately rests on a political cornerstone. As long as Al Qaeda has political appeal, people will continue to give money and operational assistance, and Al Qaeda will have the resources to act. Financial seizures, arrests, and other punitive actions stemming from intelligence, military, and law enforcement work are a race between government action and countervailing public support. Further progress depends on the United States addressing the political environment that gives context to the technical processes the United States employs.

Hostile politics, which Al Qaeda incites and manipulates, create a buffer between Al Qaeda and state authorities. These will safely cap the potential of U.S. technical efforts. The U.S. failure to address the political grievances Al Qaeda touts and exploits, or to exploit political tensions within the greater jihadist movement that Al Qaeda seeks to captain, is an untapped well of potential U.S. leverage.

Chapter 4

# The Heart of the Conflict: The U.S.-Al Qaeda Struggle's Political Dimension

*He who rules by moral forces is like the pole star, which remains in place*
*while all the lesser stars do homage to it.*

—Confucius

**A**l Qaeda presents a paradox. On the one hand, the organization should be reeling. Terrorism as a tactic is universally condemned, and the organization's professed political goals garner widespread public disapproval. On the other hand, as noted by a U.S. official, Al Qaeda terrorists "are being replaced as fast as we can kill or capture them. . . . Even if they are reduced as an organization, they've been able to enlist . . . others to do their bidding" and maintain their status within the hierarchy of terrorist groups.[1]

In order to successfully meet this challenge, the United States must focus on the political dimension of the conflict. Both U.S. and Al Qaeda policies, and the value choices associated with those policies, must be examined. The results must then be interpreted and applied according to the dynamics of terrorism and counterinsurgency.

The United States, as the leader of the international system, has shaped the global political, economic, and security context. Both prior to and since 9/11, Al Qaeda is mainly reacting to U.S. policy. The United States, as the world's dominant power, is therefore uniquely positioned to engineer a political solution, or to at least mollify the struggle's intensity.

## POSSIBLE INCIPIENT SUPPORT FOR AL QAEDA

Not only does the U.S. public, the direct target of Al Qaeda violence, reject Al Qaeda's goals, but the world's Muslim publics also overwhelmingly reject Al Qaeda's political goals. A 2006 Zogby survey polled Lebanon, Egypt, Jordan, Morocco, the United Arab Emirates, and Saudi Arabia about support for Al Qaeda's primary political goal—a single "Talibanesque, pan-Islamic state." Support never broke single digits.[2]

The world's Muslim publics—despite being extremely diverse in terms of ethnicity, geography, political situation, economic prosperity, and so forth—also overwhelmingly reject Al Qaeda's violence against civilians. The *2002 Gallup Poll of the Islamic World*—Saudi Arabia, Iran, Pakistan, Indonesia, Turkey, Lebanon, Kuwait, Jordan, and Morocco—showed strong majorities in eight of the nine Muslim countries polled condemned the 9/11 attacks. A 2006 Zogby poll of Lebanon, Egypt, Jordan, Morocco, the United Arab Emirates, and Saudi Arabia revealed mostly single-digit support for Al Qaeda's "methods of operation." A spring 2007 poll of Muslims by Pew and Terror Free Tomorrow (TFT) found six in ten people or more, in seven of ten countries, saying that "suicide bombings and other forms of violence against civilian targets" are "never justified." Majorities in Turkey and Iran, with even higher percentages in Indonesia and Pakistan, stated that attacks against civilians can never be justified. Pew also found a complete rejection of terrorist violence among very large majorities of Muslims living in Germany, Britain, Spain, and France.[3]

One possible explanation for these findings could be that, despite always claiming to target the West, Al Qaeda far more often delivers harm unto innocent Muslims. Only 15 percent of Al Qaeda's victims were Westerners from 2004 to 2008, and even this number was artificially spiked due to the Madrid and London bombings. From 2006 to 2008, only 2 percent of Al Qaeda's victims were Westerners while the rest were citizens of Muslim countries, whom Al Qaeda purports to defend. External to Iraq and Afghanistan, Al Qaeda's victims were 99 percent non-Western in 2007 and 96 percent non-Western in 2008. Overall, a non-Westerner has proven to be fifty-four times more likely to die in an Al Qaeda attack than a Westerner.[4]

Muslim publics have increasingly denounced terrorist violence the more Al Qaeda has executed post-9/11 strikes in their countries. Between 2002 and 2009, for example, support for attacks on civilians in Jordan plummeted following the 2006 hotel bombings. Support in Indonesia fell from 26 percent to 13 percent following the Bali bombings. In Pakistan, the current and foreseeable front in the struggle against Al Qaeda, which has gone from zero attacks to become the world's leading victim of suicide bombings, 87 percent of Pakistanis in 2009 rejected violence against civilians saying such acts were never justified, as compared to shortly after 9/11 when one-third stated such acts were often or sometimes justified and only 43 percent stated they were rarely or never justified.[5]

Rather than reflecting a problem with who is being victimized, these numbers are a sign of broadly rejecting terrorism as a tactic. A 2009 WorldPublicOpinion .org survey of Muslim-majority countries—Egypt, Indonesia, Pakistan, Morocco, Jordan, Turkey, Azerbaijan, and the Palestinian territories—found widespread condemnation of killing U.S. civilians as well. More than seven in ten in nearly all nations disapproved of such attacks.[6]

The reasoning for this rejection of terrorism appears twofold. On the one hand, moral sentiments in the same WorldPublicOpinion.org survey found that "'bombings and assassinations that are carried out to achieve political or religious goals' [were] rejected as 'not justified at all' by large majorities ranging from 67 to 89 percent." On the other hand, after roughly a decade of violence since 9/11, a more utilitarian sentiment appears to have also taken root with approximately half now saying that such attacks are hardly ever effective.[7]

This rejection of Al Qaeda's signature tool has spilled over into a rejection of Osama bin Laden as well, with a 2009 Pew Global Attitudes Project finding that support for bin Laden has declined considerably among Muslim publics in recent years. Of the nine prominent Muslim publics polled—Pakistan, Turkey, Indonesia, Jordan, Israel, Egypt, Lebanon, Nigeria, and the Palestinian territories—only in Nigeria and the Palestinian territories has bin Laden's standing increased or broken the 50 percent threshold. Most significantly, in Pakistan, where bin Laden is suspected of hiding, only 18 percent of Pakistanis in 2006 proclaimed confidence in him to do the right thing regarding world affairs, as compared to 34 percent in 2005 and 46 percent in 2003[8]—a trend that is unlikely to change given Al Qaeda's steadily increasing violence.

After initially raising its organizational profile, and that of its political issues, through terrorism, Al Qaeda stigmatized itself. A 2006 Zogby poll asked Middle Eastern Arab publics: "When you think about Al Qaeda, what aspect of the organization, if any, do you sympathize with most?" The most common answer was "none." A February 2009 WorldPublicOpinion.org survey of Muslim-majority countries—Egypt, Pakistan, Indonesia, Turkey, Jordan, the Palestinian territories, Azerbaijan, and Nigeria—showed strong disapproval of "groups that use violence against civilians, such as Al Qaeda."[9]

Nonetheless, Al Qaeda is sufficiently popular to remain viable despite being hunted by almost every state in the world. A 2006 Zogby poll found that Al Qaeda was perceived by a small but still notable percentage of respondents as standing up for Muslim causes (Lebanon 7 percent, Egypt 12 percent, Jordan 16 percent, Morocco 18 percent, the UAE 29 percent, and Saudi Arabia 20 percent). More importantly, Al Qaeda was more strongly perceived as confronting the United States (Lebanon 18 percent, Egypt 33 percent, Jordan 38 percent, Morocco 34 percent, the UAE 28 percent, and Saudi Arabia 36 percent). "Arabs may deplore [bin Laden's] violence, but few will not feel some pull of emotions. Amid Israel's brutality toward Palestinians and American threats toward Iraq, at least one Arab is prepared to hit back."[10]

## MUSLIM PUBLICS' PERCEPTIONS OF THE U.S.-AL QAEDA POLITICAL STRUGGLE

If Al Qaeda's sustainability derives not from what it is fighting for but rather from what it is fighting against, precisely defining the U.S.-associated political hot buttons Al Qaeda exploits is the first step to focusing U.S. efforts to mollify

Al Qaeda's sources of political strength. After roughly ten years of war, one trillion dollars, and thousands of U.S. lives with no foreseeable end in sight, it is necessary to reexamine the Bush-developed political cornerstone of the U.S. 9/11 response—that Al Qaeda is "not protesting our policies" but rather "protesting our existence," and so no significant U.S. policy changes are necessary because they would not only fail to appease U.S. attackers but would also force policy changes detrimental to U.S. interests.[11]

### Muslim Publics' Views of U.S. Political and Economic Values

At World War II's end, the United States reigned supreme at sea and the Soviets dominated on land, the aspect of military prowess that would control the fruits of the Nazi defeat. The United States, militarily backed by its lesser allies, and the Soviet Union, militarily backed by both its lesser allies and the countries it conquered in defeating the Nazis, became embroiled in a cold war. Using its military assets to temporarily hold the Soviet military juggernaut at bay, the United States, rather than proclaiming an empire, invoked the appeal of its values to create a rival politico-economic system. The goal was to ultimately be capable of producing sufficient hard power to counter the Soviets in a hot war if necessary. Power and values simultaneously intertwined to advance U.S. interests.

To obtain the political support, and thus hard-power capability, of the less powerful states it was attempting to win, the United States advocated a participatory system that involved, benefited, and constrained all actors, to include itself. The United States limited the use of force to self-defense, respected sovereignty, championed democracy, and promoted human rights. It also advocated international law with an embrace of participatory international institutions, which culminated in an endorsement of the United Nations.

Sixty years later, these political sentiments strongly resonate. A 2007 BBC poll covering both Muslim and non-Muslim countries found that in thirty out of thirty-two states, people thought the UN—the world's chief embodiment of international law, human rights, and sovereignty—is having a positive influence in the world. A 2005 Gallup International poll found 78 percent in the Middle East, as a whole, agreed that "democracy may have problems, but it is the best form of government." Separate 2006 Pew polling found that most Muslims around the world rejected the proposition that "democracy is a Western way of doing things that would not work in most Muslim countries." A 2009 WorldPublicOpinion.org survey of Egypt, Pakistan, and Indonesia, with additional polling in Turkey, Jordan, the Palestinian territories, Azerbaijan, and Nigeria, found that majorities or pluralities in every country expressed support for democracy, to include participation by religious parties, the very groups often associated with being opposed to democratic practices.[12]

The United States dovetailed these political efforts with private enterprise and an open international trading system, which, at its root, was about increasing mutually beneficial participatory economic opportunity for all. The United States' foreign aid and economic policies integrated poorer countries, particularly ones with strategic value, into the U.S.-dominated international economic system. Institutions such as the International Monetary Fund and the World Bank received U.S. backing.

Sixty years later, these U.S. economic tenets have been strongly embraced. In 2006, the BBC found publics in nineteen out of twenty countries agreed that "the free enterprise system and free market economy is the best system on which to base the future of the world." In December 2001, Pew found overwhelming majorities in the Middle East (81 percent) and Islamic states in general (81 percent) viewed the United States as the land of opportunity. Those same majorities in the Middle East (86 percent) and Islamic states in general (73 percent) revered the scientific and technical achievements of the U.S. system as well.[13]

Directly contrary to the Bush administration's contention and Al Qaeda's assertions, there is no fundamental clash in political values between the United States and the world's "Muslim publics." In fact, there are no indications that support for these U.S. political and economic principles underpinning the world system is declining.[14] Al Qaeda, not the United States, is the political and economic ideological outlier.

## U.S. Public Standing

Despite its well-regarded political values, and despite being commonly viewed as the source of these values, the United States is not an exceptionally popular country post-9/11. In a 2006 Chicago Council on Global Affairs poll, which surveyed publics around the world that represented about 56 percent of the world's population, the most common view in ten out of fifteen countries was that the United States could not be trusted "a great deal," "somewhat," or even "very much" to act responsibly in the world. Across all twenty-five countries polled, in a 2006 BBC World Service Poll, one citizen in two (49 percent) stated the United States was playing a mainly negative role in the world.[15]

The picture was even more dire in the Middle East and other Muslim-majority countries crucial to the U.S. struggle against Al Qaeda. A February 2002 Gallup poll, when 9/11 sympathy for the United States was high, found more unfavorable than favorable ratings in all but one of the nine Muslim countries surveyed. In particular, there was a general perception among Islamic states that Western nations were not fair in their stances toward Palestine in particular or Arab and Islamic peoples in general.[16]

The onset of the Obama administration has somewhat mitigated general anti-U.S. sentiment. A late 2009–early 2010 BBC World Service poll of twenty-eight countries found, for the first time since polling began in 2005, that the United States is "viewed positively on balance in 20 of 28 countries, with an average of 46 percent now saying it has a mostly positive influence in the world, while 34 percent say it has a negative influence. Compared to a year earlier, negative ratings of the United States have dropped a striking nine points on average across the countries surveyed both years, while positive ratings are up a more modest four points."[17]

The plight of the United States within the Middle East and other Muslim-majority countries crucial to the struggle against Al Qaeda, however, remains unassuaged. Apart from Indonesia, where Obama family ties are well known and U.S. favorability ratings nearly doubled, the opinions of Muslim publics throughout the Middle East reference the United States remain largely unfavorable, despite some modest movement in Jordan and Egypt. Crucially, animosity toward the United States runs "deep and unabated" in Pakistan.[18]

As explained by Steven Kull, director of the Program on International Policy Attitudes, "After a year, it appears the 'Obama effect' is real. Its influence on people's views worldwide, though, is to soften the negative aspects of the United States' image, while positive aspects are not yet coming into strong focus."[19] Given the wide interpretation that the election of the Obama administration was a rebuke to the Bush administration, the failure of President Obama to more substantively reverse public perceptions of the United States, particularly among Muslim-majority countries, strongly suggests that there are more fundamental disputes at hand with the United States than superficial political tensions that can be eliminated by changing the messenger.

By contrast, Europe's ratings have been, and continue to be, positive. A November 2006–January 2007 BBC World Survey poll found that, in twenty-four out of twenty-seven countries surveyed, 53 percent worldwide say the European Union's influence is positive while only 19 percent say it is negative. Even when European Union (EU) members were excluded from the polling, sixteen out of nineteen non-EU countries said the EU plays a constructive role in world affairs. On average, 48 percent say the EU is a positive influence while only 22 percent say it is negative. In fact, majorities around the world prefer that Europe be more influential than the United States. The November 2009 to February 2010 BBC World Survey of twenty-eight countries showed that, while down a modest four points, the EU as an organization still ranked above the United States and that key member states, such as Germany, either improved their standing or ranked above the United States as well.[20]

Such disparate ratings for two entities of the same highly respected value sets beg the question of why. The dichotomous U.S.-European approval ratings strongly suggest that U.S. policies, not Western policies, are the point of objection. The individual actor, not the actor's religious, political, or geographical identity, is the key.

## Policies versus Values

Policy is either an implicit expression of values manifested in interests, or it is a direct implementation of values. Given the strong global support for U.S. values, the source of such low U.S. standing is mostly likely the perception of a disconnect between U.S. policies and U.S. values by those on the receiving end of U.S. policies. Specifically, U.S. policies are seen as pursuing U.S. interests while setting aside, if not directly undermining, U.S.-touted values.

Polling reflects this sustained perspective among the world's Muslim publics, particularly in the Middle East. Covering U.S. policy leading up to 9/11, a Pew December 2001 survey of opinion-makers in Islamic states found, to the tune of 76 percent, that "most/many people believe" that U.S. policy caused the 9/11 attacks. Within the Middle East, a vast majority (81 percent) of opinion-makers stated that "many/most people believed" U.S. policies, not values, were the problem. A March 2002 poll in Saudi Arabia, a relative hotbed for Al Qaeda support, queried Saudi elites about their source of frustrations with the United States; the poll found that 86 percent saw U.S. policies as the source of their frustrations. Among the general public, 59 percent identified "policies" as the cause whereas only 19 percent identified "values." Reflecting U.S. post-9/11 actions, a 2006 BBC World Service Poll across twenty-seven countries found Muslim respondents overwhelmingly cited "conflicts about political power and interests" over "differences of religion/culture" as the "cause of Islam-West tensions."[21]

The Israeli-Palestinian conflict, where the United States is globally perceived to display a pro-Israel stance, is a highly visible point of contention. A 2001 Pew survey of opinion-makers found that while a range of non-Islamic societies, spanning from 36 percent in Asia to 7 percent in Latin America, cite U.S. support for Israel as a major reason for not liking the United States, the global average is 29 percent. Even in places where U.S. support for Israel is not a frontline issue and most people register a particular sympathy for neither side, such as Western Europe, the underlying current among those who do express a sympathy favors the Palestinians. A 2002 Zogby poll in France, for example, found that "70 percent of respondents said they would react more favorably toward the United States if it 'were to apply pressure to ensure the creation of an independent Palestinian state.'"[22]

The sentiments are markedly more intense among the world's Muslim publics, particularly in the Middle East, where Al Qaeda draws its strongest support. Approximately 57 percent of opinion-makers in Islamic countries in general and the Middle East in particular cited U.S. support for Israel as a major reason for disliking the United States. In spring 2001, when noted Middle East scholar Shibley Telhami polled "five Arab states—Saudi Arabia, the United Arab Emirates, Kuwait, Lebanon, and Egypt—about 60 percent of the respondents identified the Palestinian conflict as the 'single most important issue' to them personally, while about 20 percent more said it was among their top three issues. In Egypt, 79 percent identified it as 'the single most important issue.'"[23] In spring 2002 in a separate survey, approximately two-thirds of publics queried in all Arab countries stated that the Palestinian question was either "the most important" or a "very important" issue confronting the Arab peoples. Similar sentiments were found in Pakistan and Indonesia, two of the most important non-Arab Muslim states.[24]

The U.S. invasion and occupation of Iraq is also a highly visible point of contention. A 2006 BBC World Service poll of twenty-seven countries showed an overall average of 76 percent disapproval of U.S. handling of the Iraq war.[25] As of 2011, trends have not markedly changed.

Rather than quelling terrorism, the 2003 invasion of Iraq has caused the overall volume of global terrorism to skyrocket. "Comparing the period before the war [Sept 12, 2001 to March 20, 2003] and the period since, there has been a 607 percent rise in the average yearly incidence of attacks—and a 237 percent jump in the fatality rate. . . . Not only has [the war in Iraq] brought more recruits to Sunni terrorist groups," their actions have "energized militants elsewhere. This has particularly been the case in the Arab world, whose countries excluding Iraq have seen 783 percent more fatalities from jihadist terrorism since the U.S. invasion. . . . Excluding [Iraq and Afghanistan], there has been a 35 percent rise in the number of terrorist attacks globally and a 25 percent increase in attacks on Western targets."[26]

The U.S. war in Afghanistan, though largely supported by Europe, has also been a highly visible point of contention with much of the rest of the world. Despite the provocation of 9/11, a March 2002 Gallup poll of Islamic states found a majority in every country viewed U.S. military action in Afghanistan as either "largely or completely morally unjustifiable." A majority of respondents in more than half of the countries actually viewed the U.S. military actions in Afghanistan as less defensible than the 9/11 attacks. The remainder of the developing world, especially Latin America and Africa, also opposed the war.[27] As of 2011, no significant changes to the contrary have emerged.

Several secondary U.S. "high politics" policies also draw particular ire. As of 2007, approximately 68 percent disapproved of the U.S. pro-Israeli stance in the 2006 Israel-Hezbollah war in Lebanon. The U.S. hostile handling of Iran's nuclear program registered a 61 percent disapproval rating. Underwriting these specific points, 69 percent, on average, believed that the U.S. military presence in the Middle East "provokes more conflict than it prevents" as compared to 16 percent who saw it as a stabilizing force.

Several secondary U.S. "low politics" choices are also negatively rated. As of 2007, roughly 69 percent perceive Guantánamo Bay as violating international law. Human rights scandals, such as Abu Ghraib, secret CIA prisons, and the

U.S. use of torture combined to tarnish the traditional U.S. image as a human rights champion. In 1998, for example, the United States Information Agency found that 59 percent of the British and 61 percent of Germans said the United States was doing a good job promoting human rights while, as of 2007, 56 percent of the British and 78 percent of Germans said the United States was doing a bad job.[28]

### Future Possibilities

Despite adverse perceptions of the United States and its actions, a December 2001 Pew poll showed opinion leaders in both Western and Islamic countries "clearly reject the idea that Islam and the West are caught in an inevitable clash of civilizations." A 2006–2007 BBC World Service poll of 28,000 respondents across twenty-seven countries found less than one-third (28 percent) thought violent conflict was inevitable while more than half (56 percent) thought "it is possible to find common ground," the most common response in twenty-five countries. Overall, 35 percent of Muslim respondents felt that "violent conflict is inevitable" while 52 percent said that "it is possible to find common ground."

Though these findings hold, they are less pronounced among Al Qaeda's traditional areas of support. When polling only Islamic countries, 64 percent of respondents stated that the ensuing conflict would be limited to the United States and Al Qaeda with only 29 percent predicting a major conflict between the West and Islam. In Middle Eastern countries, a majority (54 percent) saw a limited conflict while a substantial minority (41 percent) saw a grander civilizational clash portending.

Consistent with these findings, a March 2003 Zogby poll of elites in Saudi Arabia, a relative hotbed of Al Qaeda support, found support for secular political leaders clearly trumped religious ones. Osama bin Laden garnered only 8 percent of the vote. The name "George Bush," without any further clarification, received 4 percent of the vote, which was higher than the Taliban's Mullah Omar, Hamas's Ahmad Yassin, and religious authority Yusuf al-Qaradawi combined.

Instead, as found in a 2006 BBC World Service poll of twenty-seven countries, 58 percent of respondents found combative and intolerant minorities, who by definition reject inviting and encompassing U.S. political and economic norms, to be the primary source of tension. There was ample blame to go around. Thirty-nine percent of respondents stated that these minorities existed on both the Muslim and Western sides of the equation. Twelve percent said that they were only on the Muslim side. Seven percent said that these minorities existed only on the Western side.[29]

### IMPLICATIONS FOR THE U.S.-AL QAEDA STRUGGLE

Al Qaeda's 9/11 strike, though operationally successful, failed politically. Terrorism is most effective when there is an incipient yet unrealized potential for the terrorists' political agenda that terrorist violence can awaken and mobilize. The U.S. population, Al Qaeda's main target public in the 9/11 attacks, however, was deafened to Al Qaeda by its violence and has firmly rejected Al Qaeda in both form and substance.

Because the probability of future violence increases in direct proportion to the distance the terrorists perceive the targeted public to be from acquiescing to their political goals, and the U.S. response has run counter to Al Qaeda's ultimate goals, Al Qaeda is likely to continue attacking. Post-9/11 U.S. policies, however, have allowed Al Qaeda to gain several of terrorism's secondary advantages. These have not only bolstered Al Qaeda, but they have also likely increased the struggle's duration at U.S. hard-power and political expense.

Most significantly, far from slithering away post-9/11 to escape the U.S. juggernaut, Al Qaeda has been, and is likely to remain, provocative. The perceived gap between U.S. values and U.S. policies has induced suspicions of ulterior U.S. motives. A December 2006–February 2007 popular survey conducted by WorldPublicOpinion.org with support from the University of Maryland's START (Study of Terrorism and Responses to Terrorism) consortium in Egypt, Morocco, Pakistan, and Indonesia found that, on average, 79 percent say they "definitely/probably" perceive the weakening and dividing of the Islamic world as a U.S. goal. At the same time, 79 percent also claim that the United States is trying to maintain "control over the oil resources of the Middle East." A majority (64 percent) even believe it is a U.S. goal to "spread Christianity in the region."[30]

These suspicions have gone so far as to induce questions about the U.S. commitment to democracy, America's signature political value. The same 2009 WorldPublicOpinion.org poll found that majorities saw only conditional U.S. support for democracy in Muslim countries, with the most common response being that the United States favored democracy only if the government was cooperative. Nearly as many stated that the United States was simply opposed to democracy in Muslim countries while only a very small minority stated the United States supported democracy regardless of its relationship to the United States.[31]

Meanwhile, pro-democracy attitudes have taken hold. Majorities or pluralities in every country in 2009 polling expressed that "'all people should have the right to organize themselves into political parties and run candidates, including Islamist groups,' including Pakistan (83 percent), Indonesia (81 percent), Azerbaijan (75 percent), [the] Palestinian territories (69 percent), Turkey (53 percent), and Jordan (50 percent)." This has resulted in an upsurge of legitimate political activity by Islamist parties, the very entities most likely to support Al Qaeda, be co-opted by it, or simply be opposed to U.S. policies.[32]

Despite U.S. proclamations to the contrary, people in Muslim societies clearly perceive the United States as being at war with Islam and Muslim peoples, and the 2009 poll showed that large majorities now agree with nearly all of Al Qaeda's intermediary aspirations of changing U.S. behavior toward Muslim countries, to promote Islamic governance, and to preserve and affirm Islamic identity. Most specifically, the 2007 survey of Egypt, Morocco, Pakistan, and Indonesia noted above, for example, found that an average of 70 percent or more in each country support Al Qaeda's intermediary objectives of pushing the United States to remove its bases and its military forces from all Islamic countries as well as pressuring the United States not to favor Israel. Two years later, another survey of Egypt, Pakistan, Indonesia, Turkey, Jordan, the Palestinian territories, Azerbaijan, and Nigeria, found that large majorities endorse Al Qaeda's goal to "push the [United States] to remove its bases and its military forces from all Islamic countries," including 87 percent of Egyptians, 64 percent of Indonesians, and 60 percent of Pakistanis.[33]

Al Qaeda's internal unity and morale has also increased. Select U.S. policies—most notably on Israel and Iraq—serve as political glue for Al Qaeda. In an age of nationalism, they help a transnational terrorist entity espousing a pan-Islamic identity resonate among disenchanted, angry, or otherwise dissatisfied Muslim groups from Morocco to Indonesia to internally unite and focus otherwise disparate, albeit not unrelated, angst and forces against the United States. They do so at a time when Al Qaeda's central node under Osama bin Laden is experiencing weakening suzerainty over both the organization itself and the greater jihadist movement writ large. With associated inflammatory policies (e.g., the U.S. military presence in the Middle East, the U.S. handling of the 2006 Israel-Hezbollah war in Lebanon, the simmering U.S.-Iran crisis, and U.S. actions that tarnish its prestigious human rights record, such as torturous secret prisons and Abu Ghraib) in the background, these U.S. policies are uniquely potent.

In turn, Al Qaeda's ability to inflict harm on the United States is rising as substantial numbers also favor attacks on U.S. troops in Iraq, Afghanistan, and in the Persian Gulf. According to the 2006–2007 poll, approximately half supported such attacks in each locale while only a third were opposed. A 2009 WorldPublicOpinion.org poll found this sentiment gaining steam with large majorities in Egypt (78–83 percent), the Palestinian territories (87–90 percent), and Jordan (66–72 percent), as well as smaller majorities in Turkey and Pakistan, approving of attacks on U.S. troops in Iraq, the Persian Gulf, and Afghanistan.[34]

As of September 2008, a full seven years after 9/11, a WorldPublicOpinion .org poll of seventeen countries found that majorities in only nine thought that Al Qaeda was behind the 9/11 attacks. Ironically, formal education and news media exposure bore little correlation to assigning blame. Rather, those with positive views of U.S. influence in the world were more likely to cite Al Qaeda (59 percent) while those with a more negative view (40 percent) cited other options, to include the U.S. government itself (22 percent), Israel (7 percent), and various other perpetrators.

Critically, Middle Eastern publics were particularly likely to name a perpetrator other than Al Qaeda. In Egypt, 43 percent cited Israel. Thirty-one percent in Jordan and 19 percent in the Palestinian territories agreed. Correspondingly, 36 percent of Turks and 27 percent of Palestinians cited the United States itself. Those who cited Al Qaeda as being responsible for the attacks range from a low of 11 percent in Jordan to a high of 42 percent in the Palestinian territories.[35]

Popularity, as a component of legitimacy, is the currency of survival in the global jihadist insurgency. Al Qaeda, if left to its own devices, rapidly depletes its stock. Neither its ultimate goals nor its means to achieve them are widely applauded. It is only by rallying against U.S. actions, which are widely viewed as not being in line with widely lauded U.S. values and are perceived as a greater evil, that Al Qaeda gains traction with its potential followers. The world's publics are not pro–Al Qaeda, but rather anti–United States. Al Qaeda is harnessing and co-opting the political outrage of disenchanted, angry, or otherwise dissatisfied Muslim groups around the world.

This is the underlying political bedrock upon which the U.S.-Al Qaeda struggle will play out, and either party ignores it to its peril. In direct contrast to the clash of civilizations thesis, cursorily summarized by President George W. Bush as "they hate us for who we are," the intensity of any conflict between the United States and various Muslim, particularly Arab, polities that Al Qaeda may exploit will be governed by clashing national interests.[36] These can be massaged, manipulated, and even resolved in a way that enduring socio-cultural clashes of political principle cannot.

The United States, as the leader of the international system, is positioned to take the initiative and politically undercut Al Qaeda. The United States is highly unlikely to dissuade actual Al Qaeda members and supporters. Rather, the U.S. political focus must be on the masses from which Al Qaeda draws its sustenance. This tack leverages U.S. capacity not against Al Qaeda's organizational capacities, which are Al Qaeda's strengths and beyond U.S. control, but against Al Qaeda's political standing, which is a malleable vulnerability for Al Qaeda that it cannot control and that the United States can significantly influence.

Critics will argue that any political change in response to terrorism is giving in to and empowering the terrorists. To the extent that a country caves to terrorists and is violating its own self-defined national interests simply to stave off another attack, such a contention is entirely correct. Such an act is knowingly and intentionally subjugating oneself to terrorist demands.

In the wake of a devastating terrorist attack announcing the emergence of a serious, potent, long-term, self-declared terrorist enemy, however, the international political and strategic landscape has been altered. A new international environment requires a reassessment of national interests in response to a new international context. Any actions then taken in line with newly defined national interests and in response to events are a prudent evolution of national policy recognizing new realities.

The only other option is to continue the same policies as prior to the threat's onset and attempt to quash the terrorists via force. Relying solely on force has the possibility of success against a very weak and isolated terrorist group as its political appeal is likely to have been low and it would likely have been doomed to failure anyway. Eliminating the group's membership may then effectively squelch the political current it embodied. A capable group speaking to potent political currents, however, is highly unlikely to be undone by force, particularly on an international level. Osama bin Laden's Al Qaeda speaks to deep underlying political currents that ensure that it will continue beyond any particular membership set.

Political change can be skirted in the short run. Yoking foreign state structures can repress harmful terrorist actions and political sentiments contrary to the status quo. The United States has done so with great effectiveness since 2001.

Unless the United States is indefinitely willing to tolerate unremitting Al Qaeda–led efforts to launch future 9/11-style attacks, at least some of which are ultimately likely to succeed, as well as the attendant domestic political changes and ever-increasing security burdens in blood, treasure, and sacrificed priorities that come from living under such a cloud, long-term security requires the United States to meaningfully politically engage the developing world's Muslim publics. This is the population where Al Qaeda lives and from where Al Qaeda draws the majority of its support. Only that public can refuse Al Qaeda sanctuary and cooperate with state authorities to defeat it. No U.S. effort focused against such a culturally based, transnational terrorist entity from a specific realm of world society can succeed with weak support from those publics.

## CONCLUSION

U.S. political and economic values have permeated the international system since World War II. They are now highly respected. Yet the United States remains deeply unpopular.

From the perspective of Al Qaeda's actual and potential followers—disenchanted, angry, or otherwise dissatisfied groups throughout Muslim countries—U.S. policies, for which U.S. political values are a yardstick by which to measure both the ends and means of these policies, are to blame. Major U.S. actions post-9/11 (e.g., the U.S. invasion of Iraq, the perceived U.S. disregard for human rights, perceived U.S. unilateral tendencies, and so forth) have generated resentment. This is so not because of any significant differences in political values among the culturally disparate societies supporting either the United States government or Osama bin Laden's Al Qaeda. Rather it is because of the differing degrees of political power and conflicting interests between the United States and the societies supporting Al Qaeda, and the way the United States furthers those interests, particularly when they conflict with self-professed U.S. political values. In a political struggle like terrorism, these self-inflicted wounds to U.S. credibility and legitimacy are gaping.

Al Qaeda—whose own agenda and means of pursuing it is highly unpopular with both the U.S. public, its target, and the world's Muslim publics, the audience from whom Al Qaeda hopes to rally support—capitalizes on this situation by shrouding its own unpopular agenda in opposition to unpopular U.S. policies. The support that Al Qaeda receives is thus largely not pro–Al Qaeda. Rather, it is an expression of anti-U.S. sentiment. Al Qaeda co-opts this sentiment and serves as an instrument of that anti-U.S. expression.

Force alone speaks past the fundamental nature of the inherently political U.S.-Al Qaeda conflict. Al Qaeda taps into potent and widely felt political currents, and it will continue beyond any particular membership set so long as the drivers of the situation—the political grievances that motivate membership and drive nonmembers to provide support—go unaddressed. Absent the ability to capture or kill all Al Qaeda members, responding with force alone, which can yield short-term gains, all but guarantees ever increasing U.S. casualties and financial costs in a long-term struggle where time is not on the U.S. side.

The United States must narrow Al Qaeda's political, and thus operational, breathing space. Points of contention, as well as possible solutions, are clear. As the leader of the international system, the United States is in a position to marry its power to popularly accepted political values in making and executing U.S. policy on issues relevant to Al Qaeda in furtherance of U.S. national advantage that will suffocate Al Qaeda.

The chief target of U.S. political actions is not Al Qaeda's actual members and adherents. They are already dedicated to a U.S. downfall and, even if they can be dissuaded, focusing on them would be inefficient. The world's Muslim publics, not states, where Al Qaeda resides and finds operational sustenance, must be the target U.S. audience. Draining Al Qaeda's political support there by lessening ire toward the United States will reduce its operational capacity by leaving it no political, and thus operational, breathing space.

Despite generally unfavorable views of the United States, there is still a general public sentiment around the world that peaceful accommodations can be made. The United States is not inherently hated and doomed from the start. The raw potential for the United States to garner international political support exists.

Chapter 5

# A Question of Importance:
# The Obama Administration and Iraq

*This is the devilish thing about foreign affairs: They are foreign and will not always conform to our whim.*

— James Reston

The Obama administration took office on the cusp of major changes. The temporary stability wrought by the 2007 U.S. troop surge was poised to give way to Iraq's indigenously driven political evolution as the impending drawdown of U.S. political, economic, and military resources steadily decreased U.S. influence. Issues critical to Iraq's viability, however, still remained unaddressed.

The 2007 U.S. troop surge dealt Al Qaeda in Iraq (AQI) a strategic defeat, but it survived. The power vacuum formed by the gap between Iraqi state capacity and the withdrawing U.S. presence will give AQI and other insurgent groups a new window of opportunity. As of 2010, AQI has begun to replay its previously almost-successful strategy of sectarian killings targeting Shiite civilians and leaders to incite civil war and sink the entire U.S. venture.

The Obama administration is confronted by a largely dysfunctional Iraqi state riven by unresolved security, governance, and economic issues that are fundamental to Iraq's long-term viability and whose successful resolution will be unlikely without U.S. involvement. How will the administration assess the role and importance of AQI? How will events in Iraq impact both bin Laden's Al Qaeda central and the greater jihadist movement, as well as U.S. efforts against them? Consequently, how will the Obama administration assess these needs against numerous competing U.S. priorities?

## THE OBAMA ADMINISTRATION'S INHERITANCE
### The Rise of Al Qaeda in Iraq

The 2003 U.S. invasion created an Al Qaeda haven. With force levels insufficient to either occupy Iraq or quell a post-invasion insurgency, the United States failed to provide security. At the same time, poor political planning for the invasion's aftermath exacerbated both regional and internal Iraqi political tensions, and a largely dysfunctional Iraqi state unable to provide social services resulted.[1]

AQI under Abu Musab al-Zarqawi exploited this failed-state environment to harness a "new generation of Islamic radicalism." In a year's time, AQI co-opted and united fractious, indigenous Sunni actors under a single standard to become a "dominant force in the Sunni insurgency." Having sworn fealty to Osama bin Laden's Al Qaeda, AQI internationalized the struggle and ultimately became bin Laden's flagship frontline franchise.[2]

Inside Iraq, AQI's forces swelled. Foreign volunteers, the vast majority of suicide bombers, became abundant. By mid-2005, an estimated three thousand foreign fighters—primarily from Saudi Arabia, Syria, North Africa, Jordan, and Kuwait—found their way to Iraq. Led by al-Zarqawi, AQI became one of the few "foreigner brigades" to seize and hold towns such as Fallujah and Al Qaim before honorably retiring in the face of overwhelming U.S. firepower.[3]

Outside of Iraq, al-Zarqawi used his political following to build an international network consisting of associates of at least twenty-four groups in nearly forty countries in the Middle East, Africa, Asia, and Europe. Looking inward, this network funneled recruits to support AQI's Iraq-based suicide bombers and resistance fighters. Looking outward, this outreach effort recruited, trained, and dispatched foreign operatives back home for future action.[4]

Within the global jihadist insurgency, al-Zarqawi was positioned to challenge Osama bin Laden for leadership. European intelligence reports reviewed by *Time* magazine in 2005 suggested that al-Zarqawi rivaled bin Laden for influence among Middle Eastern and European jihadists. "'He function[ed] as a role model. . . . Groups . . . believe[d] it [was] a great honor to be able to carry out attacks in his name,'" said August Hanning, chief of Germany's foreign intelligence.[5]

### Prior to the 2007 U.S. Troop Surge

While occasionally engaging U.S. forces, al-Zarqawi's AQI, from the start, emphasized overlaying terrorism atop a Sunni Iraqi guerilla effort directed at U.S. and largely Shiite national government forces. Working through terrorism's four-step process, AQI tried to affect the political environment, not the military balance, to influence the war's outcome.[6]

First, AQI chose its target set—Iraq's Shia population. Long repressed under Saddam Hussein, they rose to control the state after 2003. Foreign support, overtly from the United States and illicitly from Iran, bolstered their position.

Second, AQI slaughtered innocent Shia. Horrific car bombings and suicide attacks shockingly and randomly killed civilians on an unprecedented scale. From the March 2003 U.S. invasion to June 2005, Zarqawi was credited with executing 479 suicide car-bomb attacks, killing 2,174 people and wounding 5,520.[7]

AQI engineered a niche by exploiting pre-existing Sunni-Shia political cleavages, and it changed the tenor of the violence that defined the country. "Zarqawi's attacks on Shiite mosques and police stations, U.S. intelligence officials believe, were the main reason for the creation of the fearsome Shiite death squads. These in turn . . . created renewed support among the Sunnis for the insurgency." This Shia militia retaliation against the Sunni population in response to AQI-initiated attacks spurred Sunni insurgents into at least a marriage of convenience with AQI. What began as a guerilla war against U.S. forces devolved into a sectarian conflict.[8]

Third, AQI's message became apparent: that changing the government, not just policy, was the only acceptable solution. Shia, who were religious heretics in AQI's eyes, were the pillar of Iraq's new government, and so most closely wed to U.S. interests. Religious validity intertwined with realpolitik significance.

Spiraling sectarian violence permeated Iraq's communities with fear. Social and political complacency evaporated as Iraq's decades-old, Saddam-era social fabric disintegrated. By 2006, Iraq verged on civil war.

Fourth, the targeted publics—Iraqi Shia society directly and the U.S. public indirectly—were to begin to press their respective authority centers for change, and AQI's efforts nearly succeeded. Spiraling violence precluded any significant progress on core national issues critical to Iraq's social, economic, and political stability found in the Bush administration's benchmarks. American public opinion polling showed no appetite for sustaining the U.S. troop presence, much less increasing it. Left unchecked, these political and military trends placed the U.S. effort in a politically and militarily unsustainable position, and they would have almost certainly undone the U.S. effort.

### The 2007 U.S. Troop Surge

Rather than accede to these mounting pressures, however, President Bush launched a 30,000-strong U.S. troop surge to reverse U.S. fortunes. These forces were employed in a new U.S. strategy composed of four interlocking, sequential steps meant to capitalize on ripe conditions. The insurgency's political and military drivers were undermined, and the fighting was quelled.[9]

First, the United States surged forces in a timely and focused manner to protect the Iraqi population. The U.S. strategy until 2007 had emphasized hunting enemy fighters and rapidly shifting security responsibilities to Iraqi forces, which proved incapable. New U.S. forces dispersed from large-scale bases into outposts spread among the population to create a critical mass of security so that the population, from all sects, would be able to cleave to the government out of choice vice cooperating with the insurgents out of fear or lack of an alternative.

Second, the United States simultaneously rapidly bolstered indigenous security capability. Iraqi forces increased in both quantity and quality. They worked alongside U.S. troops to fill the security vacuum and increase state sovereignty at militia expense.

For the first time, U.S. and allied forces dispersed in both Sunni and Shia zones of control. Sunni tribes now had options beyond Al Qaeda. The Shiite population had options beyond Moqtada al-Sadr's death squads. Corresponding U.S. political pressure on both the government of the Shiite prime minister, Nouri al-Maliki, and Shiite factions complemented these military efforts.

Third, the number of combatant factions was reduced. Moqtada al-Sadr, the Iraqi Shiite potentate most closely allied to Iran and under whose purview most Shiite death squads operated, opted to discontinue fighting. The increased number and focus of U.S. forces inspired newfound confidence in U.S. capability to protect the Shiite tribes, and the increased U.S. force structure made it, and its Iraqi national government allies, deadlier foes.

Fourth, the United States co-opted a pivotal insurgent faction. Rather than fight the Sunni tribes, who were both assisting and assisted by Al Qaeda, U.S. forces hired the tribes to combat AQI's growing influence under the banner of the Sunni Awakening.[10] In return, the United States ceased hostilities against the Sunni insurgents, paid them, militarily supported them against Al Qaeda, and induced the Iraqi state to make promises of patronage and largesse.

This aspect of the surge capitalized on incipient conditions. Devoid of its own territory or an Afghan-style third-country sanctuary, AQI depended on its Sunni sectarian backers for logistical and operational assistance as well as for protection from the United States, Iraqi authorities, and other insurgents. Al-Zarqawi, however, burned many of his political bridges through his violent methods and "inspired almost as much fear among his Sunni confederates as he did in his victims . . . frightening his Sunni hosts into silence or cooperation with his unique combination of cruelty and competence: cross al-Zarqawi and you would die, along with your family, perhaps horribly." With Sunni tribes hosting al-Zarqawi already fighting the Shia, a faction of Sunni chiefs forced him to relocate, which led to his death in a June 2006 U.S. airstrike.[11]

AQI, however, proved an enduring organization, not a personality-dependent al-Zarqawi creation. Abu Hamza al-Muhajir, bin Laden's publicly anointed al-Zarqawi successor, "pushed the sectarian violence into a new era" with an unprecedented rate of roughly five thousand violent acts per month by spring 2007.[12] Only AQI's operations external to Iraq slowed and did not become a fully active operational wing.

Ultimately, however, the success of the U.S. troop surge dealt AQI a strategic defeat. Subsequent AQI leaders, such as Abu Hamza al-Muhajir and Omar al-Baghdadi, took AQI to ground. They traded AQI's highly visible, ideology-driven, jihadist-oriented role and ambitions for more local concerns, and AQI effectively became just another Sunni militia. In contrast to when it began, U.S.

officials estimated that AQI's roster of several thousand fighters became almost 90 percent Iraqi "both in terms of leaders and foot soldiers" post-surge. AQI created, but abdicated leadership of, a pan-Sunni umbrella group, and it eased pressing its social dictates that differed from Iraqi customs.[13]

The overall volume of Sunni insurgent fighters was estimated at 20,000–30,000 men. "Foreigners [made] up 10 percent of the insurgents—probably less than that." AQI was only a small portion.

Yet AQI permanently altered the Iraqi political landscape. "'Sectarianism is al-Zarqawi's legacy,' says Mokhtar Lamani, the Arab League's permanent envoy to Iraq. 'The main thing that all Iraqis share now is being afraid of one another. And everybody's afraid of what is in the future.'" Al-Zarqawi's efforts have planted the potential for "plenty of fighting . . . for years."[14] Concern is rife about a return to ethnic conflict as U.S. power recedes. So long as exploitable conditions exist, small numbers of AQI and their disproportionate impact cannot be discounted.

Abu Musab al-Zarqawi's impact, however, went beyond Iraq. His signature invention—Internet-focused media manipulation—was a pioneering terrorist operational technique. He was the first to exploit the Internet's chief virtues—no broadcast standards or censorship—to disseminate propaganda and spread tactics. His raw, unedited, piercing, and timely advertising "set a new standard of ruthlessness. . . . Videos later posted in Thailand showed people being beheaded by militants 'who looked into the camera and said one word: Zarqawi.'" Being unprecedented only magnified this strategy's power. Other groups recognized this and adopted the strategy even when their own tenets contradicted its use. The Taliban, who had banned all human images, for example, developed a video department.[15]

Al-Zarqawi also diversified and fragmented global jihadism. As a frontline leader, his cyber-world legend rivaled that of bin Laden, who, while respected, remained in hiding. Al-Zarqawi became a de facto threat to bin Laden's previously unilateral putative dominance in captaining the jihadist movement.[16]

Writ large, this precedent has enabled other aspiring leaders to non-confrontationally challenge bin Laden while pursuing their own more narrow agendas within the broad outlines of greater jihadist ideology. This move has the potential to come at the personal expense of bin Laden's operational command. Global jihadist adherence to bin Laden's preferred agenda may also suffer.

## MOVING FORWARD
### Scene Setter

The Obama administration inherited the most peaceful and stable Iraq since the 2003 invasion. A legitimately elected Iraqi national government was in place. Both the antigovernment insurgency and the intra-sectarian conflict that raged from 2004 to 2007, though still ongoing, had been subdued to manageable levels. Casualty rates for U.S. and allied forces were at their lowest levels since the 2003 invasion.

The ostensible stability wrought by the U.S. surge, however, is largely a veneer. Iraq's fighting transitioned from an initial anti-U.S. effort to become a domestic civil struggle for power in a post-Saddam Iraq.[17] The Iraqis have largely failed to use the surge-induced window of opportunity to make progress on the Bush administration's benchmarks—specific economic, security, and governance objectives with quantifiable measures of progress central to Iraq's viability as a country.

Security underpins all U.S. and Iraqi national government political efforts. Of the eight security benchmarks, Iraq fully met one, failed to meet two, and partially met five by 2010. This cornerstone for U.S. efforts is weak.

Iraq was most successful during the U.S.-led surge. Iraq fully established joint security stations in neighborhoods across Baghdad, which then closed in 2009 per the U.S.-Iraq security agreement. Follow-up efforts to assist U.S. forces by providing additional brigades ultimately arrived late and understaffed, and commanders only somewhat had the necessary authority to make tactical decisions free of political influence.

More significantly, Iraq's post-surge efforts to build capable and durable security forces have been only partially successful. Though Iraqi forces have reached more than 500,000 personnel, Iraq has also failed to significantly increase the number of forces that can operate independently, and they remain untested in a sectarian conflict environment. In September 2010 General Babakir Zebari, who was then chief of staff of the Iraqi armed forces, predicted that U.S. forces would need to remain in Iraq until 2020, and U.S. officials have also acknowledged U.S. aid beyond 2011 will be necessary.[18]

Though sectarian violence is down from its 2007 high, this has been significantly enabled by post-invasion ethnic cleansing. Much of the Iraqi population is now in highly segregated neighborhoods. With roughly 2.5 million Iraqis internally displaced and another 2.5 million overseas, this tenuous situation likely marks only a temporary respite.

The reduction in militia control is equally tenuous. The al-Maliki government has slow-rolled the effort to bring the militias—overwhelmingly Sunni insurgents (80 percent) formerly sustained by a U.S. payroll but also some Shia ones from competing factions—under government control to give the state a monopoly on the use of force. Less than 2 percent had been inducted one year after the 2007 U.S. troop surge, and only approximately 50 percent of the 100,000 members of the Awakening were receiving any kind of government support, and even that was months in arrears. Only about 5 percent of fighters had been given permanent government jobs by March 2009. By July 2010, less than half—roughly 41,000 of 94,000—of the Awakening's fighters had been offered government jobs, and only 9,000 former Awakening fighters had been brought into the security forces.[19]

The Maliki government's attitude was perhaps best summed up by Zuhair al-Chalabi, the head of the National Reconciliation Committee, which is charged with healing Iraq's sectarian divides, when he stated that "fighting the Al Qaeda organization does not mean that you are giving service to the government or the people, and that you deserve gifts, rank, presents, or benefits." The former Sunni insurgents' sense of political abandonment has been exacerbated by systemic efforts of the Shia-dominated government to confiscate weapons and systematically demote former Awakening members who did manage to get into the security forces. As explained by Muthana al-Tamimi, the head of Diyala's provincial council security committee, "The Awakening needs government support. They're not getting it, so they're an easy bite for terrorists."[20] With little, if any, loyalty to the national government, these Sunni and Shiite militia stand-downs in deference to the central government can be ended at any time.

Meanwhile, AQI has begun a serious recruitment campaign. Threats of retribution for having left AQI or the insurgency for the national government and failing to rejoin AQI are complemented by offers of roughly $100 more per month to Sunni members of the security forces than what the Iraqi government is paying. As explained by Nathum al-Jubouri, a former Awakening Council leader in Salahuddin Province who quit the movement in fall 2010, the "Awakening members have two options: Stay with the government, which would be a threat to their lives, or help Al Qaeda by being a double agent. . . . The Awakening is like a database for Al Qaeda that can be used to target places that had been out of reach before," and Iraqi government officials have noted to the press that there are potentially thousands of Awakening fighters on the government payroll who covertly aid the insurgency. While many of the sheiks who had associated with Al Qaeda in Iraq have not intimated a possible return to violence, several thousand Awakening fighters quit, were fired, stopped showing up for duty, or ceased picking up paychecks between spring and fall 2010, a time period that coincides with an increase in post–2007 U.S. troop surge violence and the start of the ever-deepening ethnic fissures stemming from the March 2010 parliamentary election stalemate.[21]

Within a sufficiently secure environment, good governance creates loyalty and political stability. Of the eight governance benchmarks, Iraq fully met two, failed to meet two, and partially met four by 2010. The seeds of long-term conflict remain.

Iraq was most successful with its surge-related governance benchmarks. It created an "Executive Steering Committee" to establish political, media, economic, and social services committees to support the U.S. troop surge by ensuring crucial development activities arrived hand in glove with security improvements. Iraq also ensured the rights of minority-party political participation through Article 37 of the Iraqi constitution, which has been implemented.

Crucially, however, Iraq has failed to establish a durable and inclusive governing structure. Iraq's Sunni leadership agreed to enter the political process in 2005 conditional to a constitutional review to make changes in key clauses with which the Sunni confession took issue. Though a constitutional review committee was formed, a decision required the consensus of all major factions, and no substantive results have been achieved, thus trying Sunni patience.

In this vein, forming semiautonomous regions has stalled. As noted in 2008 by former Iraqi national security advisor Mowaffak al-Rubaie, "A system devolving power to the regions is the route to a viable Iraq." Controversial territorial issues, however—such as a referendum on the status of Kirkuk, which has 13 percent of Iraq's known oil reserves and whose possession the Kurds see as an inviolable need—have been indefinitely postponed for fear of the tensions they would create. In October 2010 the prime minister, Nouri al-Maliki, continued a series of postponements begun in 2007 of the first census in twenty-three years for fear of its impact on political stability because of the Kurdish-Arab tension on this crucial issue.[22]

Iraq still lacks effective, apolitical, nonsectarian enforcement of law and order by respected and capable security forces. "Amnesty International and Human Rights Watch have accused him [al-Maliki] of operating secret prisons in which Sunni suspects have been tortured." Favored sectarian interests and insurgent groups are provided safe haven.[23]

The Iraqi military still shows difficulty making decisions independent of political and sectarian actors, particularly the prime minister's office. Al-Maliki has replaced divisional army commanders with his appointees. Provincial command centers have been brought under his control. He has also moved to dominate the intelligence agencies. The Baghdad Brigade answers directly to al-Maliki's office, and it has frequently been used to move against his political opponents.[24]

Amnesty for former insurgents, many of them Sunnis, has stalled. At the surge's height, U.S. forces held more than 50,000 prisoners, of whom only 10 to 20 percent were deemed hard-core, irreconcilable AQI members. Though a law to grant amnesty to non-terrorists among the 25,000 insurgent prisoners held by the Iraqi government passed February 13, 2008, only 6,300 had been released two years later.

Oppressive de-Ba'athification laws that disenfranchised Iraq's Sunnis have yet to be fully reformed. Former members are still subject to prosecution. Former Hussein regime security personnel are still denied the chance to return to their former jobs. Validating Sunni worries, this law became a significant tool in the hands of de-Ba'athification officials to affect the outcome of the March 2010 elections against Sunni interests.

Iraq has only been partially successful in arranging and holding national elections. To Iraq's credit, it established an Independent High Electoral Commission, it passed a law stipulating the powers of provincial governments, and it passed implementing legislation for national elections. Unfortunately, national elections set for no later than January 31, 2009, were not held until March 2010, and they did not produce a clear, decisive result. This has cast a pall on their legitimacy, and it has turned them into a source of instability.

The ongoing U.S. drawdown only exacerbates the latent storm brewing in a degrading security situation by removing an externally imposed, steadying hand. Though Iraqi politicians cannot totally disregard U.S. desires if they hope to successfully negotiate a $13 billion arms package and leave the door open for soliciting a continued, stabilizing U.S. presence beyond 2011, the United States' influence, which is in direct proportion to its military presence, is steadily dwindling. As voiced by prominent Kurdish lawmaker Mahmoud Othman, "The Americans will leave Iraq with its problems, thus their influence has become weak." As noted by Shiite lawmaker Sami al-Askari, a close ally of Nouri al-Maliki, "The weak American role has given the region's countries a greater sense of influence on Iraqi affairs." According to Mahmoud Othman, "The Iranian ambassador [now] has a bigger role in Iraq than [U.S. Vice President Joseph] Biden."[25] The implications for Iraq's stability, as well as U.S. interests, are ominous.

If Iraq's Sunnis, who as a result of numerical disadvantage and political disunion have a relatively weak hand, come to feel disenfranchised, this could serve as a catalyst for AQI, as well as other Sunni militias, to rise again and renew sectarian violence. The United States would then be confronted with what to do with its limited and increasingly strained supply of military, economic, and political resources. Immediate trade-offs among U.S. interests with respect to Iraq, Afghanistan, Al Qaeda writ large, and especially Iran, would become necessary.

Meanwhile, it is to Iran's advantage to exclude Iraq's Sunnis and bolster the supremacy of Iraq's Shia, particularly the Sadrist faction. Such an outcome would keep Iraq's internal conflict simmering—thus leaving it weak, semi-stable, and Iran-dependent. The Iraqi state would remain generally pro-Iran, and, the United States would either be expelled or kept vulnerable and bogged down.[26]

With a sufficiently secure environment established and governance structures in place to create stability, economic progress creates opportunity and incentive for all. Of two economic benchmarks, Iraq failed to meet one and only partially met the other by 2010. Stability-producing economic development is uncertain.

Iraq has failed to enact national-level legislation to ensure the equitable distribution of oil and gas resources among Iraqis without regard to sect or ethnicity. This would build national cohesion, trust, and stability that would give all Iraqis a stake in Iraq's future as a unified country. Without legal codification, the sharing that does occur could be canceled or adjusted at any time according to the whims of Iraq's political leadership at the time. The rush by Chinese and European firms to develop Iraq's oil and gas fields combined with the willingness of local actors, particularly the Kurds, to cut deals outside of the central government only exacerbates this situation and increases the need to act quickly.

Iraq partially met its goal of allocating and spending $10 billion in its 2007 capital budget for reconstruction projects and job creation, to include the delivery of essential services, on an equitable basis. Expenditures, however, have been slow and decreasing. Sunni areas have not benefitted equally from the Shia-led government's reconstruction efforts.[27] The government's ability to deliver electricity, clean water, medical care, and so forth has not significantly improved, and an efficient, corruption-free method for authorizing and enacting reconstruction remains lacking.

The lingering U.S. presence has thus far mitigated the impact of these security, governance, and economic failures. These seeds of future conflict, however, will only become more potent as time passes and U.S. influence decreases as U.S. forces inevitably draw down. The uncontrolled, unguided unfolding of these unresolved issues the Bush benchmarks were meant to address could easily wreck the stability achieved to date.[28]

### Initial Choices

In February 2009, President Obama announced that his goal was "a way forward in Iraq that leaves Iraq to its people and responsibly ends this war." His administration publicly embraced the Bush administration's U.S.-Iraq security agreement, which took effect January 1, 2009, that called for a timeline-driven approach, not a conditions-based approach, to turning over security responsibility to Iraqi forces while steadily reducing, and eventually eliminating, the American military presence no later than the end of 2011. Not only did the Obama administration adhere to slated withdrawal timelines, such as pulling U.S. forces from Iraq's urban areas by June 2009, but it also went further by announcing an end to all U.S. combat operations by August 31, 2010.[29] It further instituted an interim drawdown goal of having only 50,000 U.S. ground troops by September 1, 2010, which was down from the 95,000 present in May 2010 after Iraq's parliamentary election and markedly below the 142,000 the Obama administration inherited in January 2009.[30]

The troop reduction is not, however, as genuine as it appears. The Congressional Research Service noted in July 2010 that the number of private security contractors has risen by 26 percent during the drawdown. The United States now fields a hybrid force wherein roughly one of every four or five U.S. combat personnel is a private contractor. While the vast majority of the roughly 90,000 contractors perform combat service support duties, such as logistical support, and fulfill combat support obligations, such as intelligence analysis, roughly 15,000 are performing straight-up security work, which includes everything from base security to advanced weapons training to providing personal and supply line protection. The demand for contractor personnel, particularly those directly engaged in security work, is only likely to rise as the U.S. military presence progressively dwindles.[31]

The remaining U.S. "transition force" to aid Iraqi national self-sufficiency was to have a threefold purpose. The bulk of the effort would train, equip, and advise Iraqi security forces as long as they remained nonsectarian. More directly, it would conduct targeted counterterrorism missions as needed. Lastly, it would protect ongoing U.S. civilian and military efforts within Iraq.[32]

A temporarily stable Iraq made the administration's initial decision to proceed with its desired troop withdrawals an easy one. The armed services' ability to field a volume of troops is limited. A tangible, immediately deteriorating situation in Afghanistan, which the Obama administration has touted as the true Al Qaeda central–connected threat to U.S. national security, was contemporaneously juxtaposed against a somewhat stable Iraq. Not only was any future Iraqi violence or instability not a predetermined certainty, but, after U.S. forces stabilized the situation in 2007, the United States had the potential to politically absolve itself of responsibility and blame the Iraqis for future violence, thereby providing plausible political cover for a U.S. departure amid chaos.

The destabilizing March 2010 Iraqi national election did not bolster the Obama administration's desire for an easily continued and irreversible U.S. withdrawal. Iraq's Sunnis were particularly inflamed by al-Maliki's exploitation of the de-Ba'athification process for sectarian political gain, which mobilized his voters and effectively reversed a trend of slowly decreasing sectarian polarization. The Kurds, the holders of the balance of power in Iraq's tri-confessional arrangement, exploited the Sunni and Shiite Arabs' courting for alliances by pressing for increased regional Kurdish autonomy, control of oil, and control of disputed Iraqi territory. Al-Maliki's refusal to step aside after failing to gain the largest number of votes increased unemployment, worsened services, and spiked cynicism among voters who risked their lives to participate in the March 2009 elections as Iraq took world-record time to form a government.[33]

Al-Maliki finally announced a broad-based, inclusive government in late December 2010. The new council of ministers, which was expanded to a total roster of thirty-four members, included ten members from Iraqiya, the multi-sectarian, Sunni-backed bloc that finished slightly ahead of al-Maliki, as well as eight members of the Sadrist faction. Notably, Sunnis were named as speaker of the parliament, a position which drives the legislative agenda, as well as finance minister—steps that may stave off feelings of disenfranchisement that could reignite the Sunni insurgency.[34]

No serious urge to substantively and substantially compromise among either the various political blocs or ethnic communities, however, has emerged.[35] Al-Maliki produced a large, unwieldy, and jury-rigged set of alliances. As summarized by Reidar Visser, author of "A Responsible End? The United States and the Iraqi Transition, 2005–2010," it is "an open question whether the government will be able to decide on key legislation, which is really needed."[36]

The Maliki-led government resulting from the 2009 election, however, is likely to be relatively stable. As summarized by former U.S. Ambassador to Iraq Ryan Crocker when speaking of al-Maliki, "If the Sadrists decide to walk at some point, Maliki can say, 'fine.' . . . If Iraqiya pulls out, it won't force a vote of no confidence. He's got a lot of latitude. Some of the alliances may not hold up. And that may be OK with him."[37]

It also empowers Iraq's Shia. Al-Maliki appointed himself acting minister for defense, interior, and national security. This has effectively guaranteed that Iraq's Shia community will be protected by and control the state, most specifically through his personal rule.

This Shia dominance, however, will likely be rocky. Mr. Sadr's return to Iraq in early 2011 to lead his rejuvenated political organization, which is now more powerful than at any time since the 2003 U.S. invasion, has witnessed him continue to cast his movement as a more mature form of anti-U.S. resistance. When Iran-allied Sadr's increasing sway is set against his known conflicts with al-Maliki, most specifically over al-Maliki's likely request for a continued American presence beyond 2011, political turbulence, which could become security turbulence, is likely.[38]

A security vacuum is forming as of late 2010/early 2011. As one senior U.S. officer stated to the *Los Angeles Times*, "The American military isn't on the scene. The Iraqi security forces are still not trusted in most areas, and the government of Iraq is absent."[39] All major factions are preparing for the possibility of future conflict, a step which in itself only makes such conflict more likely.

AQI, which exists hand in glove with the Sunni insurgency's regenerating potential, is stepping into the void. Bolstered by a surge in financial aid and the renewed influx of foreign fighters, AQI remains a powerful force in Mosul and is also an ongoing threat to U.S. forces as they prepare to draw down.[40]

AQI's third generation, which has proven to be just as ruthless and cunning as its predecessors, has reintroduced al-Zarqawi-style violence, and warned of "dark days soaked with blood." On August 25, 2010, AQI launched a series of coordinated attacks in thirteen cities consisting of hit-and-run shootings, roadside mines, and more than a dozen car bombs killing at least fifty and wounding hundreds. The number of Iraqi civilians killed increased by 50 percent in the month following the March 2010 election, and bombings, sometimes killing or wounding hundreds, have returned as a fact of life.[41] In total, Iraq witnessed some of its highest casualty totals in two years from late summer to early fall 2010, and no readily apparent signs of this trend reversing existed.

All of this occurred despite the U.S. military's killing of thirty-four of AQI's top forty-two leaders by spring 2010. As explained by a senior U.S. officer to the *Los Angeles Times*, "Without good support for the Awakening, [Al] Qaeda is starting to morph back into areas." New to this generation of AQI, they appear to be willing to cut deals with and employ Shia to further their attacks, a situation reflecting not just Shia poverty but also desperation and an extreme lack of faith in the Iraqi government.[42] "The message the insurgents want to deliver to the Iraqi people and politicians is that we exist, and we choose the time and place," said Wael Abdel Latif, a judge and former lawmaker. "They are carrying out such attacks when the Americans are here, so just imagine what they can do after the Americans leave." Though AQI has not reestablished suzerainty over whole towns as it once did, its presence is being felt in Sunni areas, most notably Anbar and Diyala provinces, as well as in Shiite areas, particularly Wasit province south of Baghdad, and its footprint is spreading. The then–minister of defense, Abdul Qadir al-Obeidi, acknowledged in 2010 the "definite signs of regeneration."[43]

Pessimistic about Iraq's political and security trajectory and their future prospects, Iraq's Sunnis, who have always been beset by internal divisions, have begun to unify. Militarily, nearly 250 people representing twenty different groups, to include the 1920 Revolution Brigades and the al-Rashideen Army, which formed to fight the U.S. occupation, met in April 2010 in Istanbul, Turkey, to find common ground after a history of failed attempts to successfully band together. In May 2010, Iraq's outlawed Ba'ath party held a public meeting in Damascus, Syria, to announce its rebirth. Though these groups didn't have large constituencies prior to the March 2010 election, they have now positioned themselves to co-opt popular dissatisfaction.[44]

Iraq's Shia, though divided along factional lines, have also been preparing themselves for potential conflict. In response to the surge in bombings, Moqtada al-Sadr has called for reconstituting his Mahdi Army, which proved the most effective at challenging U.S. and Iraqi national government forces and was most often associated with Shiite death squads that played into AQI's spiral of violence.[45] The al-Maliki-led bloc has increased its political machinations in a divide-and-conquer strategy against Iraq's Kurd and Sunni confessional interests while co-opting state forces in pursuit of its sectarian Shia agenda.

Iran has opted to manipulate the security situation. Attacks against the Green Zone surged from late summer to early fall 2010. A senior American military commander speaking to the *New York Times* stated that Iranian-backed militias were behind the attacks, which exert pressure indirectly on the United States, through swaying U.S. public opinion, and directly on the prime minister, Nouri al-Maliki, who ran on a platform to restore order and security.[46]

The United States has redeployed its remaining forces in response to these post–March 2010 election tensions. The remaining U.S. forces—45,000 combat troops ostensibly reassigned to training and support roles as "Advisory Training Brigades" or "Advisory Assistance Brigades" despite being armed and going on combat patrols with Iraqi forces—were posted strategically around the country.[47] One brigade each went to Baghdad and Anbar province. A thin but significant presence was posted along the Iranian and Syrian borders, both of which have historically served as gateways for weapons and fighters. A significant force was dispatched to northern Iraq, where Kurdish units loyal to the Kurdish regional government and conventional Iraqi army units from the national government have come close to a shooting war in disputed territories along what has become known as the "trigger line."

Special effort was devoted to AQI and Shiite militias. Roughly 4,500 Special Operations Forces (SOF) will remain through the U.S. drawdown.[48] Their primary purpose has been designated as targeting terrorist networks and partnering with Iraqi special forces to preclude a reigniting of the spiral of sectarian violence.

Many experts close to the situation assess that the various competing factions are simply biding their time until the U.S. departure. Most commonly, they predict the collapse of the U.S.-backed regime or an intense civil war as the U.S. force posture weakens. Such a violent internal conflict would likely breathe new life into AQI.[49]

### Future Choices

An already revived AQI, and by extension Al Qaeda central, will claim victory in Iraq when the United States eventually leaves by virtue of being the last ones on the battlefield. They will likely receive significant credit in the eyes of Al Qaeda's actual and potential followers. Anything short of a very peaceful and well-functioning Iraqi state will be seen as a U.S. failure. The overall record of violence, suffering, and despair to date will be credited to the United States. The question, therefore, is what will be the impact on the greater bin Laden–led global jihad of a revived AQI?

When AQI first formed and bin Laden was in hiding, al-Zarqawi filled the role of the hands-on, unifying, operational jihadist commander repelling invading U.S. forces from a historically significant Muslim land. He publicly boosted Al Qaeda central by giving it a highly visible beachhead at the jihadist front while, in turn, he gained legitimacy, media attention, money, and recruits by using the Al Qaeda name.[50] Many potential Al Qaeda supporters viewed AQI as leading the militant political Islamist global insurgency in bin Laden's name, and AQI's prominence will almost certainly rise again if violence in Iraq escalates.

AQI, however, is highly unlikely to significantly boost the jihadist movement or compete with bin Laden's Al Qaeda for stewardship. Following al-Zarqawi's death AQI survived by maneuvering to the top of the post-Zarqawi insurgency by becoming, in effect, a Sunni militia with an almost entirely Iraqi membership to counter the Shiite death squads it inspired. AQI and the Iraqi Sunni insurgency are now intertwined, and AQI is now a transnational jihadist entity in name only. Further, as stated in a 2005 letter from al-Zawahiri to al-Zarqawi, AQI's mass killing of Iraqi Shia tarnished it in the eyes of many coreligionists, who, particularly relative to non-Muslims, view Shia as fellow Muslims regardless of stripe.[51]

AQI and bin Laden's Al Qaeda central have effectively traded places. With U.S. effort shifting away from Iraq to Afghanistan and Pakistan, the region where bin Laden purportedly resides, Al Qaeda central is now once again at the jihadist front. In contrast to AQI's internal transformation, bin Laden's Al Qaeda remains very much an international entity. Apparently seeing himself as leading a long-term global insurgency, wherein popularity with a global audience is the currency for both victory and survival, bin Laden has maintained his popularity by curbing the implementation of his full ideology (i.e., purging Shia, particularly Arabs), as he realizes that killing innocent Muslims, particularly Arabs, and even Shia, is looked down upon by many Muslims around the world and may eliminate potential Al Qaeda troops and supporters.

One factor, however, could counter these trends speaking against AQI's future global significance—U.S. involvement, real or perceived, in Iraq. A fight between Iraqi Sunnis, Shia, and Kurds loses global significance without U.S. involvement. AQI gained prominence by co-opting anti-U.S. rage and successfully channeling it into operational victories against U.S. forces and their allies. Osama Bin Laden's Al Qaeda cannot politically usurp a truly local fight.

## CONCLUSION

Iraq has made tremendous strides since the 2007 U.S. troop surge rescued it from the brink of sectarian civil war. A national election widely viewed as free and fair was held. Leaders and sects, who just three years prior were effectively fighting a civil war, came together to form an inclusive, broad-based government. Civilian deaths compared to one year earlier made Iraq a far safer country than Mexico.[52]

Iraq's progress and stability, however, are largely a veneer. Fundamental security, economics, and governance issues that go to the heart of Iraq's viability as a state are in dispute both within and among Iraq's major ethnic confessions. The short- to medium-term political environment is unlikely to be conducive to their resolution. Desired or not, Iraq is on the cusp of significant political evolution due to the U.S. drawdown, which is simultaneously reducing U.S. sway.

Iraq's slowly deteriorating political and security environment, which is both induced and exacerbated by a combination of the U.S. drawdown and Iraqi political gridlock, has stoked each ethnic community's political fears and ambitions. Iraq's Kurds, Sunnis, and Shiites have all begun to reconsolidate their forces in the event of post-U.S. sectarian conflict. Each faction has hardened its political positions and pressed its demands to exploit the emerging chaos for sectarian gain that has come largely at national expense.

This simmering situation has given AQI a new operational window to impact Iraq's political landscape, and AQI is rejuvenating. Foreign fighters are again beginning to flow into Iraq. AQI funding is increasing. Iraq has witnessed a rebirth of AQI-inspired intercommunal violence.

Though AQI may still seriously impact Iraq's future to the detriment of its peace and stability, AQI is highly unlikely to return to prominence on the world stage. It has effectively become a Sunni militia in both membership and agenda, and its previous mass killing of Shia significantly discredited it among many coreligionists. Of equal importance, Iraq is losing visibility as the Obama administration shifts its focus to Afghanistan and Pakistan.

Conversely, Osama bin Laden's Al Qaeda central is poised to regain any lost stature. The Afghanistan-Pakistan region, where bin Laden and his organization purportedly reside, is the Obama administration's central front. Al Qaeda central's tactics have not disproportionately sullied its jihadist credentials, and it remains a truly transnational terrorist entity with a global presence.

The United States could, however, reverse AQI's likely trajectory. Increasing the United States' commitment to Iraq in what is otherwise a local fight with little to no jihadist relevance and visibility would give AQI a stage. Directly or indirectly, Iraq touches on multiple U.S. interests—Gulf stability, oil, Iran, Israel and the Palestinians, Turkey and the Kurds, and U.S. domestic politics, among others, are all affected. The U.S. incentive to reinvest itself in Iraq between 2010 and 2020 to preclude it from imploding will be significant.

Extensive research on intercommunal civil wars, such as Iraq's, where different segments of society fight one another for power, shows that conflict has roughly a 50 percent reoccurrence rate within five years of a ceasefire. The odds further increase when "lootable" natural resources, such as oil, are stake. At the same time, if a strong external power commits to a peacekeeping and mediation role, which is the U.S. role in Iraq today, then odds of a renewed civil war drop to less than one in three as communal leaders realize that attempting to achieve their domestic goals by force will not be successful.[53]

The Iraqi national government is highly likely to request a prolonged U.S. commitment and indefinite U.S. political, military, and economic assistance in some form. Unfortunately, the United States is overextended. The Obama administration will have to prioritize. No ideal outcome securing the preferred U.S. position for all of the affected issues exists. Tradeoffs will have to be made.

Chapter 6

# A Question of Priorities:
# The Obama Administration and Iran

*The definition of insanity is doing the same thing over and over again and expecting different results.*

—largely attributed to Albert Einstein

The U.S.-Iranian relationship was as antagonistic as ever at the Bush administration's close, and the administration's policies had largely failed to achieve their aims. At the same time, Iran's stark military and political empowerment by the 2003 U.S. invasion of Iraq altered the strategic balance in the Persian Gulf in Iran's favor. As never before, Iranian interests must be taken into account.

The Obama administration has led with a broad engagement effort to appeal to mutual U.S.-Iranian interests dovetailed with selective coercive efforts against clearly conflicting interests.[1] As outlined by Secretary of Defense Gates, "Perhaps if there is enough . . . pressure placed on Iran, diplomacy can provide them an open door through which they can walk if they choose to change their policies. And so I think the two go hand in hand."[2]

The United States, however, increasingly lacks the ability to dominate the region and impose a new order. The faltering U.S. regional position—tied to the largely flailing U.S. efforts in Afghanistan and tenuous success in Iraq—consumes massive quantities of resources that limit U.S. military, economic, and political options elsewhere. Barring a remarkable turn of events, this trend is unlikely to change in the near term.

Iran touches on numerous Obama administration issues and agendas—terrorism, proliferation, oil, Israel and the Palestinians, regional stability, Iraq, Afghanistan, and domestic U.S. politics, among others. None can be ignored. All cannot be addressed at once. The Obama administration must not only choose what objectives to pursue, but also how to pursue them.

## THE OBAMA ADMINISTRATION'S INHERITANCE

Iran viewed itself as being in a potentially precarious situation immediately post-9/11. Juxtaposed with a politically empowered United States, Iran's historical ties to groups that the United States could characterize as terrorists, such as Hezbollah, and its publicly acknowledged holding of senior Al Qaeda leaders[3] made Iran politically vulnerable post-9/11. Meanwhile, Tehran was encircled by U.S. forces successfully engaged on Iran's eastern and western borders in Afghanistan and Iraq while the U.S. Navy boasted of a powerful armada in the Gulf.

Iran responded by reaching out. It offered immediate assistance to the U.S. war effort by allowing over-flights by U.S. planes into Afghanistan, search-and-rescue services for U.S. pilots, and aid for refugees. Iran participated in regional discussions about Afghanistan in a constructive manner.[4] Iran even went so far as to offer the United States a "grand bargain" to resolve outstanding bilateral issues and map a new future.[5]

The Bush administration, however, responded by publicly labeling Iran a member of the "axis of evil." Internationally, this eviscerated Iran's political incentives to amicably engage. Domestically, this discredited Iranians who had pushed for engagement with the United States.[6]

Meanwhile, post-9/11 U.S. actions however, dramatically improved Iran's regional position. The U.S. invasion of Iraq destroyed the only Arab force able to contain Iranian influence, and a Shiite-dominated state with close ties to Iran has risen to power.[7] The unfinished U.S. invasion of Afghanistan created a window for Iran to play the spoiler through a double game of aiding insurgents while engaging the Afghan government with massive reconstruction contracts as it simultaneously provided countering diplomatic leverage, as exemplified by when President Hamid Karzai responded to U.S. chastisement about corruption by extending a state welcome to President Mahmoud Ahmadinejad, who used the occasion to denounce U.S. interference in the region. Regionally, with the United States safely bogged down, Iran, acting via non-state proxies, can needle U.S. interests in Lebanon and Israel via Hezbollah and Hamas.

Iran's clerical regime has also solidified its domestic base. Treating the Green Movement following the 2009 presidential election as an embryonic insurgency, the Iranian Revolutionary Guard Corps (IRGC), per established counterinsurgency theory, quickly delivered harsh and decisive action. As of early 2010, according to the *New York Times*, Iran had arrested more than one thousand people, sentenced eleven regime opponents to death, hanged two, squashed rallies, and held numerous show trials. Throughout, the regime has effectively controlled the media and manipulated the information flow to weave a narrative supportive of its actions.[8]

Iran has also made significant progress on its nuclear capabilities. In June 2010, the UN's International Atomic Energy Agency (IAEA) stated that Iran had produced a stockpile of nuclear fuel that, with further enrichment, would be enough for two nuclear weapons. Though no solid, incontrovertible evidence has emerged on hidden activity, the fall 2009 disclosure of a previously undeclared nuclear site at Qom, and a *New York Times* report that the 2007 National Intelligence Estimate identified ten to fifteen suspect sites, only suggests further Iranian progress while exacerbating the almost total lack of bilateral U.S.-Iranian trust born of decades of acrimonious relations.[9] Secretary of Defense Robert Gates stated in June 2010 that Iran could produce a workable nuclear weapon in one to three years.[10] Western experts estimate an Iranian warhead could be ready by sometime between 2012 and 2014.[11] Though Iran denies any plans or actions, U.S. estimates as of 2010 were that, with sufficient foreign assistance, Iran could produce a nuclear-capable intercontinental ballistic missile (ICBM) able to reach the United States between 2015 and 2020. An April 2010 report to Congress noted that Iran already had missiles that could strike all of Israel.[12]

While early 2011 press reporting notes that the Stuxnet computer virus, whatever its origins, has wreaked havoc with Iran's enrichment capabilities and induced a delay of possibly three years when coupled with export restrictions and other steps, Iran's timeline for being able to make a bomb and subsequent weaponry advances has simply been lengthened. The United States has some breathing space. Iran's overall trajectory and its nuclear inevitability, however, remain unchanged. The United States cannot avoid the issue.[13]

Meanwhile, Iran's once-controversial nuclear program has politically evolved. Enrichment as a right has become non-negotiable across the Iranian political spectrum. Exploitable fissures in Iran's internal politics are few to nonexistent.[14]

While definitely serving as a hindrance to Iranian prosperity, the U.S.-driven economic sanctions have neither hindered the regime's survival nor forced it to fundamentally alter its policies in line with U.S. interests.[15] In fact, additional sanctions have only sparked increased Iranian defiance and a reduction in what little international cooperation on the nuclear issue it does offer. Meanwhile, the United States has strained some of its international ties in this effort.

Iran has also gained indirect sway over Al Qaeda central's AQAP affiliate. Yemen is a state on the verge of collapse. It is contending with separatist efforts in both the north and south of the country, a domestic refugee crisis stemming from internal fighting that has overwhelmed state capacity, a foreign Somali refugee crisis further taxing state capacity, a national water supply that may dry up by 2015, and an oil supply that will likely deplete within ten years. At the same time, Yemen also is host to hundreds of Al Qaeda operatives and the only Al Qaeda affiliate to directly attack the U.S. homeland, which makes it uniquely critical to the broader U.S. struggle against Al Qaeda. Iran can exploit northern Yemen's Shiite rebellion against Sanaa to needle both Yemen and Saudi Arabia, two crucial U.S. allies against Al Qaeda. As of 2010, Saudi Arabia has already accused Iran of interfering to Saudi detriment, a situation that could result in a low-grade proxy war. At the same time, the combination of such a dire national situation with U.S. dependence upon Yemen only strengthens Iran's position, while both easing the execution and magnifying the impact of any of its actions.[16]

Most crucially, however, Iran has gained direct influence over Osama bin Laden's Al Qaeda central. Press reporting notes that while Osama bin Laden led much of his organization to Pakistan after 9/11, other Al Qaeda operatives fled to Iran, which had historically allowed Al Qaeda members safe passage. Most notably, Saif al-Adl (an Egyptian-born longtime aide to Osama bin Laden wanted in connection with the 1998 East Africa embassy bombings) led Abu Hafs the Mauritanian (an Osama bin Laden advisor who helped merge bin Laden's organization with Egyptian Islamic Jihad to form the modern Al Qaeda), Saeed al-Masri (Al Qaeda's longtime chief financial officer), Sulaiman Abu Ghaith (Al Qaeda's longtime spokesman), Mustafa Hamid (a noted Al Qaeda trainer), members of Osama bin Laden's family (including his son Saad), and an unknown number of lesser members out of Afghanistan and into Iran. They remained free until 2003, when Iran placed them under house arrest as both a buffer against an Al Qaeda attack and as a bargaining chip with the United States.[17]

Al Qaeda now uses Iran as a de facto safe haven. According to the U.S. Department of State 2009 Country Report on Terrorism, a publication that has taken a consistent approach since Al Qaeda fled to Iran in 2003, Iran, despite requests from the international community, "has remained unwilling to bring to justice senior al-Qa'ida members it has detained, and has refused to publicly identify those senior members in its custody. Iran has repeatedly resisted numerous calls to transfer custody of its al-Qa'ida detainees to their countries of origin or third countries for trial. Iran has also continued to fail to control the activities of some al-Qa'ida members who fled to Iran following the fall of the Taliban regime in Afghanistan."[18] In March 2010, Gen. David Petraeus stated before the Senate Armed Services Committee that "Al Qaeda continues to use Iran as a key facilitation hub, where facilitators connect Al Qaeda's senior leadership to regional affiliates." While Iran does "periodically disrupt this network by detaining select Al Qaeda facilitators and operational planners, Tehran's policy in this regard is often unpredictable."[19]

As of 2010, according to press reporting, Iran appeared to be loosening its grip on Al Qaeda by permitting operatives to travel outside of Iran, which could allow Al Qaeda to replenish its ranks following a deadly U.S. missile campaign and Pakistani ground incursions into the FATA. These departures began in late 2008 as the Bush administration stepped up international efforts to sanction Iran for its nuclear program. Most notably, Saad bin Laden, who is a son of Osama bin Laden, was permitted to leave in the company of several other Al Qaeda members. Other operatives—primarily money-men and planners, the lower-level workhorses Al Qaeda needs to replenish its ranks—have since followed.

Tracking these operatives is extremely difficult, and U.S. officials have publicly expressed concern that these movements could foretell Iran permitting more senior and prominent managers to move.[20]

Rather than Al Qaeda being the issue prism through which the U.S. views Iran, Iran has become the U.S. issue prism for Al Qaeda. Al Qaeda has subsequently become a function of competing, and only somewhat tangentially, related U.S. interests. Perpetual Iran-U.S. tension makes Al Qaeda into an Iranian lever, which only gives both actors further opportunities.

Time is on Iran's side. Militarily, the U.S. ability to take conventional action against it steadily decreases as the ongoing U.S.-led efforts in Afghanistan and Iraq keep U.S. forces bogged down and unable to divert to a third major ground action—a critical military arbiter whether the objective is regime change or compelling Iranian policy changes regionally, particularly in Iraq and Afghanistan.[21] Diplomatically, the increasing strain of the Afghan war and securing gains in Iraq is causing U.S. allies to increasingly abandon the fight despite these efforts' outcomes, as of 2011, being unclear. Regionally, important conflicts in which Iran plays a significant role and has significant leverage over the United States— Iraq, Afghanistan, Lebanon, Yemen, and the plight of the Palestinians—are not trending to U.S. advantage. Strategically, increased time only brings Iran closer to nuclear weapons. Politically, the United States is burning increasing amounts of capital to coax and coerce a fractious and reluctant international system into an increasingly tenuous coalition behind the U.S. viewpoint, with ineffective results.[22]

Iranian leadership is keenly aware of these post-9/11 changes. Iranian political leadership statements, a barometer of perceived relative power, have largely gone from being conciliatory after 9/11 to being confrontational. As of the Obama presidency, U.S. policy is at a pivot point.

## MOVING FORWARD
### Initial Choices

The administration has staked out U.S. interests relative to Iran—the success of U.S. efforts in Iraq and Afghanistan, precluding Iran from developing nuclear weapons, securing U.S. economic interests, combating terrorism, and securing regional allies, most notably Israel. Tensions with Iran will certainly be present. The administration, however, has evinced flexibility in a velvet-on-iron approach. Implicit is the idea that a constructive, mutually beneficial U.S.-Iranian working relationship not mired in stalemating conflict and rancor, distinct from a friendship, is possible.[23]

President Obama initially appeared to take regime change off the table. In his 2009 Now Ruz message President Obama acknowledged the legitimacy of Iran's theocratic regime not only by speaking to it instead of around it to the

Iranian people, but also by using its preferred name, the Islamic Republic of Iran. He also signaled no regime change subtext by calling upon Iran to "take its rightful place in the community of nations."[24]

President Obama stated he was "committed to diplomacy that addresses the full range of issues before us, and to pursuing constructive ties among the United States, Iran, and the international community."[25] As a lead-up to more contentious issues, the Obama administration's initial forays were on non-confrontational issues of mutual interest, such as countering the narcotics flow from Afghanistan's porous border. In a marked break from President Bush, who routinely required Iran to essentially cave on the points to be discussed as a precondition to direct U.S. interaction, President Obama offered to negotiate "without preconditions."[26]

On the forefront issue of Iran's nuclear capability, the sole and ultimate guarantor of regime survival, the Obama administration has intimated at accommodation. As noted by former Department of State expert Mark Fitzpatrick, "There is a fundamental impasse between the Western demand for no enrichment and the Iranian demand to continue enrichment,"[27] and the Bush administration's position boiled down to an all-or-nothing stance. President Obama's stance of "don't develop a nuclear weapon," however, allows for more flexibility.[28] It implies the permissibility of a civilian nuclear program, which, in effect, contends that Iran seeks nuclear weapons capability, but not necessarily the weapons themselves.

President Obama has also displayed cultural awareness to facilitate dialogue. His Now Ruz message was the first for a sitting U.S. president. Significantly, he has dropped the phrase "carrots and sticks," which the Iranians assert should only be used when talking about donkeys.[29] Having stated that it neither needs nor wants nuclear weapons and that Islam actually forbids them, calling upon Iran to live up to its cultural and religious principles only serves as a natural political opening for negotiations, and it allows the United States the political high ground.

The administration has followed up its inducements with focused pressure upon key Iranian actors, notably the IRGC, to compel policy changes. Unlike the Iranian military, which defends the country, the IRGC's express purpose is to safeguard Iran's theocratic regime. The United States assesses therefore that the IRGC, which is estimated to control up to 40 percent of Iran's economy, handles the regime's most delicate issues, such as Iran's nuclear program and terrorism-related activity abroad.

Executive Order 13382 designated the IRGC a nuclear proliferator. A vigorous and targeted sanctions campaign has followed. Covert action against Iran's nuclear program has also been increased.[30]

Executive order 13224 labeled the IRGC a terrorist entity. Between 2007 and 2010, U.S.-led forces have captured more than twenty members of the Qods Force, an elite IRGC unit, as well as Iran-backed Hezbollah and regular IRGC forces who were members of "covert Iranian networks providing advanced weaponry and training to our enemies in Iraq."[31] Kenneth Katzman, a senior Iran analyst at the Congressional Research Service, allows no "indication that the Obama administration is backing away from continuing the strategy of acting to disrupt Iranian covert networks." The Obama administration has also created new multiagency "threat finance cells" to uncover terrorist financing data, which are then shared with military units that either apprehend or kill Iranian operatives. The administration has also retained Stuart Levey, Bush's undersecretary of the treasury for terrorism and financial intelligence, to help starve Iranian companies and banks of Western capital.[32]

On a separate but not unrelated note, the Obama administration has engaged Syria to try to flip this Iranian ally and key lever on U.S. efforts in Iraq that is bound to Iran in regional affairs primarily by anti-U.S. glue. The Obama administration is uniquely positioned to do so because of the distinctive U.S. ability to serve as a mediator that can be both an inducer and a guarantor for Israeli-Syrian talks as Syria seeks the return of the Golan Heights and Israel seeks moderated Syrian support for Hamas and Hezbollah, which also impacts U.S. interests in Lebanon and the plight of the Palestinians. "Over time, as Syria sees the benefits of contact with the West," Iranian behavior can then be leveraged.[33]

More broadly, the Obama administration has looked after its Arab allies. Per the *New York Times*, the administration has placed anti-missile defenses in four countries around the Persian Gulf.[34] Indirectly, U.S. interests in Persian Gulf oil, allied assistance against Al Qaeda, and those countries' assistance with Iraq and Afghanistan are secured.

The United States and Iran are intrinsically linked into, fall out on opposite sides of, and are not yet strong enough to impose their respective wills in the region's disputes. The Obama administration's position, as elaborated by Adm. Dennis Blair, then director of National Intelligence, is that "Iran 'can have its security without nuclear weapons. And that it can advance both its economic prospects and its own view of where it is in the region, and in the world, without the use of the backing of extremist groups and possessing nuclear weapons.'"[35] This essentially adds up to devising a new Gulf security system. U.S. engagement presents Iran the opportunity to consolidate its gains to date and achieve U.S. recognition of its regional status.[36]

Despite the initial appearance of a sharp break, the Obama administration has shown that it retains many of the same underlying Bush administration premises that have proven so ineffective. Conflicting political and strategic demands have maintained unresolved inconsistencies in the U.S. position. These have precluded effective engagement by muddling U.S. efforts and denying Iran clear paths to walk toward a more productive relationship.

The Green Movement has both caused and highlighted internal U.S. contradictions. Its challenge, not just to the 2009 national election results, but also to the regime's clerical nature is the most organized, broad-based, pro-democracy challenge to the regime since its inception. Regime defensive politics have emphasized nationalism, religion, and charges of foreign influence, particularly by Americans, and this has shrunk the political window for bilateral compromises. The U.S. proposals speak not only to Iran's core national interests, but also to the regime's root political identity, and thus its domestic legitimacy and survival. Amid such internal political stress, asking Iran to put itself in a position of being able to claim anything other than a meaningful victory against a traditional adversary, who has historically denied the regime's legitimacy and called for its overthrow, is highly unlikely to yield productive results.

The administration must now choose between Iran's actively repressive clerical government and oft-touted U.S. rhetoric on American political values, as embodied in human rights and supporting protestors citing these U.S.-validated inalienable rights. Nothing can be done without engaging Iran's clerical regime, yet engaging the regime and abandoning the Green Movement leaves the United States open to charges of political expediency.

This political conundrum has led to strategic confusion. Criticizing the clerical regime's internal political repression indirectly takes a step toward undoing much of the administration's legitimizing of the clerical regime simultaneous to the Iranian protestors increasingly challenging not just the clerical regime's actions, but the validity of the regime itself. At the same time, as the United States exploits Iran's political strife by failing to support the regime, fruitful negotiations become increasingly less likely. Regime change and the curbing of Iran's nuclear potential are placed at odds. Hedging political bets effectively subordinates curbing Iran's nuclear weapons potential to regime change, and it links them by making regime change the means of execution.

Though the administration has claimed to seek rapport on a variety of issues, and the multiple regional disputes offer Iran opportunities for political and strategic advancement at reasonable U.S. expense, President Obama has stridently made the nuclear question the issue prism for U.S.-Iranian relations. The administration is attempting to begin a rapprochement on perhaps the most politically charged, sensitive, and contentious bilateral issue.

Not only is it a particularly difficult issue to make the cornerstone of a new relationship but, given the multitude of U.S.-Iranian bilateral concerns, most notably Al Qaeda, it is a woefully inefficient approach, particularly when the administration itself estimates that the national security of the United States and its allies will not be irrevocably harmed if Iran acquires nuclear weapons. Gary Samore, a senior nuclear proliferation advisor, and Bruce Riedel, the Afghanistan-Pakistan policy review chief, have written that "if Iran acquires nuclear weapons, it is likely to behave like other nuclear weapons states, trying to intimidate its foes, but not recklessly using its weapons. As such, Iran will be subject to the same deterrence system that other nuclear weapons states have accommodated themselves to since 1945."[37]

U.S. security will certainly be indirectly impacted. A flurry of regional nuclear reactor building has coincided with Iran's increasing capabilities. Twenty-five countries, ten of them in the greater Middle East, have since announced plans to acquire a nuclear capacity,[38] and all of the rest of the greater Middle East, with the sole exception of Lebanon, have at least expressed an interest.[39] Arms purchases in 2010 by Saudi Arabia, the UAE, Oman, and Kuwait totaling $123 billion and consisting of fighter jets, command and control systems, existing equipment upgrades, radars, and missile defenses, which are at least tacitly meant to compensate for impending unconventional inferiority, show that a conventional arms race has already begun.[40] Israel, which has declared that an Iranian nuclear weapons capacity is an existential threat that cannot be permitted, has intimated punitive military strikes. Questions about U.S.-led nonproliferation efforts, U.S. deterrence policies, particularly extended deterrence, and tangentially connected regional economic and political issues— oil, terrorism, Iraq, Afghanistan, Lebanon, Yemen, and the plight of the Palestinians—all surface.

Again, however, strategic confusion exists. Existing U.S. policy has made Iran's nuclear program the common and enabling link in this impending evolution of the Middle East for these otherwise independently existing issues that exist in their own unique circumstances. Iran's nuclear program is not interchangeable with the issues that it impacts, either in the substance of the impact or in the ease with which the United States is able to impact their outcomes. Resolving the nuclear issue will not preempt the others. Priorities must be parsed.

The net result has been that Iran has "not taken advantage of the many opportunities to begin to build trust and confidence," particularly on the nuclear issue, the cornerstone of the administration's approach.[41] In fall 2009, Iran rejected an administration offer to send the bulk of its enriched uranium abroad at one time for one year and receive internationally monitored quantities of nuclear fuel in return, an arrangement that would have left it sufficient nuclear material for its civilian nuclear program, scientific experiments, and medical needs while, from the U.S. perspective, depriving Iran of sufficient fissile material for nuclear weapons construction.[42] In 2010, Iran announced that it would begin large-scale enriching of uranium to 20 percent, which has some limited medicinal applications in very limited quantities, and from which the technical leap to 90 percent, whose only purpose is for weapons, is minimal.[43] Iran has also announced the construction of new facilities,[44] of which Iran stated it would not notify the IAEA about until they were nearly ready for operation.[45] In tandem, Iran announced an increase in the number of machines producing reactor-grade uranium, an incremental step that could increase Iran's ability to highly refine uranium necessary for nuclear weapons.[46] Lastly, Iran brought the Bushehr facility online, Iran's first operational nuclear plant out of a goal of twenty.[47]

All the while, Iran has refused to answer IAEA questions "about the possible existence in Iran of past or current undisclosed nuclear-related activities involving military-related organizations, including activities related to the development of a nuclear payload for a missile." Iran has also denied the IAEA information regarding its operations to manufacture centrifuges, possible work on laser enrichment, and mining and milling of uranium. Iran has even gone so far as to bar IAEA inspectors. Tehran "has not provided the necessary cooperation to permit the [IAEA] to confirm that all nuclear material in Iran is in peaceful activities," and the IAEA is slowly losing its ability to effectively perform its duties.[48]

### Future Choices

As stated by senior House Democrats in a letter to President Obama, "Engagement must be serious and credible, but it cannot be open-ended."[49] In the eyes of the United States and its allies, particularly Israel, Iran's 2010 actions remove any pretenses of Iran not having outright weaponization or the clear capacity for turn-key weaponization as an ulterior motive. The failure of such a genuine and proactive outreach politically positions the United States for coercive action.[50] The administration is rapidly being faced with three options—military action, a broad policy of containment, or more sanctions.[51]

Limited airstrikes directed against Iran's known WMD capacity is the primary military possibility. The prospect of either a full-scale war to depose Iran's clerical regime or meaningful ground incursions to attack Iran's purported WMD infrastructure is unlikely with U.S. ground forces consumed by Iraq and Afghanistan and no U.S. ally with a potent deployable ground force showing political will. If not a unilateral U.S. strike, an Israeli attack, either independently with U.S. permission or in support of a U.S. launch, is likely.

The benefits are several. Even if it fails to eliminate Iran's WMD capability and simply delays Iran's inevitable WMD acquisition, advocates prefer it to a permanently altered regional dynamic. Internationally, the specter of military action may serve as an effective catalyst to President Obama's engagement efforts. Domestically, the inclusion of a military possibility may broaden political support for President Obama's approach as people rally to the flag, and an opening is created for the American political right to support the president by claiming vindication for finally executing a policy they have often touted.

The odds of a successful strike eliminating Iran's WMD capacity, however, are low, and "security analysts in Israel and America have warned . . . that such a strike would at best delay, rather than stamp out, Iran's nuclear program." The full scope, scale, and details of Iran's WMD programs are not known. Any damage from a one-time operation would, ultimately, likely be repairable. There is no guarantee that a strike would even delay Iran's efforts. This, in turn, begs the question of whether any military action would be a one-time affair or a multistep endeavor spread out over time, which would inevitably ratchet up Iran's response.

The United States' already wobbly regional strategic position would likely become more precarious. "Analysts expect that Iran would step up support for anti-American militants in the Gulf, as well as for militias fighting U.S. forces in Iraq and Afghanistan."[52] Al Qaeda will be both politically and operationally strengthened.

Since the United States is unlikely to get international backing for preemptive action following the Iraq WMD debacle, U.S. public standing would likely plummet. While first-world U.S. allies and regional partners may turn a blind eye, the likelihood of receiving assistance from the rest of the developing world on other issues, most notably Al Qaeda, will most probably markedly decline. From Al Qaeda's perspective, claims of wanton U.S. aggression against possible Muslim progress will have been validated, and Al Qaeda will be positioned to operationally co-opt this newfound political rage.

If Israel unilaterally attacks despite U.S. admonitions, the United States might publicly denounce the attack. This would produce an open break in the U.S.-Israeli alliance, the first since the 1956 Suez crisis. Whether true or not, Israel will commonly be perceived as acting with U.S. blessing. Al Qaeda will make political hay, which translates into more operational capacity.[53]

If Israel attacks unilaterally with U.S. permission or in conjunction with U.S. forces, the Israeli political and security outcomes, as well as their impact upon U.S. interests, could be far worse. Israel may possibly fall victim to subsequent military efforts by Iranian proxies seeking to exploit Israel's precarious strategic situation for their own gains. Hezbollah, with its increased and potent armory, could make trouble from Lebanon. Hamas could attempt to seek gains in Gaza. Negotiations over the plight of the Palestinians, already anemic, would likely grind to a halt, and this would most likely induce more domestic violence inside Israel, which will only make negotiations more difficult and likely raise tensions with the United States. Again, Al Qaeda would be positioned to co-opt, and possibly act upon, the outrage.

The United States could also suffer more explicitly. Iran is in a position to wreak political and military havoc on the U.S. position in Iraq. As evidenced by press reporting that Iran has forwarded antiaircraft missiles to Taliban insurgents while already providing monetary support and incentives to kill U.S.

soldiers, actions which appear to correlate with times of increased U.S. pressure on its nuclear program, Iran could also likely destabilize the already tenuous U.S. position in Afghanistan.[54] The U.S. naval presence in the Gulf and the Strait of Hormuz, critical choke points in U.S. military and energy supply lines, would also be vulnerable. Due to Iran's established pattern of using surrogates, America's global economic, political, and military presence would also have to be considered to be at risk.

Economically, the 2008–2010 global downturn would likely be prolonged. The price of oil could be expected to rise immediately by ten to twenty dollars per barrel, if not more. A corresponding spike in insurance rates would likely hike the price even further. The U.S. stock market and, to a lesser extent, that of Israel, would likely fall precipitously.

Lastly, any U.S. hope for domestic change inside Iran would likely fall victim to the strikes. Iranian nationalism will likely be stoked, and the position of the clerical regime will be further solidified. The Green Movement, even if it did not unite behind the regime to oppose aggression against Iran and thus lose its independent standing, would likely have to, at a minimum, go to ground to survive if the clerical regime did not seize the security crisis to vanquish it outright.

Though Iran could respond more passively instead and play the victim in order to build international political standing at U.S. expense, Iran could also go beyond these medium-intensity steps. It could take direct military action against Israel, whose cities are within range of Iranian missiles, or against U.S. forces in the region. Economically, Iran could try to close the Straits of Hormuz, which would spike oil prices with some estimates reaching $150 per barrel, a serious blow to the nascent 2010 economic global recovery.[55]

Possible second- and third-order effects create the potential for the region's politico-military situation to rapidly spiral out of control. Israel, for example, has already threatened to hold the Syrian and Lebanese governments responsible if it is struck by Hezbollah. Would military action spiral? Would all weapons use remain conventional? With such economic and political calamity broadly dispersing pain to all who are wedded to the region—the United States, China, Russia, Europe—would such a chaotic situation force consensus or exacerbate existing tensions and spill over into other issues? In the wake of any ensuing hostilities, how much would defense budgets rise? What, in turn, would be the impact on the 2010 nascent global economic recovery?[56]

A Soviet-style containment policy provides an alternative to military action. To be meaningful, it would have to include an extension of the U.S. nuclear umbrella to Arab allies, increased security guarantees to Israel, increased political, economic, and military ties and aid to the United States' Arab allies, and a large forward-based U.S. military presence throughout the region, which to a significant degree has already rejected a large, overt U.S. presence. Most crucially, it would also necessitate freezing Iran out of the benefits of the global political and economic system.

Neither the United States nor its local allies, however, can muster the containment approach's voluminous regional military requirements in the near- to medium-term. U.S. regional allies do not possess substantial conventional capabilities, and U.S. forces are fully occupied in long-term wars in Iraq and Afghanistan. U.S. regional allies also do not possess any unconventional capability, and the United States has intentionally kept unconventional weapons from its regional policy tool kit.

U.S. economic capacity to forcefully implement a Cold War–style containment strategy is also in doubt. Near- to medium-term massive U.S. budget deficits, entitlement spending obligations, voluminous war-related expenses that can reasonably be expected to continue for at least five to ten years, and repair efforts to stave off the near-collapse of the global financial system and revive the lagging U.S. economy amid a global economic downturn have brought the United States to its economic limits. Economic space to sign ally-benefitting trade deals and to provide heavy direct U.S. economic aid, as well as the political will to expend significant resources to this end during this time of economic crisis and ongoing wars, are in short supply.

The chief stumbling block, however, is politico-economic factors beyond U.S. and close-ally control. After World War II, the United States, of its own accord, was able to provide a set of mutually overlapping military, political, and economic opportunities alternative to the Soviet Bloc and its inferior military, political, and economic systems. In the early twenty-first century, however, the world system is more diversified, and the United States is a preponderant, not hegemonic, actor. Comprehensive cooperation from the world's other major powers, most notably veto-wielding Russia and China, would be necessary for the requisite and interlaced political, economic, and military policy choices to be effective, particularly if executed by sanctions. Capitalizing on the major powers' diverging interests, Iran is able to separately and diversely secure its military, political, and economic needs in a multipolar world.

China's economic needs, which have been the Communist Party's unswerving priority for roughly two decades and have turned China into an economic powerhouse, make it unlikely that one of the world's most potent economies will cooperate in a U.S.-led comprehensive containment effort. Iran is China's second-largest oil supplier at 12 percent of Chinese consumption,[57] and China is systematically integrating Iran into its economic engine. In 2004, for example, China Petroleum and Chemical Corporation signed a $70 billion deal to develop the Yadavaran oil field and buy 10 million metric tons of liquefied natural gas from Iran per annum for the next twenty-five years. More than

$5 billion in contracts to expand or build four Iranian refineries have since been signed.[58]

China is also unlikely to cooperate in order to gain strategic advantage. Maintaining Iran's viability and independence from U.S. efforts voids effective unilateral U.S. control over a critical region and its resources. China's significantly increasing military capabilities, which are increasingly challenging the U.S. security hegemony in East Asia, and its rising economic clout,[59] which in part stems from U.S. reliance upon China as an economic and fiscal savior in an increasingly interconnected global economy, suggest a decade of increasing tension and competition, not cooperation. China is assuming a more prominent role in the international system, and it employs client state North Korea while facilitating de facto regional surrogate Iran to effectively stymie the United States and occupy U.S. energies.[60]

Since the mid-1990s, Russia has dangled possible cooperation with the United States. At the same time, Moscow has maintained its connections to Tehran and undermined U.S.-Russian unity. U.S. logic—Russia's status is diluted every time another country acquires nuclear weapons, Russia has no interest in living next to a regime able to strike it with nuclear ballistic missiles, Russia has a sizable Muslim population that Iran could exploit, and the Middle East peace process is hurt because any increased Iranian standing allows it to better bolster those opposed to the process—has not prevailed.[61]

The Russian-Iranian relationship is not one-dimensional. Russia may see value in keeping Iran nuclear-free. It may, however, value its substantial commercial and military trade with Iran even more.

Russia would also likely lose strategic advantage if it joined a U.S.-led containment policy. Russia, as with China, maintains Iran as a regional foil to void unilateral U.S. control over a critical region and its resources. Even if Russia accepts U.S. logic, Russia may not believe Iran can be stopped. In that situation, Russia's best angle would be to offer hope to the Obama administration that it could be induced to cooperate. It could then win concessions on other matters for as long as possible while seeking a position of privilege with Iran when it goes nuclear.[62]

As a third option, internationally binding UN sanctions, effectively constitutes "containment lite." The Obama administration is "laying the groundwork for the kind of very tough ... crippling sanctions that might be necessary in the event that ... [its] ... offers are either rejected or the process is inconclusive or unsuccessful."[63] Easing the U.S. burden, containment's military aspect is gone. Easing U.S. and allied burdens, the political aspect is made easier by only requiring agreement to enact specific, substantive sanctions targeted at Iran's nuclear program to induce it to halt its nuclear activities vice economically and politically freezing Iran out entirely.

Again, China is unlikely to either take or permit significant action. Seriously tough economic sanctions would likely spike Chinese oil costs, and this would threaten its economic juggernaut, which is the Communist Party's strongest claim to continued domestic legitimacy.[64] This would also undermine the means by which China has financed its twenty-one-fold purchasing power parity increase in military expenditures from 1988 to 2007 to develop forces capable of challenging the United States, thus affecting Taiwan and the United States' Pacific alliances.

In fact, ineffective sanctions are China's ideal situation as U.S. allies abstaining from the Iranian market does not hurt China or Iran. China National Petroleum Corporation, for example, signed a $5 billion dollar contract with the National Iranian Oil Company to develop the massive South Pars field. This, however, was only after Iran assessed that France's Total SA, which had already signed an agreement to develop these fields, was stalling.[65]

China's mode of economic development dovetails with its foreign affairs philosophy since the 1950s of "noninterference in internal affairs." Iran need only maintain a modicum of actual cooperation and the appearance of a spirit of earnestness in engaging with the international community on nuclear and other issues to provide China a sufficient fig leaf to block a more comprehensive approach.[66] By slowing down sanctions implementation, China is not just reducing that tool, but it is also effectively delaying decisions to authorize the use of force.

Russia is also unlikely to either take or permit significant action. The Iran issue, bolstered by U.S. attempts to expand its logistical bridges into Afghanistan through the Soviet sphere of influence in Central Asia, gives Russia significant leverage. While Iran is unlikely to have been the key driver in multiple recent U.S. concessions—declaring Russia's continued illegal military occupation of Georgia as "no obstacle" to U.S.-Russian cooperation, posing no public objection to Russian control of a Crimean naval base through 2042, and not publicly contesting the suggestions of Vladimir Putin, the Russian prime minister, of undermining Ukrainian sovereignty by merging Russian and Ukrainian industries—it is also highly unlikely to have been of no significance.[67] At the same time, because the West won't buy Iran's natural gas, delaying vice immediately preventing Iran's nuclear progress, while also preventing normalized relations with the United States and the West, increases Russia's leverage over Europe and Cental Asia as its main gas supplier while also increasing Russian leverage over Iran.

Meanwhile, lesser powers have sought to exploit this great power tension. Brazil and Turkey, for example, floated a proposal similar to President Obama's earlier offer about sending uranium abroad. This potentially placed the United States in the role of being an obstacle to a diplomatic solution. It also allowed both Turkey and Brazil not only to gain global stature, but also to exploit U.S. vulnerability to increase their standing with Iran while bolstering their leverage against the United States on other U.S.-related regional issues.[68]

These U.S.-Russian-Chinese tensions effectively transformed the administration's 2010 keynote effort against Iran from "crippling sanctions" into more of a symbolic political victory. The toughest clause banned states from accepting Iranian nuclear-related investment abroad, a statement that only addressed rumors of Iranian ventures in Venezuela and Zimbabwe while leaving Iran's now self-sustaining domestic nuclear industry untouched.[69] All of the key points, filtered through Russian and Chinese desires and leverage, largely perpetuate the status quo.

Tightening financial restrictions to cut off Iran's access to outside financing and banks is likely the most effective means of squeezing Tehran, and the 2010 effort required financial institutions that established reasonable grounds to believe Iranian banks or other firms were evading sanctions to block any transactions related to banned activities. Expanding the lists of IRGC-linked individuals and entities subject to asset freezes gained traction. There was, however, no comprehensive ban on financial dealings with the IRGC.[70]

Expanding the lists of IRGC-associated individuals and entities subject to travel bans also gained support. There was, however, no agreement on which individuals and entities linked to the IRGC will be targeted. The countries likely to honor travel bans are not Iran's key patrons, and Iran's key patrons are highly unlikely to suffer any consequences from not honoring them. As Iran is an advanced country, travel is easy, and core constituencies can always come to Iran.

The anti-Iran international arms embargo was expanded, and it now includes key hardware such as battle tanks, combat aircraft, and missiles, yet there was no comprehensive arms embargo as sought by the United States and France. Crucially, Iran is still permitted to purchase light weapons, to include the highly sophisticated Russian S-300 surface-to-air missile system, which can most likely hobble any airstrike on Iran's nuclear facilities.[71]

A new framework for carrying out inspections of suspect cargo on the high seas was also included. There was no requirement, however, that states board Iranian vessels suspected of carrying banned items. As evidenced by similar efforts against North Korea, the political will to take such tension-inducing steps on a routine basis, even once the authority is in place, is low.[72]

Lastly, and most significantly, the administration's 2010 efforts yielded no mention of a U.S.-backed proposal for halting new investment in Iran's energy sector. Despite being a crude-oil exporter, Iran's lack of refining capacity makes it a gasoline importer. No restrictions were placed on Iran's lucrative oil trade, its chief source of hard currency and government revenue.

Cognizant of this vulnerability, Iran has taken unilateral interim steps. Iran dropped its reliance on gasoline imports from 40 percent to 25 percent of its needs. An elaborate rationing system decreased consumption by nearly 20 percent in the first six months of 2010 alone. It has also developed a strategic reserve able to meet domestic needs for at least eighty days.[73]

Meanwhile, as evidenced by the hundreds of European, Asian, and South American firms on hand for Tehran's annual oil fair in May 2010, there is a "whole network of companies in the Gulf that are prepared to trade refined products to Iran" despite U.S. wishes. China's refinery investment on the horizon will markedly increase Iran's domestic capacity. Iran will likely not only become less vulnerable, but also more economically, and thus politically, globally integrated.[74]

The Obama administration, in concert with key allies such as Australia, Canada, and Europe, has initiated a series of unilateral sanctions meant to fill some of the gaps. The Comprehensive Iran Sanctions, Accountability, and Divestment Act, for example, imposes penalties on foreign firms that sell refined petroleum to Iran or assist Iran with its domestic refining capacity. It requires U.S. and foreign businesses who have U.S. government contracts to certify that they have no prohibited business with Iran. It also restricts or bans from the U.S. financial system foreign banks that deal with the IRGC or other blacklisted entities.[75]

While sound in theory, these steps lack impact in context. Iran is simply not critically dependent upon the United States or its close allies for the very points of vulnerability the law seeks to exploit. Without multilateral backing, Iran will continue to evade restrictions and meet its needs, albeit at higher financial and possibly political cost.

Reflective of the administration's strategic confusion, sanctions advocates also argue that increased pressure will cause the regime to collapse, and that now is the time to act. They say that large-scale political protests have weakened the regime's foundation. Its protector, the IRGC, is besieged, and Iran's military has warned that its toleration for repression has limits.[76]

The clerical regime's foundations, however, are relatively strong. Contrary to the Green Movement's claims of electoral fraud, the Iranian public generally accepts the 2009 presidential election as legitimate. Analysis of multiple public opinion polls conducted by the University of Tehran, WorldPublicOpinion.org, and GlobeScan leading up to and following the 2009 presidential election shows that the majority of the Iranian public (52–57 percent) planned to vote for Ahmadinejad, and an even larger majority (55–66 percent) claimed to have done so after the election. Prior to the election, 57 percent expected Ahmadinejad to win, and more than 70 percent saw him as the legitimate president. In total, roughly 80 percent saw the 2009 election as free and fair. While this does not disprove election irregularities, the Iranian public did not blatantly reject Ahmadinejad as the Green Movement vociferously claims.[77]

Also contrary to the Green Movement's criticism, the Iranian public generally supports the regime's clerical nature. Large majorities of the Iranian public endorse the concept of Islamic scholars being able to veto laws contrary to sharia. This sentiment even held true with a majority of opposition leader Mir-Hossein Mousavi's supporters.[78]

Postelection public opinion polling shows little change in Iran's internal political balance. Comparison findings from early 2008 and late 2009 by WorldPublicOpinion.org show those siding with the Iranian opposition amid Iran's more repressive post-election climate holding relatively steady, with those consistently expressing very critical views of their government experiencing a loss of only 4 percent (17 percent to 13 percent). Similarly, the number of Iranians consistently expressing moderately critical views of their government slid only six points (46 percent to 40 percent). Meanwhile, the number of Iranians consistently expressing positive views of their political system associated with Iran's conservatives rose by 11 percent (36 percent to 47 percent). Roughly one-fifth of these conservatives, who make up 10 percent of the Iranian public, take a militant position against the United States.[79]

Comparing Iran's Green Revolution to Eastern Europe's nonviolent color revolutions is inaccurate. Eastern Bloc dissidents have had three forces on their side: nationalism, because communism was imposed by a foreign power; religion, because communism suppressed the church; and ideology, because democracy was a sought-after alternative to a bankrupt predecessor. The Green Movement only partially has democracy to the extent it was truly subverted, an uncertain fact, and the regime has suppressed this venue by fusing religion and nationalism backed by force against its political opposition, whom the regime has worked to denounce and discredit through its control of the media.[80]

The political resistance movement will likely survive underground. It will very likely exist, however, as an isolated, yet virulent, current in Iranian society that is unlikely to serve as the vanguard of a general public uprising. Its views, loudly voiced, have been rejected by the masses. The Obama administration's supplying of computer hardware and software to the resistance movement to assist them in evading government censors and increasing their communications only risks tainting what could otherwise possibly become a potent force in the future in order to forgo changes in current U.S. policy.[81] A continuation of Iran's existing policies is the most likely outcome for the foreseeable future. The Iranian public, as of 2010, was simply not in a prerevolutionary mindset that could either fundamentally reorient Iran's internal politics or its foreign policy. Any internal conflict within the government of Iran's military and security apparatus has either been absent or insufficient to fundamentally alter the government's repression of its political opposition.[82]

Ironically, increased sanctions are likely to strengthen the IRGC, the regime's key coercive pillar and guarantor of existing policies.[83] Depriving Iran of foreign capital to increase and diversify legitimate investment only concentrates wealth. The IRGC, which reportedly controls up to 40 percent of Iran's economy,[84] has significant and increasing holdings throughout key sectors of Iran's legitimate economy—banks, manufacturing, the oil sector, communications, mining, construction, and so forth. While sanctions are making access to foreign capital more difficult, Iran's banks are shouldering the burden. In September 2009, for example, the Iranian Labor News Agency reported that the debt of Iran's eleven state-run banks to the Central Bank rose tenfold since 2005 to a total of $32 billion. The state, particularly the IRGC, is being empowered in the process. On the flip side, as the Guards already, at least implicitly, control much of the contraband smuggling into Iran. Any sanctions-induced growth of the black market will only funnel more money to the Guards rather than undercutting them.[85]

Paradoxically, high-profile or particularly effective sanctions will also likely harm U.S. interests. If the sanctions themselves don't drive the people closer to their government, those advocating change will have their patriotic credentials questioned if perceived to be acting in response to U.S. pressure. The ability to disagree with government policies of a state increasingly under siege will slowly evaporate. Meanwhile, an increasingly empowered IRGC is only likely to more effectively compete for political power with the regime's traditional clerical elites, particularly the reformists. The IRGC's conservative political and strategic sway, and that of their conservative political allies, will likely grow, and Iran will likely become more recalcitrant.[86]

Absent rapidly collapsing the regime, a highly unlikely prospect, sanctioning a country does not necessarily translate into altered policies. North Korea, Cuba, and Burma, for example, have been economically isolated for decades to little effect. In a timeline wholly unsuitable to U.S. interests in Iran, Libya was sanctioned for decades before it adjusted its orientation. As noted by Richard Haass, president of the Council on Foreign Relations, "The history of sanctions suggests it is nearly impossible to craft them to compel a government to change on an issue it sees as vital to national security. They can affect a government's calculations, but it's [sic] not a solution."[87] Adm. Michael Mullen, chairman of the Joint Chiefs of Staff, has stated that he believes Iran will continue to pursue nuclear weapons even if sanctions increase.[88]

Iran is a country whose clerical government has been under siege by the world's now-dominant power since its inception. Nuclear weapons, and the inherent deterrent capacity they possess, could well be perceived by the Iranian regime as its key to survival. With public pressure mutable and the regime's core constituencies benefitting, dramatic policy change is unlikely unless the United States provides a viable, substantive alternative that speaks to Iran's self-defined interests.[89]

The United States is on the cusp of resetting the pre-2003 Iraq war stage. Continued sanctions will most likely lead to continued Iranian resistance. Iran can reasonably be expected to reduce cooperation with outside inspectors and levy unspecified threats of retaliation.[90] This will, in turn, create an intelligence black hole and lead to "ominous strategic uncertainty."[91]

From the point of view of regional states, the largely symbolic U.S.-led sanctions approach risks entrenching Iran as a Middle East power while failing to end its nuclear program as the United States seeks to avoid a war. The absence of hard deadlines or clearly forecasted responses to Iran's actions only aggravates regional fears. Disconnects between these actors' differing interests, as well as the differing timelines pulling them in different directions, are not conducive to U.S. interests. U.S. political and strategic latitude to redress the situation is only likely to decrease over time, and the ensuing intensity of any conflagration is likely to increase.

Israel worries that "the [United States] is moving away from preventing a nuclear Iran to containing a nuclear Iran—with deterrence based on the Cold War experience. . . . Israel, in contrast, still believes a nuclear Iran must be prevented."[92] Israel allows that it can and will unilaterally strike Iran if necessary.[93]

Fearing Iranian regional domination, numerous Gulf Arab states are now seeking assurances that the United States will not undercut their security interests in a deal with Iran.[94] Too much perceived compromise by the United States could invite U.S. Arab allies to undermine U.S. efforts. Saudi Arabia, for example, is offering tacit support for an Israeli strike.[95]

Syria, on the other hand, benefits from a prolonged U.S.-Iran standoff. Its position is akin to Russian dealings with Iran. Syria, by providing the appearance that it can be brought along, can obtain U.S. concessions on other issues, particularly the Golan Heights.

In the interim, Syria's bargaining position only strengthens the more potent a regional actor it becomes. Increasing its leverage through Hezbollah by proxy, and thus giving it political breathing space from Israeli threats while reaping strategic gains, Syria, as noted in spring 2010 press reporting, sharply altered regional balances by providing Hezbollah with Scud missiles. These have a 430-mile range and would enable Hezbollah to attack Tel Aviv and Jerusalem instead of being limited to Israel's northern areas, which have historically been subject to Hezbollah's short-range and largely inaccurate missiles.[96] Despite serious losses in the 2006 war, an April 2010 Pentagon report stated that Hezbollah, in addition to receiving $100–$200 million in cash per year from Iran, has rearmed itself beyond prewar levels.[97]

## CONCLUSION

The defining trait of the U.S.-Iranian relationship is stalemate. Numerous U.S. interests in the Middle East and South Asia—Iraq, Afghanistan, Israeli security, Lebanon, Gulf security, the Palestinians' plight, oil and global economic stability, Al Qaeda and other militants, and greater regional political stability, all of which Iran has a stake in and where common ground with the United States potentially exists—cannot be secured without Iranian assent. At the same time, Iran can survive, but not prosper, without U.S. assent.

With a regional power balance and underlying trends favoring Iran, however, time is on Iran's side. The absence of progress by the Bush administration on U.S.-Iran bilateral issues, particularly the nuclear issue, has not only allowed these issues to develop counter to U.S. interests, but it has also reduced both U.S. maneuvering room and the resources the United States could potentially bring to bear. At the same time, the sense of urgency surrounding these issues, particularly the nuclear issue, as well as Iraq and Afghanistan, has increased.

President Obama's initial velvet-on-iron approach, underwritten with a general spirit of accommodation, combined targeted inducements with tightly focused coercion and regional U.S. maneuverings to simultaneously hem Iran in while highlighting a path to achieving an interest-based modus vivendi devoid of rancor. It has largely failed. Iran has not only rejected U.S. offers, but it has also directly taken actions contrary to U.S. desires on nearly all points.

The administration undermined its approach through two crucial points of implicit strategic confusion that still persist. Despite assessing that a nuclear-armed Iran would be bound by the principles of deterrence and restraint that has guided all nuclear powers, the administration has made the nuclear question, the most contentious issue in U.S.-Iran relations, its issue prism. As evidenced by its technical assistance to the Green Movement and the shaping and timing of U.S. actions around the Green Movement's viability, the administration has also subordinated its numerous goals to the hope of regime change, which is highly unlikely.

President Obama's proliferation and Afghanistan-Pakistan advisors, "Samore and Riedel forecast that Iran is 'at least two to three years away' from being capable of building a nuclear weapon, and note that there are several stages between capability and deploying a bomb—stages at which the United States could still work to freeze the program and contain Iran's behavior."[98] After that, the Middle East will be politically and militarily transformed. A new strategic framework is needed.

Military strikes will likely be counterproductive. The United States lacks both the military capacity and the necessary understanding of Iran's nuclear programs to strike decisively. Regardless of the damage, the harm to U.S. interests in Iraq, Afghanistan, the plight of the Palestinians, Israeli security, oil and global economic stability, and regional political stability would be severe, not to mention the political, and thus operational, gain Al Qaeda would reap. Iran would at best be delayed, and its reasons for needing a program would be consummately validated while leaving little room for negotiating a new future.

A Cold War–style containment approach to freeze Iran out of the international system is impractical. Iran secures its political, economic, and military needs in a globalized, multipolar world in which the United States is a preponderant but not hegemonic power. The United States has neither the ability nor the political will to dominate and channel the world's political, economic, and security systems as it did after World War II. In addition, this is a long-term tack when competing U.S. interests demand immediate attention.

A "containment lite" approach of intensive, internationally binding UN political and economic sanctions on select political, economic, and military issues is unlikely to be more successful. Iran's key points of vulnerability—access to the global financial system, Iran's energy industry, Iran's military capacity, and Iran's access to the world community—are controlled by U.S. competitors, notably Russia and China. They are unlikely to jeopardize meeting their economic needs or undermining their strategic leverage against the United States by seriously weakening Iran. Again, this is still a long-term approach, and competing U.S. interests demand immediate attention.

Unilateral U.S. sanctions are equally unlikely to be successful. Iran is simply not dependent upon the United States or close U.S. allies to meet its needs. Only multilateral adherence can give sanctions teeth. The timelines for the key actors to this step, however, only add to the challenge and are even more adverse to U.S. interests.

With Iran's nuclear program now self-sustaining and forestalling the inevitable not a viable policy option, U.S. choices must now be about consequence management.[99] Leading Iranian objectives—regime security, recognition and exercise of Iran's regional stature, and economic prosperity—remain not only fundamentally unaddressed, but they are also directly endangered by the current U.S. posture. The task of U.S. diplomacy will be to use the enticements at its disposal, primarily Iran's integration into the regional order—a powerful incentive that Iran cannot obtain without U.S. concurrence—to induce Iranian cooperation on key U.S. interests and alter its positions on the select issues that are utterly inimical to U.S. interests.[100] A coherent hierarchy of U.S. priorities tied to realities on the ground to enable logical execution is necessary.

Chapter 7

# A Question of Leverage:
# The Obama Administration and Pakistan

*The whole leverage thing, it's a difficult thing to gauge.*
—John Paxson

**P**resident Obama readjusted the United States' strategic focus from Iraq's Sunni Triangle back to the eastern Afghanistan-Pakistan border, where Osama bin Laden's Al Qaeda central purportedly resides. The modern political boundary of this remote mountainous area divides the Pashtuns into 12 million on the Afghan side and 27 million on the Pakistani side. It is this historic, fiercely independent set of tribes that today comprises the overwhelming majority of Al Qaeda's insurgent militant allies and indigenous protectors through whom the United States must fight by way of the Afghan and Pakistani governments.

The problem, as articulated by Shuja Nawaz, director of the South Asia Center of the Atlantic Council, is that "they don't recognize the border. They never have. They never will."[1]

Per Bruce Riedel, the leader of the Obama administration's initial Afghanistan-Pakistan policy review, "The short answer is that the combination of aggressive military operations on the Afghan side, and working energetically with the Pakistani government to shut down these Federally Administered Tribal Areas and Baluchistan safe havens, creates the synergy which we hope will then lead to their destruction."[2]

Pakistan, however, is a less than ideal partner. Weak Pakistani state capacity, combined with conflicting U.S. and Pakistani interests exacerbated by the lack of a supportive regional consensus behind U.S. aims, has seen minimal Pakistani progress to destroy Al Qaeda and its indigenous Islamic militant allies within Pakistan. It has also witnessed Pakistan manipulate regional Islamic militancy, particularly the Afghan insurgency, for its own gain largely at U.S. expense. With the U.S. position in Afghanistan under duress and Osama bin Laden's Al Qaeda and its affiliates planning and launching ever more attacks, time is not on the U.S. side.

*The Federally Administered Tribal Areas of Pakistan*

Nonetheless, the United States will have to continue to work with Pakistan, a sovereign nation. The Obama administration must now employ increasingly limited political, economic, and military resources to adjust a strategic context that calcified in a manner inimical to U.S. interests during the Bush administration. Roughly a decade after 9/11, the outcome of the United States' Pakistan-based efforts against Al Qaeda is still uncertain.

## THE OBAMA ADMINISTRATION'S INHERITANCE
### Islamabad's Interaction with Al Qaeda and Afghan Militants

Al Qaeda's post-9/11 flight into Pakistan's FATA and the Afghan Taliban's flight into FATA, Baluchistan, and Khyber Pakhtunkhwa—the Pakistani hinterlands—presented the opportunity for a U.S.-Pakistani hammer and anvil strategy. After initially refusing, citing domestic politics and a lack of military capability, President Pervez Musharraf, in winter 2003–2004, dispatched 70,000 of Pakistan's Frontier Corps, a paramilitary auxiliary, into the FATA to flush out Taliban and Al Qaeda fighters after the unmasking of Abdul Qadeer Khan's nuclear activities.[3] Clashes between Islamabad's forces and the militants became frequent.[4]

Pakistani pressure eased markedly in fall 2006, however, when, in response to domestic political pressure and rising tensions with India, Islamabad signed the Waziristan Accord with FATA tribal elders, some of whom were concentric with militant leadership. In return for the removal of federal troops, the tribes agreed to police themselves and prevent Al Qaeda and Taliban violence. Federal troops were to return if the tribes failed in their obligations.[5]

While sound in theory, the deal failed in practice. Cross-border attacks into Afghanistan tripled. The tribes were, and have been, either unwilling or unable to control their territory. Al Qaeda and the Afghan Taliban gained a de facto safe haven.

Nevertheless, in February 2007, Islamabad pronounced the treaty a success. Islamabad even announced plans to salvage the deal after insurgent tribal spokesmen pronounced the treaty dead following Islamabad's July 2007 storming of the Red Mosque, the Pakistani militants' theological center of gravity. Even after insurgents killed scores of federal troops in retaliation, Islamabad signed more such agreements.[6]

Following Musharraf's turbulent succession, the ascension of Pakistani People's Party leader Ali Asif Zardari, whose political base went beyond the military and the Islamists formerly queued behind the Musharraf regime, enabled a more dogged pursuit of Al Qaeda and its indigenous allies. Pakistan, however, still did not unilaterally capture a single ranking Al Qaeda commander. The new civilian government was weak, and rapid policy deviations may not have been possible, as shown by the military intelligence services' rejection of

Zardari's order to report to the minister of the interior vice military channels.[7] Without disallowing this possibility, an alternative explanation is that Pakistan sought to manage, not defeat, Al Qaeda and its local militant allies.

Pakistan has had a roughly thirty-year relationship with Islamic militants. After the 1979 Soviet invasion of Afghanistan, Pakistan became the conduit for billions of U.S., Saudi, and private donations to the resistance, and Pakistan chose to allocate the bulk of its support to the most intense Islamic militants at the expense of royalist, tribal, nationalist, or secular political factions. Following the jihad, Pakistan stoked and manipulated Islamic militants as a plausibly deniable force-multiplying proxy to compensate for conventional military and political weakness to help secure Islamabad's regional strategic objectives.

Most prominently, the Taliban took Kabul in 1996, only two years after its founding. "'We created the Taliban,' Nasrullah Babar, the interior minister under Benazir Bhutto, [stated in 1999]. 'Mrs. Bhutto had a vision: that through a peaceful Afghanistan, Pakistan could extend its influence into the resource-rich territories of Central Asia.'" The Pakistani military's Inter-Services Intelligence Directorate (ISI) provided assistance to the Taliban regime, to include its military and Al Qaeda–related terrorist training camps, to further this vision.[8]

Since 9/11, Pakistan's military and civilian leaders have played a double game. On the one hand, Pakistan assures the United States that it is vigorously repressing Islamic militants. On the other hand, it aids and abets those same militants.

"Publicly, Pakistan and the militants are enemies. Privately, they are friends." Bowing to Bush demands, for example, in 2002 Musharraf arrested approximately two thousand militants, many of whom had trained in Pakistani camps, but nearly all were then quietly released. Similarly, Musharraf promised shortly after 9/11 to rein in the roughly 25,000 madrassas, many of which U.S. assessments claim are militant incubators, but he never acted.[9]

By March 2009, citing electronic surveillance and trusted informants, the U.S. government publicly stated that the Islamic militants' campaign in Afghanistan is made possible in part by direct support from ISI's S Wing, which is responsible for activities external to Pakistan. The U.S. government further claims that ISI has divided its support among three major factions.[10] Though none is directly under ISI control, all heavily depend upon ISI assistance.

ISI operatives meet regularly with Mullah Omar's commanders in Quetta, where they routinely discuss political and military strategy. Though the overwhelmingly Pashtun Taliban has been able to finance its low-cost military operations through wealthy Persian Gulf donors supplemented by the drug trade, ISI has routinely provided fuel and ammunition to help sustain attacks. When commanders need to replenish losses, ISI operatives go to the madrassas and muster recruits.[11] "We are saving the Taliban for a rainy day," one Pakistani official stated.

The Haqqani network is also a Pakistani foil and, according to one senior ISI official, "We [Pakistan] are not apologetic about this." It was a stunning admission for a purported U.S. ally in 2006: Sirajuddin Haqqani, an Afghan, leads a mix of foreign fighters and predominantly Afghan Pashtuns as one of the most ruthless U.S. opponents. Jalaluddin, his father, is a longtime associate of Osama bin Laden.

Gulbuddin Hekmatyar, a ruthless Islamist commander who was often Pakistan's lead surrogate during the anti-Soviet jihad, also receives assistance. After moving on to serve briefly as prime minister of Afghanistan before helping spur the post-Soviet civil war, he is now the leader of the Hezb-e-Islami/Gulbuddin (HiG), an Islamist political party with a potent military wing that has a following among Pashtuns. Though no longer at his apex, he remains an influential figure.

Pakistan's January 2010 detention of Mullah Berader, Mullah Omar's military deputy, who is credited with rebuilding the Taliban following the U.S. invasion into a force of roughly 20,000, for example, was a potentially significant victory. Proper exploitation could have achieved a treasure trove of intelligence and yielded significant strategic U.S. gains. The details of the case, however, explicitly confirm Pakistan's double game.[12]

The Pakistanis, however, denied time-sensitive access. Two weeks passed before U.S. interrogators were able to pose direct questions, and the Pakistanis waited four months before providing regular access. Inherently time-sensitive command and control data were rendered useless.

The Pakistanis also failed to extract actionable intelligence of strategic importance, which Berader almost certainly had as Mullah Omar's military deputy. He did not disclose the location of any senior Taliban leaders or provide any useful information regarding the group's financial backers. He also would not divulge the identities of ISI members who worked with the Taliban. Berader spoke only "about the general dynamics of the tribes," said a senior U.S. intelligence official in a position to know.[13]

To ensure future control, Pakistan has announced that it will put Berader, an Afghan citizen, on trial instead of relinquishing custody. This precludes his unhindered Afghan/American exploitation. As of fall 2010, according to press reporting, Berader was living comfortably in an ISI safe house.[14]

Berader, however, was not taken alone. He was arrested with at least two senior Afghan Taliban figures "who would have been recognizable as insurgents the United States would want in custody." Subsequent roundups led to the capture of as many as twenty-two other ranking individuals who had been enjoying the protection of the Pakistani government for years. They included some of the Taliban's most senior commanders, such as Mullah Abdul Qayyum Zakir, who replaced Berader and is reputed to be more ruthless and less compromising. All, save for Berader, however, were quietly freed.[15]

The Afghan government began reaching out to Taliban leaders in late 2009 to explore prospects for a deal. The talks were in their incipient phase, and both sides had staked out extreme positions. Yet, according to press reports, Afghan officials assessed a Taliban readiness for peace as the two sides discussed the conditions under which formal talks could begin.

Speculation at the time, which received a boost from Karzai's public outrage upon the announcement of Berader's capture, was that these detentions were meant to scuttle secret Karzai-Taliban peace talks. In fall 2010, a Pakistani official speaking anonymously to the press confirmed this hypothesis when he explained, "We picked up Berader and the others because they were trying to make a deal without us. We protect the Taliban. They are dependent on us. We are not going to allow them to make a deal with Karzai and the Indians."

The twenty-two other detained Taliban leaders, according to the same Pakistani official, "were warned against carrying out future negotiations without their permission. A former Western diplomat, with long experience in the region, confirmed that the ISI sent a warning to its Taliban protégés. 'The message from ISI was: no flirting.'" Press reports citing a Pakistani spiritual leader close to the Taliban high command confirmed that the Afghan Taliban lacked independence, or were even the dominant force, in their own decision-making. "'When we try to act on our own, they stop us,' the Pakistani spiritual leader said."[16]

The United States and its allies, while displeased with the situation, have come to accept it. Despite much rhetoric, U.S. foreign assistance has never been made conditional upon Pakistan withdrawing its support for these militants. Voluminous U.S. economic and military aid, which is implicitly if not explicitly accompanied by U.S. political blessing, has flowed uninterrupted.

After committing to Iraq shortly after 9/11, the subsequent lack of U.S. economic and military capacity to undertake any meaningful, new, unilateral action in Pakistan combined with an absence of U.S. government and public political will to invade yet another country has forced the United States to continue to rely upon Pakistan as a regional proxy. Even though action by Pakistan against Afghanistan-oriented militants is not guaranteed, Pakistan is both materially enabled and, through increasing Pakistani dependence upon U.S. aid, increasingly pressured toward acting on immediate U.S. goals. Meanwhile, important secondary U.S. objectives, such as protecting Pakistan's nuclear arsenal, are simultaneously secured by building the Pakistani state's capacity. This U.S.

position, however, is a catch-22 likely to perpetuate existing dynamics to long-term U.S. detriment at best.

The United States is in a vicious cycle of giving preference to short-term operational success at the cost of long-term U.S. strategic detriment and Pakistani political evolution. Post-9/11 U.S. administrations have relied upon Pakistan's army—the most coherent, stable, and effective of Pakistan's institutions—as a day-to-day center of gravity for acting on U.S. interests. This situation positions the Pakistani military establishment to control defense and security policy and rebuff its own civilian officials—as exemplified by General Ashfaq Kayani, the Pakistani army chief, informing President Zardari that Pakistan's historical refusal to issue a "no first strike" nuclear policy was "irreversible" and the Pakistani military rebuffing President Zardari's efforts to place ISI under civilian control. This imbalance has progressed to the point that General Kayani led a 2010 meeting of federal Pakistani officials before attending a series of meetings in Washington—a first in Pakistan's history.

Empowering Pakistan's army as a policy executor simultaneously empowers the army's self-furthering, India-centric, threat-based strategic perspective. International tension with India, with whom Pakistan has fought three wars since independence, induces a need for domestic unity and an emphasis on national security through a strong military capable of decisive action. This combination has served as an ever-present excuse to circumscribe civilian political activity, and the army has ruled for more than half of Pakistan's history.

Post-9/11 U.S. military aid has helped Pakistan's military enact this dynamic. Billions of dollars that would not have arrived otherwise have allowed Pakistan to acquire F-16s and better tanks. While these weapons are good for fighting India, and they permit Pakistan to perpetuate and stoke international military and political tension, they have little counterinsurgency value. More military capability only increases the military's domestic stature, which only increases its political sway. At the same time, any internal ethnic dissension with the army's Punjabi-dominated Pashtun cadre is quelled as the military remains India-focused.

Counterproductive military attitudes are perpetuated. Historically a secular institution, Pakistan's military is increasingly being led by Islamist-minded officers. As described by a Western military officer with several years in the region, "There is a growing Islamist feeling in the military, and it's inseparable from anti-Americanism. The vast majority of Pakistani officers feel they are fighting our war. There is a lot of sympathy for the Taliban. The result is that the Pakistanis do as little as they possibly can to combat the militants."[17]

Counterproductive public attitudes are also stoked. With Pakistani and Muslim casualties increasing as the war drags on, the popular perception is that

Pakistan is fighting America's war at Pakistani expense. The political will of the Pakistani public to support U.S.-connected actions, and the Pakistani authorities' political will and maneuvering room to undertake military action on U.S. behalf, only decrease over time.[18]

Structural political and ethnic imbalances are also perpetuated that keep the military and its narrow coterie empowered at the expense of developing a broad-based national government, which would almost certainly dilute the military's power and thus most likely broaden the range of Pakistan's interests and political flexibility to U.S. advantage. In particular, the Punjabi-dominated army provides material assistance to the Pashtun Taliban as a counterweight to secular Pakistani Baluchistan separatists. An established pattern exists, both in Quetta and Karachi. First, government-owned land is seized illegally or purchased with assistance from ISI. Second, a mosque and religious school go up with money coming from the Gulf. Third, small houses pop up around the mosque complex and the area becomes a no-go zone for both outsiders and government authority, such as police. In Baluchistan, there are actually no-go areas for Baluchis.[19] So long as Afghan militants are manipulated against internal Pakistani insurgents to state benefit at little to no cost, while simultaneously furthering Pakistan's foreign policy objectives, this policy is unlikely to change.

Post-9/11 U.S. economic aid has underwritten this entire arrangement. Billions of dollars that would not have arrived otherwise fueled a boom during Musharraf's tenure for the socioeconomic and urban elite that lubricated any political discomfort. This foreign assistance, whose continued flow was intertwined with and dependent upon the Pakistan military's actions, became so important that one retired Pakistani general stated in 2008 that "the Pakistani economy would collapse without it."[20]

Strategic institutional concerns within the Pakistani military remain perpetually unaddressed. In the background is the popular perception that the United States abandoned Pakistan after the Soviet defeat, and that the United States will do so again. As evidenced by the weapons it is acquiring, Pakistan has only a transient loyalty to its U.S. backers and retains an India-centric orientation. Absent alleviating this fear of abandonment, Pakistan has every incentive to prolong the current situation, and thus U.S. aid, by doing just enough to mollify U.S. demands for action against Al Qaeda and its indigenous militant allies.

The United States becomes more ensnared as time progresses. The more U.S. aid strengthens the Pakistani military, the more the United States depends upon it. As the militant threat perpetually worsens over time and further strains U.S. resources, which are most intensely consumed through direct U.S. action in Afghanistan and elsewhere around the world, the more the United States is induced to provide aid to Pakistan. At the same time, a more empowered Pakistani military is also able to defy the United States and stoke the regional conflicts and domestic arrangements that provide it political preeminence. Pakistan's double game, and the circumstances that support it, are mutually furthered in perpetuity.[21]

### Pakistani State Interaction with Al Qaeda and Pakistani Militants

A delicate balance between the state and Pakistani militants existed post-9/11. Harboring Al Qaeda and associated militants, ruling non-settled areas at state expense, such as portions of FATA, and any select directed activities were permissible. Attacks on the state's security forces, significant violence against civilians, or unsanctioned attacks on the government were verboten.

The military employed and manipulated Pakistani militants to do its bidding. Per "a Pakistani source who follow[ed] the issue, high-level American officials have shared with their counterparts in Islamabad some intelligence indicating that renegade ISI elements helped Baitullah Mehsud's group train for the December 2007 assassination of Pakistan's former prime minister Benazir Bhutto, whose widower, Asif Ali Zardari, . . . [became] . . . the country's president. (U.S. officials either declined to discuss that point or said they couldn't confirm it.)"[22]

The Pakistani government's 2007 Red Mosque attack killing nearly one hundred people after a series of Islamabad incursions into the tribal areas generating militant and tribal resentments, however, upset this delicate militant-state balance. With growing strength in the FATA set against chaotic national politics, the militants, historically a fractured lot, united. In December 2007, Baitullah Mehsud announced an umbrella organization of roughly forty Pakistani-based militant groups named the Tehrik-e-Taliban Pakistan (TTP), otherwise known as the Pakistani Taliban.[23]

The TTP had global significance almost from its inception. Following a 2008 meeting between Baitullah Mehsud and Ayman al-Zawahiri in South Waziristan, as publicly noted by Brigadier General Mahmood Shah, Pakistan's senior security official in the tribal areas until 2005, "'Pakistan told the [United States] that Baitullah Mehsud came directly under Al Qaeda,' Brigadier Shah said. 'The Pakistani government was very sure that he was Al Qaeda.'" Alleviating any doubt, Amir Rana, director of the Pakistan Institute for Peace Studies, stated in 2010 that the TTP "is the local partner of Al Qaeda in Pakistan."[24]

The TTP's external orientation of combating the neighboring U.S. invasion in Afghanistan quickly combined with ensuring FATA's independence, which in practical terms meant methodically and potently attacking the Pakistani state as U.S. pressure forced a grudging Islamabad presence ever deeper into FATA. Police officers, the most ubiquitous government presence, have been particularly emphasized, and in Khyber Pakhtunkhwa (KP), for example, attacks against police went from 113 in 2005 to 1,820 in 2007, with a corresponding rise in the death toll from 9 to 575. Targets have also included judges, tribal elders with government ties, Pakistani military forces, elected representatives, infrastructure like Pakistan's largest military hardware factory, and links to Pakistan's foreign backers like the Islamabad Marriott, which is frequented by the international community. In fall 2009, the militants launched a series of coordinated assaults on Pakistani police stations and military bases throughout the country that included seizing the national army headquarters. Attacks have also taken place or been stopped in Pakistan's largest cities—Islamabad, Lahore, and Karachi.[25]

Violence against civilians also rose dramatically. Historically nonexistent in Pakistan, suicide bomb attacks went from two in 2002 to fifty-six in 2007, and Pakistan surpassed Iraq in 2008 to become the world leader in suicide-bomb deaths. Attacks against noncombatants, in whatever form, doubled from 890 in 2007 to 1,839 in 2008, and casualties rose correspondingly from 1,240 in 2007 to 2,293 in 2008. The Islamabad-based Pak Institute for Peace Studies assesses that more than three thousand Pakistanis died in terrorist attacks in 2009. In total, roughly seven thousand civilians have died in terrorist attacks from 2003 to 2010.[26]

Al Qaeda spokesman Adam Gadahn called upon the various Pakistani militants to put aside any differences and establish an Islamic state within Pakistan,[27] and in 2009 Pakistani Taliban took over the KP's Swat Valley. They illegally displaced authorities in the neighboring districts of Buner and Dir to give themselves a Delaware-sized area under their direct control roughly seventy miles from Islamabad. In an Islamabad deal, which the militants subsequently violated by setting up training camps, they gained legally recognized suzerainty.

The militants also made their presence felt in Peshawar, the KP's capital—through which flows roughly 75 percent of supplies for U.S. and allied forces in Afghanistan—by seizing heavy weapons and shutting down the Kohat tunnel. By March 2009, Taliban fighters were patrolling inside city limits, were kidnapping local officials, and had attacked military headquarters.[28] In spring 2010, they launched suicide vehicles against the U.S. consulate and nearly destroyed it.

Subsumed into a larger Islamic militant cause, the TTP is no longer FATA or Pashtun-centric. "It is well documented that recruits from southern Punjab are fighting in Khyber Pakhtunkhwa and tribal areas. . . . They—Lashkar-e-Janghvi, the Sipah-e-Sohaba Pakistan, and Jaish-e-Mohammad—are allies of the Taliban and Al Qaeda," according to 2010 minister of the interior, Rehman Malik.[29] Originally created by the military to battle India in Kashmir, Punjabi groups, who "have surpassed many of their peers in the technical ability and the viciousness of their attacks," are particularly dangerous because they move easily between the tribal areas for training and Punjab for action. "One Pakistani security official estimated that 5 to 10 percent of militants in the tribal regions could be Punjabi."[30]

These groups constantly cross-fertilize. Overlapping social ties and agendas combined with a loose organizational structure has led to various groups swapping personnel, resources, and, occasionally, sharing targets. Some individuals are members of multiple groups at the same time.[31]

Though connected to the antistate TTP mix, some of these Punjabi groups have also operated in the Pakistani state's interests by helping to further its double game. Jaish-e-Mohammad, for example, has broadened its mission and trained thousands to fight U.S. and NATO forces in Afghanistan. In 2008, press reporting noted an alliance between the Pakistani Taliban and anti-India militant groups in Punjab province to target NATO supply convoys in Karachi.[32]

Nonetheless, these groups constitute a threat to the Pakistani state. The minister of the interior acknowledged in 2010 that Punjabi groups were "now active" in Punjab, the Pakistani heartland that serves as a major recruiting ground for the army, and are trying to "destabilize the country." "Southern Punjab, a backward, underdeveloped area run in many parts by traditional feudal families, is fast emerging as an important hub in Al Qaeda's global jihad, with many suicide bombers and gunmen recruited from the province. Militant groups such as Lashkar-e-Taiba [Army of the Pure], which carried out . . . November [2009's] . . . Mumbai attacks, have grown steadily in the area."[33]

This militant encroachment into inner Pakistan has sparked U.S. concern over Pakistan's nuclear security. In competition with India's force of sixty to eighty warheads, Pakistan is estimated to have seventy to ninety nuclear weapons. Pakistan claims these are stored unassembled under the control of a ten-thousand-strong security force commanded by a two-star general. Though denied access to the weapons directly, the United States estimates that they are spread throughout the country, mainly south of Islamabad.[34]

The Pakistanis have been actively working to increase their nuclear capacity relative to India, which Pakistan claims gained an unfair advantage through the Bush administration's civilian nuclear deal. Pakistan fears this increase in domestic fissile material could be turned into bomb fuel, though India has no such history. In Pakistani eyes, a similar deal is a crucial U.S. compromise to show that Pakistan is on the same level as its rival India. Such a deal would also alleviate fears in Islamabad that the United States secretly harbors intentions of dismantling Pakistan's nuclear capacity.[35]

Pakistan also claims that it should be allowed to build up its nuclear arsenal to counter the larger conventional forces of India. Despite the devastating 2010 floods and an unexpectedly massive need for economic recovery and physical reconstruction, Pakistan has continued to forge ahead in building the Punjab-based Khushab III military site, which has a total of three reactors. When fully operational by as early as 2011, it will be able to produce enough fuel for ten missiles per year, or roughly half of Pakistan's total annual nuclear-weapons production capacity.[36]

Though the United States has low concern that a weapon could be taken directly from a storage site, U.S. concern is high that a weapon could be stolen while in transit, particularly in response to an India-related crisis. The United States is also worried that Pakistan's opaque network of nuclear facilities, equipment, and scientists could be either pilfered by militants or that Pakistani nuclear establishment sympathizers, either government or military, could provide assistance. Pakistan's history of proliferation, such as Abdul Qadeer Khan's nuclear black-market activities, which provided weapons technology to Libya, Iran, and North Korea, roots these fears firmly in reality.[37]

A secret, multiyear, $100 million program begun under Bush to increase nuclear facility physical security and train Pakistanis in nuclear security is struggling. "American officials have never been permitted to see how much of the money was spent, the facilities where the weapons are kept or even a tally of how many Pakistan has produced. The facility Pakistan was supposed to build to conduct its own training exercises is running years behind schedule."[38]

Fanning U.S. fears, Pakistan publicly condemns certain Punjabi militant groups while discreetly allowing them to operate under the radar to enhance its double game. "To facilitate their operations, some extremist organizations have created humanitarian front groups with different names that raise funds for building schools and healthcare clinics. What's not known is how much of that money gets channeled to militant activities. 'Usually when the government bans these militant groups, they suddenly start welfare work,' said Yusuf Khan, a Karachi-based analyst. 'During the earthquake in Kashmir in 2005, Jaish-e-Mohammad began helping people and rebuilding. That's their technique: to become philanthropic and get sympathy.'" The leaders of Lashkar-e-Taiba, now known as Jamaat-ud-Dawa, and other groups freely build compounds and campaign with politicians as their foot soldiers fight in the FATA.[39]

In contrast to the FATA-based TTP, however, Pakistan's response to the Punjabi TTP presence is slightly more of an accommodation to hard realities than wanton manipulation. The infrastructure that propels the insurgency—recruiting, fund-raising, bivouacking, procurement, transportation, and ideological promotion—is in Pakistan's cities. Karachi, a violent city of 18 million with 3,500 madrassas and an ethnically diverse population that allows TTP militants to blend, is acknowledged to be crucial to the militants by both Karachi's politicians and the militants alike. Existing FATA counterinsurgency tactics—missiles and military operations—are not politically feasible in Pakistan's teeming metropolises.[40]

The TTP's organizational coherence somewhat dissipated after Baitullah Mehsud's death. Spring 2010, for example, witnessed the kidnapping/killing of

Khalid Khawaja and Amir Sultan Tarar (otherwise known as Colonel Imam) in North Waziristan by the TTP-associated Asian Tigers. Both men were well known former ISI officers with a long history of training and supporting militants in the tribal regions, including Mullah Omar and Osama bin Laden. This organizational fragmentation has effectively resulted in the FATA becoming a no-man's-land.

The TTP's capabilities, however, were not neutered. Hakimullah Mehsud, Baitullah's successor, unleashed bombings throughout Pakistan that killed more than six hundred people in the last three months of 2009.[41] The TTP also tried to bomb New York City's Times Square.

From Al Qaeda central's point of view, co-opting the TTP represents yet another successful example of piggybacking upon local militants and interweaving into local politics to obtain a secure indigenous foothold while engaging in a mutually beneficial operational relationship. "The [TTP–Al Qaeda] alliance is based on more than shared ideology. 'These are tactical alliances,' said a senior American counterterrorism official, who spoke on condition of anonymity because he was not authorized to discuss intelligence matters. The Pashtun Taliban and Arab militants, who are part of Al Qaeda, have money, sanctuary, training sites and suicide bombers. The Punjabi militants can provide logistical help in Punjabi cities, like Lahore, including handling bombers and target reconnaissance."[42]

This TTP–Al Qaeda alliance has deepened the U.S. fight. The United States has been drawn into the quagmire of Pakistan's social, political, military, and economic problems that fuel Pakistani militancy and endanger the Pakistani state, upon which the United States is utterly dependent. Given the threat disparity—the empowerment of the Pakistani army at the cost of the killing of Pakistani civilians, which Islamabad is apparently willing to tolerate in moderation, versus the Al Qaeda–connected strikes against the U.S. homeland and the real possibility of U.S. defeat in Afghanistan, neither of which the United States is willing to tolerate—any future U.S. actions must address Pakistan's domestic dimension.

This TTP–Al Qaeda alliance, as borne out by the Lashkar-e-Taiba 2009 Mumbai assault, has also shown the fragility of the U.S. regional position. If Pakistan did not direct the militants, this independent militant group unwittingly enhanced Pakistan's double game by causing severe tensions between two historic, nuclear-armed rivals, which secured the Pakistani military's domestic position, deflected U.S. pressure, and induced the United States to Pakistan's side in restraining India. If Pakistan did direct the militants, then the Mumbai attacks reflect the Pakistani security establishment's skill and control in using Islamic militants in plausibly deniable brinkmanship to manipulate the United States and preserve its double game.

Under U.S. and domestic pressure, Pakistani forces have directly engaged militant forces. Managing short-term militant violence rather than eliminating the militants or gaining strategic advantage, however, appears to be the objective. The double game's foundations survive.

Most visibly, a large-scale Pakistani army assault in the summer of 2009 displaced the vast majority of militants. By spring 2010, officials claimed 2,677 law enforcement officers and 5,288 civilians had died in the fighting since 2007. State sovereignty was returned to the KP's Swat Valley.[43]

Approximately two to four thousand Taliban fighters were pitted against four Pakistani brigades totaling 12,000 to 15,000 men. "But the soldiers largely stay[ed] inside their camps, unwilling to patrol or exert any large presence that might provoke—or discourage—the militants, Swat residents and political leaders [said]. The military . . . also [did] not aid a small village that locals say [was] widely known as the Taliban's headquarters in Swat. Nor [did] troops destroy mobile radio transmitters mounted on motorcycles or pickup trucks that . . . the leader of the Taliban in Swat, Maulana Fazlullah, [had] expertly used to terrify residents."[44]

Islamabad's calibrated retaking of the Swat valley and neighboring Buner and Dir districts perpetuated its double game. Pakistani sovereignty was restored and the militants were checked. Yet no significant militant leadership figures were captured or killed. Because no cordons were employed, militant forces escaped to occupy the surrounding hills and continue to offer resistance. Pakistani forces, whose presence is now larger than during the height of the fighting, remained as an occupying force fending off guerilla attacks. Curfews still applied. Assassinations of anti-Taliban political leaders became common. By 2010, large segments of the population had yet to return, and the press was still not allowed in the area.[45]

Pakistani forces have also defended against TTP encroachment on major cities and other "settled areas" near the FATA. In summer 2008, the Pakistani army began to fight back against Pakistani Taliban positions and forces that had begun to encroach on Peshawar. While Pakistani Taliban were not routed, their presence has been held at bay and their momentum stopped.

Pakistani forces also conducted offensives in six of the seven tribal agencies bordering Afghanistan over roughly eighteen months from late summer/early fall 2008 to spring/summer 2010. Islamabad disrupted the militant mini-state in Bajuar. Pakistani government forces also recaptured the Kohat tunnel, a road more than a mile long used to carry U.S. and NATO supplies from Karachi, the chief U.S. regional supply point. Most significantly, however, Pakistan sent 28,000 troops into South Waziristan, where the Pakistani government claimed 80 percent of the Pakistani Taliban's attacks were planned, and the TTP's major attacks dropped from twenty-four in 2009 to only four by mid-2010. By summer

2010, Pakistan had roughly 140,000 regular and paramilitary forces stationed in the vicinity of the Afghanistan-Pakistan border, backed up by 100,000 in reserve to rotate in, manning more than nine hundred small mud-and-rock outposts and roadside checkpoints in the frontier.[46]

Untouched North Waziristan, meanwhile, became a militant epicenter. The Afghan-oriented networks of Jalaluddin Haqqani, whom ISI admits continue to spend up to fifteen days each month in North Waziristan and whose son Sirajuddin has offered increasing support for Al Qaeda in online forums, as well as the networks of Gulbuddin Hekmatyar and Mullah Omar, have a presence. Besides Al Qaeda and the TTP, whose attempts against the New York City subway and Times Square emanated from North Waziristan, militant residents include "vehemently anti-Shiite groups, several Central Asian and Chechen groups, and, by some accounts, Lashkar-e-Taiba, blamed for the deadly 2008 attack in Mumbai. Training is available for Pakistanis and foreigners who come and go at will."[47]

The Pakistani military, though present, is docile. "In the near-border towns of Miran Shah and Mir Ali, armed insurgents seem to be in charge. They hang out in the fly-blown restaurants and crude Internet cafes, drive around in green Ford Ranger pickup trucks stolen from the Afghan police, and openly carry weapons—all in the shadow of large Pakistani military encampments."[48]

Despite the fact that ISI, for the first time in Pakistan's sixty-three-year history, stated that Islamist militants, not India, were the gravest threat to Pakistan's national security, Pakistan claimed it simply did not have the forces available to launch new attacks. In lieu, Pakistan has framed its large-scale clearing efforts in the adjacent tribal areas and small, targeted operations closer to North Waziristan as "shaping operations" for the coming battle. While claiming it is preparing to launch attacks, Islamabad has stated that any expanded campaign will happen completely on its own terms, and it has warned the Obama administration not to push so hard that it uses up any goodwill it has fostered.[49]

Pakistan, however, has adequate military muscle. Its military boasts 650,000 active troops, 500,000 reservists, and 300,000 paramilitary members. In fact, as its FATA offensives continued, Pakistan simultaneously held a military exercise with 50,000 troops on the Indian border, where Pakistan maintains 350,000 active-duty forces.[50]

Despite all of the militant violence, Pakistani public opinion supports this force lay-down. A 2010 Pew Research Center poll found that 53 percent of Pakistanis considered India to be the biggest threat to national security. The Taliban, by contrast, polled 23 percent, and Al Qaeda polled a mere 3 percent. India is still widely accused by Pakistani politicians and media of stealing water from Pakistan by building dams on shared rivers, undermining Pakistani interests in Afghanistan, and funding a separatist insurgency in Baluchistan.[51]

Pakistan's desire to perpetuate its double game is a more likely explanation for not attacking North Waziristan. Local news reports revealed that Pakistan gave Gul Bahadur, the dominant local warlord, a choice between facing a Pakistani military offensive and driving out TTP militants. Rather than fighting the TTP, Bahadur persuaded them, at least temporarily, to vacate their North Waziristan sanctuaries under his sway and physically distance themselves from other militant groups, such as the Haqqani network, the Afghan Taliban, and Al Qaeda, whose presence went conspicuously unmentioned, to eliminate a pretext for a government assault. These moves, which blunted calls for a Pakistani offensive, preserved a lack of central government control in North Waziristan, maintained the central government's FATA ally, and allowed all of the militants most directly threatening the United States to live to fight another day.[52]

By extension, Pakistan's victories in the other tribal agencies must now be questioned. Press reporting in winter 2010–2011, for example, noted that the Haqqani network sought to move from North Waziristan to the adjacent Kurram agency. Such a move would preempt any danger from any eventual U.S.-induced moves by Islamabad into North Waziristan.[53] Pakistan's failure either to attack or to actively prepare a timeline to do so in light of U.S. concerns and the Pakistani Taliban's failed attack on Times Square effectively constitutes a thinly veiled "no" as Pakistan hedges its bets for a post-U.S. Afghanistan. The message to the United States is clear: Pakistan considers India to be its primary enemy, and U.S. needs will be better met once Pakistan's security needs relative to India are better addressed.[54] Pakistani leverage only strengthens as the U.S. plight in Afghanistan worsens.

Pakistan has stood firm against U.S. action in FATA beyond drone strikes. In 2010, for the first time, U.S. forces employed hot-pursuit authorities by reaching into Pakistan when attacked, and four times in mid-fall 2010 U.S. helicopters engaged militants on the Pakistani side of the border, sometimes breaching Pakistani airspace. After the fourth time, during which three Frontier Corps troops were killed and three were wounded, Pakistan responded by shutting down for eleven days the Khyber Pass border crossing at Torkham, one of two major land crossings to Afghanistan, while also threatening to stop protecting U.S. and NATO convoys, which are routinely attacked as they traverse nearly the entire length of Pakistan and cross through enemy-held terrain. Roughly 150 trucks of equipment were destroyed on Pakistan's roads and in its storage facilities in the interim.

To limit the event's fallout, however, Pakistan also let other supply lines continue. This strongly indicated that Pakistan wished to illustrate its displeasure with recent U.S. actions and make a point by highlighting U.S. vulnerability while not inducing a rupture in U.S.-Pakistani cooperation. In light of the U.S. failure to find alternative supply lines, which has left U.S. forces with having to bring roughly 80 percent of nonlethal supplies through Pakistan, this U.S. vulnerability is likely to persist.[55]

The 2010 floods only served as yet another excuse to further delay government attacks. By any objective standard, the flooding that beset Pakistan was horrific. At one point, approximately one-fifth of the country was underwater. Casualties included more than one thousand killed, over 1 million homes destroyed, and more than 21 million people injured or made homeless.[56]

Pakistan's military capitalized on the chaos to promote itself at civilian expense. The Pakistani army, for example, has engaged in humanitarian relief, reconstruction, and maintaining supply lines that militants regularly ambush. These are all responsibilities within the civil bailiwick that the army has not actively worked to shed.

At the same time, Pakistan made no effort to mobilize its extensive armed forces to either maintain pressure on the militants or to increase it during this time of vulnerability and displacement, from which the militants were not uniquely sheltered. Further, the government did not prevent the various militant groups from performing humanitarian work during this disaster to aid the suffering population, thereby permitting the militants to further ingratiate themselves with the public. American officials could not criticize the government's focus on its own population during such a time of national distress without being perceived as utterly callous.

Pakistan's employment of its forces has also been conducive to furthering its double game. Al Qaeda–associated militants are a well-trained and formidable full-time force that routinely employs AK-47s, other modern small arms, and heavy weapons.[57] The Pakistani front line, by contrast, regularly consists of the Frontier Corps, a paramilitary entity, and the Frontier Constabulary, a law-enforcement entity, both of which are part-time forces with minimal training, raised from the local tribes in contested areas. More than $100 million in U.S. aid since 2005 has built these forces to 70,000-strong and improved salaries, weapons, training, and infrastructure significantly, which has resulted in improved discipline and reduced mass desertions. Government casualties, even when they win, however, are still routinely high.[58]

Pakistan can trumpet to the United States the great sacrifices it is making, which have totaled roughly two thousand soldiers from 2008 to 2010, when the war against the Pakistani Taliban began in earnest.[59] This provides the state-to-state moral and practical standing to rebuff further U.S. pressure. At the same time, ever-increasing losses build political pressure to limit military action against the militants, which feeds domestic support to Pakistan's ulterior double game motives.

Public support for reducing Pakistani military activity where the militants reside is also increased. Collateral damage has often been extensive. Frontier forces, which have only sparingly been supported by more modernly equipped and better trained Pakistani regulars, have routinely invoked indirect fire from artillery and helicopter gunships to even the odds. When it is employed, the regular army, which is trained for mass battles against Indian armor and infantry, routinely inflicts even steeper civilian casualties and extensive property destruction.

Supporting manpower and recruitment dynamics then undermine the local police, who are critical to the "hold and build" phase after an area is cleared. Militant groups pay roughly $20,000 per person to suicide bombers' families, but policemen's survivors are given only $6,000. The average Taliban foot soldier earns roughly $170 per month while the average police officer (there is one officer for every 364 square miles in the NWFP) earns only $80 per month, a figure which only lends itself to corruption that further undermines state legitimacy.[60]

The resulting exodus of refugees from militant-Islamabad fighting, which creates both physical space for the militants to occupy as well as political space between the people and the state that the militants can exploit, has made Pakistan the world's leader in internally displaced persons at roughly 3 million people.[61] Even if the population is not inherently pro-Taliban, resentments against the government increase for its perceived lack of concern for civilian life and property. In some cases, local populations have rejected the presence of Pakistani federal troops because they know this will bring violence from the Taliban to their doorstep, which will only unleash indiscriminate government attacks. Toleration for the insurgents thus increases. This is the exact opposite effect necessary for separating the insurgents from the population.

Tribal elders from South Waziristan refused to return despite Pakistani army claims that the region was safe.[62] "Many Pakistanis remain skeptical of military victory declarations they have heard many times before. 'Pakistanis generally are not yet clear as to what the military establishment is up to with respect to dealing with non-state actors and militant Islamic forces. . . . The [Pakistani] Taliban network, and its leadership, is still intact and still capable of launching strikes across Pakistan.'"[63]

Islamabad has enlisted the aid of tribal militias, commonly known as *lashkars*, to compensate for these military weaknesses. A traditional response to dangers against the tribe, these temporary, normally lightly armed and supplied militias, which can vary dramatically in size but are traditionally forty to fifty men, answer to tribal authorities and have a fixed area of responsibility. Historically, *lashkars* have been involved in settling intertribal disputes or expelling any threatening or unwanted foreign entity from tribal land, which, in contemporary times, includes Al Qaeda–associated militants, the Americans, and even Pakistani federal troops.

The *lashkar* strategy has been compared to Iraq's Sunni Awakening, where U.S.-supported Sunni tribes evicted Al Qaeda and associated militants. Unlike in Iraq, however, Pakistan's Al Qaeda–associated militants are relatively independent and have more military potency than the tribes. The net result is likely to be increased chaos that Islamabad can exploit to perpetuate its double game.

The militants generally field higher caliber personnel. The militants, who have undergone military training, have both light and heavy weaponry. The *lashkars*, by contrast, are equipped only with the members' personal weapons, many of which date from the 1980s, and have no formal military training. Per one Pakistani officer, "You put these people up front and you will get them chewed up."[64]

The militants, backed by a substantial support structure developed over decades of fighting, also have superior logistics. The *lashkars'* logistics, by contrast, consist of the food and ammunition the members bring with them. As evidenced by the fighting in Bajuar, where the *lashkar* ran out of ammunition after three days, *lashkars* cannot keep troops in the field for any meaningful period of time.

The militants also have better command and control. In military fashion, they employ a unified chain of command that moves forces over the battle space as needed. Because *lashkars* are geographically restricted based on tribe, however, they cannot present a coordinated presence before a coordinated enemy, and so they can be destroyed piecemeal. Per one Pakistani observer, "If you deploy the *lashkar[s]* on an ad hoc basis, they can be an embarrassment."[65]

The militants are also often better motivated. At least at the leadership level, they fight out of incentive to achieve their religious, cultural, and political goals. Many of the *lashkars*, however, are fighting out of coercion. In fall 2008, for example, Abdul Rehman, a tribal elder of the Orakzai area, stated that "we were pressured by the government to take action because they warned, 'If you don't take action you will be bombed.'"[66]

The militants are further advantaged by Pakistan's circumscribed intent, which seeks to have the *lashkars* hold the militants in check while preventing the *lashkars* from being able to either challenge Pakistani forces or become independent of them. "Great care is taken to make sure the *lashkars* do not become a threat to the military itself. 'We do not want a *lashkar* to become an offensive force,' said one of the [Pakistani] generals, who spoke frankly about the *lashkars* on the condition of anonymity. For that reason, the military was willing to lend supporting fire from artillery and helicopters but would not give the militias heavy weapons."[67] Instead, as exemplified when it gave 30,000 rifles to Peshawar's citizenry, Pakistan has distributed small arms, a growing portion of which will inevitably end up in militant hands. Revolting tribesmen in Iraq, by contrast, awoke to millions of dollars and the direct support of the U.S. Third

Infantry Division. At best, Pakistan's support for the tribal militias has been "episodic" and "unsustained."[68]

Attempting to blunt the growth of these forces, the militants have responded asymmetrically by systematically killing pro-government tribal leaders who raise and direct *lashkars*. Al Qaeda–associated militants killed over five hundred elders from 2004 to spring 2009. Al Qaeda–associated militants also killed more than 150 *maliks* (tribal chieftains) from 2005 to fall 2008, all but destroying the tribal system.[69]

This has further swayed the supporting manpower and recruitment dynamics in the militants' favor. Without empowered tribal figures, there is no one with standing in the eyes of the region's uneducated youth. Most of the Taliban's leadership and foot soldiers come from the lower Pashtun classes. There are increasingly fewer voices to speak against the sway of generous militant salaries, which, when combined with religious and cultural prestige, are a hefty recruitment incentive.

Even if successful, the *lashkars* may effectively transform into unaccountable, untrained, and empowered private armies, who may acquire their own agendas. As of winter 2010–2011, for example, the leading commander in the Matani area near Peshawar increased his demands for money and weapons on threat of ceasing cooperation with the authorities. Meanwhile, the Taliban have begun to seek to persuade these newfound power brokers to switch sides.

The likely impact upon long-term FATA governance will be a multi-sided, Pashtun-centric civil war pitting tribes against the militants, as well as each other, while stoking intratribal conflict. None of the tribes, who supply the vast majority of both militant fighters and local government forces, has total solidarity, and some support the government or the militants more wholesale than others. Forming *lashkars* forces questions of loyalty, religion, and politics that risk exposing and creating tribal rifts. The ample supply of weapons in the region combined with the traditional Pashtun emphases on courage/manliness, revenge, and a strong proclivity for independence that collectively compose a sense of honor, which must be strenuously defended, makes the situation ripe for large-scale, intense, and prolonged violence. Meanwhile, the *jirga*, the traditional tribal council system for dispute resolution, has been severely weakened through not just the killing of tribal elders, but also by the militants purposefully displacing it.

Pakistan's double game is eminently preserved. The *lashkar* strategy effectively divides the Islamic militants into two categories—those focused against the Pakistani state and those focused against Afghanistan. By aligning only against the Pakistani Taliban attacking Islamabad, Al Qaeda and its associated close allies are preserved, and the militants are indirectly encouraged to focus against foreign forces and their Afghan allies. Islamabad is able to increase its forces without distracting itself from India, and the increased casualties, largely stemming from lower-quality forces being poorly employed, better enables Islamabad to rebuff U.S. criticism. With Pashtuns fighting one another instead of the Punjabi-dominated Pakistani state, both Pashtun nationalists and the militants are preoccupied and potentially weakened. Meanwhile, this slew of internal security problems bolsters the army's position at the forefront of foreign and security policy while allowing it to check Pakistan's civilian government in the name of threats to national security.

Lastly, Pakistan has pursued accommodations with the Islamic militants. "It's a very close relationship. The army and the Taliban are friends. Whenever a Taliban fighter is killed, army officers go to his funeral. They bring money to the family."[70] Islamabad's offensives—none of which Pakistan has unquestionably won—have routinely ended in compromises that leave the politico-military situation fundamentally unchanged. The double game is perpetuated.

The agreement ending the 2008 offensive into South Waziristan against Baitullah Mehsud is emblematic. Members of the Mehsud tribe agreed to refrain from attacking the Pakistani state and setting up a parallel government, which, in essence, is accepting the rule of law, and thus the legitimacy of the Pakistani state. Sending fighters into Afghanistan was not addressed in the agreement. As noted by Maj. Gen. Jeffrey Schloesser, the top U.S. commander in eastern Afghanistan in 2008, Pakistani offensives did not slow the influx of Pakistani-based fighters against U.S. and allied troops.[71]

The mechanics of the negotiations further perpetuate the problem set. Instead of engaging the region's tribal elders, the traditional means of maintaining social order and stability, talks routinely take place directly between the militants and the Pakistani military. This empowers the militants over the tribal elders in the Pakistani military's absence, and it makes the army, not the tribes, the primary enforcement mechanism for any agreements. Given the tribal areas' exclusion from federal administration and the military's reluctance to intervene, the militants are essentially being released on their own recognizance.

In 2009, however, Pakistan began to make deals at the expense of state sovereignty. To escape U.S. drone attacks, Islamic militants pushed into Pakistan's "settled" areas in search of a new haven, the most prominent of which became the Swat Valley, a Delaware-sized area with roughly 1.5 million people within reach of Peshawar, Rawalpindi, and Islamabad. The Malakand Accord, signed with Sufi Mohammed of the Movement for the Enforcement of Islamic Law, offered the militants a ceasefire and an Islamic system of justice.

President Asif Ali Zardari's government insisted the legal change would only allow the limited application of sharia through the local courts.[72] This was the first time, however, that the Pakistani state had surrendered such a large portion of land, given land from Pakistan's settled areas, or ceded writ of the state. Even in Musharraf's many deals with the militants, he never countenanced major changes in Pakistan's political or legal system. Even in Afghanistan, where the Taliban control multiple provinces, Kabul has never conceded the writ of the state, and it insists that these areas remain contested.[73]

Even before the militants accepted, the government enacted the deal. Advocates saw it as a way to exploit militant fractiousness. Some would be neutralized through peace deals, which husbands state resources. Others would be defeated in battle.

This treaty giving the militants legal and political space, however, apparently emboldened rather than placated them. The militants immediately set up training camps, and the number of fighters quickly tripled. Within weeks, the militants expanded their control into two neighboring districts, Buner and Dir, which brought the militants to within sixty miles of the capital. This validated jihadist ideologue Abu Bakr Naji's 2004 treatise, *The Management of Savagery*—which rebuffs earlier Al Qaeda theoreticians by arguing that the key to advanced jihad is to first hold territory and then impose a government that enforces Islamic law, which the Taliban did by blowing up two hundred girls' schools, hanging policemen, setting up sharia courts, and establishing parallel governance.[74]

Swat was not an example of the militants embodying the sentiments of the local population. In the previous year's general elections, Swat's largely secular and pro-democracy Pashtun population voted overwhelmingly to oust a regional government of Musharraf-installed Islamic fundamentalists. Islamabad's posture actually let the militants have Swat.

A string of militant attacks in fall 2009 against Pakistani police stations and military bases that culminated in militants seizing the Pakistani army's national headquarters finally built government momentum to act. "There has to be consensus in the face of what is clearly now a war," said Sherry Rehman, a ruling party lawmaker. "We have to treat this as a battle for Pakistan's survival."[75]

Islamabad's pain threshold, however, is high, as is its assessment of its ability to control the militants, relative to the gains derived from its double game. Reminiscent of Swat, Pakistan massed 30,000 troops to take on ten thousand indigenous militants backed by roughly two thousand foreign fighters in South Waziristan in fall 2009. The fighters largely melted away, however, and they sustained relatively few casualties by avoiding Pakistani firepower. Islamabad, meanwhile, sustained roughly two thousand casualties, which included a disproportionately high number of officers. Per past offensives, the Pakistanis declared victory and largely withdrew their forces. Though this large-scale Islamabad invasion clearly sent a message to the militants, the situation on the ground remained effectively unaltered.

## Pakistan's Economic and Governance Situation

President Zardari returned Pakistan to a parliamentary system when he signed the eighteenth amendment in spring 2010. Many of the Pakistani presidency's powers that had been assumed under Musharraf devolved to the legislature. Most significantly, Zardari ceded to the prime minister the right to appoint the head of the military and to dissolve parliament—a 1980s-era tool that various political factions have used to destroy rival governments with the military's blessing, which then had a reason to seize power amid chaos.[76]

In the long term, these changes could restructure Pakistan's politics. With the legislature now dominant over the presidency, the provinces, not Islamabad, will gain the upper hand. The provinces are likely to eventually have the right to legislate, to control their own education programs, and, most significantly, to govern their own finances.

While this could lead to increased instability and possibly even Pakistan's disintegration if handled poorly, this transition could also lay the foundations for long-term peace and prosperity. This reorientation could serve as the basis for transitioning from the top-down messianic zeal of pan-Islamism central to the founding of Pakistan—a country carved from Muslim-majority areas of British India in 1947 to become the first modern state based on Islam and whose name means "land of the pure"—to a bottom-up nationalism fueled by an emphasis on local cultures and languages. It could lead to a new national identity not inherently in conflict with the West and a government focused more on development for Pakistan's impoverished masses than the contemporary focus on regional expansionism and power politics cloaked and justified in religion. The end result could be not just a more prosperous Pakistan but also a more peaceful and stable international system devoid of the leading facilitator of the Islamic militancy that perpetuates global terrorist threats, such as Osama bin Laden's Al Qaeda.[77] Pakistan's domestic situation, however, is not a conducive facilitator.

Pakistan's economy remains anemic. In a country of 173 million with a rapidly growing and youthful population, less than 3 percent growth equates to a recession. Roughly 6 percent or more during Musharraf's military dictatorship with a peak of 8 percent in 2005, growth was just 0.6 percent in 2008, the first year of restored democracy. Pakistan's GDP fell to less than 3 percent in 2009. Though the United States staved off a Pakistani collapse following 9/11 by orchestrating an extension of its $13.5 billion in foreign debt, the 2008 global credit crisis brought Pakistan back to the brink.[78]

Pakistan is in a negative loop. From 2008 to 2010, virtually all of the world's governments have attempted to stimulate growth by cutting interest rates and increasing government spending. By contrast, Pakistan raised interest rates and reduced overall government spending to try to control its budget deficit and bring down its 20 percent inflation. Only a November 2008 infusion of $7.6 billion in International Monetary Fund loans staved off another Pakistani financial collapse.[79]

Unending political and security turmoil only hinders economic growth. When the Pakistani Supreme Court barred popular former prime minister Nawaz Sharif from holding office, for example, the markets fell 5 percent. Between April 2008 and spring 2009, as internal violence rose, the Pakistani stock market declined from an all-time high of 15,000 points to roughly 5,000 points. A Pakistani foreign ministry study showed a loss in 2009 of $35 billion due to multinational companies pulling out of Pakistan citing security, and $68 billion in losses were predicted for 2010.[80]

Pakistan's increasing military activities have only worsened its plight. FATA-related military expenditures were poised to widen Pakistan's fiscal deficit to as much as 5.5 percent of GDP in 2010 compared to a target of 4.9 percent. With capital already fleeing, Pakistan has had to free up more money for launching FATA offensives, which, as of 2011, have no end in sight.[81] Pakistan's rickety civilian government, still in the shadow of a military dictatorship, has opted to cut social spending, which could ease poverty in both the short and long term, in lieu of defense spending. In the second half of 2008, for example, Pakistan spent less than $900 million of the $2.5 billion it had planned for development.[82]

The micro effect on people's daily lives has been dramatic. Electrical blackouts stemming from the government falling behind on payments to power companies have not only caused riots, but the electricity shortages have also reduced economic activity even further, which has reduced wages. At the same time, prices skyrocketed following the government's removal of fuel, food, and utilities subsidies. A fall 2008 International Republican Institute (IRI) poll found that 73 percent of Pakistani adults said their personal finances had deteriorated, and 59 percent expected things to get worse. By 2009, wheat cost 2.5 times as much compared to 2007. The cost of cooking oil had tripled. From Zardari's 2008 election through 2010, the cost of sugar has tripled and the cost of flour has doubled.[83]

The immediate economic impact of the 2010 floods on Pakistan's already dysfunctional economy has been estimated at roughly $43 billion. Growth predictions for 2011 have dropped from 4.1 percent to 2.5 percent.[84] Finance minister Abdul Hafeez Shaikh, a former officer of the World Bank, noted in fall 2010 that Pakistan's economy, already "teetering on the brink," was headed for the "abyss," and by fall 2010 the state had only enough revenues in reserve to pay two months of salaries.[85]

By contrast, "Even in bad times, Pakistani militant groups draw donations from sympathizers across the country and in the oil-rich Middle East; some also make money from criminal enterprises. 'Their economy doesn't go down—their narcotics, their smuggling, their kidnappings. . . . The militants have plenty of money and can simply offer either income to the unemployed or a better income' for those who have jobs. . . . And joining militant groups also 'carries much greater status and honor than most menial jobs.'"[86]

The socioeconomic foundation upon which to build a prosperous future is, by and large, not present. Unlike India after the 1947 partition, Pakistan maintained a dichotomized society with a small, narrow, landed upper class and masses of subservient, landless workers. Opportunities for socioeconomic advancement are slim.

Poor governance compounds socioeconomic tensions. Successive governments have failed to execute land reform. Health care has never been widespread or affordable. The state has also failed to provide basic education, which has yielded a 40 percent illiteracy rate.

Progress has been slow. A program announced in 2008 to reign in madrassas preaching militancy, for example, had not gotten off the ground as of 2010 due to a combination of bureaucratic inertia and fears of a backlash from powerful conservative religious groups. In the meantime, as state-sponsored education has become ever more expensive for poor parents, the number of madrassas actually increased between 2007 and 2010 from 13,000 to 17,000. Experts estimate that at least several thousand madrassas produce militant students.[87] Ikram Sehgal, the chairman of Pathfinder G4S, Pakistan's largest private security firm, estimates the throughput at 7,000 to 15,000 "hard core" students each year.

Corruption further erodes governance capacity. The court system is notorious not just for slow decisions, but also for a lack of impartiality. The problem is so endemic that Transparency International ranked Pakistan the forty-sixth most corrupt state among 180 countries.[88]

The problem is particularly acute when it comes to dealing with insurgents. As of 2010, the United States estimates that roughly 2,500 prisoners have been held for more than one year with no contact with family members, lawyers, or humanitarian groups. Pakistani officials are admittedly aware of the problems. According to one expert, however, "there is no clear solution: Pakistan has no applicable military justice system, and . . . their courts are not up to the task of handling such a large volume of complex terrorism cases. There is little forensic evidence in most cases, and witnesses are likely to be too scared to testify."[89] Furthermore, hundreds, if not thousands, of Baluchis have been detained without charges and held incommunicado in secret, leading some American officials to suggest "the Pakistanis have used the pretext of war to imprison members of the Baluch nationalist opposition that has fought for generations to separate from Pakistan.[90]

This situation plays into the Pakistani Taliban's hands. Pakistan's heavy-handed treatment alienates the population. The various militants, who have gained popularity in part by issuing swift and Quranic-based justice, present themselves as a positive alternative. At the same time, the U.S. image is tarnished by extension.

The holding of thousands without trial risks violating the Leahy Amendment. This law requires recipients of U.S. military assistance to abide by international human rights laws and standards. The U.S. aid flow to Pakistan, which has totaled $18 billion in military and development aid with another $3 billion slated for 2011, is jeopardized. Fall 2010 witnessed strong State Department criticism of Pakistani security forces' human rights practices and a U.S. refusal to train or equip about a half-dozen Pakistani army units.[91]

The worst socioeconomic indicators are in the tribal areas. While roughly two-thirds of Pakistani women as a whole are illiterate, estimates for the FATA state that only 3 percent of women are educated. No area is poorer or has less civil infrastructure. The militants have created what Amnesty International calls a "human rights free zone" where they enforce their ideology through a combination of fear and violence. No credible social alternatives now exist.[92]

State-backed FATA governance is collapsing. Formally, the FATA is still ruled using the Frontier Crimes Regulation, a colonial era–law implemented by the British to suppress and manipulate the tribes, and which relies upon tribal leaders interfacing with their people on behalf of the government. With so many pro-government tribal elders killed by the militants or having fled the area, however, the underpinnings of the system are disappearing.

As noted by Pakistani-American lawyer Mahboob Mahmood, the militants exploit this situation by "promising more than just proscriptions on music and schooling. They are also promising Islamic justice, effective government and economic redistribution. . . . The people of Pakistan are psychologically ready for a revolution."[93]

The militants' five-step process in the takeover of Swat is representative:

First, the Taliban struck directly at competing points of power, which consisted of landlords and elected officials, who were usually the same people, and weak police. They made small symbolic demands of minor inconvenience and subtle conveyances. Over time, these gave way to overt threats of violence and acts of intimidation.

Second, they simultaneously exploited class resentments of the general public. The militants particularly emphasized issues where the people had unresolved cases against the elite in the notoriously slow and corrupt court system. By allying with the general public in these disputes, the militants increased their public support.

Third, as landlords and other authority figures fled, the Taliban rewarded the masses. They divided the spoils of the departed leaders among the public.

The masses not only saw immediate material improvement in their lives, but they also got a sense of revenge.

Fourth, the Taliban took ownership of the local economy. If peace came quickly, they either instigated their own businesses or fulfilled the role of the departed landlords and other leaders on more amicable terms that delivered them a cut of the profits. If violence was prolonged, fighting itself became the economy, and the militants paid better than the government.

Fifth, militant group leaders ascended over truly local figures. This enabled highly organized Al Qaeda–associated Islamic militants to co-opt the whole area, now engulfed in local turmoil, into the greater militant cause. The local people were then in a position where they either could not oppose the militants without undue risk to their personal safety, or they supported the militants of their own volition.[94]

The great danger is that these conditions so effectively exploited by the Taliban in Swat exist throughout much of the country. In the hinterlands, it is a distinct likelihood that the Pakistani government, while not formally disintegrating, could simply lose suzerainty over much of its territory and degenerate into a series of tribal fiefdoms or militant-controlled mini-states.[95] In Pakistan's heartland, such dynamics inspire and enable antistate militancy.

Force, while necessary, is not sufficient to address this problem. The economic structure and mismanagement of the country to date contains the seeds for the Islamic militants to become self-sufficient and get beyond the control of the state. As noted by Shuja Nawaz, a Pakistani-American military expert, "The army is overstretched, so we have to start dealing with the causes of the militancy—the vast gap between rich and poor, the lack of governance—that Pakistan has neglected for so long."[96]

The 2010 floods have spiraled political tensions. Public anger at the ruling elite has swelled as landowners were accused of flooding the lands of the poor to save their own. As Pakistan has become increasingly dependent upon foreign donors, the United States wants to see taxes raised on Pakistan's wealthy landed and commercial class, which would require changes to Pakistan's tax structure, in which only 2 million people out of 170 million pay income tax and exceptions for the wealthy or politically connected are not uncommon. Criticism of the armed forces, the United States' chief proxy, and, by extension, of the United States, has risen as defense spending maintains at 13.6 percent for 2011 even as the civilian population suffers. Pakistani civil-military relations took a turn for the worse when General Kayani presented a list of corrupt civilian ministers the army wanted to see purged as a step to taking control of the plummeting economy, cracking down on corruption, and improving the government's faltering response to the floods.

In the background, the Supreme Court has threatened to repeal the amnesty of President Zardari, who visited his family's chateau in France during the floods, and this would open him to standing corruption charges. Instead of unswervingly leaping to Zardari's aid during this hour of need and vowing assistance, the United States stated that the international community could not be expected to provide all of the money needed to recover. With the U.S. government seriously worried about the possibility of major unrest, this was essentially a vote of little confidence in its democratically elected Pakistani counterpart.[97]

Nonetheless, extra-constitutional political change—an army intervention in politics to install a Bangladesh-style technocratic government, the removal of Zardari, or a military coup—is unlikely. As of 2011, Pakistan's situation is dire, and options are few. Anyone taking on responsibility for managing and fixing its problems under these circumstances would almost certainly have their reputations destroyed,[98] and, as of winter 2010–2011, public opinion polling shows that the Pakistani public holds the military in far higher regard than the civilian government.[99]

Al Qaeda benefits. The U.S. image and its already contentious causes are tainted by association with Pakistan's democratically elected ineptitude. Al Qaeda spokesman Adam Gadahn, meanwhile, has stated that the poor military and civilian response shows that the government does not care for the poor. As an alternative, Al Qaeda has urged Pakistani Muslims to support Islamist insurgents.[100]

## MOVING FORWARD

The United States must pursue two dovetailing interests—salving its efforts in Afghanistan and pursuing Pakistani-based Al Qaeda and its allies. Pakistan is both a crucial venue and enabling interlocutor. More than a means to an end, Islamabad also stands as a cause in itself.[101]

### Initial U.S. Choices—The State Level

The United States could simply abandon Islamabad and work with other states in the region, namely India, or component parts of Pakistan, such as Baluch, Pashtun, and Sindhi tribal leaders and provincial governments, to secure its interests.[102] The administration, however, rejected this approach. The collapse or severe degradation of the Pakistani state endangers multiple U.S. interests with no guarantee of success or alternative if it fails.

The proliferation risk, either intentional or illicit, from Pakistan's fully developed nuclear weapons establishment would likely rise markedly. Nuclear materials, knowledge, equipment, personnel, or even weapons could fall into the hands of Al Qaeda or associated terrorists. Or, countries adversarial to the United States, such as Iran, could benefit, as occurred under the A. Q. Khan network.

U.S. efforts in Afghanistan would be endangered. The most critical U.S. supply line would either be cut or seriously endangered. Increased Pakistani military pressure against militant sanctuaries would be highly unlikely.

Regional chaos would likely result. Iran, Russia, and India, directly or indirectly, would be hard pressed not to act. The resulting tensions would be both politically and operationally exploitable by Al Qaeda.

Al Qaeda–associated militant control that gives Osama bin Laden's Al Qaeda geographic sanctuary would likely increase, as would Al Qaeda's ability to infuse itself into the world system. "Pakistan isn't Afghanistan, a backward, isolated, landlocked place that outsiders get interested in about once a century. It's a developed state . . . [with] a major Indian Ocean port and ties to the outside world, especially the [Persian] Gulf, that Afghanistan and the Taliban never had."[103]

The administration has instead tried to strengthen the Pakistani state. The Obama administration's steps to date, however, are not game-changers. Though they make headway, they do not secure U.S. interests, and time is not on the U.S. side.

The administration's economic actions are a dramatic increase. The United States played a leading role in arranging a donors' conference in Tokyo in mid-April 2009 that raised approximately $5 billion dollars in new aid intended for health, education, governance, and developing democracy. From U.S. coffers, the Obama administration decided it would triple nonmilitary aid to Pakistan to $1.5 billion per year for the next five years to build roads and schools.[104]

These steps will likely curry U.S. and Pakistani political favor, but they are also wholly inadequate and do not substantively address the problems of a low U.S. public standing coupled with weak Pakistani state capacity. Pakistan has over 180 million people with a 40 percent illiteracy rate. U.S. priorities, as expressed in dollar allocation, are still clearly on the military side of the equation. U.S. civilian aid donations, while aimed at what many argue are the root enablers of the militants' domestic insurgency and the social viruses that weaken the vibrancy of the Pakistani state and its body politic, are woefully out of scale to the task at hand.

The Obama administration has taken steps to keep fissile materials adaptable to weaponization out of the hands of terrorists. It called for "a new treaty that verifiably ends the production of fissile materials" at the Nuclear Security Summit in 2009, and the sixty-four-nation Conference on Disarmament has agreed to negotiate the Fissile Materials Cut-off Treaty to cap the production of weapons-grade enriched uranium and most forms of plutonium. Specific to Pakistan, one U.S. proposal was to ship some of the spent fuel used in Pakistan's civilian nuclear power plants to the United States. Another proposal was to create a joint program to secure or destroy radioactive materials that could be used to make a nuclear device.[105]

Pakistan, in direct contradiction to U.S. efforts, however, subsequently blocked the conference from starting discussions. As described by Ashley Tellis of the Carnegie Endowment for International Peace, "Pakistan thinks it's going to be forced to cap its fissile material stocks and wants to make sure it has as much as it can get before then." Rose Gottemoeller, the U.S. assistant secretary of state in charge of arms control, even went so far as to rebuke Pakistan at the UN in October 2010 for slowing down treaty negotiations.[106]

Fearing potential U.S. political or military action against its arsenal, Pakistan is still withholding the details of its nuclear establishment. The United States does not know the edges of Pakistan's nuclear picture. The United States has no idea how deep or broad the problems truly are. Meanwhile, low U.S. political standing and public suspicion of U.S. motives only increase the potential to complicate any formal political cooperation.

The Obama administration's nonproliferation policy is exacerbating Pakistan's security fears stemming from regional power imbalances, which China is exploiting by deepening its nuclear ties to Pakistan as a counterbalance for U.S. support to India, and U.S. counterterrorism efforts are highly likely to suffer given the gravity Pakistan attaches to its nuclear program. Pakistan can exploit U.S. vulnerability by pacing its cooperation on bilateral U.S.-Pakistan issues to display its pique. Meanwhile, Pakistan is increasing its nuclear infra-structure, which only increases the chances for terrorist access.[107]

In the conventional realm, bilateral negotiations following the New York City Times Square bombing—during which the U.S. side essentially said, "Sorry, if there is a successful attack, we will have to act" unilaterally within Pakistan—appear to have produced a strategic decision by both the United States and Pakistan to improve cooperation. As of 2010, for example, Pakistani officers began taking advantage of previously more or less unused cross-border intelligence compiled at two joint coordination centers on the Afghan side of the border.[108] The Obama administration has increased the scope and volume of on-the-ground U.S. assistance to Pakistan.

The overall Obama administration increase more than doubled the Pakistan-based U.S. force presence to roughly two hundred troops in 2010. The administration has sent additional CIA operatives and technicians. It has also stationed roughly fifty U.S. military personnel to secure avionics, weapons, and data systems on board the first four of eighteen new F-16 fighter jets, which will upgrade the thirty-year-old U.S. aircraft that comprise the mainstay of Pakistan's air force to enable nighttime air operations for the first time.[109]

The administration also dispatched and enlarged a Special Operations training and advisory contingent from 80 to 140 troops in two locations.

Previously, the Bush administration had sent more than seventy military advisors and technical specialists, mostly from U.S. Army Special Forces, who were aided by a small British contingent. They provided intelligence and training that produced a dedicated counterinsurgency force within Pakistan's Frontier Corps that would not get diverted to Pakistan's routine disputes with India and that was knowledgeable in local geography, language, and culture. The resulting five hundred–man commando unit has been credited with capturing or killing more than sixty militants, including five ranking Taliban commanders. More than 1,100 Pakistani special operations troops were trained in 2010 alone.[110]

The Obama administration's efforts against Al Qaeda's indigenous militant allies, however, are highly unlikely to yield time-effective results. Pakistan's military, which boasts 650,000 active troops, 500,000 reservists, and 300,000 paramilitary members, has the raw strength to crush the Islamic militants. Token training of such a large force trained and deployed for conventional war with India is unlikely to yield substantial results against unknown thousands of militants. In fact, the Bush administration's National Security Council concluded this piecemeal, train-the-trainer approach was so indirect that it would take approximately twelve years to field an effective counterinsurgency force.[111]

This Frontier Corps force is also not as dedicated as initially intended. The Frontier Corps relies heavily upon the conventional army, which provides all of the Frontier Corps' officers and air support, and so the force cannot operate independently or with agility.[112] This lack of operational independence, particularly when set within the context of Pakistan's double game approach, makes any actual capability the United States does instill in the Frontier Corps dubious. Under political authorities with a differing agenda, any such military potential could also be used contrary to U.S. interests just as easily as it could be used to support them.

The U.S. intelligence buildup was meant to parallel the U.S. military effort to intensify pressure on the Afghan Taliban and its allied insurgent groups conducting attacks in Afghanistan. Noting that intelligence sharing goes both ways, and that targets are monitored inside both Afghanistan and Pakistan, bilateral dialogue produced plans to set up a joint military intelligence–processing center on the outskirts of Peshawar. Negotiations began to set up another center near Quetta, the Pakistani city where U.S. officials claim the Afghan Taliban is based. These fusion centers were meant to bolster Pakistani military operations by providing them direct access to U.S. intelligence, to include real-time video surveillance from U.S. drones using new surveillance and eavesdropping technology deployed by the National Security Agency (NSA).[113]

Pakistan's double game, however, undercuts any such intelligence-sharing progress. The ulterior purpose of both sides is to leverage and monitor their counterpart as to what the other is doing in insurgent areas. From the U.S. point of view, the fusion centers serve to make the Pakistanis more dependent upon U.S. intelligence, which makes it less likely they will be able to curtail drone strikes or other programs that draw significant opposition from Pakistani public opinion. The United States also gains physical presence "to see what they are actually doing versus what they say they're doing." From the Pakistani point of view, the fusion centers offer insight into U.S. capabilities and a chance to monitor U.S. military operations in both Afghanistan and Pakistan. Meanwhile, Pakistan has also been slow to issue visas for additional U.S. personnel, and it has continued to harass U.S. military and civilian officials at military and police checkpoints. The centers have effectively been converted from collaborative springboards to points of leverage within a bilateral context.[114]

The Obama administration has also ratcheted up Bush-era drone missile attacks, which Pakistan secretly approves and assists. These strikes insert a U.S. presence where U.S. and allied forces have little or no access and the writ of the Pakistani state is weak. They are ultimately, however, a tool to bide time rather than a path to victory.[115]

The Bush administration broadened its initially narrow selection and launching criteria from precisely targeted, named individuals to permit indirect and circumstantial evidence—"pattern of life" analysis, evidence collected by surveillance cameras on the unmanned aircraft, targeting information supplied by Pakistan, and so forth. As explained to the *Los Angeles Times* by a senior U.S. counterterrorism official, "We might not always have their names, but . . . [the] actions [of these people] over time have made it obvious that they are a threat." Once deemed a lawful target, there does not appear to be an obligation to warn or attempt to detain that person before attacking.[116]

Not only did the Obama administration continue these Bush-era changes, but the administration also broadened this tool to the Pakistani Taliban. Under the TTP, the FATA has become a "witches' brew" of interlocking militant groups who have attacked U.S. forces in Afghanistan, the U.S. homeland and its interests abroad, and the Pakistani state. For all practical purposes, drone strikes have effectively changed from sniper attacks against a subset of enemy leadership to modern-day "cannon fire" against any enemy forces in sight.[117]

The strike volume has risen markedly. Surpassing the Bush administration's initial 2007 foray of five launches and its 2008 escalation to thirty-six firings, the Obama administration registered fifty-three strikes in 2009. Following the retaliatory U.S. volley responding to the Al Qaeda attack by suicide bomber on a CIA post in Afghanistan, the Obama administration was on pace for nearly doubling the U.S. strike volume to approximately one hundred attacks in 2010, by which time it averaged two to three strikes per week.[118]

These strikes have achieved tactical success with strategic impact by efficiently killing enemy leadership using limited resources. From 2004 to 2010,

U.S. airstrikes killed at least fifteen senior and mid-level Al Qaeda leaders. At least four senior and five mid-level Afghan Taliban leaders had also been killed.

"[T]he enemy has [also] lost not just operational leaders and facilitators—people whose names we know—but formations of fighters and other terrorists." By 2010, these strikes had killed roughly twelve times as many low-level fighters than mid- to high-level leaders since their use intensified starting in summer 2008. Drone strikes are now executed against safe houses, training camps, and other FATA hiding places.[119]

Drone attacks were one of the few ready and working tools producing tangible results that the Obama administration inherited, and the administration found them immensely expedient as a leading counterterrorism tool. The drone strikes permit the administration to blunt criticism that it is weak on national security, particularly as it seeks to apply and negotiate the civilian justice process to terrorism, which Republicans have criticized as coddling. Viewed as a way to kill terrorists at low to no risk to U.S. personnel, the strikes garner significant support from both Democrats and Republicans. Killing also sidesteps the more difficult issue of how to detain, question, and prosecute enemy operatives—a set of decisions still unresolved ten years after 9/11. A possible harbinger, the administration has prepositioned drones in the Horn of Africa.[120]

The drone program has also helped to invigorate and sustain the U.S.-Pakistani relationship. At the Obama administration's start, the drones were a ready and workable tool amid a broadly quasi-functional relationship. Because they inflict tangible, visible losses and are a technical process that the United States can execute unilaterally, they enabled the administration to claim continued progress against Al Qaeda and its allies while sidestepping more contentious issues, such as North Waziristan, amid efforts to mend the broader strategic U.S.-Pakistani partnership. If the relationship improved, the drone strikes were a ready-made collaboration opportunity. Pakistani agents are sometimes present at U.S. bases, and they have taken on an increased role in target selection and strike coordination. Per Pakistani security expert Ikram Sehgal, the intelligence enabling drone strikes improved precisely because Pakistani cooperation increased.[121]

Whether by intent or design, the drone strikes have essentially gone from being a tool for implementing a U.S. strategy to being the U.S. strategy. Unfortunately, the drone attacks—whose focus is overwhelmingly Osama bin Laden's ranking Al Qaeda operatives, a demonstrated yet clearly present secondary priority on Pakistani Taliban senior leadership, and a possible, yet-to-be-substantively-realized tertiary emphasis against Afghan Taliban—are a stop-gap measure. Strategic success has yet to materialize.

Killing both the leadership and rank and file of Al Qaeda and its militant allies can only hurt. May 2010, however, witnessed the killing of Sheikh Saeed al-Masri, Al Qaeda's tenth third-in-command. At the working level, where the targets' names are not known and operatives perform the core rear-area support functions, the attrition rate is not sufficient to produce a crippling effect. Al Qaeda and its associated militant groups have shown themselves to be systemic organizations, not a unique and limited amalgamation of irreplaceable individuals.

The scale of the fight favors insurgents drawn from the general population over missiles from a limited number of drones. The militants will persevere despite any losses so long as their political agenda and strategy remain popular and continue to draw recruits. By June 2010, for example, roughly 70 percent of the 140 U.S. drone strikes conducted since their inception have been against the Pakistani Taliban, the Haqqani network, and Al Qaeda, and yet the volume and lethality of these militants' efforts was rising.[122]

While there has been no 9/11-scale attack inside the United States since the drone campaign became the norm, there was also no large-scale attack after 9/11 prior to the drone campaign. There have been numerous other U.S. actions since 9/11—deposing the Taliban, establishing the global financial dragnet, stepped-up global intelligence and military operations, building a global political coalition, and so forth. The drone strikes have at best likely correlated with this absence of large-scale attacks inside the United States rather than been the cause of it.

While the gain from drone strikes is indirectly reaped in the future, the disadvantages are directly present in the immediate. The increasing pace only magnifies the juxtaposition. As of 2011, their net strategic and political impact verges on undermining the U.S. long-run effort.

The drone strikes' impetus is now expanding the list of U.S. attackers, whom Al Qaeda is transforming into frontline units in its global anti-U.S. struggle. Qari Hussein of the Pakistani Taliban, for example, announced on YouTube that the Times Square attempt was "revenge for the global American interference and terrorism in Muslim countries, especially in Pakistan." In a similar vein, Yemen's AQAP announced that the Christmas 2009 airliner bombing by Umar Farouk Abdul Mutallab was revenge for U.S. bombings in the Yemeni-Saudi border region. Not only does the United States inherit a new enemy, but it also inherits the domestic social, political, and economic problems that provide an Al Qaeda offshoot its niche in that society.[123]

Attempting terrorism's gold standard, a successful attack inside the United States, has significant rewards. As noted by Bruce Hoffman, a terrorism expert at Georgetown University, "The message may be 'the U.S is pounding us with drone attacks, but we're powerful enough to strike back;' it's certainly enough to attract ever more recruits to replace those they're losing."[124]

The U.S. drone strategy has also garnered international condemnation. The United Nations faulted the United States in June 2010 for being "the most prolific user of targeted killings in the world." The "strongly asserted but ill-defined [U.S.] license to kill without accountability is not an entitlement which the United States or other states can have without doing grave damage to the rules designed to protect the right to life and prevent extrajudicial executions." Following the U.S. example, many other countries are engaging in targeted killings and seeking unmanned aircraft to "permit targeted killing at little or no risk."[125]

The overall reaction of the Pakistani public, which has endured the most such attacks, has been strongly negative. To the tune of 77 percent in 2009, Pakistanis in settled areas overwhelmingly opposed the drone strikes. They are broadly perceived as an intrusion on Pakistani sovereignty that kills vast quantities of innocent civilians. In fact, a 2009 Gallup poll commissioned by Al Jazeera Television found that 59 percent of Pakistanis in settled areas view the United States as the greatest threat to Pakistan's security.[126]

Ironically, FATA residents, the very people subject to the strikes, displayed significantly more tolerance for these attacks so long as drone strikes remained fairly focused in target and limited in volume. A 2009 poll of 550 tribal area residents by the Aryana Institute for Regional Research and Advocacy, an independent think tank in Islamabad, found that many of the FATA residents objected to the influence of the militants on their lives. "They say they're unable to dance their traditional dances, or assemble without the permission of the local militant commander. These things trespass on their honor code, their lifestyle, and their culture." As such, 58 percent said that they did not think the strikes increased anti-American sentiment. In fact, in some tribal areas that had not been targeted, such as the Malakand district, residents actually requested drone strikes. In a region with little to no government presence anyway, little concern existed for violations of Pakistani sovereignty.[127] A separate poll by the Community Appraisal and Motivation Programme, which has polled the FATA for years, found that roughly two-thirds of FATA residents wanted the drone strikes to continue.

That sentiment, however, may be changing in 2011 with the Obama administration's "cannon fire" approach, which is steadily affecting a broader population. Polling by the Community Appraisal and Motivation Programme noted that residents still disapproved of Al Qaeda (more than 75 percent), the Pakistani Taliban (more than 66 percent), and the Afghan Taliban (60 percent). Simultaneously, however, a New America Foundation poll of FATA residents found that only 16 percent now say that the strikes "accurately target militants" with 48 percent saying that the strikes "largely kill civilians."

Innocent civilian casualties elicit serious enmity throughout both the FATA and Pakistan's settled areas. It is a commonplace puzzle in the Pakistani public mind how a weapon using advanced technology such as lasers and infrared cameras can also kill innocents. Even when allowed for as an inevitable aspect of war, there is a common sentiment that Pakistanis should operate the drones, not Americans.

Speculation about the number of civilian casualties is wild, and they only trend higher with time. On the low end, a U.S. counterterrorism official in 2010 noted to the press that collateral damage stood at 5 percent for a total of less than 30 with more than 500 militants killed. On the high end, the *Long War Journal* Web site, which uses news reports and contacts within the security establishments in Afghanistan and Pakistan to track drone strikes, estimates roughly 1,100 militants were killed in 2009. Pakistani news reports claim that drone strikes killed 708 civilians in 2009 alone.

The strikes inflame anti-American sentiments. Among middle- and upper-class Pakistanis in the major cities, where it is not an uncommon belief that the United States will attack Pakistan from its ever-increasing bases in Afghanistan because it secretly wants to colonize Pakistan or take Pakistan's nuclear arsenal, roughly 60 percent approved of suicide attacks by 2010 against U.S. forces, which are commonly perceived to be in the Afghanistan-Pakistan region to wage war on Islam or steal the region's natural resources. In an about-face from 2009, nearly 90 percent of FATA residents voiced a desire for the United States to stop pursuing militants in their backyard as support for the Pakistani army, whom nearly 79 percent would not object to running the FATA, has risen. Pakistani nationalism, which is stoked with every strike, is becoming ever more synonymous with anti-Americanism.

U.S. strategic disadvantage is accruing. Heavy use of the drone strikes appears to be driving FATA residents—the very people who live in close proximity to the militants and are best able to assist in action against them—away from the United States in a fight where public perception and popular support are crucial. FATA support for and hope in the Pakistani military, as compared to the civilian government, only enhances the role of Pakistan's military in its governing process and more deeply entrenches the building blocks of Pakistan's double game. Meanwhile, no matter what regime is running Pakistan, the state's room for public political maneuver is decreasing, which, in turn, limits the Pakistani state's ability to operationally support U.S. forces in private.[128]

Al Qaeda's strategic footing is becoming sounder. Al Qaeda and its allied local militants usurp the burgeoning anger at the United States and its Pakistani government ally, who is criticized either for being complicit or being too weak to stop the U.S. strikes, to rally recruits and funding to build operational capacity. Because striking remotely from drones is viewed as cowardly, unmanly, and, for a superpower, proof of its moral inferiority and turpitude in a culture that values direct and personal combat as a sign of bravery and manliness, Al Qaeda's stature rises in the eyes of potential supporters with its defiance and the perpetual U.S. targeting of it.

One approach to countering these various charges of civilian casualties, violations of sovereignty, and, to some degree, U.S. cowardice, would be to acknowledge the drone strikes. This would bring them into the open. Third-party scrutiny would then be possible.

Such a step, however, is unlikely to succeed. Cultural and security factors would still continue to hinder accurate accountings. More significantly, per a 2009 WorldPublicOpinion.org poll, 93 percent of Pakistanis believed that Obama was "seeking to impose American culture on the Islamic world," and 90 percent agreed that Obama "wanted to weaken and divide the Muslim world." The United States is not taken as a credible actor, and so any protestations or data in U.S. favor are likely to mean little.[129]

Pakistan would then be confronted with the problem of openly siding with the United States to selectively kill its citizens at U.S. behest. It would not only then be accountable for any errors killing civilians, and but also for being too weak to prevent U.S. errors. The Pakistani government, upon whom the United States is utterly dependent, would likely have its public room for maneuver, and thus indirectly its ability to assist privately, seriously curtailed.

The capability presented by the drone program—the ability to accurately project military power into areas denied to U.S. forces for political or tactical reasons— is a potentially valuable tool in the U.S. arsenal. It is not, however, a solution by itself. It puts two key U.S. regional objectives, killing Al Qaeda's leadership and strengthening the Pakistani state, at odds. It also antagonizes the political dimension of the U.S.-Al Qaeda struggle to Al Qaeda's political benefit, and thus ultimately to its organizational gain, through enabling short-term tactical U.S. gains while ceding to Al Qaeda the strategic initiative.

Reflecting the path of post-9/11 U.S.-Pakistani relations to date, one of the most powerful means of U.S. influence is money, and the Obama administration has steadily increased U.S. assistance. Military aid has averaged $1.5–2 billion per year since 2001. The Obama administration announced plans in fall 2010 to increase annual grants for Pakistan to buy U.S. defense equipment, as well as a new request for additional military aid expected to total roughly $2 billion over five years to pay for equipment Pakistan can use in counterinsurgency and counterterrorism operations. This assistance not only helps develop Pakistan's raw military capacity, but it also politically eliminates plausibly citing excuses of insufficient capability or funding to act.[130]

## Initial U.S. Choices—The International Level

### *Afghanistan-Pakistan-U.S. Interactive Dynamic*

There has been a failure to synchronize military activity. As noted by Andrew Bacevich, "The chief effect of military operations in Afghanistan so far has been to push radical Islamists across the Pakistani border. As a result, efforts to stabilize Afghanistan are contributing to the destabilization of Pakistan." U.S. drone strikes have only further encouraged the militants to take aim at Pakistan itself, as happened in Swat.[131]

A Pakistani anvil to backstop a U.S. hammer has been either weak or absent. Consistent with Pakistan's double game, this has almost certainly been largely intentional. As noted by Pakistani journalist Ahmed Rashid, "Right now is crunch time for Afghanistan and the Afghan Taliban, and this is a card Pakistan has held for nine years and is not about to throw away because of increased American pressure."[132] Time, which increasingly correlates with increasing U.S. desperation, has become one of Pakistan's chief forms of leverage to exact further concessions from the United States in this U.S. hour of need.

### *Regional Perspective*

Following in the footsteps of its predecessor, the Obama administration has failed to build a supportive regional consensus for its efforts in Pakistan. The administration's competing regional priorities have further placed U.S. proliferation and terrorism objectives at odds. The fight against Al Qaeda has suffered.

The administration has continued to embrace the Bush strategic view of empowering India to counter China. Conferring such preferred strategic treatment upon the country that Pakistan views as its chief security threat, however, can only bolster the mindset and political dynamics that contribute to Pakistan's double game. Meanwhile, China, which has historically played Pakistan as a counter against India for its own purposes, has agreed to thirty-five pacts that are anticipated to dwarf Obama administration efforts by bringing in as much as $30 billion of investment into Pakistan from 2011 to 2016. Akin to Iran, China, whom Pakistan views as its closest friend in Asia, is undercutting the United States.[133]

More broadly, the administration's counter-proliferation efforts against Iran and counterterrorism efforts against Pakistan-based Al Qaeda and its Afghan militant allies are working at cross purposes. In an apparent quid pro quo for not blocking a fourth round of United Nations Security Council (UNSC) sanctions against Iran, the administration, which has strongly advocated for restrictions on the spread of nuclear technology, has not seriously objected to China's spring 2010 agreement to supply Pakistan's increasingly unstable Punjab province with two new nuclear reactors.[134]

The administration's attempt to establish credible new international counter-proliferation norms was seriously undermined. This deal is a clear violation of international guidelines forbidding nuclear exports to countries that have not signed the Nuclear Non-Proliferation Treaty (NPT) or do not have international safeguards on reactors, limits which China agreed to in 2004 when it joined the Nuclear Suppliers group. This deal undercuts U.S. credibility in sanctioning Iran, and it denies the United States the ability to more broadly take the moral and political high ground.

The potential risk from Al Qaeda and its associated militants was increased. Inside Pakistan, the reactors are going to a region of increasing instability, which only increases the risk of Al Qaeda and associated militants' theft or sabotage during construction. Outside Pakistan, the regional balance is made less stable. While this deal brings Pakistan a step closer to parity with India, it is a piecemeal step that does not accord Pakistan strategic parity, and so an increasingly nuclear-capable country remains politically and strategically isolated, which only feeds Pakistan's need for its double game. Furthermore, U.S. policy in Afghanistan and Pakistan, home to a flailing hot war against Al Qaeda and its allies, is apparently being subordinated to U.S. policy on Iran, which now only has increased incentive to work against an already faltering U.S. position in Afghanistan due to the fourth round of sanctions that this deal helped purchase.

### Future U.S. Choices

The United States cannot even maintain a presence in Afghanistan without help from Pakistan, which handles roughly 70 percent of all U.S. supplies. The United States must work through the Pakistani state, particularly the interests of Pakistan's military, in order to reach U.S. interests. Unlike Afghanistan, however, Pakistan is not utterly dependent upon U.S. assistance, though it prospers markedly more with it. Paralleling a common perception of U.S. leverage on Iran, an administration official when speaking of Pakistan has noted, "It's not good when your national security interests are dependent on a country over which you have almost no influence."[135]

It is not the case, however, that the United States—the most economically, militarily, and politically powerful country in the world—has no leverage to work the Pakistan situation to its advantage. Internal to Pakistan, U.S. efforts are filtered through the prism of the Pakistani state, particularly the Pakistani army, which has interests that are not inherently concentric with those of the United States. External to Pakistan, however, the United States can leverage its political, economic, and military resources unfiltered to impact the stimuli to which both the militants and the Pakistani state respond. Manipulating these external factors holds the potential to move beyond Pakistan's double game, which is the key to increasing U.S. leverage and freedom of action to secure U.S. interests.

## CONCLUSION

Internal security in Pakistan is deteriorating. Nearly 4 million Pakistanis now live under Taliban rule in the tribal agencies.[136] In 2009, a total of 7,200 soldiers and militants were killed in addition to 1,300 civilians—a level of bloodshed that is comparable to Afghanistan. The militants have gone beyond defending the FATA to attacking the state and settled areas.

State governance capacity is not improving. The political and economic inequalities found in Swat, which are the seeds of dissension exploited by the Pakistani Taliban, are found throughout the country. An ever-corrupt and incapable justice system only intensifies public misgivings. A failing educational system is producing ever more militants.

The Pakistani economic situation is tenuous at best. Growth has plummeted since the fall of Musharraf, and it remains anemic. The country remains afloat on foreign assistance.

The United States has attempted to bolster the Pakistani state as an anvil to the U.S. hammer by bolstering the three key pillars of counterinsurgency—security, governance, and economic development. To aid security, drone missile strikes have been increased and broadened, efforts have been made to secure fissile material, and the United States has also offered troops, intelligence, and military equipment. To assist governance, foreign aid has been used to promote better practices and increase state capacity. Economically, development aid, which was not a priority under the Bush administration, has seen an unparalleled increase to $1.5 billion per annum for at least five years.

The Obama administration's plan, however, has not proven to be a game-changer. With over 180 million people, the majority of whom are beset by illiteracy and live in dire poverty in some of the most dense urban concentrations and sparse rural patterns in the world, Pakistan is the world's sixth most populous country holding roughly 4–5 percent of the global population, and the scale of U.S. assistance, while unprecedented from the U.S. viewpoint, simply does not match either the scale or scope of the problem set. No new substantial governance has occurred at the national level to draft laws addressing underlying socioeconomic inequalities, government corruption, or health, education, and welfare shortfalls, which are the root causes of the regional insurgencies that give Al Qaeda geographic and political sanctuary. As evidenced by the growing militant threat in Pakistan and the insurgent resurgence in Afghanistan, U.S. security assistance in the form of intelligence, troops, equipment, and money has also fallen short. Actual and potential economic growth, which remains anemic and tenuous, is effectively limited through Pakistan's internal structural flaws.

The manner in which U.S. resources have been applied to influence the timeline of the U.S. effort against Al Qaeda, and Afghanistan in particular, places the inevitability of a U.S. victory in doubt. Unlike in Afghanistan, administration efforts are conducted one degree removed through Pakistan's good offices. These U.S. assistance efforts, therefore, are processed through the prism of Pakistan's national interests as defined by the Pakistani military, and so they have been applied to meet U.S. interests only to the extent that they first meet Pakistani interests.

In practical terms, this has meant Pakistan tamping down but preserving and managing threats to the United States—the Afghan Taliban, the Haqqani network, Hezb-e-Islami/Gulbuddin forces, Osama bin Laden's Al Qaeda, and other associated militants—while securing immediate and unacceptable threats to Pakistan, such as the Pakistani Taliban and its offshoots. De facto Pakistani safe havens—primarily the FATA and, to a lesser extent, Baluchistan—are preserved. The U.S. effort in Afghanistan is kept on the strategic defensive, and its ultimate viability, much less success, is kept in doubt.

This double game plays on a U.S. dependency upon Pakistan born of U.S. military and economic inadequacy combined with a lack of political will to expand the fight, as contrasted against the threat posed by Al Qaeda and its associated militants, who have adequate means and willpower to carry out their strikes. Pakistan gains a continued flow of U.S. aid to preserve a social and political order that would otherwise collapse while securing Pakistan's regional security, most notably by keeping India at bay. Crucially, Pakistan's leverage only increases over time as U.S. resources to act independently reduce and U.S. desperation increases as Al Qaeda and associated militants score operational and political gains.

The administration's approach of working through the Pakistani state and its various organs has likely reached the limits of its potential. After having inflicted initial damage to Al Qaeda and associated militants immediately following 9/11, the interests of key internal actors, namely the Pakistani military establishment, preclude significantly addressing core U.S. objectives beyond keeping the militants most threatening to Pakistan in check. Any future changes of strategic significance will need to be induced by changing Pakistan's domestic situation, over which the United States has little control, and through adjusting Pakistan's international context, over which the United States has substantial control, to alter the stimuli to which Pakistan reacts in order to bring Pakistan's behavior in line with U.S. interests.

Chapter 8

# A Question of Willpower:
# The Obama Administration and Afghanistan

*Losing hurts twice as bad as winning feels good.*
—Sparky Anderson

The Bush administration's initial accomplishments were significant: deposing the Afghan Taliban, routing pre-9/11 Al Qaeda, and establishing a new democratic regime. The U.S. strategic position, however, tenuous at best due to a quick shift in focus to Iraq, began to falter. By 2009 a U.S. National Intelligence Estimate described Afghanistan as being on a "downward spiral."[1]

Rather than abandon flagging U.S. efforts, President Obama embraced them by affirming that "the United States has made a lasting commitment to defeat Al Qaeda, but also to support the democratically elected sovereign government of . . . Afghanistan. That commitment will not waver. And that support will be sustained."[2]

President Obama also narrowed the means of implementation for this "war of necessity" in order to "disrupt, dismantle and defeat al-Qaeda in Afghanistan and Pakistan, and to prevent its capacity to threaten America and our allies in the future."[3] Rather than domestically securing Afghanistan according to the vision of the Bush administration, which sought to make Afghanistan into a beacon of "reform and democracy" throughout the Muslim world to manifestly display an alternative "to fanaticism, resentment, and terror,"[4] the Obama administration stated that it simply sought to ensure that Afghanistan would not "be used as a base to launch attacks against the United States."[5] Though this approach potentially affords the United States significantly more latitude, and it implicitly lowers the bar for U.S. success, the Obama administration's task was no easier because Afghanistan's once malleable strategic context had congealed in a way that was inimical to U.S. interests.

The administration's chief approach has been a national-level counterinsurgency campaign. If it does not outright defeat the Taliban and its militant allies, it should at least subdue the insurgency to locally manageable levels and force it to the bargaining table with the U.S.-backed Afghan national government. The preservation and dominance of this U.S.-created entity should then be able to guarantee that Al Qaeda will be denied the sanctuary it found pre-9/11 under Mullah Omar's Taliban.

Roughly a decade after 9/11, the outcome is still uncertain. Extensive military and economic resources, as well as political will, have been irrevocably drained. The U.S.-led war effort is now at a crucial make-or-break point. Key strategic choices are nearing, and Al Qaeda's potency hangs in the balance.

## THE OBAMA ADMINISTRATION'S INHERITANCE

Regional experts initially estimated roughly $5 billion per year for ten years to create the basic trappings of a state able to counter any Taliban or Al Qaeda threat. Agriculture, which is the crux of Afghanistan's economy; road building, to link major hubs and enable the economy; and creating army and police forces for internal security would be the nascent government's functioning priorities in addition to providing justice, education, and health systems. The result would be a center strong enough to keep law and order, but also not strong enough to undermine Afghanistan's historically preponderant tribal system. Afghanistan would not become a superpower, or even a modern country, but it would be functional, stable, and secure.[6]

The Bush administration, however, abruptly turned to Iraq. Exploiting this neglect, the Taliban and their allies began an insurgency. By 2009, though incapable of ruling, the insurgents were positioned to erase much of the United States' and Afghan central government's progress to date and severely hinder, if not outright block, future U.S. and allied efforts. Admiral Mullen, chairman of the Joint Chiefs of Staff, called the situation "serious" and "deteriorating."[7]

### The State Level

The growth of the Afghan economy post-9/11 has been the shining light in what has largely proved to be a long and dark tunnel to a brighter future. The Afghan economy has continued to expand at double-digit rates since 2005, and the 2009–2010 fiscal year saw a stunning 22.5 percent increase in real gross domestic product (GDP). Inflation has generally remained low, and was a mere 2 percent in fiscal 2009–2010. Roughly 85 percent of the population has access to basic health care, which is up from only 8 percent in 2001.[8]

The average Afghan's plight, however, remains dim. Approximately 2.8 million people are internally displaced. Unemployment is at roughly 40 percent. Nearly 40 percent of the country is in extreme, abject poverty—which equates to living on approximately one dollar per day without electricity or clean running water. Roughly one-third of the population is literate, and illiteracy is at roughly 89 percent in the rural countryside, which is where roughly 75 percent of the population lives.[9]

Capital flight is massive. Afghanistan's 2009 GDP totaled roughly $13.5 billion, and nearly $3 billion is estimated to have legally left the country. Such a large amount cannot, however, just be attributed to drug money moving to safer havens. Diverted U.S. aid and logistics dollars must also be involved.[10]

Opium production, which some estimates place at more than 50 percent of the economy, denies the Afghan government revenue.[11] Not only does poppy earn significantly more than any other crop, but it can be stored for years in paste form, which can then be brought to market anytime after harvest, thus making it an ideal product in an unstable conflict zone. Even if it is supplanted today, its detrimental effect upon state revenue is likely to remain for years.[12]

Even if the opium problem were tamed, the central government still lacks a significant revenue collection enterprise. Afghanistan's budget for the 2008–2009 fiscal year, for example, was $7.2 billion, but its tax system corralled only $1 billion in 2009. The Afghan central government remains utterly dependent upon foreign aid.[13]

International donations, however, are flagging. Of the five international donor conferences held since 9/11, roughly $11 billion of the $44.5 billion governments claim to have pledged has actually been the re-announcing of existing pledges instead of new monetary contributions. The practical result is that Afghanistan's National Development Strategy, a document approved by the international community outlining the development priorities over the next four years, was underfunded by $3.1 billion in 2009. A $22.3 billion shortfall is projected from 2010 to 2014.[14]

Afghanistan's natural environment holds great potential. Vast mineral riches—primarily consisting of the world's last untapped reserves of iron, copper, lithium, gold, uranium, precious gems, and other raw materials—were discovered in 2010; they could be worth up to nearly $1 trillion. Roughly 15 trillion cubic feet of natural gas have been discovered. Afghanistan also has more than 1.5 billion barrels of oil.

These finds could become a sustainable new backbone for an economy heretofore dominated by agriculture, opium, and war. Afghanistan, however, lacks a technological, legal, and business infrastructure sufficiently devoid of corruption to develop this potential. Most likely, at least five to ten years, and probably decades, will be necessary to unlock it.[15]

Ironically, these finds are likely to prove a boon to the militants. Such a geographically-based mass of potential wealth is likely to spur more factional fighting for control. From Al Qaeda's perspective, its followers will likely either believe the United States knew about these natural deposits in advance, or they will portray Obama's 2010 surge as an effort to secure U.S. exploitation. Either way, fighting will likely intensify and development will likely be delayed.

Meanwhile, the Afghan state finds its once substantial domestic and international support evaporating. In the wake of the Taliban's fall, the U.S.-backed government initially claimed victory by its mere existence. Roughly a decade later, it must deliver to meet people's rising expectations, needs, and wants. The state's capacity to do this, however, is virtually nonexistent.[16]

President Karzai, derisively dubbed the "mayor of Kabul," heads a national government whose writ effectively ends at the Kabul city limits. Provincial officials, often the only sign of the national government in Afghanistan's predominantly rural society, are not safe in their capitals. They rarely leave these isolated islands of government without U.S. protection.[17]

When the government is actually present, the Afghan population largely perceives the Karzai government, whom the British assess to have "lost all trust," as feckless and corrupt. Petty corruption is estimated to have doubled from 2007 to 2010, and, according to Transparency International, Afghanistan ranked second in corruption in 2009 only to Somalia after placing forty-second in 2005.[18] U.S. and NATO military command surveys of the Afghan public in 2010 found that 83 percent of Afghans reported that corruption affected their daily lives. A 2009 survey by the United Nations Office of Drugs and Crime found that the scale of the corruption equaled nearly 25 percent of Afghanistan's economic output, or roughly $2.5 billion, which makes bribery rival Afghanistan's opium trade proceeds of $2.8 billion. Roughly one in seven Afghans was asked for bribes when they needed a document or a license, medical treatment, or to have their rights protected in court. In a country with per capita economic output of just $425 per year, the average bribe was $160, a crippling tax on some of the world's poorest people. The September 2010 run on Kabul Bank, one of the nation's most prominent and which was shown to have engaged in corrupt lending practices favoring politically connected personalities, to include one of President Karzai's brothers, shows that Afghanistan's corruption is not just individual but systemic. American contracting practices, which inject large quantities of cash into a weak state with a strong presidency for a variety of services, without which U.S.-led forces cannot function, only further enables graft while generating further political instability by enriching some Afghans and enraging others.[19]

The Taliban have worked hard to undermine what little Afghan national government capacity does exist. From spring 2009 to spring 2010, the Taliban increased by 45 percent their systematic assassination campaign against lower-level government officials and workers such as policemen and municipal officials, who often lack the bodyguards and other protection of more senior officials. This renders existing government structures dysfunctional while making replacement personnel harder to find.[20]

The U.S. Agency for International Development's (USAID) civil service training institute responded with a goal of graduating 15,000 to 16,000 civil servants before the end of 2010. Despite training large numbers of people, the threat levels make it difficult to find people willing to serve in the most fought-over provinces, which are where the need for government services is most crucial. As of 2010, for example, only roughly 25 percent of the provincial jobs in Kandahar had been filled, and the figures for Helmand were little better. Hand in glove, the Taliban have been increasingly targeting contractors, who actually implement USAID's efforts, with one hundred killed in just the last six months of 2009 out of a total of 289 since 2001.[21]

The international community's efforts to build governance capacity are a double-edged sword. On the one hand, they train and help equip thousands of would-be civil servants. On the other hand, the salaries offered by numerous development-oriented nongovernmental organizations, the U.S. armed forces, civilian components of the U.S. government, international governmental organizations, and other foreign entities are disproportionately high compared to those of Afghan civil servants, and so the cream of Afghan society is drawn away from serving its government. Afghan civil servants providing key government services, for example, can earn anywhere from $50 to $200 depending upon their level and their duties, but someone can make $80,000 working for the foreigners simply as a translator.[22]

The popular public perception is that Afghanistan has received billions in international aid, a view which is rooted in fact, and so public expectations for Afghanistan's material improvement and government services have risen dramatically. Such a massive quantity of money has the potential to dramatically impact such a poor country. Unfortunately, as of 2010, there is little to show for it in people's daily lives. Kabul only obtained twenty-four-hour electricity in 2009. Modern and inclusive education and health systems are still lacking. Agriculture reform and modernization in Afghanistan's agrarian society are absent. A widespread road network to enable economic prosperity is still largely missing.[23] Conversely, an exceptionally rich minority is now building opulent "poppy palace" mansions in Kabul.

As explained in spring 2010 by a commander from the Taliban—who not only have a reputation for honest and fair, if somewhat ruthless, adjudication consistent with the Quran and tribal codes, but have also set up a complaint department for commanders who abuse the populace—"People don't trust foreigners because they are backing warlords. People are fed up with crime and brutality and that's a big problem for the Americans. We're well positioned."[24]

Taliban recruitment directly benefits. A congressionally mandated Pentagon report in spring 2010 notes that "a ready supply of recruits is drawn from the frustrated population, where insurgents exploit poverty, tribal friction, and lack of governance to grow their ranks." Bounties for NATO soldiers and equipment are used to both motivate and sustain existing and new fighters, a step which also undermines U.S. jobs programs meant to dissuade low-level nonideological fighters suspected of fighting, out of necessity, for money.[25]

Taliban shadow governments have strengthened. These can include courts, jails for criminals, detention centers for Afghan national government soldiers, tax levies, basic social services, and conscription. By 2010, the Taliban had shadow governors in thirty-three of Afghanistan's thirty-four provinces.[26]

The disputed 2009 presidential election, which, in contrast to international criticism, the Afghan public generally perceived to be more or less fair and valid despite roughly one-fourth of the ballots being thrown out, complicates the entire post-Taliban democracy, not just Karzai's administration, by raising questions of legitimacy.[27] In the eyes of the central government's supporters, the United States has a valid local partner, albeit one whose ineptitude taints the U.S.-led foreign presence by extension. In the eyes of insurgents and their potential supporters, however, the electoral corruption charges only provide increased motivation, and it makes it less likely they will settle for negotiations with an illegitimate power center in lieu of total victory.

The fall 2010 parliamentary election has only added fuel to insurgent claims of the Karzai government's weakness and illegitimacy. Roughly one-fourth of the ballots were eliminated due to fraud. Several elected candidates were disqualified by the Electoral Complaints Commission, and explanations were not always provided.[28]

Apart from the obvious fraud, the credibility of the national government was also undermined due to the election's skewed results. Many parliamentary candidates were too fearful to campaign due to the deteriorating security situation, which prevented at least 938 of 6,853 polling centers from even opening— most of them in the south and east where the insurgency is strongest and thus a legitimate government presence is even more crucial.[29] In the Pashtun-majority Ghazni province where Pashtuns held six seats in the previous parliament, for example, the eleven lawmakers elected belonged to the Hazara ethnic minority because insurgent activity derailed the vote in most Pashtun areas. Writ large, Pashtuns, Afghanistan's largest ethnic community, lost at least twenty seats to other groups, an outcome that has stirred up ethnic tensions.[30]

Underwriting everything, Afghanistan's security situation continues to trend negatively. After the 2001 U.S. invasion swept away the Taliban regime, the insurgents controlled ten districts by 2010. The Afghan government was on the defensive in 92 of 121 of the districts deemed crucial to stabilizing the country and defeating the insurgency, out of Afghanistan's total of 398. Nowhere did the Afghan government hold full control or did the population completely support the U.S.-backed central government. In fact, while the Afghan people either supported or were sympathetic to the insurgents in forty-eight districts, popular support for Karzai's government was strong in only twenty-nine districts, and the population was neutral in forty-four districts.[31]

Mullah Omar has announced that the Taliban have embarked on a strategy of attrition through a counter-surge. The 2009–2010 seasonal movement of fighters from FATA to Afghanistan proved the largest to date.[32] In a guerilla war like Afghanistan, such a strategy is aimed at diminishing the foreign forces' supporting public's will to continue by increasing casualties and creating perceptions of a stalemate. Concurrently, the insurgents have also strategically dispersed their forces to spread thin the foreign presence, to preclude the foreign forces from concentrating strength and being effective in any one locale while increasing U.S. and allied casualties.[33] Following the U.S. invasion of Helmand, the Taliban opened a front in the previously peaceful and lightly defended Pashtun-minority north, most notably in the provinces of Badakhshan, Balkh, Samangan, Kunduz, Taqhar, and Baghlan. Strategically situated Baghlan, which controls the northern end of the Salang pass linking Afghanistan's north with the rest of the country while also serving as Afghanistan's gateway to Central Asia, saw insurgent attacks more than double in the third quarter of 2010 as the insurgency has diversified to include previously anti-Taliban Tajiks and Uzbeks by tapping into disillusionment with the Karzai government. Northern U.S. supply routes intended to bypass Pakistan are now threatened.[34]

A spate of attacks in 2010 has also disrupted Afghanistan's west, most notably in Herat Province. U.S. bases as well as Afghan facilities have been targeted. The formerly largely peaceful West had been under consideration for being turned over to Afghan control.[35]

The insurgents have also reorganized. Press reporting from late 2010 notes that insurgents are increasingly setting aside historic rivalries. Though commonly inspired, previously distinct operational rivals—HiG, the Haqqani network, and the Taliban—have begun granting one another safe passage through their areas of control, sharing new recruits, and coordinating their propaganda responses to U.S. and allied actions on an ad hoc, informal basis. Islamabad agrees with the new U.S. and NATO assessments.[36]

Insurgent violence has grown faster than the increased pace of U.S.-led violence and forces. Overall, attacks on the U.S. and allied forces rose 300 percent from 2008 to 2009. Total attacks against coalition forces, to include roadside improvised explosive device bombings (IEDs), increased by roughly 83 percent from September 2009 to March 2010 compared to the year prior.[37]

In particular, roadside IED bombings skyrocketed 94 percent in spring 2010 compared to spring 2009. April 2010, by which time IED attacks had increased 236 percent compared to one year prior, witnessed 1,059 IED attacks, one of the highest numbers on record, and was well on track to beat 2009's IED total of 7,228. By contrast, 2003 witnessed only 81 such attacks.

President Karzai has issued a decree banning the import of ammonium nitrate, the primary ingredient in insurgent IEDs that is also a key ingredient in Afghanistan's most common fertilizer. Despite a U.S.-led effort dubbed Global Shield to curtail shipments from Pakistan's single manufacturer as well as the ammonium nitrate and precursor chemical trade from European allies, staggering amounts of ammonium nitrate flow from Pakistan despite an ostensibly sizable Pakistani security presence in the FATA and at the border. In fall 2010, for example, U.S. forces made a seizure in excess of 50,000 pounds. As of late 2010, the United States estimated that hundreds of tons flowed in from Pakistan each month.[38]

IED attacks are the equivalent of "the surface-to-air missile system for the mujahideen back in the Soviet era." Nearly two-thirds of U.S. and allied combat fatalities are caused by IEDs. Militarily, such a weapon gives the Taliban tactical advantage. Politically, IEDs give the Taliban the strategic initiative through antagonizing the U.S. public by increasing U.S. casualties while creating a sense of inevitable hopelessness about the war effort.[39]

Suicide bombings, unknown throughout the anti-Soviet jihad as well as during the subsequent civil war, are now commonplace. By spring 2010 they were occurring at the rate of about three per week. The UN attributes the increasing numbers of complex attacks combining suicide bombers and small-arms fire to increased links between Taliban fighters and Al Qaeda.[40]

The Taliban's perseverance and the fighting's intensity has spiked U.S. and allied casualty levels. It took 2,520 days for the war to take five hundred American lives, but it took only 627 days for the war to take the next five hundred. The U.S. casualty rate doubled from 2009 to 2010 and broke one thousand in June 2010, the deadliest year to date. More than an additional one thousand NATO troops have been killed since 9/11. Of these two thousand plus international losses, of which roughly 60 percent were American, almost half occurred in 2009 and 2010. In 2010, on average, two soldiers died each day.[41]

The U.S.-led international forces, taking an enemy-centric approach, have also brought a new ferocity to the fight as of 2009–2010 that has resulted in extensive insurgent losses. Special operations forces—a NATO-led special operations force, an all-American unit, and a team of Afghan forces with U.S. advisors—have been killing four to six targets per day, a pace three to four times more intense than Iraq ever saw. Nearly four thousand SOF missions from May to August 2010 killed hundreds of mid-level leaders inside Afghanistan from the Taliban and the Haqqani network while killing over one thousand rank-and-file troops and detaining more than another thousand. Over a 90-day period ending November 11, 2010, NATO statistics show "Special Operations Forces were averaging seventeen missions a night, conducting 1,572 operations over three months that resulted in 368 insurgent leaders killed or captured, and 968 lower-level insurgents killed and 2,477 captured."[42]

These 5 percent of U.S. troops, which are credited with racking up 90 percent of the operational successes in enemy-centric efforts, have been complemented by the surge's conventional forces, which have conducted population-centric efforts throughout the country. The strategically important southern provinces of Helmand, Kandahar, and Nimruz now have a sizable international presence where nothing substantial had previously existed. U.S. forces have also moved into the mountainous east, particularly Konar province. As of fall 2010, these forces, for the first time, are backed by U.S. battle tanks.[43]

Despite taking heavy losses, U.S. military and intelligence officials assess that the insurgency is maintaining its resilience. "Taliban commanders who are captured or killed are often replaced in a matter of days. Insurgent groups that have ceded territory . . . seem content to melt away temporarily, leaving behind operatives to carry out assassinations or to intimidate villagers while waiting for an opportunity to return." Senior insurgent leadership continues to provide strategic guidance.[44]

Such heightened violence has increased collateral damage. Overall, the United Nations estimates that civilian casualties rose 20 percent in the first ten months of 2010 compared to the same period in 2009. This equated to more than five thousand civilian deaths.[45]

Responsibility, however, is not evenly divided.[46] UN statistics show that insurgent-induced casualties rose by 25 percent in the first ten months of 2010 as compared to 2009,[47] and U.S. and UN statistics more broadly show that insurgents are responsible for 80 to 90 percent of all civilian casualties. In 2009, the Taliban killed at least 1,630 Afghan civilians, which is a 41 percent increase over 2008 and three times as many as U.S. and allied foreign forces.[48] The UN reports that suicide and IED attacks, which are aimed at foreign forces but are often carried out where Afghan civilians congregate, "caused more civilian casualties than [any] other tactic."[49] While not a viable long-run strategy to wean the population away from the Karzai government and its U.S. backers and win public loyalty, such coercive tactics disrupt government aid efforts and only further limit the national government's ability to provide services to its people, who commonly blame the government for not preventing the attacks.

Conversely, even as U.S. forces have surged, the United Nations cited an 18 percent drop in civilians killed by U.S. and NATO forces for a total of 742.[50] Even as the number of security incidents (ambushes, roadside bombings, suicide bombings, rocket attacks, and so forth) rose to a high of 6,716 events,[51] the total number of 2010 incidents in which U.S. or NATO forces wounded or killed noncombatants declined by 10 percent compared to 2009. Instances of insurgent-caused casualties, by contrast, rose by 5 percent.[52]

Inadequate troop levels, however, still force a heavy reliance on airpower. U.S. and allied warplanes flew 1,462 close air support missions in 2009, a 25 percent increase over 2008.[53] Airstrikes, as well as ordnance expended, were up 50 percent in the second half of 2010 with roughly 2,600 attack sorties, and Secretary Gates ordered a second carrier to take up station off the coast of Pakistan to keep up with ever-increasing demand.[54]

Though the number of civilians killed by U.S. and NATO fixed-wing aircraft declined by 65 percent in the first ten months of 2010 as the volume of strikes rose, such highly visible attacks, which cause 60 percent of Afghanistan's war-related casualties, have caused a burgeoning sense of ill will toward U.S. and allied forces. After several high profile incidents, U.S. generals have imposed restrictions on the use of airpower. As articulated by Gen. David Barno when he commanded U.S. forces in Afghanistan, he was "very concerned that if the killing of local Taliban leaders with airstrikes produced civilian casualties, the tactical benefit would not offset the strategic damage it did."[55] An April 2010 study by the staff of the U.S.-led International Security Assistance Force (ISAF) then-commander, Gen. Stanley McChrystal, who has dubbed the results "insurgent math," showed that there was a 25 to 65 percent spike in violence for up to five months after NATO forces, by whatever means, killed civilians.[56]

Even though public opinion surveys show that Afghans continue to blame the Taliban rather than NATO forces for the country's violence and instability, U.S. and allied forces continue to take a disproportionate share of the blame for civilian losses, particularly through airstrikes. Taliban-caused casualties have yet to meaningfully backfire on the insurgents, as evidenced by their ample ability to recruit and surge forces. In fact, anecdotal evidence indicates that when civilian-killing IEDs do explode, the Taliban will often claim that it was the Americans who planted the bombs, and "many people believe them." October 2010 polling in Afghanistan's southern provinces showed that only 31 percent of Afghans believed that NATO forces were protecting the population, and 65 percent said that foreign forces kill more civilians than do the Taliban.[57]

Negative Afghan assumptions about the United States only increase the U.S. challenge. October 2010 polling in Afghanistan's southern provinces showed that 72 percent say foreigners disrespect their religion. In Helmand, only 8 percent out of a sample of one thousand young men knew of the 9/11 attacks. "The poll results convey a stark reality about this war: People in the Pashtun region of southern Afghanistan resent foreign fighters. Most don't comprehend why they have come or how they might offer a better future than would the Taliban. They feel that America and its allies don't respect their traditions."[58]

Unfortunately, "the alternative is popular support for the insurgency, which renders the ISAF mission unachievable." The number of Afghans who rated U.S. and NATO forces as "good" or "very good" dropped from 38 percent in

December 2009 when President Obama announced his new strategy to 29 percent in March 2010, at which point the U.S. troop surge was starting to flow
and violence was rising. In October 2010, separate polling found that 50 percent
think recent military operations are bad for the Afghan people, 58 percent think
it is wrong to work with foreign forces, and 55 percent oppose military operations against the Taliban in their area.[59] "'Many people now perceive ISAF as
an occupying force,' said Anne Jones, a humanitarian activist and author who
has lived in Afghanistan. '[They] are no longer part of the solution; they have
become part of the problem.'"[60]

If Afghanistan is to be compared to Iraq's darkest days in 2005–2006, at
least 600,000 troops should have been present at the Obama administration's outset. The new administration, however, found only 30,000. As of 2010, the start
date for the administration's surge, the total international presence of 150,000, of
which roughly 40,000 had national exceptions barring them from combat, was
supported by still growing and largely unreliable Afghan police and military
forces of roughly 200,000—numbers which are still roughly only one- to two-
thirds of the prescribed total at best.[61] Because the requisite troop levels necessary to negate the need for airstrikes and the bar for political will to take extra
casualties are so high, and U.S.-induced civilian casualties are unavoidable, sentiments toward the United States and its international allies are likely to continue
to be negative as U.S. forces remain strong enough to cause pain but not strong
enough to solve the problem.

U.S. and allied force capacity has been so inadequate that Taliban-run protection rackets are commonplace. Millions of dollars have been funneled into
Taliban coffers through U.S. and internationally funded development projects
that routinely endure a 20 percent "protection tax." Logistical and security contractors, whose total numbers rival if not surpass U.S. government personnel,
routinely pay this protection money to Taliban and Al Qaeda–associated militants in order to ensure their survival and mission accomplishment, without
which U.S.-led efforts would fail. In fact, Taliban are regularly paid to tip off
trucking contractors when attacks on a convoy are planned, but that information is not passed to U.S. military convoys, whose vehicles are routinely struck
by IEDs.[62] Unfortunately, local security personnel routinely undergo little or no
vetting, making such practices difficult to counter effectively.

Enduring critical troop shortages ensures that the presence of the private
security forces that directly enable this corruption remains ubiquitous. The
Afghan Ministry of the Interior states that there are fifty-two licensed private
security companies and an unknown number of unlicensed firms performing
security work, which is primarily guarding embassies, bases, convoys, and
development projects. While some estimates place total private security

personnel at 26,000 people, 19,000 of whom work with the U.S. military, other estimates run as high as 40,000.

President Karzai's August 2010 directive to disband private security contractors by December 2010, which was subsequently rolled back to February 2011, is a game-changing decision. Private security guards were to be restricted to compounds and buildings, and they were not to be authorized to escort supply, diplomatic, or nongovernmental organization (NGO) convoys. Afghan private guards are to have the option of joining the Ministry of the Interior, which has offered to buy the contractors' weapons and equipment. Foreign security guards in the convoy protection business will presumably take up other duties.[63]

Short-term security dynamics are unlikely to favor the U.S.-led effort. The burden for Afghanistan's fledgling security forces, which were already overburdened when augmented by private security firms filling a security vacuum, is only increased before they reach critical mass and can assume these additional responsibilities in an orderly manner. The demand for U.S. troops to fulfill these escort and base security roles will spike just as they are needed elsewhere, such as Kandahar, during the U.S. surge window. Large numbers, possibly thousands, of armed indigenous men will likely become unemployed and ripe for recruitment by the insurgency.[64]

Long-term U.S. strategic maneuvering room is also likely to decrease. Afghanistan has multiple centers of money and influence. Until this decree, the international community repeatedly went to other domestic actors—warlords, tribal figures, provincial personalities, and so on—to obtain labor, security, influence, and political access. Centralizing security in an actively contested country significantly strengthens Karzai's control over development projects, cash flows, and provincial security initiatives, such as the Petraeus-favored tribal militias. This increased control over political favors and patronage allows Karzai to lead Afghanistan as a more unified actor while simultaneously strengthening his own hand over his domestic rivals. With the international community now increasingly channeled through Karzai's government, and thus dependent upon him, Karzai is better positioned to negotiate on more equal footing with both the international community and the United States. The latter, from Karzai's point of view, has proven an unreliable and inconsistent partner leading a coalition that fails to speak with a single, coherent voice or act in unison, and this stop gives Karzai leverage.[65]

As conveyed by General Petraeus in a fall 2010 television interview, the net result is that U.S. efforts have not "reversed the [insurgents'] momentum in all areas by any means. In some we have reversed it, in some we have blunted it, in some perhaps the Taliban are still trying to expand." As expounded by a senior U.S. military official, "The Taliban [aren't] strong enough to take over the country. But they don't have to be. They are strong enough to end its progress—and they are doing that relatively successfully."

Indeed, following roughly a decade of ever-increasing U.S-led efforts to suppress them, the Taliban and their militant allies view Afghanistan's expanded and escalating violence as a sign pointing toward their ultimate victory. As one U.S. military official noted to the press, "They don't believe they are losing yet." The fight is highly likely to continue.[66]

## The International Level

There is no international consensus actively aiding Afghanistan, which is a pawn among local powers with conflicting relationships. In fact, rising anticipation of a U.S. withdrawal has sparked increasingly intense jostling among both regional and foreign powers over how to manipulate the impending U.S. drawdown to their benefit and capitalize on the emerging post-U.S. political dynamics. Little, if any, of this maneuvering is to U.S. benefit.[67]

Iran's sway is increasing. Akin to Pakistan, it is playing a double game. As of 2010, the Iranians "literally have the ability to ratchet this thing [the Afghan insurgency] up or down at their will, with not much stopping them."[68]

On the one hand, Iran is nurturing a relationship with the Afghan insurgency. This malign influence has mainly consisted of supplying rifles, ammunition, some medium and heavy machine guns, and some IED equipment. A small number of Taliban has been sent to Iran for military training in weapons, sniper rifles, guerilla warfare tactics, and munitions handling. Iran's paramilitary Qods Force has been helping to train the Taliban and direct some attacks, primarily in western and southern Afghanistan, though some evidence also suggests a presence in the north as well. Press reporting notes that Iranian military advisors have also been training Taliban fighters in Afghanistan on the use of surface-to-air missiles, which are a potential game-changer, to U.S. detriment, if the insurgents are able to use such weapons effectively. Despite U.S. worries, as of early 2011, shoulder-fired antiaircraft missiles and Iraq-style, Iranian-produced explosively formed projectiles (EFPs), the particularly potent IEDs intended to defeat U.S. armor, have yet to materialize on the battlefield.[69]

On the other hand, Iran has been nurturing a relationship with the Afghan government. In Afghanistan's western provinces, Iran has become Afghanistan's leading investor in the sensitive areas of electricity and water. Iran has also maintained a nonhostile stewardship over its 1 million Afghan refugees, and Iran's influence is felt through remittances and the possibility of forced expulsion. To curry favor with key personalities, Iran has provided cash ranging from $1 million to $6 million every other month to officials in the Afghan presidential palace.[70] As shown by Iran's surprise blockade of winter 2009–2010 fuel imports, Iran is also willing to use its economic links coercively as well.[71]

Iran also has leverage over key catalysts. Iran can try to engage the United Front, the last vestiges of its former Northern Alliance ally that now forms the anti-Karzai parliamentary bloc. Having renewed lapsed ties with Pakistan post-9/11, Iran can also help increase or decrease Pakistani vulnerability to U.S. pressure on Afghan policy.[72]

While Iran could use its power and influence conducive to U.S. interests, the U.S.-Iran struggle, largely centered on Iran's nuclear program, makes Afghanistan a pawn. Iran will almost certainly seek to avoid a strong, pliant American client state to avoid U.S.-dominated geographic encirclement. Iran is effectively "'playing both sides in the Afghan war by supplying arms and training that help the Taliban keep the war going, but not enough to help them win power.' At the same time, the Iranians are inflicting casualties on the United States 'to put a check on the West's ability to dominate and to embarrass the West and to string'" out the fighting to U.S. strategic disadvantage at Iranian gain.[73]

India's strategic presence and sway are also increasing. At the public level, India, in a hearts-and-minds offensive to strengthen old ties, has roughly four thousand personnel throughout the country engaging in nation-building, and India spends roughly $1.2 billion per year, its largest foreign aid program, on health care, food, and infrastructure in Afghanistan. Hand in glove, there are a large number of Indian intelligence operatives in Afghanistan working to counter Pakistani influence and place limits on Taliban militants. To support this strategic presence, India has opened an airbase in Tajikistan, its first outside of India.

Pakistan, however, has not accepted this Indian presence. India blames ISI for the 2008 blast at the Indian embassy, which was carried out by the Haqqani network and killed fifty-eight, including the Indian defense attaché. Though the Indian government has yet to assign blame for the second attack on its Kabul-based embassy, killing seventeen in October 2009, Pakistan is suspect. Per regional affairs expert Ahmed Rashid, "Kabul is the new Kashmir. . . . This is where the real proxy war between the two countries is being fought."[74]

As of 2010, Pakistan, a non-unitary actor, is still firmly driven by the double-game dynamics that empower its army at the expense of the civilian government and that keep its antagonism with India alive. The November 2008 Mumbai attacks that killed over 170 and closed India's financial capital for three days were executed entirely by Pakistanis and wiped away at least five years of diplomatic progress. The October 2009 bombing in Kabul then came one day after Pakistan's foreign minister, Shah Mehmood Qureshi, announced that relations between India and Pakistan were thawing and that peace talks might resume. With Pakistan's perception of the U.S. commitment to Afghanistan, and thus to Pakistan and the rest of the region, in doubt, Pakistan's actions vis-à-vis India in Afghanistan, as well as its general disposition to the region, is unlikely to change.[75]

Regional U.S. strategic capacity remains unsteady. In Pakistan, which as of 2010 funneled roughly 75 percent of U.S. supplies from Karachi's port through the Khyber Pass, U.S. supply routes have become increasingly untenable due to the Taliban's sustained campaign to cut these primary lines as they pass through Pakistan, particularly in the FATA. Russia appears to have backed off of pressuring Kyrgyzstan since 2008 to close Manas airbase, a crucial air hub supporting Afghanistan, but Kyrgyz domestic instability, as evidenced by the April 2010 uprising that deposed President Kurmanbek Bakiyev—a corrupt dictator whom the new government says the United States placated at the expense of democracy for its base—has made that base's future uncertain. Meanwhile, the United States has been casting around for overland routes through Russia and former Soviet Central Asia, which is in Russia's sphere of influence, while U.S.-Russian ties are at a post–Cold War low.[76]

Key U.S. allies in Europe are wavering. A fall 2010 European Union report stated that the international effort in Afghanistan is failing and the time has arrived to begin looking for an exit strategy. All of the key combat contingents—the Netherlands with 2,200 troops, Italy with 3,400 troops, Canada with 2,800 troops, and England with nearly 10,000 troops—have either announced withdrawal dates, none of which extends past 2014 at the latest, or have completed their departures. Interim additional contributions in response to U.S. calls were tendered largely in the hundreds vice thousands, even for civilian experts, and the refusal to curtail national exceptions has limited the utility of what forces remain. Germany has vetoed dispatching NATO's rapid-reaction force.[77]

Barring a significant turn of events, this situation is highly unlikely to change. As stated to the press by Rob de Wijk, a member of the Atlantic Council's Strategic Advisors Group, NATO's "shift in emphasis from protecting territory to defending strategic interests requires NATO to transform the [territorial] armed forces of all member states into deployable armed forces, remove obstacles for risky 'away' operations and forge a new understanding of solidarity." Yet, "Even with their Afghan commitments, total defense spending among NATO's European members fell from $311 billion in 2001 to $272 billion in 2009." The most powerful and capable members, such as England, continue to significantly cut defense spending in response to economic pressures, and the organization as a whole continues to scale back.[78]

The announced U.S. withdrawal, regardless of when it actually happens, has brought the same key pre-9/11 players to the fore—India, Russia, Iran, and Pakistan. The rapid return of pre-9/11 actors and dynamics shows how little the United States has structurally altered the international system to achieve its goals and institutionally sustain that success. The region's future, though uncertain, is foreboding.[79]

## MOVING FORWARD

President Bush's post-9/11 invasion combated both Al Qaeda and Afghanistan's Taliban, Al Qaeda's state protectors. Both were Afghanistan-based. The two were inseparable.

The core of Al Qaeda, however, is now primarily in Pakistan, not Afghanistan. Why is it relevant to the U.S.-Al Qaeda struggle if Mullah Omar's Taliban and associated militants, such as the forces under Gulbuddin Hekmatyar and Jalaluddin Haqqani, rule Afghanistan? Why must U.S. forces mount sustained combat operations against them in Afghanistan if the core of Al Qaeda, which poses the direct threat to the U.S. homeland, is in Pakistan?

### Initial Choices—The State Level, Rejected

Vice President Joseph Biden's "counterterrorism approach" recognizes this conundrum and advocates narrowly focused operations against Al Qaeda to achieve the ultimate intent of the 2001–2002 U.S. invasion—defeating Al Qaeda terrorists to prevent them from killing Americans. This strategy involves a limited troop presence in Afghanistan with a heavy emphasis on pinpoint attacks, largely via drones and special operations forces, against Al Qaeda in Pakistan. Meanwhile, U.S.-trained Afghan forces would have the lead in engaging the Taliban-led insurgency, which would be countered by U.S. forces only as necessary as it impacted U.S. capability to strike Osama bin Laden's Pakistan-based Al Qaeda.

All terrorist entities must execute core functions. They must manifest an organizational structure consistent with their stated political goals and then raise and move money, weapons, and recruits to sustain it. They must also communicate, both internally to execute operational activity and externally through terrorist attacks and propaganda to communicate their political message, or their viability as an agent of political change is lost.

State pressure hinders these efforts. As the terrorists are forced underground, their ability to raise and move money, weapons, and recruits is hampered. Communication becomes a potentially mortal threat in the face of government monitoring, for it can unravel the entire group's organizational structure and membership in addition to its activities.

State authorities need voluminous, time-sensitive intelligence to identify the suspects, confirm guilt, locate, and strike terrorist operatives. To a certain extent, this can certainly come from state monitoring of electronic communications, but that can easily be defeated through countermeasures, such as employing couriers instead of using electronic devices. Humans must provide the rest.

The limiting factor on U.S. efforts to capture and kill Al Qaeda operatives in a timely manner is the ability of U.S. intelligence to identify, validate, and locate targets. The absence of a substantial unilateral capability would make the

United States dependent upon the services of third-party countries. Their differing interests and capabilities, as amply demonstrated by Pakistan's double game, however, rule them out as reliable U.S. surrogates. The Pakistani public's conflicted sentiments toward Pakistan's various militant groups further complicate the picture.

A unilateral U.S. presence is necessary, and it must be focused against Pakistan-based Al Qaeda and its terrorist allies. Pakistan, however, has forbidden extensive U.S. deployments on its soil. This U.S. force presence must therefore be based in Afghanistan, the area most directly adjacent to the problem areas inside Pakistan.

Two target sets must be pursued simultaneously. Senior leadership guiding the organization must, obviously, be struck. More crucial to degrading organizational capacity, however, is to also attack the terrorist entity's battle staff at the middle-management level. This not only hinders the organizational machinery in place to execute the group's core functions, but it also eliminates those likely to replace senior leaders.

This counterterrorism approach is efficient and politically savvy. The United States would be able to leverage limited and highly skilled U.S. forces, as well as technology, their chief advantage, directly against Al Qaeda, the United States' foremost enemy. Given the still significant and lingering U.S. troop commitment in Iraq, whose subsequent drawdown depends upon events beyond U.S. control, this economy-of-force approach stays within U.S. resource limits. Shifting the bulk of the fighting to indigenous forces also shirks the bulk of political-support-sapping casualties, thus making this long-term fight easier to sustain. Leaving indigenous personnel to sort out their own disputes also prevents the United States from becoming entangled in nation-building and enables U.S. efforts to remain focused on core U.S. interests. Unpalatable political and policy choices that impact both domestic and foreign affairs, stemming from allocating the United States' limited political, economic, and military resources, will be made less likely if not altogether avoided.

The cornerstone argument supporting this position is that allowing Al Qaeda's local insurgent allies to succeed in their Afghanistan-centric aims will not hinder the U.S. effort against Al Qaeda. Implicit in this argument are three distinct but intertwined assumptions: that Al Qaeda is and operates as a terrorist entity, that it can be separated from its local insurgent militant allies, upon whom it depends for survival, and that Afghan forces can secure their own country against a Taliban-led insurgency, thus freeing up U.S. forces to focus on Al Qaeda in Pakistan. None, however, is valid.

Mullah Omar's Taliban rebuffed the United States to the point that they were willing to confront the United States directly rather than surrender Osama bin Laden. U.S. efforts have been unable to force a formal break after nearly a decade. Any claims by a new Taliban regime about not supporting Al Qaeda could not be accepted at face value. Even if it did not actively provide state sanctuary, a new Taliban regime would, at a minimum, either intentionally or unintentionally out of weakness, likely give Al Qaeda de facto safe haven.

Apart from political, cultural, and ideological factors, Al Qaeda and the Taliban are linked through mutually reinforcing operational activity. Post-9/11 Al Qaeda has interwoven with the Taliban and other insurgent forces. In addition to fielding some stand-alone field units, it provides training on IEDs and suicide bombings, intelligence, and propaganda, to help wage an increasingly lethal insurgency while still launching terrorist attacks abroad.

The counterterrorism approach's premise of indigenous forces broadly providing security to suppress the Taliban-led insurgency and sustain the U.S. presence is highly unlikely to be viable. As evidenced by its failure in Iraq, the very strengths cited by the advocates of the "counterterrorism approach"—a narrow political focus, economically employing military, economic, and political resources, and avoiding nation-building—nearly sank that U.S. effort. The rapid training and fielding of Iraqi forces while reducing U.S. efforts to strikes on Al Qaeda resulted in intensified sectarian conflict for which the nascent Iraqi armed forces were neither militarily capable nor politically motivated to handle. Only when the 2007 U.S. troop surge partnered with host-nation units, pacified population centers, and provided tangible political and security guarantees to build an enduring state structure—steps only a credible, powerful outside actor could take—was the problem set tamed.[80]

Afghanistan in 2010 is little different than pre-surge Iraq. It has an ethnically based insurgency, hostile and intervening neighbors, a weak state and weak armed forces, an insufficient U.S. force presence, a dismal economy, and a politically exacerbating Al Qaeda presence. The counterterrorism approach's virtues from the U.S. perspective—a narrow political focus, economically employing military, economic, and political resources, and avoiding nation-building— become vices in context.

The Taliban have three consecutive goals. They seek to expel foreign forces, the Karzai government's lifeline. They seek to undermine the Karzai regime's governance, which will turn both the Afghan public and foreign support away from it. And they ultimately seek to reestablish a state under Mullah Omar.[81]

A Taliban-dominated state would constitute a U.S. strategic defeat. Even though such a victory would be won largely on the backs of local Afghan insurgent foot soldiers, Al Qaeda would lay claim as the steward of global Islamic militancy and its history of alliance with the Taliban, and it would be able to convert this major political victory into increased operational capacity. Failing to subjugate Afghanistan's Taliban and associated local militants fails to shrink Al Qaeda's bubble of political and operational safety, and an unfettered Al Qaeda would almost certainly incubate to greater intensity. The United States would be deprived of a regional position to unilaterally secure its interests, and so it will fall victim to Pakistan's double game even more as U.S. dependency upon Pakistan's military and intelligence capabilities increases. Regional U.S. leverage, particularly over Afghanistan and Pakistan, would almost certainly decline as the U.S. commitment would appear minimalist and wavering just as pressure to act in the face of such a setback leaves the United States with few assets in the region, and thus limited immediate options. Serious threats of U.S. retribution—political, economic, or military—are unlikely to be a powerful lever following a U.S. military retreat. A U.S. defeat in Afghanistan would hand an enduring strategic advantage to Al Qaeda, which has refused to relinquish its fight against the United States.

Precluding a Taliban victory is not a sufficient step to defeating Al Qaeda, but it is a necessary step.[82] Al Qaeda and the Taliban are politically and operationally intertwined and have refused to separate, so a fight against one is a fight against both. The United States, therefore, must work through the Taliban and other indigenous Al Qaeda insurgent militant allies in order to get to Al Qaeda proper. Because Al Qaeda and its local militant allies were neither vigorously pursued nor manipulated against one another immediately following the U.S. invasion when the situation was still extremely fluid, U.S. power must now be reused to refight the same battle at an increased cost in blood and treasure to undo a new post-9/11 status quo inimical to U.S. interests.

### Initial Choices—The State Level, Accepted

When ordinary people lose faith in their government, and by extension its foreign supporters, "the lion of the people will turn on you," and all is lost. So, the Obama administration has embarked upon a national-level counterinsurgency campaign. This will bolster the Afghan national government's legitimacy, the singular pole around which all counterinsurgency strategy revolves, by providing a mutually reinforcing spiral of security, the primary effort of which underwrites all progress; economic development, which in turn provides incentive to the masses; and better governance, which enables and creates loyalty.[83] A successful effort will drive a wedge between the insurgents and the public and deprive the indigenous insurgents and Al Qaeda terrorists of political and geographic space as combative militant entities.

A counterinsurgency campaign, however, is not predicated upon the insurgents' destruction. This is impossible because they embody a political sentiment. Rather, it is premised upon co-opting and reintegrating them into a new political order.

The military impact is immense. The goal line shifts from a comprehensive and decisive military victory won and maintained by U.S. and foreign forces to reducing the insurgency "to a manageable level . . . that's not a strategic threat and can be managed by the Afghan army."[84] The Taliban has deep political roots among Afghanistan's Pashtuns, who represent roughly 40 percent of the population. Degrading the Taliban, vice defeating their forces, and bringing them to the table are feasible given U.S. military and economic constraints set against fungible U.S. political will.

Politically, the goal line also shifts. Rather than dictating terms through military subjugation of the enemy, herein defined as all actors combating the authority of the central government, a truce is reached. Political negotiation, not military action, manifests future political arrangements.

As explained by Abdullah Anas, a former cohort of bin Laden and mediator on behalf of the Taliban, "The Taliban are in a strong position now, but that doesn't mean they can control the state. Afghan people will not give them loyalty again and they know that."[85] An ABC/BBC poll in February 2009 found that 58 percent of respondents saw the Taliban as the greatest threat to Afghanistan, and that nearly 70 percent said it was "good" or "mostly good" that U.S. forces overthrew the Taliban, who garnered only a 7 percent favorability rating.[86]

Negotiations offer the Taliban the prospect of legitimacy and increased popular support. The administration's military-civilian surge to stanch security, governance, and economic trend lines that favor Taliban ascendancy is meant to give the United States and the Afghan national government a position of strength in future negotiations. To reach this point, the Obama administration faces four sequential and interrelated tests. All four must be hurdled to achieve success. As of 2011, the outcome is uncertain.

### Test 1. Security

U.S. and coalition forces must raise security writ large throughout the country so that credible Afghan elections, both presidential and parliamentary, can be held and government can carry out basic functions—economic development with a particular emphasis on agriculture, roads to connect the country, law and order, and justice, education, and health services. Afghanistan's elected government is the political fig leaf for the presence of U.S. and coalition forces. These forces, in turn, constitute the linchpin to a sustained and successful U.S. regional presence to combat Al Qaeda in Pakistan by furthering the Kabul regime.[87]

To do so, the administration is obligated to control the ill-defined, 1,550-mile-long, Taliban-dominated border areas with Pakistan. This open porthole of violence from Pakistani militant sanctuaries is the source of instability and failing state control throughout all of Afghanistan. U.S. and allied troops must secure the most strategic of the hundreds of traditional border crossings used by the Afghan and Pakistani populations along the FATA and Baluchistan.

U.S. forces must also venture into the Pashtun homeland of southern Afghanistan, whose men overwhelmingly provide the insurgency's manpower. As of 2010, as was the case in 2009, U.S. and coalition forces there were "at best, stalemated."[88] U.S.-led forces must work with Afghan forces to clear and hold towns and villages to increase security for the local population, which will then be positioned to turn away from the insurgency and empower the central government at the insurgents' expense.

Together, these objectives are meant to induce a game-changing strategic shift in U.S. favor in the balance of forces. If successful, the insurgents inside Afghanistan could be overwhelmed. Akin to the situation in Iraq, the Obama administration is seeking to resolve its security challenge through a concurrently executed four-step process.

*Step 1. A Dramatic U.S. Troop Increase for Time-Sensitive Security Effect*
The Obama administration immediately began adding to the 33,000 U.S. troops on the ground it inherited to "to stabilize a deteriorating situation in Afghanistan, which [had] not received the strategic attention, direction, and resources it urgently" required. In February 2009, President Obama dispatched 17,000 troops. In November 2009, following a second policy review throughout the fall, President Obama ordered the dispatch of another 30,000 U.S. combat troops, which were to be bolstered by roughly 3,000 support troops executing intelligence, road clearance, medical support, and other specialties. President Obama also called upon U.S. allies, primarily Europe, to increase their forces by 5,000–10,000 troops. All told, by fall 2010, roughly 140,000 foreign troops, of which approximately 100,000 were American, were deployed.[89]

From this position of strength, an initial, conditions-based, "ground-up" drawdown to transition to Afghan control is to begin in summer 2011 and be completed by the end of 2014, the date President Karzai has assessed that Afghanistan could assume control for its own security. With a goal of completing the handover by the end of 2012, new areas will be identified to begin the transition every few months, though U.S. forces will remain in an "overwatch" position if needed. Akin to Iraq, tens of thousands of U.S. troops will likely remain to provide mentoring, training, and other assistance. Press reporting notes that "an 'enduring partnership' agreement being negotiated between NATO and Afghanistan will extend security support indefinitely. A bilateral U.S.-Afghanistan accord, similar to the 'strategic framework' signed with Iraq when troop-withdrawal deadlines were set there in 2008, will promise long-term economic, diplomatic, and security cooperation."[90]

Prior to the U.S. drawdown, the Iraq surge witnessed a major influx of troops to rapidly increase U.S. capability and strategically alter the balance of power. Five brigades totaling approximately 30,000 troops arrived and took up their duties within five months. There was a timely and effective concentration of mass against enemy forces.

The slow pace of the U.S. troop surge in Afghanistan, however, precluded a similar concentration. The total dispatch of troops was dispersed over roughly eighteen months, and it was not fully in place until early fall 2010. Peak U.S. strength will have been disproportionately present during the Afghan winter, whose ferocity combined with Afghan topography and a lack of infrastructure effectively suspends the fighting season until spring.

The Obama administration's self-imposed July 2011 deadline to begin a conditions-based drawdown also truncates the surge's political impact. While pragmatic troop constraints would likely have limited the Iraq surge's practical military impact to approximately eighteen months, Bush's effort signified nearly unbounded political determination, a salient factor given that all guerilla wars are essentially contests of political will. During a time when the United States is attempting to halt the insurgents' momentum and deprive them of the upper hand, the Taliban have effectively been told that they only need to endure to win. According to press reporting, "U.S. officials said Taliban operatives have adopted a refrain that reflects their focus on President Obama's intent to start withdrawing troops. . . . Attributing the words to Taliban leader Mohammad Omar, officials said, operatives tell one another, 'The end is near.'"[91]

Also unlike Iraq, which was the clear and unhindered Bush priority, Afghanistan must compete with Iraq for resources. U.S. forces in Afghanistan only outstripped those in Iraq in mid-2010. The influx of new forces into Afghanistan is predicated upon the stability and progress of an only tenuously stabilized Iraq, a situation over which the United States has ever-decreasing control as its troop levels decline.

The net gain of allied foreign forces beyond political symbolism with a real military impact is likely to be negligible. The foreign troop commitment more than doubled between 2007 and 2010 from roughly 17,000 to roughly 44,000 troops, which are drawn from a combination of forty-four NATO and non-NATO countries.[92] Members' self-imposed operational caveats, however, routinely bar the direct combat that is in demand. With drawdowns from all of the major combat contingents already scheduled and those same key players refusing to meaningfully raise their efforts in response to the Obama administration's calls for increases, real allied combat power is declining.

Afghanistan's population distribution further works against the U.S. troop surge in securing the population. Iraq was a predominantly urban society grappling with an urban insurgency, and this enabled a concentrated combat troop presence with limited U.S. forces. Afghanistan, however, is a rural society plagued by a rural-based insurgency. Approximately 50 percent of Afghans live in villages of three hundred people or less, and 75–80 percent of the population lives in a rural environment. Roughly 30,000 villages, most of which have only a slim connection to Kabul due to challenging topography and the absence of a modern communications grid and national infrastructure, dot the countryside of Afghanistan's nearly 30 million people, a figure roughly 5 million larger than Iraq.[93] Afghanistan will witness not only a higher minimum requirement for the U.S. force total, but U.S. forces will also have to be more dispersed.

The Taliban's strategy further magnifies this dynamic. Iraq saw Baghdad as the primary battlefield with a few select provinces playing a crucial role. Afghanistan's Taliban, however, have sought to open multiple fronts, which forces geographic dispersion and denies U.S.-led forces concentrations of mass. When combined with a mountainous topography and little to no national infrastructure yielding a weak U.S. supply chain, outposts spread among a widely scattered populace become tactically vulnerable and can be overrun if insurgents mass.[94]

To some degree, these factors are naturally mitigated. Roughly 65 percent of the population lives within thirty-five miles of the main road system, which approximates ancient caravan routes. This shrinks the U.S. geographic focus substantially. The U.S. and coalition forces can protect major population centers such as Kabul in the northeast with its 5 million residents, and Kandahar and Lashkar Gah where 80 percent of the southern population lives.[95]

Significant geographic and political space, however, will still likely be ceded. By the end of 2010, the U.S.-led force reached approximately one third of the Afghan land mass and affected roughly 60 percent of the population.[96] While certainly a step in the right direction and an effective use of existing forces, this still left approximately two thirds of the Afghan countryside in non-coalition hands and 40 percent of the population fending for itself and trapped between the Al Qaeda-associated militants and the U.S.-backed Kabul government.

By default, this puts U.S. forces on the strategic defensive. The United States is in a situation resembling that of the Soviets wherein they occupied the cities but the insurgents controlled the countryside, which is Afghanistan's center of gravity. Due to the limited geographic coverage, there is ample space for insurgents to simply avoid any temporary increases in U.S. forces and live to fight another day. The insurgents hold the initiative.

Strategically inefficient troop deployments have squandered some resources. Most significantly, the U.S. Marine Corps has deployed in lightly populated areas such as Nimruz, which the Marines cannot hold in its entirety and whose borders the Marines cannot seal, and Helmand, the leading opium-producing province.

Any damage to Taliban income from being deprived of poppy-related revenue is highly unlikely to be significant given that the Taliban derive adequate if not greater revenue from overseas donors, bribes related to U.S. trucking convoys, and other criminal activity. In fact, Taliban operations are so cheap, according to a former CIA analyst, that "they can be continued indefinitely" with the chief cost being paying fighters, who generally receive higher wages than underpaid Afghan government soldiers.[97]

By contrast, securing Kandahar, the capital of the Pashtun belt, strikes directly into the region most supportive of the insurgency. Approximately 1 million people live in its greater environs. It also has immense political value as the Taliban's home city.

The untimely arrival of U.S. surge forces and the dispersion of those forces throughout Afghanistan, however, have prevented a timely and effective application of concentrated mass. Unlike in Marjah, where U.S.-led forces cleared the city by force to provide security in order to begin the hold-and-build phases, the Kandahar offensive has had to take a "rising tide" approach. U.S.-led security, governance, and economic efforts have been ramped up to pressure the insurgents' operating space in an attempt to "squeeze" them from the city vice forcibly expelling them, a move which would almost certainly be contingent on the Taliban not launching a counter-surge or simply going to ground and retaliating with an asymmetric response, such as the four to five daily assassinations in and around Kandahar that have been occurring since mid-June 2010.[98] While possibly effective in the long run, timely results are highly unlikely for the administration's periodic reviews and wavering U.S. political will.

No matter how effective, the U.S. surge is unlikely to directly confront the United States' chief adversary. Baghdad was the nerve center of the nation. AQI chose it as the field of battle and presented itself. Afghanistan, by contrast, has no such Al Qaeda center of gravity. Osama bin Laden's Al Qaeda has only a diffuse presence in Afghanistan intermingled with the various insurgent groups. At best, U.S. forces will defeat the Taliban, HiG, and the Haqqani network, key Al Qaeda surrogates in a necessary but not sufficient step toward victory and expend significant resources in the process.

*Step 2. Rapidly Increase Indigenous Military and Police Forces to Augment U.S. Forces*

The administration intends to dramatically expand indigenous forces to augment U.S. and allied efforts. Iraq witnessed the rapid creation and expansion of a domestic U.S.-backed security establishment built upon the Hussein regime's residual police and army capacity, which was of high quality by regional standards. A similar replay of events in Afghanistan, however, is unlikely.

The Afghan National Army (ANA) is both undersized and weak. Progressing from being 58,000 strong in 2008, which was short of its assessed ceiling of 75,000, the ANA achieved its goal of roughly 134,000 troops by October 2010. Only 30 percent of forces ranked in the top two tiers of combat readiness, however, and a 2010 audit by the Special Inspector General for Afghanistan Reconstruction found that even this ranking was likely excessively positive. Subsequent rankings on a five-point scale, which measures quality of leadership as well as troops' dependability and loyalty, have assessed roughly half of all army units at three or better, but effective and independent action is still largely elusive. Further increases call for 171,600 troops by October 2011.[99]

The Afghan National Police (ANP) is also undersized and weak. Progressing from roughly 80,000 at the start of 2009, the ANP achieved its goal of approximately 109,000 officers by October 2010. As of 2010, however, they did not maintain a presence throughout the entire country, and they boasted only 3 percent in the top two tiers of readiness. Generally speaking, they are widely considered both ineffectual and corrupt, as evidenced by roughly 25 percent of the ANP's roster estimated to be ghosts on the payroll while officials embezzle their salaries, and 15 percent of the force testing positive for drug use. Further increases call for 134,000 officers by October 2011.[100]

Voracious recruiting has led to concerns of Taliban infiltration. Numbers mean little if they are not reliable. This sentiment is particularly acute among the police.[101] Critically, in areas where the insurgency is strong, public faith in these state institutions is lacking. October 2010 polling in Afghanistan's southern provinces showed that only 52 percent of the public thought the Afghan army was effective, and only 39 percent thought similarly about the police. Sixty-one percent believed that Afghan security forces would be unable to provide security in areas from which foreign forces withdrew.[102]

International trainers have been perennially undersupplied. The goal of keeping roughly 5,200 U.S. and international trainers in Afghanistan, however, saw only 3,600 on the ground by spring 2010. International pledges have consistently either been inadequate or gone unfulfilled. The Afghan security forces are positioned for gradual, not rapid, expansion.[103]

Exacerbating this problem, attrition has proven significant. U.S. plans call for a combined total of 305,000 Afghan military and police personnel by October 2011. Officials, however, put the rate across the police and military forces at 3 percent per month.[104] To meet this called-for increase of roughly an additional 56,000 security personnel, U.S. forces would need to train more than 140,000 people, which is greater than the size of the entire 2010 Afghan army.[105]

Attrition in units operating in southern Afghanistan is particularly high. Attrition rates for the police in the south are nearly double those of the overall force. Attrition rates for the army in the south have hit an annualized rate of

45 percent as compared to about 24 percent for the army as a whole. Benefits such as hazard pay, salary increases, and providing safe transportation home for leave have helped stanch the flood, but the problem remains. To this end, U.S. forces have attempted to provide the rudiments for Afghanistan's future forces. In fall 2010, U.S. forces provided Afghan forces with more than 7,700 armored Humvees to better protect their soldiers and police, while giving the Afghan army more than 117,000 M16 and M4 rifles, which are far more accurate than the ubiquitous AK-47s they had employed.[106]

The Obama administration has also attempted to create a new security infrastructure. The construction of military bases, military and police academies, military hospitals, and so forth is aimed at "establishing enduring institutions" and creating "irreversible momentum" that will sustain itself following a U.S. departure. Only then will a U.S. drawdown be possible.[107]

The Pentagon's approach of recruiting and fielding forces quickly with the intent of improving their fighting and managerial skills over time, however, has also proven problematic. Marjah, an ostensibly Afghan-led operation, was actually spearheaded by the United States, and Afghan units performed poorly. U.S. forces routinely find their Afghan comrades' military prowess lacking.

The United States has responded with attempts to upgrade the quality of the initial training. Significantly, literacy training has been introduced, but only an estimated 14 percent of the combined army and police forces can read or write at a third-grade level. The provision of U.S. equipment and training to develop indigenous force multiplier capabilities—indirect firepower (mortars and artillery), airlift and reconnaissance, aerial surveillance equipment, and medical evacuation capabilities—has improved Afghan capabilities, but they remain lagging relative to the U.S.-driven timeline. In fact, Afghanistan's air force is not slated to be self-sufficient and at full operational capacity until 2016.[108]

In total, the administration plans to spend $20 billion in less than two years to speed the growth of Afghanistan's police and army. The administration's Afghanistan training ramp-up has been estimated to cost roughly $11.6 billion for 2011, and spending will likely remain at that level until a U.S. drawdown. Though critics chafe at the cost, it is significantly cheaper than the roughly $7 billion per month spent on U.S. operations. Post-drawdown spending, as of 2010, was estimated at $6.2 billion per year through 2015, assuming an increasingly unlikely meaningful summer 2011 withdrawal.[109]

Undergirding these forces is a weak support structure. Afghanistan's budget of roughly $3.3 billion, excluding security and defense costs, is supported by only roughly $1 billion in revenues. The Obama administration requested an additional $14.2 billion from Congress in a 2010 supplemental alone for training, equipping, and mentoring Afghan army and national police forces.[110]

Per the classic analysis of the arithmetic of insurgencies by James T. Quinlivan in his article "Force Requirements in Stability Operations," suppressing armed conflict and building governance—as has occurred in Bosnia, Kosovo, and Northern Ireland—typically have required one international "force provider" for every twenty residents, a formula that would necessitate in excess of 1 million troops for Afghanistan.[111] The U.S.-led effort in Iraq, between foreign and indigenous government security forces, involved 700,000 soldiers and police, plus 100,000 demobilized insurgent volunteers. If Afghanistan is to be compared to Iraq's darkest days in 2005–2006, at least 600,000 troops will be needed.

Afghanistan's raw numbers, however, call into question the surge's ability to achieve its goals as it is currently constructed. At its peak, the U.S.-led Afghanistan surge will have roughly 100,000 U.S. troops, 40,000 allied troops (whose use is severely restricted by national exceptions), and somewhere between 150,000 to 300,000 Afghan soldiers and police (who vary wildly in capability) slated to last for only about six to nine months. They will be attempting to provide security to roughly 30 million people, 5 million more people than in Iraq, for a country that is 25 percent larger with a more challenging topography and population distribution.[112] Using Iraq as a baseline, these forces will still be roughly only one-third to two-thirds of the prescribed total at best.

By comparison, during King Mohammad Zahir Shah's reign in the 1970s, when the country was at peace and reasonably stable, the Afghan army was 200,000 strong. Even then, the goal was 250,000 men. Now there is an active insurgency combined with an international terrorist presence. More forces are needed for a more prolonged period of time.[113] While early 2011 press reporting notes informal plans to raise total security personnel levels 30 percent to roughly 400,000, no firm plans exist and no timeline has been outlined.[114]

To further help offset this shortage and provide security in areas devoid of a government presence, the United States, after two failed efforts, is raising tribal militias entitled Afghan Local Police (ALP), which General Petraeus has dubbed "community watch with AK-47s." Eight districts, primarily in eastern and southern Afghanistan, will be part of the initial rollout. Most significantly, new forces will be created in the Arghandab region of Kandahar and the border provinces of Paktika and Paktia. Each village will be allocated no more than a few hundred fighters. Thirty to thirty-five districts will participate, with about thirty villages in each district receiving these local police units.[115] Ultimately, the U.S.-backed program allows for an initial goal of ten-person teams in roughly nine hundred villages by March 2011 in order to increase security in some of the violent and remote parts of Afghanistan.

To build the force quickly, salaries are lucrative, yet calculated. Recruits are offered roughly $120 per month, which is about 60 percent of an Afghan policeman's salary to avoid creating manpower drains. A small stipend for food is also granted. In total, recruits will earn a total amount of $1,440 per annum. By contrast, 2009 per capita income was $370, and even less in poor rural areas where the program will focus. Though the publicly stated goal as of 2010 was ten thousand of these local police, 2011 U.S. planning has already begun for more than twice that number.[116]

These local police units are composed of local male volunteers. Candidates will be recommended by village elders. Nonideological, demobilized insurgents, though not the target audience, are a prized demographic. Those selected then go through a training course conducted by U.S. Special Forces troops on how to run checkpoints, conduct patrols, and marksmanship.[117]

To ensure these groups do not become a parallel police force or spin off to become militias, these forces will be closely linked to local Ministry of the Interior elements. Local U.S. Special Forces detachments will also play an advisory role. Intended as a temporary measure, plans as of 2010 called for disbanding the units within two to three years or incorporating them into the national police.[118]

By contrast, illegally armed groups are composed of unscreened and untrained members. They are beholden to local commanders, not the national government, and their duties remain not just uncircumscribed but also unmonitored.[119]

Afghanistan's unique characteristics, however, make Iraq-style gains unlikely as the formation of the Afghan militias does not inherently reduce insurgent numbers. In Iraq, virtually all of the tribal militias that were stood up during the Awakening were carved from within the ranks of the Sunni insurgents. By contrast, the U.S. effort in Afghanistan is largely attempting to draft noncombatants into the fight to contest the insurgents.

The target enemy is also not inherently vulnerable. In Iraq, the former Sunni insurgents turned on AQI, a politically isolated and militarily insignificant terrorist entity that was dependent for its survival upon the very people who became militia members against it in response to an onslaught of terrorist attacks, assassinations, and other physical and cultural brutalities. The Taliban are also dependent upon the very people that the Petraeus initiative seeks to muster, the southern Pashtuns. The Afghan context, however, differs significantly and lessens, but by no means eliminates, the chances for this U.S. initiative.

The Taliban are not politically isolated, as was AQI with its purist, non-Iraq-centric ideology. The Taliban have deep political and social ties to Afghanistan's large and historically dominant southern Pashtuns. The broad-based insurgency they are leading has become identified with Pashtun tribal grievances and complaints against the corrupt, U.S.-backed national government.

The Taliban are also not militarily insignificant. AQI killed innocent civilians and conducted low-scale, albeit frightening, assassinations of political leaders. The Taliban, by contrast, are well-trained, well-armed and disciplined insurgents who have been fighting U.S. troops for years.

The Taliban's military vulnerability to the ALP is likely low. The ALP consists of newly raised, lightly armed, poorly trained police of unknown reliability. Any susceptibility has most likely been reduced even further by the fact that the various and competing insurgents have vowed to unify their efforts and step up attacks in their own counter-surge to U.S. efforts.[120]

The political options are also different, and far less palatable than was the case with AQI. In Iraq, the losing and beleaguered Sunnis stood to gain employment and political power curried by U.S. favor if they defeated AQI, or continued AQI-induced casualties and political repression if they lost. In Afghanistan, the historically dominant southern Pashtuns stand to gain access to a beleaguered, corrupt, largely ineffective government primarily run by their historical tribal enemies as the United States withdraws and leaves the Afghan people to their fate. Or, they can choose their kinsmen, who have shown themselves to be attentive to local needs and cultural dictates as they appear closer to an increasingly inevitable victory and increasingly provide social services. Even if successfully recruited into the ALP, southern Pashtuns not aligned with the Taliban may still be reluctant to take on their own kinsmen, particularly when the alternative is a weak, corrupt, foreign-backed government.

The ANA exemplifies this dilemma. Pashtuns account for roughly 43 percent of the ANA, but very few are southern Pashtuns, whose numbers generally consist of 1–3 percent of monthly new recruits. (Ostensibly national forces then become foreign invaders in southern provinces.)[121]

Lingering political divisions may be reanimated and militias may return. The nascent U.S.-backed central government following the 2001 U.S. invasion was far weaker than many of the warlord forces, militias, and insurgent groups with whom it had to contest, and so the United States embarked on a largely successful multi-year, multimillion-dollar effort to elevate the central government by disarming rival entities. This simultaneously left much of society dependent upon the new central government for security, and thus vulnerable to the armed insurgents because the government was unable to provide that security. These disarmed entities of only tentative national loyalty never truly lost the ability to re-muster, however, and many of their political grievances remain unsatisfied. Rearming the populace gives them license to reanimate as there is no guarantee that the Ministry of the Interior and U.S. supervision will ensure their loyalty or control.

As with Iraq, creating such a force builds expectations on the part of its members, who now play a unique and potent role in domestic security that requires a consistent outlay of resources amid changing political priorities. Afghanistan's socioeconomic situation is highly unlikely to have dramatically improved to the point where alternative gainful employment will be easily accessible when their services are no longer required. Iraq saw its insurgency begin to reanimate in 2010 at the expense of state sovereignty because its militia members were not properly supported by the state. The burden of continuing this program will soon be placed on the tottering Afghan national government as areas are transitioned to Afghan control. The continued maintenance of these Afghan forces is a real question given the impending decrease in international support after a U.S. drawdown and President Karzai's acknowledged lack of support for creating militias for fear it would lead to a return of chaos and warlord rule.[122]

The state is only tenuously empowered. Iraq witnessed all security forces, even the militias, as an arm of the state, and the militias served as a minority complement to state forces. In Afghanistan, the tribes are being placed between the insurgents and the government, and there is no binding check on the system to prevent the tribes from siding with the insurgents should they decide that is where their chances are best. The ALP forces make the tribes both less dependent upon and poised to combat the reach of the central government, as they are simultaneously empowered to settle tribal scores by force of arms racked up over decades of fighting. While this may fight off insurgents, it does not effectively project security provided by a strong central government and increase the capacity, writ, and standing of the state.

The government's overall political stability is also made more dubious. Security and state sovereignty will not be reliably obtained until there is a real Afghan national police presence in all thirty-four provinces and roughly four hundred districts, and until the Afghan National Army is able to project its power throughout the country. The ALP initiative creates a heavily armed populace under the immediate command of local leaders combined with third-country interest and influence in an Afghanistan bereft of a capable central government. This is the combination of factors that led to the Afghan civil war in the 1990s.

The ghost of Afghanistan's post-Soviet civil war is a permeating subtext. Post-9/11 Afghanistan witnessed a historically repressed and embattled minority sect, the Tajiks, take control with U.S. backing. The subsequent insurgency, drawing almost exclusively upon the significant Pashtun plurality, particularly the southern Pashtuns, began directly targeting U.S. forces, who, by default, took sides in a local civil war on the side of the underdog. This latent context for violence cannot be ignored as an increased presence of U.S. troops and allied forces is poised to expand the fighting.

*Step 3. Reduce the Number of Combatant Factions*
The Obama administration also seeks to sideline potent enemies. Moqtada al-Sadr's forces, a pivotal Iranian-backed Iraqi Shiite militia, stood down. The

same domestic and foreign factors, however, are unlikely to stand down meaningful segments of the Afghan insurgency.

Moqtada al-Sadr's domestic operational breathing space and national-level political support evaporated. After Iraq's Sunni community defected from AQI to the United States and the prime minister, Nouri al-Maliki, began to crack down on rogue Shiite militias, Iraq's previously three-sided game of U.S./national government forces, Sunni insurgents, and Moqtada's militias morphed to set Moqtada's forces alone against a united Sunni/U.S./national government front. In response, Moqtada folded militarily and engaged his opponents politically through the auspices of the central government rather than try to act as a spoiler and risk annihilation.

No domestic pressures are present in Afghanistan to induce key factions to stand down. The insurgents have one common enemy, the United States and, by extension, the U.S.-backed national government. With the overall military balance trending in the insurgents' favor, no faction is in such a desperate position as to need U.S. support and turn against its rivals to ensure survival, though jockeying for position after the U.S. withdrawal and post-U.S. internecine warfare is likely. In fact, the militants have announced a united counter-surge. With all of the insurgents, particularly the Taliban, excluded from the national government, they have nothing to lose and everything to gain politically by continuing the fight, a situation that is complemented by a militarily winning hand, and that can only improve their leverage in future negotiations.

Neighboring states also worked to calm Iraq's insurgency. A successful U.S. effort would have created a stable and Shia-dominated regime, a situation very much in Iranian interests, and so Iran kept the Shiite militias in check. At the same time, Iran calibrated the fighting to keep U.S. efforts bogged down in order to keep the United States at a disadvantage, while being careful to avoid overt blame for U.S. problems and risk retaliation.

American efforts in Afghanistan are not producing a situation conducive to the interests of key regional powers. Rather than supporting the U.S. effort, they are working to keep the insurgency boiling. This situation is highly unlikely to change in the short to medium term.

Iran benefits from a struggling U.S. position in Afghanistan. Ever more U.S. political, economic, and military resources will be consumed and so cannot be redirected against Iran. In the interim, Iran gains a pressure point on a key U.S. interest.

Pakistan gains leverage through its double game as the fight continues. Precluding a strong, independent Kabul—the main U.S. goal—furthers Pakistan's regional security through increasing its strategic depth and perpetuating U.S. dependence. Favorable domestic arrangements for Pakistan's military are also perpetuated. By proxy, China's regional leverage also increases.

Lastly, Russia gains leverage from a flailing U.S. position. As U.S. links with Pakistan experience progressively more tension, the precarious U.S. logistics tail increasingly flows through Russia and its sphere of influence. This creates a key U.S. vulnerability as U.S.-Russian relations suffer through a post–Cold War low.

### Step 4. Co-opt Insurgent Groups

The Obama administration's intent is to co-opt pivotal insurgent actors into the U.S.-backed political order to create broad-based stability. In Iraq, the United States co-opted the Sunnis and turned them into militia allies directed against a common enemy (AQI) that directly threatened the entire U.S. enterprise while enrolling this crucial constituency in the new political order. The actors' identities and goals, the role of Osama bin Laden's Al Qaeda, the influence of third countries, and differing social dynamics, however, make it unlikely that similar circumstances will meld together to co-opt and redirect meaningful segments of the Afghan insurgency. As a result, instead of being a path to building a greater whole, negotiation has become war by other means.

The actors' identities and goals are a complicating factor for U.S. interests. Iraq was fundamentally a local affair where Iraqi Sunnis displaced by Iraqi Shia sought to regain lost power in a secular state, and any foreign fighters were subsumed into the local fight. Stability, not the victory of a particular faction, was the U.S. goal. While Afghanistan is also fundamentally a local affair with Pashtun tribes seeking to regain lost power and historical dominance against the U.S.-backed minority northern tribes, Afghanistan's militant actors and their aspirations are more complex and have global implications. U.S. interests, which by definition limit the flexibility of any outcomes, dictate a deeper involvement in the internal structure of any future Afghan state. Future negotiations will be more difficult.

It is a misnomer to label all Afghan insurgents as Taliban or to assume that all are fighting for direct control of the Afghan state. As summed up by the former Afghan minister of the interior, Ali Jalali, "There are three kinds of opposition—the traditional insurgency of people who have been mistreated by the government and is [sic] not ideology-backed, the classic ideological Taliban-type movement, and the global movements using Afghanistan for their own purposes."[123] In a mutually reinforcing dynamic, two domestic themes, one ideologically driven and one not, enable Al Qaeda–led, globally focused jihadists, and vice versa.

The easiest part will be engaging the insurgency's nonideological foot soldiers who are tired of fighting. No political decisions or concessions by the United States are necessary. To the extent such efforts reduce enemy forces, the United States gains leverage in any future negotiations. Dennis Blair, the former director of National Intelligence (DNI), has assessed that "two-thirds of insurgents have local grievances and can be mollified by the government."[124]

A draft of the Afghan Peace and Reintegration plan for low-level fighters states that if a Taliban member seeks amnesty, he must renounce violence and swear allegiance to the Afghan constitution. He must also submit to fingerprinting and retinal scans. After his tribal members have vouched for his sincerity, he will be given courses in literacy and Islam, which are to be followed by a manual labor job. Roughly $160 million in foreign aid has been pledged to execute this program, which will be run by a "High Level Peace Council" composed of parliament members, military officers and, possibly, former insurgents, to make policy recommendations. They would operate under the stewardship of a secretariat run by a cabinet-level chief executive who would have day-to-day responsibility and coordinate with NATO and UN officials. This economic assistance, coupled with guarantees of military protection after defecting, is meant to meet defecting insurgents' immediate needs and enable them to build a new life apart from war.[125]

The more difficult problem is the disconnect between what the U.S.-sponsored reintegration plan offers, which is mostly job opportunities, and the grievances of the insurgency's ideological fighters and leadership. Per former DNI Blair's assessment, they are "fed up with what they see as a profiteering and exclusionary government that has strayed from Islamic principles, and they oppose the presence of nearly 100,000 U.S. troops in their country."[126] Given that the U.S.-backed government would collapse without a continued U.S. presence, and the insurgents have refused to relinquish ties to Al Qaeda, there is potentially little overlap between insurgent objectives and U.S. goals upon which to build a mutually beneficial political future. As proof of this, less than 3 percent of estimated insurgents have sought amnesty one year into the effort.[127]

The insurgency, writ large, has time on its side and little incentive to compromise. According to an interview, published in the London *Sunday Times* in spring 2010, with two of the Taliban's senior Islamic scholars who are in touch with the Quetta *shura* (the Afghan Taliban-in-exile's decision-making council), "The Taliban believe they are winning and are able to negotiate from a position of strength." President Obama has conceded that the United States is not winning.[128] The announcement of the summer 2011 start date for the U.S. withdrawal, and a culmination date of 2014, means the insurgents need only survive to win. As a result, the insurgents have offered uncompromising terms in response to Karzai's feelers:[129]

In stage one, hostilities would be reduced. The insurgents would stop burning schools and targeting reconstruction teams. The United States would stop house searches and release prisoners.

In stage two, a new system of government would be chosen. The insurgents seek an "Islamic emirate" based solely on their dispensation of sharia. This is a marked difference from the current Islamic republic, where a version of sharia not adjudicated by the insurgents' Islamic scholars coexists with a parliamentary republic.

Lastly, stage three would involve setting a deadline for the withdrawal of foreign forces. This is a fundamental insurgent goal. The Karzai administration, dependent on foreign forces for its survival, has allowed that foreign troops are in Afghanistan on only a temporary, albeit undefined, basis.

These terms strongly suggest the insurgents are simply stalling until the inevitable U.S. departure and the depletion of U.S. political will. Militant efforts to reduce hostilities strike at a core part of U.S. counterinsurgency strategy and would fundamentally preserve, if not increase, the militant balance of power. The subtext of the militants' vision for a political future effectively equates to U.S. capitulation, and the withdrawal of all foreign forces ensures not only that the United States will have no way to secure its interests, but that there will also be no effective opposition to the militants' desires.[130]

With trends running in their favor, individual insurgent groups have shown no signs of actively turning on one another to gain a favored position in a flailing U.S.-backed system. As outlined by Abdul Salam Rocketi, a former Taliban corps commander in Zabul Province and near Jalalabad who is now an independent member of parliament, the Taliban "want Afghanistan for themselves. If the Americans stay, the Taliban will fight. . . . [After] the Americans leave, the internal fighting will begin."[131]

Absent a decisive and comprehensive military victory over the assorted militant forces, co-opting and redirecting militant factions is a necessary U.S. tack.[132] Unlike Iraq's Sunnis, no one insurgent group is uniquely disadvantaged, and thus ripe for being co-opted to ensure its own survival. The administration must decide which insurgent group is most pivotal to future Afghan stability. It must then militarily pressure and politically manipulate that entity.

After being swept away by the 2001 U.S. invasion, Osama bin Laden's Al Qaeda is publicly suspected of basing itself in Pakistan's FATA. As of 2010, Michael Leiter, the director of the National Counterterrorism Center, estimated the FATA-based core at "more than 300." It is purportedly composed primarily of Chechens, Uzbeks, Arabs, European Muslims, Tajiks, and Turks.

The Afghan-based fighting force, which moves into Afghanistan through the mountains along the Durand Line, consists of anywhere from fifty to six hundred fighters inside Afghanistan. Al Qaeda has effectively shifted from hiding in a rear area behind the firepower of its allies following the 2001 U.S. invasion to combating U.S. and allied forces on the front lines inside Afghanistan in a parasitic relationship with Taliban and associated insurgent allies.[133] Looking at ISAF press releases from March 2007 to 2010, the *Long War Journal* has been able to detect the presence of Al Qaeda or affiliated groups, such as the Islamic Movement of Uzbekistan and Lashkar-e-Islam, in sixty-two different districts in nineteen of Afghanistan's thirty-four provinces, particularly Afghanistan's northern and eastern provinces. Lashkar-e-Taiba and other Pakistani-based, Al Qaeda–affiliated militant groups often help facilitate safe passage.[134]

Reflecting the interwoven and international nature of the Afghanistan/Pakistan-based Islamic militancy, Afghanistan, with its porous borders and weak state sovereignty, has become a launching point for Al Qaeda–connected Uzbek, Tajik, and Chechen networks. They have accompanied the Taliban into their new front in northern Afghanistan. From there, they are using the region as a base from which to engage in insurgencies in former Soviet Central Asia and Russia, which has been combating militants in Chechnya and Dagestan for over a decade.[135]

While some stand-alone units of "white Taliban" foreign fighters have reemerged in Afghanistan's southern provinces, Al Qaeda has primarily interwoven itself with the other numerically larger and more powerful indigenous insurgent groups through providing training on IEDs and suicide bombings, intelligence, and propaganda. As explained by Bruce Hoffman, a terrorism expert and Georgetown University professor, "The numbers aren't large, but their ability to help local forces punch above their weight acts as a multiplier. They've learned from their previous experiences, when their foreign fighters were front and center."[136]

Unfortunately, Al Qaeda cannot be co-opted. It is the steward of a global jihadist movement. Its primary reason for existence is anti-American activity.

The local perception of Al Qaeda in Afghanistan remains potent. October 2010 polling in Afghanistan's southern provinces showed that 81 percent think Al Qaeda will return if the Taliban returns to power. Seventy-two percent think Al Qaeda will then use Afghanistan as a base for attacks against the West.[137]

Crushing Al Qaeda in Afghanistan, however, is impossible. Set against a purported Pakistani sanctuary, Al Qaeda's niche role as a frontline enabler instead of a direct combat force gives it political influence and standing while shifting the bulk of the military burden to others. The United States and its allies must fight through Al Qaeda's indigenous militant allies, an extremely difficult and inefficient prospect that broadens and deepens the U.S. fight both militarily and politically. Only by bringing Al Qaeda's indigenous militant allies under control will the United States position itself to manage the Al Qaeda presence.

The Haqqani network, originally founded by Jalaluddin Haqqani to fight the Soviets and now run by his son Sirajuddin, is a force of roughly ten thousand fighters based in the FATA that largely operates in Afghanistan's Khost, Paktia, and Paktika provinces. The network's adoption of suicide bombings and complex urban assaults has made it the ranking threat to U.S. military gains and Afghan political stability. The Haqqani network's more militant forces include foreign fighters from the Persian Gulf and elsewhere in Central Asia as well as

Pashtuns largely drawn from madrassas. The Haqqanis maintain sway over the areas they inhabit and finance their operations through targeting the population with assassinations, kidnappings for ransom, timber smuggling, donations from wealthy Persian Gulf individuals, and other shakedowns instead of seeking popular support.[138]

Within militant circles, the Haqqani network plays a crucial bridge-building role, and its direct links to Osama bin Laden's Al Qaeda plugs it into the heart of the insurgency. "Like his father, [Sirajuddin] Haqqani has thrived in part by maintaining delicate alliances with the border region's militant factions. Haqqani holds a seat on Al Qaeda's leadership council, analysts say, and receives ample funding from Arab backers. In North Waziristan, where the Haqqanis run religious schools and militant training camps, he has mediated disputes among factions of the Pakistani Taliban, from which he plucks fighters."[139]

Crushing the Haqqani network would deal a strong blow to the regional insurgency. It would likely sow dissension in the ranks among the various militant groups in Pakistan. It would remove one of Afghanistan's most potent sources of both military and civilian casualties. Al Qaeda would lose a crucial local protector, medium of insurgent influence, and indirect link to Pakistan's ISI. The ISI's double game would be significantly undercut.

The Haqqani network, however, is not well suited for being co-opted into the new U.S.-backed order to foster future stability. Not attempting to sell either a brand of governance or development, the Haqqani network simply seeks to expel the U.S.-led foreign forces and their Afghan surrogates, and so it does not have a local agenda the United States can subsume. Its narrow geographic Afghan purview deprives it of broad standing. Its close ties to Osama bin Laden's Al Qaeda further remove it from consideration as a governing entity. Pakistan has already urged the Haqqani network, which is ideal for its double game, to vacate the FATA into Afghanistan, thus making sure that any future movement into North Waziristan would do it little harm.[140]

Gulbuddin Hekmatyar's forces, the military arm of Hekmatyar's faction of the Hezb-e-Islami political party, a local Afghan offshoot of the Muslim Brotherhood, consist of roughly three to four thousand fighters based in the FATA and Pakistan's Khyber Pakhtunkhwa, particularly the Jalozai and Shamshatoo refugee camps. Hekmatyar's forces (Hezb-e-Islami/Gulbuddin [HiG]) operate primarily in Afghanistan's northern and northeastern provinces of Baghlan, Kunduz, Kunar, Laghman, Paktia, and Kapisa, with a presence along the crucial Kabul–Torkham highway. They consist primarily of Pashtuns augmented by foreign fighters.

Hezb-e-Islami/Gulbuddin plays a spoiler role within the insurgency. In the north, HiG-Taliban infighting has broken out, and HiG has begun leveraging the Afghan national government against the Taliban, who previously defeated Hekmatyar's militia in 1995, which forced him to flee to Iran and many of his commanders to defect to Mullah Omar's forces or retreat to Pakistan. Hekmatyar's engagement in peace talks for roughly two years lends the possibility of a peace separate from the Taliban and the Haqqani network.

Neutralizing HiG would deal a strong blow to the regional insurgency. It would weaken the insurgency's northern front, which threatens roughly one-fifth of Afghanistan's provinces as well as strategic transportation arteries upon which U.S. forces depend. It would also lessen the need to spread the already limited international troop presence thin, which endangers U.S. efforts in the south and east. Al Qaeda, to whom HiG publicly swore allegiance in 2006, would lose a local protector. Since HiG is a historic favorite of ISI in Afghanistan and an enabler of ISI's insurgent activities in India, Pakistan's double game would be significantly undercut.

HiG has governing potential. Hekmatyar has a possible surrogate connection in parliament: the Hezb-e-Islami/Afghanistan, which holds roughly one-third of government offices, maintains a presence throughout the country, and claims thousands of supporters. Unlike the Haqqani network, Hekmatyar has held tentative peace talks with the Karzai regime.

Hezb-e-Islami/Gulbuddin forces, however, are not well suited for being co-opted into the new U.S.-backed order to foster stability. Hekmatyar's standing among Afghans plummeted when he shelled Kabul and killed thousands of civilians at the start of the post-Soviet civil war, during which he was credited with numerous atrocities. HiG's relatively concentrated geographic focus combined with its ideological militancy, which only drives it closer to Al Qaeda, deprives it of broad standing nationally. HiG was the most militant faction of the anti-Soviet resistance, and Hekmatyar's notoriously mercurial nature and ruthless ambition make him an unreliable partner. Since HiG is ideal for its double game, Pakistan is unlikely to take significant action against this key ISI ally in the run-up to negotiations or to allow it to be a truly independent actor in any future government.[141]

The Taliban is a force that fluctuates depending on the season from roughly 10,000 to 40,000 overwhelmingly Pashtun fighters under roughly 1,700 field commanders, who answer to roughly two hundred key figures, all of whom are in Pakistan, particularly Karachi, with ISI support.[142] They predominate throughout Afghanistan's south and east, but are also present in the west and north where somewhat smaller Pashtun communities also reside. The insurgency's workhorse, the Taliban has a farmer-heavy insurgent cadre. Even more so than HiG, the Taliban has a political agenda, and they are seeking to restore the state deposed by U.S. forces following 9/11.

The Taliban is the cornerstone of the regional insurgency. The Taliban's Afghanistan efforts give Al Qaeda, with whom the Taliban has ties, de facto leverage over the United States at little cost while the United States expends massive amounts of blood and treasure and the Taliban take the casualties. The Taliban's size combined with its governing agenda permit the smaller, more militant groups political and military latitude as free riders in the greater anti-Karzai effort, though they all maintain links with one another. The Taliban also maintain links with the Pakistani Taliban, by whom the Afghan Taliban is somewhat endangered as the Taliban brand-name gets besmirched by TTP actions against the Pakistani state.

Crushing the Taliban is critical to crippling the insurgency. Al Qaeda's chief means of effectively pressing the United States by exploiting a parasitic relationship with indigenous militants would be gone, and Al Qaeda's efforts to claim a state to obtain sanctuary would be dealt a crucial blow. The primary rival to the Afghan national government would be eliminated, and HiG and the Haqqani network would both likely become politically isolated and militarily outgunned. ISI's double game would be lethally undercut. In addition, destroying the original Taliban would politically undercut the Pakistani Taliban.

The Taliban is crucial for the new U.S.-backed order because it will be nearly impossible to construct a viable and enduring settlement without, at a minimum, taking account of their concerns and, most likely, at least attempting to include some of their leaders. Despite being widely unpopular in Afghanistan, the Taliban have identified their insurgency with grievances about corruption and tribal equity that resonate widely among Afghanistan's Pashtuns, who account for 40–50 percent of the population. Though the vast majority of Pashtuns are not in the Taliban, nearly all of the Taliban are Pashtun. Where the Pashtuns dominate, such as the south and east, the Taliban's movement is blended with the local economy and tribal politics. An enduring peace, as reflected by Afghan history, will not occur until a power-sharing arrangement is achieved between Pashtuns, Afghanistan's historical rulers, and non-Pashtuns, such as the current U.S.-backed Tajiks.

The Taliban have the potential to be palatably co-opted into a new political order. They have coherence but not popularity in the political realm, and the basis for their popularity—Karzai regime failures and a Western presence—can be mitigated and are within the power of the United States and its allies to control. Though they have not renounced their ties to Al Qaeda, the Taliban have displayed an independence from Al Qaeda, and there are multiple cultural, ethnic, social, religious, political, and tactical differences that the U.S.-led effort could exploit. Fundamental to Pakistan's double game, they would likely come under Pakistani pressure, but they would also likely have the ability to stand independently if given the opportunity.[143]

The Taliban have the potential to reprise the role of Iraq's Sunnis. They are the most powerful rebelling force, and so they not only drive the insurgency, but they are also the fulcrum on which it pivots. They desire domestic political power, and so they are both malleable and have motivations that make it possible to co-opt them into a new governing structure. The United States, however, is confronted with a set of challenges in subduing the Taliban that was not present when suppressing Iraq's insurgency.

U.S. efforts, however, have focused on the Haqqani network, and they have taken a battering in Afghanistan. "Coalition leaders . . . hope that pitting . . . [allied forces] . . . against the Haqqanis will eventually open a trail that leads to Al Qaeda leader Osama bin Laden and his deputy, Ayman al-Zawahiri."[144] This approach not only has a low chance of success, but it also fritters limited U.S. combat power away from winning Afghanistan as Pakistan's double game keeps the Haqqani network alive.

Further complicating the situation is the lack of a consensus from key regional actors supporting the insurgency's taming. The U.S. war in Iraq witnessed Iran benefitting from an insurgency strong enough to keep the United States bogged down but not weak enough for U.S. forces to defeat it, which would have freed up U.S. forces for action against Iran while forcing Iran to confront the remaining mess in Iraq. Pakistan similarly benefits through its double game from a perpetually struggling U.S. presence, whose increasing dependency on Pakistan only increases Pakistani leverage. On the flip side, Iran also benefitted from taming the Sunni rebellion, whose defeat was very likely to lead to a Shia-dominated, Iran-allied state. Afghanistan, however, differs dramatically in that Pakistan also benefits from a victory by the insurgency, which would empower its Taliban surrogate and restore pre-9/11 strategic advantages.

Both the United States and its allies, upon whom the United States is far more dependent in Afghanistan than it was in Iraq, show signs of fading political will. Dutch and Canadian combat units have withdrawn, substantial new troop pledges have not been forthcoming, and foreign troops are not curtailing national exceptions. The administration has announced deadlines of 2011 to start the U.S. pullout and 2014 to end it, though an unspecified supportive relationship for the Afghan national government will continue.

These timelines have led to a lack of unity between the host-nation government and the United States against the insurgents. As explained by Amrullah Saleh, President Karzai's former intelligence chief, in a press interview, President Karzai has lost faith in the Americans and NATO to prevail in Afghanistan and deal with militant sanctuaries in Pakistan now that they have gone untamed after nearly a decade of fighting. Rather than harden Afghanistan against its neighbor, President Karzai has struck a more compromising tone toward Pakistan and the Taliban. While President Karzai is highly unlikely to simply surrender to his Taliban adversaries, the possibility exists that U.S. interests will suffer as President Karzai, the Taliban, and other local actors work toward a deal.[145]

Unfortunately, no commonly accepted vision for Afghanistan's political future exists. Gen. David Petraeus and Undersecretary of Defense for Policy Michèle Flournoy could articulate to a June 2010 Senate panel only that a post-2011 Afghanistan would be stable, have a stronger army and police force, and have a long-term relationship with the United States. Ideally, as noted by British diplomat Simon Shercliff, a steady-state situation will result where Afghanistan will be "robust enough to sustain its own economic and political stability, and repel the likes of al Qaida from setting up shop there." President Obama's only caveats have been that the U.S.-backed order not be deposed and Al Qaeda not have a presence.[146]

A political strategy should identify "a pathway to the future shape of a peaceful Afghanistan and its relationships with its neighbors and the wider world." Because no pathway exists, U.S. efforts to encourage the defection of insurgent groups, much less their redirection, have become a tactic disconnected from an ill-defined goal. Conflicting approaches and contradictory statements by the United States, the Karzai-led regime, and U.S. allies, which imply and reflect conflicting assumptions and visions, have resulted. From the militants' point of view, there is no clear interlocutor, no clear path to follow, and no clear potential end-state to evaluate to make a decision.

Even if the United States is able to make the plight of the Taliban so desperate that they become successfully subsumed into the U.S.-backed order, whatever process is established for doing that will be more complicated than what was used in Iraq. Today's Taliban—which, by all accounts, is fielding ever more fighters—is less amenable to top-down control. Age, the ramifications of Afghanistan's recent history, and the nature of the insurgency all play a role.

There is a generational disconnect between the Taliban's leadership cadre, which comes from the anti-Soviet generation, and the fighter cadre battling U.S.-led forces, which denies the Pakistan-based leadership unwavering command and control. According to a senior Taliban intelligence officer who spoke to *Newsweek* magazine in May 2010, roughly 80 percent of the group's fighters are now in their late teens or early twenties. Half of the field commanders are thirty years old or younger, with the best young fighters seeing rapid promotion due to heavy losses. NATO estimates claim the average age of Taliban commanders has fallen from thirty-five to twenty-five because NATO forces have been killing so many of them.[147]

They feel less loyalty to, and are therefore less swayed by, orders from commanders hiding in Pakistan who have never braved the unprecedented U.S.-brought lethality.[148] "These younger commanders and their fiercely loyal fighters are increasingly removed from the dense networks of tribal kinship and patronage, or *qawm*, and especially of friendship born of common experiences, or *andiwali*, that bind together the top figures in the established insurgent groups like the Quetta Shura and the Haqqani network. Indeed, it is primarily through *andi-wali*—overlapping bonds of family, schooling, years together in camps, combat service, and business partnership—that talks between the adversaries, including representatives of Hamid Karzai, Afghanistan's president, and Mullah Omar, the Taliban's ultimate leader, have continued over the years.

These new Taliban warriors, however, are increasingly independent, ruthless, and unwilling to compromise with foreign infidels and their associates. They yearn to fight, and describe battle as going on vacation from the long, boring interludes of training and waiting between engagements. They claim they will fight to the death as long as any foreign soldiers remain, even if only in military bases."[149]

The mainstay of the fighter cadre is of the appropriate age to bear a grudge against the Americans, who deposed the Taliban's Islamic state only to restore the ethnic groups and warlords that Mullah Omar's fighters drove from Kabul during the 1990s. Casualty-causing actions by U.S.-led forces since, such as airstrikes, and cultural affronts, such as U.S. treatment of Afghan women and conducting house searches, are simply ever more salt in the wound. Compromises will likely be harder according to one expert who noted, "We may be killing off tired older commanders who are willing to negotiate and replacing them with younger, more embittered ones."[150]

These ideologically oriented commanders have an anti-Western zeal that was absent during the anti-Soviet jihad and that can only make negotiations more difficult. As explained by a senior Taliban intelligence officer in his mid-forties to a *Newsweek* reporter, "These young men feel they are fighting not only for the survival of Islam in Afghanistan, but for Islam's survival everywhere. . . . These young men have seen and suffered more, and have a much stronger emotional and religious commitment than we ever did." Ehsan Zahine, head of the Tribal Liaison Office, a research center, notes that the assassination policy is "creating a bunch of young guys who have been trained in the madrassas and have one word in their heads—jihad." As noted by Ali Ashraf, the director of the FATA Research Center in Islamabad, "The suicide bombers come from this class. If the leadership comes into this class, it's going to be extremely dangerous."[151]

This generational disconnect is only exacerbated by the insurgency's decentralized, self-sufficient nature. Though the FATA serves as a safe zone for both fighters and leadership to retreat to and sustain rear-area support functions, the U.S. military estimates that roughly 75 percent of insurgents fight within five miles of their homes.[152] The separation of time and distance coupled with a lack of abundant technology only loosens the grip of the Taliban's senior leadership.

Should the United States attempt to manipulate tribal elders, Afghanistan's traditional leadership cadre, against the militants, the approach will likely be positive. This group has been shunted aside through raw power by the Taliban, who traditionally come from the lower Pashtun classes, yet the elders still retain cultural standing, respect, and moral authority. Complementing their social and political virtues with means, such as money and political support, could yield results.

Such an approach, however, is likely to be painstaking. Iraq's tribal leaders, who could reliably command the obedience of the vast majority of insurgency fighters and existed in a coherent hierarchy, formed a centralized fulcrum the United States could engage and manipulate. Afghanistan's tribal leaders, however, have no clear hierarchy, are divided among sixteen main ethnic groups, must compete with warlords, and have a history of autonomy. As noted by Daniel Markey, a former South Asia expert at the State Department, "If you make a deal with one guy, you have a deal with one guy, and not his whole clan."[153]

### Test 2. Governance

Governance is also a multipart challenge. The government's ability to provide basic services—roads, electricity, health, education, and so forth—is virtually nonexistent in the provinces, and it only decreases the farther one gets from Kabul. As noted by Andrew Exum, an analyst at the Center for a New American Security who has served as an advisor to the U.S. military in Afghanistan, "If you ask Afghans or U.S. military commanders what matters most to them, the answer is almost always local governance."[154]

Southern Afghanistan, where the insurgency is strongest, is particularly bereft of national government presence and support. By 2010, six provinces did not have buildings for their governors, and others had no electricity. In many districts, more than half of the positions were vacant due to fear of the Taliban targeting government officials while educated, well-qualified applicants routinely took employment with safer, much more lucrative contracting opportunities with the international community. In one particularly hard-hit district, only five of seventy-five positions were filled.[155]

Kabul-based President Karzai has long been wary of building up rival power centers in the provinces. In March 2010, for example, the Afghan government finally approved a long-overdue mechanism to allocate money to district governors, who have little to no funds to begin development projects or hire staff. A U.S. official, however, noted that it could take up to two years to implement the new policy and actually deliver money to the district level.[156]

The Obama administration has responded by surging civilian experts. As summarized by an administration official, "We've been at war eight years, and we realize now we're starting from scratch because very little work has been done building a credible Afghan partner."[157] The goal is to create a strategic shift in state capacity by building effective institutions, which reduce the overall level of ineptitude and corruption that undermines support for the national government and, by extension U.S. forces.

The U.S. government's civilian development capacity, however, is sorely lacking. The 2009 dispatch of 20,000 troops and the U.S. invasion of Helmand was to be accompanied by a civilian surge to extend the protective and supportive bubble of central government, but it never materialized. The Department of State has prepared a civilian response core of deployable civilian experts to crisis zones, but it consists of only a few hundred officers hired on a temporary basis. The Agency for International Development, once a force of tens of thousands of officers who directly planned and executed development projects overseas during the 1960s, has shrunk for decades, and it now primarily serves as a coordination node to hire contractors to do its work. As with the State Department, the positions USAID is advertising for Afghanistan in order to field experts in a timely manner consist of only small numbers of officers hired on a temporary basis.

These failures showed in the Marjah operation, which was to be a showpiece of the administration's counterinsurgency strategy. The "government in a box" of a sufficient number of competent Afghan civilian follow-on administrators to take on municipal and district-level functions after U.S. forces cleared the area never materialized, and this gave the Taliban an opening to stage a comeback. Taliban challenges to U.S.-provided security produced refugees who, absent government services, had little incentive to stay or fight back as the Taliban returned to contest the area and disparage international efforts. In summer 2010, Gen. Stanley McChrystal, then commander of U.S. forces in Afghanistan, publicly termed Marjah a "bleeding ulcer" for U.S. efforts in the south.

Only nominally under government control by 2010, Kandahar—the Taliban's founding city, the Pashtun community's de facto capital, and Afghanistan's second-largest city with roughly 800,000 to 1 million people—will be the pivot point of the U.S. war effort.[158] In contrast to Marjah, which saw U.S.-led forces storm the area on the premise that governance and economic efforts would then follow in short order, the Kandahar offensive was to be a four- to five-month operation. Taking a rising tide approach, security forces, economic assistance, and civilian-led governance efforts were to be simultaneously increased to reduce the insurgency to isolated islands before expelling it. The effort was to be civilian-led and military-enabled.

The U.S.-led Kandahar offensive, however, was delayed from spring 2010 until fall. As relayed to the press by one military official, "There's no point in clearing an area until you have the capacity to do the hold, to bring governance. . . . Without the Afghan government civilian capacity—without a district government that can provide some basic services—you'll end up with what we're experiencing in Marjah right now."[159]

Even though the number of U.S. civilians has tripled since early 2009 and is slated to reach 1,500 by January 2012, the framework into which these bodies are being placed is sorely lacking. U.S. aid is routinely spent with little or no input from local officials. It is not uncommon for extensive funds to routinely be devoted to wages and administrative costs, such as salary and security, with only a minority of operating budgets going to actual development projects. Neither funds nor detailed data on projects are effectively tracked or centrally collated for analysis.[160]

### Test 3. Economic Development

Notably absent from the Obama administration's plans are any large, new, sustained foreign-aid commitments. Rather than cutting checks to the central government, with its notorious corruption, or engaging in large-scale infrastructure projects, the administration appears to have opted for a bottom-up approach in Afghanistan. Short-term, cash-for-work public works projects to provide alternative forms of income to poppy-growing and fighting are a staple. The administration, for example, is spending $250 million in Afghanistan's south, and $90 million in Kandahar alone.

The administration has also launched broad crop-substitution efforts. These include subsidized seeds, equipment, and fertilizer to help break the poppy cycle. The intent is to enable economic activity to create both the means for the masses to better their existence and an incentive for the masses to cleave to the government.[161]

### Test 4. Political Will

The solution set timeline is potentially short while the problem set timeline is definitely long. As noted by national security policy practitioner Gen. Barry McCaffrey, "This is a generational war to build an Afghan state and prevent the creation of a lawless, extremist region which will host and sustain enduring threats to the vital national security interests of the United States and our key allies." The potential for a severe and crippling disconnect exists between U.S. aims, the supporting political willpower of the U.S. public, and U.S. challenges.[162]

Guerilla warfare is a political contest played out through military means. It pits the political will of two societies supporting their combatant forces against each other. In the case of Afghanistan, the conflict is three-sided—the Afghan public behind the Afghan national government, the U.S. public behind its fighting forces, and disaffected Afghans behind the Taliban-led insurgency. Unfortunately, these three groups are not in sync to U.S. advantage.

The Afghan public is supportive of its national government and appears prepared for the long haul. Despite Afghanistan's multitude of problems, a November 2009 poll throughout Afghanistan by the International Republican

Institute found that 56 percent of Afghans believed the country was headed in the right direction compared to 27 percent who thought otherwise. By contrast, only 30 percent had been optimistic in spring 2009. President Karzai remains popular, with 66 percent considering him the legitimate president of the country despite election irregularities. The public is behind him, with 58 percent rating his job performance as good or very good and 81 percent saying they have a favorable view of his leadership abilities. The Afghan public expresses high confidence in the Afghan army to the tune of 70 percent. Despite the U.S. receiving only a 38 percent positive rating, approximately 68 percent of the Afghan public wants to see the U.S. and foreign forces stay to preclude rule by the Taliban, which only receives a 10 percent favorability rating.[163]

Despite this durable sense of optimism, the Afghan state's ability to defeat the Taliban independent of U.S. assistance is lacking. The durability of U.S. public sentiment, therefore, is the pivot point. From the U.S. point of view, all the Taliban needs to do to win is to survive and cause sufficient pain to the United States to ensure that the Afghanistan war effort remains a controversial and not-forgotten issue, and they have shown no wavering in their ability to do so.

The cornerstone of U.S. public will is showing cracks. In a March 2009 *USA Today*/Gallup poll of U.S. public opinion, 42 percent of respondents stated that sending troops to Afghanistan in the first place was a mistake, which is in contrast to January 2002 when only 6 percent said so.[164] By October 2009, more than 50 percent opposed continuing the war. By December 2010, a record-high 60 percent of Americans said the war in Afghanistan was "not worth it." Rising casualty rates are only likely to ensure, and possibly increase, negative ratings.

The only mitigating factor is that any U.S. success is a compounding advantage that can increase political resolve, and thus lengthen the solution set timeline. Secretary of Defense Gates is keenly aware of this fact and has stated that "in virtually all of the coalition countries, the publics are going to expect to see some progress . . . some sign that we are moving in the right direction. I think the voters are sophisticated enough to know that we're not going to be done. . . . If we are making progress and it's clear that we have the right strategy then I think the people will be patient. . . . The one thing [I] think none of the publics, . . . including the American public, will tolerate is the perception of [a] stalemate in which we're losing young men."[165]

The administration is caught in a paradox. Only after a short-run increase in fighting and casualties covering the next three to five years will any material gains begin to show. Every statement that assures the U.S. public of an ever-closer end state, such as a July 2011 start date for a U.S. pullout and a 2014 end date for U.S. involvement, however, only causes concern in Afghanistan, which has already been abandoned by the United States once before. It inspires the Taliban to simply wait out the United States to achieve victory. The crux of the Obama administration's political strategy must be how to split the difference.

## Initial Choices—The International Level

The administration has initiated a new Afghanistan-Pakistan-focused contact group of "all who should have a stake in the security of the region."[166] The intent is that such a forum could not only serve as a means for Afghanistan to engage with its neighbors, but also as political cover for key members, such as India and Pakistan, to engage with one another at U.S. behest. Contrary to the Bush administration, and in line with the Obama administration's broad engagement policy toward Tehran, Iran has been included in addition to Russia, China, India, Pakistan, NATO allies, the Central Asian states, and the United Nations. No viable Afghan state, nor U.S. goals and efforts dependent upon it, will survive if it is undermined by enduring neighbors with competing, antithetical, and vested interests.

This effort has not, however, met with extensive success. The contact group is a forum and venue for interaction, not a transformative means of altering its member states' national interests, which still remain in conflict. No substantial India-Pakistan breakthrough has yet occurred. From the viewpoint of combating Al Qaeda, the United States continues to further conflicting policies in the region reference China, India, Pakistan, Iran, and the issues of proliferation and terrorism.

## FUTURE CHOICES

The administration's strategy directly addresses Afghanistan's military, political, and economic situation, and, if properly implemented, it offers a road to victory. The administration, however, has also used up most of its excess maneuvering room within the confines of existing U.S. priorities and resource allocations. Any future decisions about the means to implement this strategy will necessarily be about associated political choices to increase its efficacy, not competing strategic options. Only a decision to withdraw from the region or an outright U.S. defeat is likely to take the United States in a different direction.

## CONCLUSION

The Obama administration inherited a war on the verge of collapse. The Taliban, backed by their jihadist allies, contest the Afghan government and its international backers for sovereignty in all parts of the country. The Afghan economy, though perpetually growing, is increasingly narcotics-dominated, which deprives the state of revenue. The central government's capacity to provide critical services—security, education, health care, roads, and justice—is weak to non-existent in the countryside, where the vast majority of the population lives.

The administration rejected a narrowly focused, Pakistan-directed counterterrorism strategy focused on bin Laden's Al Qaeda. While it would have focused and conserved limited U.S. resources for the most immediate threat to U.S. security, it would have effectively abandoned Afghanistan. Doing so deprives the United States of stable regional footing and leverage over regional powers, and it gives Al Qaeda and its allies increased geographic and political, and thus operational, breathing space.

The Obama administration launched a national-level counterinsurgency strategy to deliver a Taliban defeat, a necessary but not sufficient step in defeating Al Qaeda. This tack seeks to subordinate the Taliban into the new, U.S.-backed political order, not militarily destroy them, and so a negotiated solution is the ultimate end-state. Complemented by U.S. efforts to build a supportive regional consensus, the United States has sought to increase the Afghan central government's legitimacy by raising its ability to provide security, economic opportunity, and governance so that it becomes a credible alternative to a politically unpopular Taliban—a situation that would permit the United States to negotiate from a position of strength.

The Obama administration has decidedly shifted the flow of political, economic, and military resources from Iraq to Afghanistan, which it has designated the primary front in the U.S. war on Al Qaeda. U.S. efforts, however, are flagging. The administration has launched an Iraq-style, four-step surge to reverse negative security, economic, and governance trends.

Security—the factor that underwrites and enables all progress—has not witnessed rapid progress or achieved significantly tangible results. The U.S. troop buildup is too gradual, of insufficient volume, and of too limited duration to permit a timely and sustained concentration of mass against enemy forces in a strategic manner. Indigenous forces have not increased rapidly in either quantity or quality. The various insurgent factions have unified in a counter-surge against U.S. efforts rather than sit out the fight. Attempts to co-opt the insurgents have not yet yielded results.

Governance—the provision of critical services such as education, health care, roads, security, and justice that induces loyalty and legitimacy—is not rapidly improving. Despite extensive talk, the U.S. government has not yet fielded an extensive, development focused "civilian surge," and U.S. capacity to do so in the future has not substantively improved. Corruption remains a staggering problem that continues to alienate the population.

Economic development—a means for the masses to better their lives, and an incentive to cleave to the government, that is largely a product of security and governance—is also lacking. The narcotics trade shows no signs of abating, and its growth denies the state revenue while aiding the insurgency. The Afghan government remains utterly dependent on foreign aid.

The U.S. efforts to build a regional consensus supporting the U.S.-backed Afghan state have made little headway. From the perspective of combating Al Qaeda, the United States continues to further conflicting policies in the region reference China, India, Pakistan, Iran, and proliferation concerns. Crucially, India and Pakistan remain at loggerheads.

Such slow progress has led to a fourth challenge—maintaining popular support. Guerilla wars are contests of will played out through military means where the supporting society's political agenda favoring its forces continuing the war is the real center of gravity, which is whittled away through increased casualties, perceptions of stalemate, and increased spending over time. Though the Afghan public's will remains strong, the U.S. public's desire for continuing the fight has steadily declined. NATO allies' military contributions are waning. Foreign aid is waning.

With security, economic, and governance trends in the militants' favor, the United States is in a position of weakness. The United States is highly unlikely to be able to exploit the insurgents, particularly the Taliban, through negotiation in the short term. Sustained and concentrated military and political efforts against the Taliban will be necessary to adjust the balance of power.

Progress, however, is not absent. Though modifications are necessary, the administration's strategy addresses the key centers of gravity inside Afghanistan, while U.S. regional efforts, for the first time post-9/11, seek to favorably alter Afghanistan's regional context. The Afghans are showing the necessary political resiliency to win. Because it will take time to feel the impact of these changes, the administration's strategy must continue to be refined and given time to succeed.

The potential impact of the administration's strategy upon Al Qaeda is significant. To at least some degree, Al Qaeda will claim political credit—and thus gain a bump in its operational capacity—as the Taliban, a historic Al Qaeda ally, claim that they forced the United States to the bargaining table. Depending upon the terms of the deal, however, Al Qaeda could be deprived of a safe haven. In fact, the rejection of Al Qaeda by former allies entering into a U.S.-backed state could politically isolate it, and thus operationally degrade it. U.S. resources could be both freed up and husbanded for future use.

The only alternative, by contrast, is a strategic U.S. withdrawal. This would lead to an outright Taliban victory, which, by extension, directly empowers Al Qaeda. The international chess board would be reset to pre-9/11 positions.

Conclusion

# The Obama Administration and the Way Forward

*Strategic theory must . . . study the engagement in terms of its possible results and of the moral and psychological forces that largely determine its course.*

—Carl von Clausewitz

*I'm concerned that counterterrorism is defined as an intelligence and military program. To be successful in the long run, we have to take a far broader approach that emphasizes political, social, and economic forces.*

—Edmund J. Hull,
U.S. Ambassador to Yemen
from 2001 to 2004

Al Qaeda's ability to induce political harm is born of the security threat it poses. Its organizational capacity for violence must be degraded. Only hard power can do this.

The Bush administration's resource-intensive hard-power efforts to degrade Al Qaeda's operational capacity applied military, law enforcement, and intelligence activity against Al Qaeda's combatants and support operatives. Pre-9/11 Al Qaeda leadership has been decimated, thousands of operatives have been killed or captured, and Al Qaeda central's role as a frontline jihadist leader has faded. President Obama's efforts have, with only minor changes, largely continued the Bush approach, which correlates with no more 9/11-scale attacks.

Al Qaeda's mission as a vanguard entity, however, has been accomplished: "Worldwide instigation and inspiration."[1] Al Qaeda's stewardship of the global jihadist movement has allowed it to co-opt ever-present and perpetual anti-U.S. rage, which stems from politically tone-deaf, short-term U.S. efforts to combat it set against long-term U.S. policies that animate Al Qaeda and its supporters. Al Qaeda translates this anti-U.S. political antipathy into increased operational capability, and it has gone from merely surviving the concerted post-9/11 U.S.-led onslaught to eradicate it to actually rejuvenating despite minimal public support for its own agenda and its near total failure to achieve any of its ultimate political goals or intermediary objectives. Al Qaeda remains well positioned for long-term influence over U.S. interests.

Only by moving beyond the United States' hard-power efforts against terrorism's tactical dimension—which are both resource-intensive and systematically disadvantageous to the United States—can meaningful additional progress be made. The United States has disproportionate power and influence relative to Al Qaeda over the highly malleable political issues, and their potential resolutions, that fuel the U.S.-Al Qaeda conflict. Manipulating the U.S.-Al Qaeda conflict's political aspect has the potential to capitalize on Al Qaeda's political, and thus operational, vulnerabilities, of which it has many, to magnify the impact of corresponding U.S. hard-power actions to yield operational gains for significant U.S. national advantage.

A comprehensive approach empowering U.S. hard-power actions through exploiting Al Qaeda's political vulnerabilities, however, forces strategic political choices that a tactically oriented approach largely avoids. Given that the United States has failed to destroy Al Qaeda despite roughly a decade of concerted effort, and given that the political, economic, and military trends underlying these efforts are not only inherently unsustainable but are also proving increasingly difficult to maintain even in the short to medium term, such choices can no longer be avoided. It will fall to the Obama administration, as well as its successors, to devise criteria for pronouncing U.S. national security needs in this new and unique threat-based context that are within reach of the means available as a subset of a larger U.S. foreign policy grand strategy.

## ASSESSING THE CHALLENGE

Even though it exists on both a political level and a hard-power level, Al Qaeda is primarily a political threat, not a military one. It does not threaten the existence of the United States as a country. Rather, it endangers the U.S. political character, which formulates U.S. foreign policy to further U.S. interests and to ensure U.S. prosperity.

No serious military threat to the United States exists as of the early twenty-first century. Only the rise of a rival, potent, and antagonistic great power capable of concerted action on a global scale, which does not currently exist and is unlikely to for the foreseeable future (though China may one day achieve such a status), could pose such a threat. Until such a time, transnational terrorism, as embodied by Al Qaeda and the global jihadist movement, should be the evaluative prism of U.S. security policy because Al Qaeda alone threatens, or has the potential to threaten, all of the United States' pillars of strength.

Al Qaeda obviates the benefits of U.S. geographical independence. As shown by 9/11 and subsequent attempts, Al Qaeda and its militant allies are the only current threats both capable and likely to directly attack the United States and kill U.S. citizens. It is also one of the few international actors likely to directly use violence against U.S. interests around the world.

Al Qaeda can grind down U.S. hard-power capacity. Drawing U.S. forces into quagmires such as Iraq saps U.S. resources. Necessary long-term fights, such as Afghanistan, further strain U.S. capabilities, which then cannot be employed elsewhere to secure competing U.S. interests. Meanwhile, efforts to hone U.S. forces to fight Al Qaeda and its allies force trade-offs in preparing for other contingencies against disparate actors, to include smaller and emerging powers.

Al Qaeda globally threatens U.S. soft-power appeal. Al Qaeda uses terrorism to subvert the U.S. political process that devises and implements U.S. policy so that the United States inflicts harm upon itself through distorted decision-making. By provoking an extreme U.S. reaction to its terrorist violence resulting in steps inconsistent with U.S. values, such as torturing terrorist suspects and unilaterally invading other countries, Al Qaeda besmirches not only the United States, but also the defining values it touts, such as democracy, the rule of law, and human rights.

Al Qaeda can strike at U.S. economic vibrancy. Most directly, the U.S. response to date has created a self-inflicted, crushing, and still growing, economic burden of war-related expenditures that will ultimately force fundamental domestic political and economic choices. More broadly, reduced U.S. soft-power appeal may induce a reactionary response to U.S. world engagement, upon which the U.S. economy is heavily based.

Al Qaeda can also endanger the United States' position in the world's international institutions. The United Nations, NATO, and other organizations are key nodes for the United States to exert its power and influence to both shape and execute its policies. Not only will a major U.S. lever be gone if states begin to use these institutions as rallying points to counter unpopular U.S. policies, but the United States will also risk being strategically disadvantaged should these venues be used to organize states to further policies counter to U.S. interests.

The U.S. Al Qaeda conflict's political drivers ensure a long-term struggle. To Al Qaeda's dismay, the United States is highly unlikely to stop pursuing advantageous terms of trade to meet its energy needs, or to curtail its troop presence and other support to the Middle Eastern regimes that facilitate U.S. interests. The United States is also highly unlikely to make the global repression of Muslim minorities its fulcrum issue, or to cut ties with great powers, such as Russia and China, who do so. A direct U.S. involvement and presence in Iraq and Afghanistan is highly unlikely to end in anything but the very long term.

Al Qaeda as a potent actor in the international system is highly unlikely to fade way. Al Qaeda is an organizational manifestation of an established school of religio-political thought whose members self-select. In the context of modern communications—particularly the Internet, which makes Al Qaeda's perspective ubiquitous and enduring, while solidifying and enabling existing members and supporters and facilitating recruitment—neither Al Qaeda's organizational nor its political vestiges can be eliminated. Not only are the potentially necessary hard-power steps to thoroughly destroy such an entity likely impossible, they would trample the U.S. political character in the process. The United States, therefore, must seek to manage the U.S.-Al Qaeda struggle, not to eliminate Al Qaeda.

Neither Al Qaeda's general perspective on the world nor the fact that Al Qaeda exists to manifest that perspective, however, is the primary threat to the United States. Both of these facts are merely enabling factors, albeit potent ones. The threatening aspect of Al Qaeda is that it unifies and mobilizes disparate resources from around the world and then channels them at the United States and U.S. interests.

U.S. efforts, therefore, should seek to eliminate Al Qaeda's unified global nature. This would reduce Al Qaeda to a series of localized national movements, which would in turn reduce the direct threat to the United States itself.[2] The danger will shift to U.S. interests overseas. Al Qaeda's remnants can then be defeated piecemeal by U.S. allies with U.S. backing.

## PROPOSED U.S. POLICY ACTIONS

In the interactive dynamic between political and hard power that constitutes counterterrorism policy, politics must frame the U.S. strategy and set the limits of U.S. hard-power actions. Internally, the United States must adhere to its traditional political values when devising and executing its counterterrorism policies in order to maintain credibility and deny the phenomenon of terrorism traction in U.S. politics. Externally, the United States must employ traditional U.S. political values and foreign policy emphases as a guide to devising and implementing U.S. foreign policy—the rule of law, a participatory political system emphasizing the importance of international institutions, and democratic values, such as human rights—to take account of the perceptions and interests of the segments of the world population most supportive of Al Qaeda in order to secure U.S. interests.

### Proposed Soft-Power Approach

Directing U.S. political efforts at Al Qaeda's operatives is unlikely to be effective or efficient. Al Qaeda operatives have already rejected the United States out of hand, and so the United States lacks the credibility to speak to them. Even if the United States could credibly engage them and they were open to being persuaded, the time, effort, and resources necessary to persuade a dedicated Al Qaeda operative are far out of proportion in both absolute and relative terms to the resources necessary to politically, and thus operationally, isolate and diminish that operative by influencing the general population.

Al Qaeda is a transnational, non-state actor, and so the United States must cater to the world's publics, not governments, as its core audience. It is from this center of gravity—focused within the global south in general and the greater Middle East and South Asia in particular—that Al Qaeda incubates and draws operational support. Though the United States has largely co-opted state structures from this region, it is this particular global non-state audience that the United States has most alienated. This audience cannot be controlled through force of arms. Only through the appearance of adhering to globally revered U.S. political values—most notably a participatory political system, the rule of law, and human rights—can the perception of the legitimacy of U.S. rule be created, sustained, enhanced, and then manipulated to U.S. benefit.

The United States must seek to politically undercut Al Qaeda. As the most powerful actor in the international system, the United States can significantly alter the global political landscape to its advantage. By ameliorating salient grievances in the eyes of Al Qaeda's actual and potential adherents and supporters—grievances that Al Qaeda exploits to U.S. political detriment and whose amelioration does not violate core U.S. national interests—the United States can reduce global anger directed at it and deprive Al Qaeda of political fuel, which will then lessen Al Qaeda's capacity for violence.

This can be accomplished by a three-pronged political approach. Each step creates breathing space for the others. Execution, however, must be in tandem.

First, the United States must use its leverage to bring about a negotiated settlement to the Israeli-Palestinian conflict resulting in a viable Palestinian state. The United States has extensive economic, military, and political leverage over both the Israelis and the Palestinians. The few times that serious agreements have ever been reached, or serious progress has ever come close to being realized, were as a result of U.S. involvement.

Israel will have to conclude whether or not it is truly in Israel's longterm interest to continue on its chosen path of perpetual martial conflict with the Palestinians to deny them a state—and the immediate and ever-increasing violence, suffering, and political polarization on both sides that accompanies this position. The alternative is long-term peace and stability wrought from political accommodation that, for the first time, demarcates Israel's boundaries. Israel will, in effect, be choosing whether to remain in the United States' good graces and, as a lesser power and weaker ally, succumb to U.S. interests. It can retain virtually unparalleled U.S. military assistance and political backing as it largely has throughout its history, or it can cross U.S. interests and attempt to sustain its policies without active or passive U.S. backing, since the United States should reduce its support when U.S. interests are threatened.

The plight of the Palestinians is an exceptionally powerful issue that resonates throughout the world's Muslim populace, particularly in the Middle East, where Al Qaeda generates much of its support. Al Qaeda harnesses the anger stemming from the U.S.-backed Israeli treatment of the Palestinians as a potent glue to unite a membership drawn from every Muslim society throughout the world that would otherwise have little in common. Removing this political cohesive will very likely exploit incipient internal fissures among Al Qaeda's myriad nationalities, each of whom have concerns endemic to their own country.

Second, the United States must disengage from Iraq. The negative political repercussions from Iraq are costing the United States international cooperation against a globally networked terrorist enemy. Ever-increasing U.S. blood and treasure are being steadily consumed at an unsustainable rate, thereby weakening the United States for the fight elsewhere. The war has proven an overall recruiting boon for Al Qaeda. Devoid of a U.S. enemy to fight, Al Qaeda in Iraq, once the flagship franchise, will most likely lose global relevance, and thus any strategic significance. While the U.S. presence and connection to Iraq's U.S.-installed regime is highly unlikely to completely evaporate in order to secure competing interests, the U.S. footprint, both actual and perceived, must be minimized.

No matter the details of the U.S. exit, Al Qaeda will claim a victory by virtue of being the last ones on the battlefield. The United States can, however, choose the price it will pay to reach that end. Continued U.S. military action in Iraq operates to U.S. detriment relative to combating Al Qaeda elsewhere in both political and hard-power terms.

Third, and more indirectly, the United States must alter how it manifests its political values.[3] U.S. prosperity in the twenty-first century depends on the United States' effective integration with both the developed and developing world. As the leader of the international system, it is in the United States' national interest to defend the existing political, military, and economic order to preserve U.S. primacy and ensure that the international system is structured to the benefit of U.S. citizens and the detriment of U.S. enemies. The United States will have to intensively engage the rest of the world politically, militarily, and economically, to nurture these arrangements.[4]

The United States must therefore seek to politically avoid creating an international framework that will inspire its opponents to perpetuate their opposition to the United States and unite against it. The "axis of evil" label, for example, commits both of these sins. It lumps otherwise disparate opponents together against the United States, and it gives them no options but continued opposition or capitulation on blatantly U.S. terms.

The United States must also adhere to traditional U.S. political values, principles, and foreign policy emphases. These create checks and balances to help prevent such situations from arising while offering peaceable means of dispute resolution that are fair, reliable, and predictable. Ensuring the United States adheres to the world's rules and traditional U.S. political values and foreign policy emphases—the rule of law, a participatory political system, and democratic values such as human rights—is an executable action. It will likely have a more immediate effect and enduring impact than will proactive U.S. attempts to externally force "regime change" elsewhere in the world.

The United States' adherence to its political values, principles, and foreign policy emphases must be broad and consistent, particularly when there is a potential gap between apparent hard-power desires and soft-power obligations. Selectively using U.S. political values and principles to criticize opponents, as with Iran, only makes the United States look hypocritical. Consistency, as shown in polling around the world, is a critical component to improving U.S. public standing, which is crucial to combating Al Qaeda.

Critics will argue that this philosophic approach and guide to implementation constrains U.S. actions in the face of contemporary challenges and threats. The United States' ability to secure its interests will be inhibited. Potent adversaries who do not play by U.S. rules will then have an advantage. This argument, however, fails on two counts.

Adhering to U.S. political values is fundamental to the United States' political identity. Terrorism is fundamentally a contest of political values, which are manifested in competing interests and the means to pursue them. Wantonly abandoning U.S. political values to subdue an enemy who does not threaten the United States' existence and can be subdued in due time through those values precludes intrinsic and irreparable damage to U.S. political integrity while securing national advantage by isolating Al Qaeda, because the worlds' publics revere those U.S. values that Al Qaeda rejects and seeks to combat.

A major infringement of U.S. freedom of action is also highly unlikely. While a modest imposition may result, the United States is still preeminent and holds many levers of power. Conversely, any lesser infringement upon a proposed U.S. policy is likely to ultimately increase the chances of success for any U.S. policy eventually enacted because it will account for and institutionalize the needs of other actors, thereby giving them a stake in the U.S. action. The benefits of this legitimizing of U.S. actions far outweigh any initial restrictions, which can always be reworked in time.

To this end, the United States can, and should, return to a 1990s-style embrace of international institutions. Such organizations can not only provide political cover for otherwise reticent partners, but they can also serve as a U.S. proxy and ally. American political, economic, and military strength makes these organizations much more likely to serve as pillars of U.S. strength in the post–Cold War world than as a point of constraint upon U.S. action.

Also to this end, the United States must reevaluate the role of democracy in combating Al Qaeda. The Bush administration saw democracy as an antidote to Al Qaeda. Spreading democracy, particularly if by force, is highly unlikely to preclude Al Qaeda's terrorism.

Attempting to defeat Al Qaeda through spreading democracy implies that allowing Al Qaeda's political agenda to come to the surface through legitimate institutional means will eliminate Al Qaeda's need for terrorism. Unfortunately for Al Qaeda, its political goals have very little incipient popular support. If isolated as a stand-alone issue, Al Qaeda would very likely become even further politically isolated and marginalized. Because Al Qaeda's philosophy cannot be falsified, however, its members would likely take an electoral defeat as justification of the value of their cause amid a sea of ignorance, as validation of their need to work harder, and as proof that the need for violence had not yet dissipated.

Democracy does, however, markedly reduce Al Qaeda's ability to mask itself under the guise of more germane and salient local issues, and to usurp those sentiments into support for its own agenda. The process of multiple parties competing for political support distills out various grievances and possible means to redress them among a multitude of actors. Al Qaeda's inherently unpopular platform would most likely lose out to entities spouting anti-Americanism, emphasizing nationalism, and opposing U.S. allies, as was seen in the 2005 Hamas victory in the Palestinian territories. Intentionally depriving Al Qaeda of the excuse of being denied a fair political hearing precludes reducing Al Qaeda's support to only a small core following. Such political isolation and marginalization will, in turn, reduce Al Qaeda's capacity for violence.

The framework the United States currently employs for managing the political dissent throughout the Middle East and South Asia—supporting repressive regimes and generally disavowing peaceful political Islamists—plays directly into Al Qaeda's hands in the present while incubating increased anti-U.S. sentiment for the future. Such measures can secure short- to medium-term U.S. interests until more enduring policy solutions can be devised and enacted. In the long run, however, the United States must prioritize its interests, be willing to accept local, democratically chosen political outcomes that differ from U.S. preferences, and, in light of Al Qaeda, fashion sustainable and enduring policy that takes into account the interests of other, particularly local, actors who have leverage over U.S. interests. Such an approach allows the possibility of building legitimacy for U.S. actions furthering U.S. interests not only in the eyes of foreign states but also of foreign publics, where Al Qaeda hides, and it will give others a stake in defending and owning these U.S. actions.

## Proposed Hard-Power Approach

Unlike the indirect political approach that focuses on the general public over which the United States and Al Qaeda are competing, the hard-power approach is a direct, focused assault upon Al Qaeda itself by the state using diplomacy, military, intelligence, law enforcement, and other coercive efforts to kill or capture Al Qaeda's members. Al Qaeda's activities must be neutralized. This will not only save lives, but it will also show Islamic militants writ large that engaging in terrorism is futile. Six issues are particularly important.

### WMD

The United States must work to reduce the likelihood that Al Qaeda will acquire a weapon of mass destruction. Concurring with a December 2008 report by a bipartisan congressional commission that sounded an alarm over the United States' "shrinking" margin of safety, Pentagon officials stated in June 2010 that the risk of weapons of mass destruction falling into the hands of terrorists is the gravest threat facing the United States. Some studies have predicted terrorist use of a nuclear, biological, chemical, or radiological attack by as early as the end of 2013. Rep. Peter King (R-NY), the co-author of a bill on the prevention and deterrence of possible WMD attacks in the United States, has stated that "there is nothing [he has] seen that says that this will not happen."[5]

The United States should take the lead against this threat. It can do so by: 1) securing "loose" government nuclear materials in the former Soviet Union and around the world; 2) securing uncontrolled civilian nuclear materials, as can be found in research reactors, industrial facilities, medical facilities, and so forth; and 3) initiating more intensive anti-smuggling efforts at the inter-state and non-state levels. The Obama administration's April 2010 nuclear security summit, which hosted leaders from forty-seven countries including "nuclear club" members China, France, India, and Russia, was a positive first step.[6] Much more work, however, still remains, both in terms of technical execution of political decisions as well as addressing the underlying policy issues that create openings for this threat.

### Iran

Iran-related U.S. interests in the emerging Iran-ascendant Middle East are threefold: Iran should not initiate conventional warfare against other countries; it should not use or transfer nuclear weapons, materials, or technologies; and it should not increase its support for regional or global terrorist or subversive activities.

Prohibiting conventional attacks against other states is relatively manageable. Iran's capacity to project power abroad is relatively low. American application of traditional deterrence, diplomatic agreements with key states, the stationing of U.S. troops, and clear and unambiguous statements of U.S. policy coupled with clear and actionable consequences, to include military action up to and including nuclear weapons, can mitigate these concerns.

Whether held overtly, in an Israeli-style strategic ambiguity, or even in a capacity short of weaponizing, nuclear weapons, perhaps the ultimate military weapon and political status symbol, have only limited utility. They strongly afford regime security through deterrence. Regime security, however, is very different from power projection, which is a far more nuanced and multifaceted enterprise. Iran, a country with a civilization of thousands of years whose government seeks to secure itself domestically while making itself a dominant power regionally, is highly unlikely to be the first nuclear power in history to opt for self-annihilation by flouting deterrence and nuclear restraint.

Controlling the WMD-related proliferation will be more difficult. Iran's proliferation to non-state actors is highly unlikely not just because of severe ramifications from other states if held accountable, but also because uncontrollable non-state actors could just as easily strike Iran and its interests. Iran could, however, proliferate at the state level. Such acts of policy would most likely not necessitate such a clear-cut and dire response, as competing interests would be involved in any scenario and such acts could conceivably advance Iran's interests.

Iran's support for illicit networks, whether more directly as with Hezbollah or more tacitly as with Al Qaeda—the very actors thwarting U.S. efforts in Afghanistan, Pakistan, and globally—will be the most challenging aspect. These networks' inherently shadowy nature makes it difficult for the United States to preempt them, prove their involvement after the fact, or counter their efforts. Iranian support for these actors is a direct reflection of the state of U.S.-Iranian political relations, so addressing contentious bilateral policy issues is most apt to be successful in managing this threat.

The United States, however, does not have the necessary tools in place. The United States has painted itself into such a corner that routine diplomacy, much less formal recognition, is treated as a carrot even though the United States and Iran are fundamentally bound through issues of mutual interest. At a minimum, the United States should establish an interest section in Iran and install the necessary bureaucratic apparatus to properly engage in diplomatic relations. In a U.S.-driven reset of relations, and consistent with incremental progress in a yet-to-be-determined quid pro quo, formal diplomatic recognition should follow.

Not only does the United States have insufficient leverage to compel its goals, but Iran also has virtually nothing to gain from current arrangements. The administration is or will be seeking policy changes from the clerical regime that deviate from that regime's traditional orthodoxy. Particularly in light of domestic Iranian political unrest, the political space available for compromises is narrow. Asking Iran to put itself in a position of being able to claim anything domestically other than something of a nontrivial victory against a traditional adversary, who in this case has repeatedly called for the overthrow of the regime with which it is dealing, is highly unlikely to yield productive results.

Critics of such a U.S. approach, who have historically advocated what is now termed "regime change," will cry capitulation, but Iran's clerical regime is solidly established. Recognizing this reality is not equivalent to caving on any particular issue or interest. Rather, it is a tacit acknowledgment of the declining U.S. strategic position—a fact of which both the United States and Iran already are cognizant and which is unlikely to change in the near to medium term.

At worst, such a step will have no, or little, measureable effect. Having changed nothing structural inside Iran, anti-U.S. conservatives will likely gain a short-term political boost. It may even spur Iran to the nuclear finish line. This is an outcome, however, that the United States could not prevent anyway, and where Iran would have been headed otherwise.

At best, a bridge to a more constructive relationship to secure U.S. interests is established. Iran, the dominant power of a crucial region, is nuclear-armed, hostile to the United States, and able to detrimentally influence multiple U.S. political, economic, and security interests, not the least of which are two wars where the outcome is uncertain and the future potency of Al Qaeda is at issue. The only alternative is to have no formal or functional relationship with a country whose leverage over the United States is rising as fast, if not faster, than its importance to the United States.

In this vein, the U.S.-led sanctions campaign should be modified. It has been extensively coercive with only hints of inducements. The selective rescinding of sanctions, whether held as a carrot for a final grand-bargain end state or employed along the way in steps in return for policy action, is a powerful lever whose refinement can enhance the sanctions' effectiveness.

Broad-based sanctions, such as those affecting Iran's energy industries, hurt the population as much if not more than the regime. Not only is the regime actually domestically empowered as it defends against this external repression, but it also has no reason to abandon its nuclear pursuits without a break in U.S.-Iran hostility. Engaging the Iranian public, who have little to no say over the regime's nuclear policies, to give the Iranian people spoils to fight over, would force Iran to look inward and choose among competing options for the future instead of outward to hunker against a hostile threat. Ironically, akin to Castro's Cuba, embracing Iran may help to stir increased domestic political vitality that could be far more conducive to U.S. interests.

The Middle East is on the cusp of its next politico-military evolution, and the United States can neither prevent nor control it. Positioning the United States to manage inevitable realities is prudent. In fact, by removing the strategic confusion of equating regime change with other U.S. goals, the United States will be better positioned to speak to Iran's objectives, which are backed by increasing power and influence, and so the United States will be more likely to succeed.

The United States' prioritizing the prevention of either Iran's actual possession of weapons of mass destruction or its capability to produce them as a function of Iran threatening other states or giving them to terrorists—neither of which speak to Iran's interests—over combating Al Qaeda and its de facto or du jour regional allies is counterproductive. This choice prioritizes a largely inevitable result, over which the United States has little to no control, over a direct and immediate threat to U.S. national security, to which the United States is particularly vulnerable and which it is empowered to combat. Iran has the potential for extensive leverage over Al Qaeda. As Al Qaeda and Iran are primarily bound to one another by common anti-U.S. glue, this could be a malleable point.

Attempting to combat Al Qaeda by trying to salvage Iraq and Afghanistan through a confrontational countering of Iran also undermines these U.S. efforts. Iran benefits from stable and secure neighbors on both of its borders. If it chooses, Iran can bleed the United States in both locations and prolong the fighting at low cost and low risk to itself. Both the United States and Iran, however, have an interest in seeing the Taliban-led insurgency in Afghanistan defeated and Iraq's new state, almost certainly to be Shia-dominated, succeed.

The United States can effectively co-opt Iran's help and work against Al Qaeda with respect to Israel and the Palestinians as well. Mistreating the Palestinians only provides Al Qaeda with a rallying cry. No solution can be found, however, without accounting for Hamas, which derives much support from Iran and is a crucial point of Iranian leverage against Israel and, by extension, the United States. Permitting Israel to repress the Palestinians and attempting to negate election results favoring Hamas, therefore, are counterproductive. Engaging Iran for a constructive role on the plight of the Palestinians is crucial to resolving their fate, which would resolve a U.S. strategic liability. Though Iran would potentially be aiding in removing this U.S. liability, it could potentially garner significant political gain, as well as increased strategic standing if part of a larger U.S. initiative.

### Iraq

The United States must continue to withdraw its forces from Iraq. The situation is largely beyond U.S. control. Competing priorities must be tended. Only a minimal U.S. presence must remain.

Iraq's future independent of the United States is uncertain. The best-case scenario is likely an Iranian-allied, Shia-dominated democracy that is sufficiently politically stable and economically self-sustaining that it does not disrupt its neighbors. A much more likely projection, however, is a Lebanon-like scenario. The state is likely to contest for a monopoly on violence with political parties possessing armed wings and armed groups who have political wings, along with ethnic militias. Perpetual political, security, and economic instability will ensue, setting the stage for long-term violence that ebbs and flows in sync with ever-fluctuating political chaos.

Maintaining meaningful U.S. involvement capable of significantly shaping Iraq's internal arrangements to bolster the position of Iraq's Sunnis will be tempting. Giving the Sunnis a stronger role in the government would likely help counter Iran's influence.[7] Better incorporating them into the state would also likely increase overall stability by depriving Iraq's Sunnis of a need to reinvigorate the insurgency to achieve through military means spoils they could not garner through the political system.

Domestic U.S. politics will also favor maintaining a meaningful U.S. presence. The past expenditure of such massive U.S. blood and treasure combined with partisan dynamics will present a steep challenge to any U.S. president, particularly a Democratic one who wants to withdraw U.S. forces in near totality in the face of violence and instability, which is likely to increase as the U.S. withdrawal progresses. Republicans have already gone on record favoring a continued presence.

The United States' national military and economic capacity, as well as U.S. political capital, however, has been strained to the point where the U.S. has to make conscious trade-offs between its efforts in Iraq and the rest of the world, particularly in Afghanistan and Pakistan, where Al Qaeda central purportedly resides and is protected by its most crucial allies. The United States cannot do justice to any of these separate but interrelated problem sets, much less other security issues, without either a game-changing resource decision, such as national mobilization—and all of the political, economic, and military choices and priority reallocation that entails—or scaling back the scope of the fight to a level consistent with U.S. resources. The Obama administration will have to choose between its perceptions of the consequences for U.S. interests stemming from a semi-functional Iraqi state versus a more potent Al Qaeda–connected threat most directly found in a recalcitrant and minimally accommodating Pakistan and an unsecured Afghanistan.

Al Qaeda in Iraq is likely to reinvigorate. It is highly unlikely, however, to threaten the United States, either tactically or strategically. Not only is the fighting in Iraq losing its international relevance as the United States withdraws, but Al Qaeda in Iraq has also transformed into a local, low-level Sunni militia because the Iraqi people rejected it in its truest jihadist form.

The U.S. venture in Iraq was a strategic distraction from pursuing Osama bin Laden's Al Qaeda. Continued large-scale involvement hinders U.S. efforts against Osama bin Laden's Al Qaeda central today. The U.S. resource allocation—political, military, and economic—must be minimized.

## *Pakistan*

Pakistan-related U.S. interests are threefold: Pakistan must close down the insurgent sanctuaries that blunt the effectiveness of U.S. efforts in Afghanistan; Pakistan must pursue the Al Qaeda threat within its borders; and Pakistan must secure its weapons of mass destruction, which equates to not proliferating to other states and ensuring the security of its capability against non-state actors, such as Al Qaeda and its indigenous militant allies. All are urgent. All need to be addressed simultaneously.

Ensuring the security and the nonproliferation of Pakistan's weapons of mass destruction is the most easily accomplished objective. Islamabad will not benefit if the Pakistan-based terrorist and insurgent groups attacking it acquire nuclear weapons, components, or knowledge. Islamabad is actively working to secure its weapons of mass destruction arsenal and infrastructure with U.S. assistance, though certainly in a less-than-collaborative manner. The A. Q. Khan flap combined with Pakistan's increased dependence on the United States, and thus potentially more severe consequences, makes it unlikely the affair will be repeated.

Enticing Pakistan to pursue Al Qaeda, which is increasing the regional insurgency's lethality while continuing terrorist attacks abroad, and to close down militant sanctuaries, which blunt the effectiveness of the Obama admin-istration's surge and preserve the Al Qaeda–allied militants for another day, will be more difficult. The United States cannot meaningfully dispatch troops against these tasks unilaterally due to a lack of military capacity, Islamabad's firm opposition, and almost certainly counterproductive political fallout that would likely enrage the Pakistani public, collapse Pakistan's civilian government, and possibly incite direct conflict with Pakistani forces. Despite massive U.S. military assistance, economic aid, and political support to induce Pakistani action, a 2010 year-end White House review notes that Pakistan still has not "fundamentally changed its strategic calculus" with respect to closing insurgent sanctuaries on its territories, where Al Qaeda also reportedly hides.[8]

In fact, such U.S. aid plays directly into Pakistan's double game. Playing both ends against the middle, Islamabad extorts U.S. political, economic, and military support that would otherwise be absent—and which only increases as both U.S. enemies and U.S. fears grow more potent over time—by keeping the militants in check, yet preserving them. This enlists U.S. assistance in securing Pakistan's army-dominated domestic political order while protecting Islamabad's regional position, and it preserves the militants for future manipulation in regional affairs as a tool independent of U.S. control.

The Pakistanis view their relationship to the United States as of 2010 as merely transactional. The United States makes demands and offers aid, but it declines a broad, long-term partnership. As noted in the press, "'Kayani wants to talk about the end state in South Asia,' . . . U.S. generals . . . 'want to talk about the next drone attacks.'"[9] Pakistan is in fear of reliving the 1990s when it was militarily, politically, and economically abandoned following the Soviet defeat in Afghanistan.[10]

As articulated by Ashraf Qazi, the chairman of the Council on Pakistan Relations, a Pakistani-American political action group, "It's unreasonable for [the Pakistanis] to be fully engaged and watching out for U.S. interests when their own interests aren't being paid attention to. . . . The [United States] is not taking advantage of the full set of tools it has at its disposal to make it a true partner."[11]

The United States is highly unlikely to be able to shore up Kabul enough to change Pakistan's regional strategic calculus. As of 2010, U.S. military gains are tenuous at best, and they are systemically disadvantaged by Pakistani safe havens. The Karzai regime's governance efforts, while improving, have a long way to go, and they are almost certainly unlikely to improve enough to garner sufficient public loyalty along a U.S. timeline. Though Afghanistan's economy is growing by leaps and bounds, its structural deficiencies, most notably concerning the opium trade, are also highly unlikely to be resolved along a U.S. timeline.

Pakistan is perfectly capable of subduing the region's militants should it make the political decision to act. Speaking *through* Pakistani interests, not *past* them, to U.S.-desired ends in a mutually beneficial way is both necessary and achievable. The United States can achieve its objectives through redressing Pakistan's concerns by altering the external stimuli that shape the structure of Pakistan's society and government.

With both the Pakistani state and the Pakistani people as the audience, the United States must assure Pakistan of its regional security, and it can do so by prioritizing Indian-Pakistani relations. Contrary to the Bush administration's nuclear agreement with India, which was designed to bolster India to serve as a counterweight to China regardless of its impact on Pakistan, the United States must begin formulating its policy toward India, and by extension China, with an eye toward Pakistan. The U.S.-Pakistani relationship must be tended to not just on the Indian-Pakistani border but also in Afghanistan, where Pakistan fears its regional rivals, most notably India, will secure undue influence and work against it. Only then is Pakistan likely to bring the Afghan Taliban to the table or be amenable to resolving long-standing issues surrounding the Durand line.

An unavoidable aspect of this issue is re-evaluating the U.S.-Indian relationship, which, by extension, forces a secondary set of questions for the U.S.-China relationship. China has historically played Pakistan off of India, its southern rival, and so U.S. support for Pakistan is likely to be positively received in those quarters. While India is likely to object to any such recasting of the U.S.

optic, existing U.S. ties, as well as mutual U.S.-Indian concerns about a rising China, provide ample room for further cooperation to prevail over any resulting tension due to a modified U.S. approach to Pakistan. Simultaneously, Pakistan's newfound privileges and obligations—stemming from increased involvement by and a stronger relationship to the United States—should better discipline its international behavior as Pakistan gains something of value to lose. With this region stabilized to U.S. benefit, the United States will then be able to position itself for longer-term questions, such as China.

Beyond new strategic priorities, specific U.S. actions made conditional upon Pakistani cooperation and progress in achieving U.S. goals, which are by no means exclusive to Pakistani interests, are also necessary. Particular emphasis should be given to immediate points of friction, such as the Kashmir dispute, and tension-building actions, such as the burgeoning Pakistani-Indian arms race. Pakistan's unquestioned nuclear status should be acknowledged and accepted, and it should also be brought out of the shadows and put under international monitoring. Long-term security guarantees should be considered. A favorable long-term defense relationship, as exemplified by the U.S. relationship with Egypt, Israel, and Jordan, should be afforded.[12]

Pakistan must take control of its side of the Durand Line and close down militant sanctuaries in FATA, as well as Baluchistan, from which U.S. and allied forces in Afghanistan are attacked. In the short term, this should be accomplished through direct military action. In the long term, Pakistan must absorb the Federally Administrated Tribal Areas into Khyber Pakhtunkhwa.

There is nothing inherently ungovernable about these tribal areas. The FATA—whose people are highly unlikely to shun the social, political, and economic development opportunities afforded to the rest of Pakistan's citizenry— form one of the few officially stateless pieces of land in the world, and Al Qaeda has exploited this situation to gain sanctuary. The FATA's original purpose as a buffer between Britain and Russia has outlived its time, and it is now contrary to U.S. interests.

Pakistan must also capture or kill whatever Al Qaeda central presence resides within its borders. Eliminating this key command node will lessen Al Qaeda's operational threat as a terrorist threat and further weaken the Afghan insurgency. Al Qaeda's destruction sends a message to other jihadist groups. Being destroyed by a Muslim government will significantly politically undermine Al Qaeda in a way that a death blow inflicted by the United States, its morally disreputable enemy, never could.

Islamabad must productively participate in negotiations to end the Afghan insurgency. It must bring the Taliban, HiG, and the Haqqani network to the table, or, with U.S. backing, it must prosecute and destroy them. Islamabad must not only act as a guarantor of whatever accommodations are reached, but it must also give the various Afghan insurgent groups latitude in decision and action above and beyond Pakistan's historic preferences.

Non-U.S.-centric changes will also be necessary. Pakistan must begin to reduce its support for militant groups directed against India. The changing regional strategic context reflecting a U.S. investment in Pakistan's future eliminates the need for their existence.

With both the Pakistani state and the Pakistani people as the audience, the United States should move beyond security issues and announce its political commitment to Pakistan. The United States should do so both to Pakistan as a nation and Pakistani democracy as a government. The United States should openly state that popularly elected leaders and their appointed officials are the accepted U.S. interlocutors. Such a stance supporting institutions is different than supporting individual personalities. This is an important distinction given President Zardari's chronic unpopularity and ineffectiveness, and any such announcement should be keyed to the next set of national elections.

From the Pakistani army's point of view, this will serve as a warning that U.S. aid comes with strings attached. Overthrowing the elected civilian leadership is not permissible, and so U.S. principles and actions will coincide. The timing allows the civilian government more time to recover from the devastating 2010 floods while allowing the United States to capitalize on the Pakistani military's generally low, albeit improving, public standing following the Musharraf dictatorship and help cement it under civilian control. In the highly unlikely event of imminent or occurring truly catastrophic events in the government-versus-insurgent struggle, the United States could always justifiably intervene or rely on the military, akin to the U.S. posture in 2010, by citing a temporary need to engage the lesser of two evils for the greater good.

From the Pakistani public's point of view, such a step will likely increase U.S. standing. It will be an example of marrying U.S. political values with U.S. policy, which in turn furthers U.S. interests. Such a U.S. action speaks directly to the layer of society in which Al Qaeda incubates. Improved U.S. standing, which by definition comes at Al Qaeda's expense, can only empower future U.S. actions, give the Pakistani state breathing room to act in line with U.S. interests, and degrade Al Qaeda's operational capacity.

With both the Pakistani state and the Pakistani people as the audience, the United States should also commit to improving the economic plight of the Pakistani public. Rather than just perpetuating existing arrangements, which are commonly accepted as corrupt and ineffective, U.S. assistance should simultaneously help empower a healthy Pakistani civil society and state governance capacity. In particular, Pakistan's education system should be targeted, with an eye to displacing the madrassa system that incubates militants with a secular-oriented education that will enable Pakistan to better develop its own human capital and compete in the world market. Both unilateral and multilateral efforts will be crucial.

The Obama administration's announced increases of civilian aid are substantial, and they should continue. They are a tangible expression of U.S. goodwill. They not only have the potential to deliver an immediate impact, but they can also be selectively targeted to achieve the maximum political effect.

Significant and prolonged direct U.S. foreign aid alone, however, lessens the requirement for the Pakistani state to form a bond with its citizenry through taxing and spending decisions, which are the decision points of a democratic process that forges political consensus. The Pakistani public does not favor the rule of Islamic militants. By voting spending to combat them, both the Pakistani state and the Pakistani public would take ownership of the fight against Al Qaeda and its associated militants. Al Qaeda and associated militants could lay no claim to responding to U.S. repression, and Al Qaeda would be strategically undercut.

Significant and prolonged direct U.S. foreign aid also stunts domestic political and economic change by artificially perpetuating the status quo. Corruption and kleptocracy is directly enabled. The Taliban's exploitation of the very political and economic conditions that it rode to domination in the Swat valley, whose politico-economic situation is very similar to much of the rest of the country, is readily enabled. Providing economic opportunity through the secular economy and the Pakistani state to potential supporters of Al Qaeda only drains the swamp of potential Al Qaeda support by providing other outlets for economic improvement. Al Qaeda's operational capacity would most likely be degraded.

Significant and prolonged direct U.S. foreign aid will also systemically sacrifice U.S. national advantage. Particularly in the case of Pakistan, which offers the twin threats of terrorism and the possibility of nuclear black markets, the Pakistani state, particularly its military, has adeptly blackmailed the world community. Pakistan has not only come to depend on foreign aid, it has also come to expect foreign aid. The return on such payments in terms of the number of militants captured or plots stopped has been disproportionately negative.

Alternative means of aid requiring Pakistan to take visible and proactive actions versus gaining aid with little to no transparency will likely achieve greater U.S. policy success. The United States should establish an international trust for Pakistan managed by an international organization of standing, such as the World Bank. It would function in a manner akin to that of the trust set up for Afghanistan. Pakistani entities will have to contribute to their own aid programs, develop plans for execution, adhere to international accounting standards, and make expenditure data transparent and available to all, particularly the Pakistani public.

The advantages are several. Actual and potential Al Qaeda adherents and supporters would not be able to claim that Pakistan was a client state doing U.S. bidding, thus making it easier to justify violence. Countries could donate to Pakistan and assist in combating Al Qaeda without the stigma of cooperating with the United States. Countries that failed to deliver promised aid would be publicly identified and shamed, thus adding a measure of enforcement to claims of support. The actual needs of the Pakistani public would be addressed, not pet interests of donor countries or the desires of a corrupt Pakistani state. The financial burden of assisting Pakistan would be expanded beyond the United States, which would potentially tap far greater resources while likely gaining a more enduring basis. A Pakistani public mobilized and empowered by improvements in their lives, stemming from the Pakistani state's cooperation with the international community versus being subsidized by it to maintain current conditions, will likely set the stage for public demands and state enactment of fiscal reform, tax reform, anticorruption efforts, and better overall governance.

Pakistani military and civilian leaders will likely pose objections. They will likely decry such an act as infringement on their sovereignty. They are free to refuse such an offer, which should be highly publicized to the Pakistani people. They may also state that the civilian government will fall without unfettered access to aid. Poor governance tarnishing the name of democracy, however, is a far greater threat than a temporary military dictatorship taking over to do U.S. bidding in the short term before it discredits itself and a more popular democratic government returns.[13]

The United States can bilaterally complement these efforts. It can lower trade barriers and tariffs for Pakistani textiles and other products. The United States can also work to obtain such trading privileges for Pakistan with other U.S. allies in both bilateral and multilateral forums.[14]

In conjunction with these steps—broad security, political, and economic approaches and their specific actions—the United States must also begin to scale back the U.S. drone missile program. When selectively used, this program can inflict pinpoint casualties among ranking personalities that may induce a strategic impact. The Obama administration, however, has broadened the target set and increased the volume of strikes to the point that these strikes have been converted into the equivalent of modern-day cannon fire across the border. As evidenced by polling in both the FATA and in Pakistan's settled areas, this U.S. approach is building ever more virulent anti-U.S. sentiment. In the long run, this undermines the U.S. range of action in Pakistan by limiting the Pakistani state's range of political movement relative to the United States while giving Al Qaeda a more secure political sentiment within which to hide, which only increases its operational capability.

The strikes have failed to strategically alter the U.S.-Al Qaeda balance. Such a military capability has a role on the battlefield, but these strikes in themselves are not a policy that can defeat Al Qaeda. While they should continue, these strikes should be narrowed in focus and tamped down in volume as the new security, political, and economic approaches take effect and Pakistan's effectiveness increases against Al Qaeda and associated militants.

### Afghanistan

The Obama administration must continue to increase and sustain its commitment to Afghanistan. The Afghanistan theater is a unique haven for Al Qaeda that cannot be duplicated. The Obama administration has attempted to improve security, the underwriter of all governance progress and economic development, through a four-step, Iraq-style surge. Each stage of this Iraq-style surge is both necessary and possible. Though the Obama administration's strategy has positioned the United States to succeed, changes are necessary for the Afghan context.

Arbitrary deadlines not keyed to conditions on the ground must be eliminated. There is fundamentally a contest of wills between the United States and a Taliban-led insurgency. Al Qaeda and the Taliban have time on their side, and they are willing to wait out the U.S. presence.

U.S. and allied troop levels must continue to rise. Roughly two-thirds of the Afghan countryside and approximately 40 percent of its population have gone untouched by U.S. efforts at their 2010 peak, and thus have been effectively ceded to the insurgents. The possibility that even more forces may be necessary must be permitted. Rather than just a spike, troop levels must continue to remain elevated.

Indigenous forces must be increased beyond initial planning. Approximately 500,000 to 750,000 forces, if not more, are needed. Both increased pay, so that government salaries are at least competitive with the militants, if not better, as well as combat support and combat service support equipment, which the United States was willing to provide in Iraq but has been reluctant to provide in Afghanistan, must also be employed to improve quality and reduce attrition.

The numbers of trainers must be substantially increased. As noted by Bruce Riedel, "In the long term, the ticket in Afghanistan is an Afghan army that is large enough. It will be a lot cheaper to pay for an Afghan army than a U.S. expeditionary force." Roughly seventy Afghan soldiers can be fielded per year at the cost of a single U.S. soldier.[15]

Trainers, and the derivative local forces, however, are not a substitute for additional U.S. combat and support troops. As shown by the failed effort to rush in newly trained Iraqi forces and abdicate the frontline U.S. role, such new forces lack the political and technical wherewithal to substitute for U.S. forces. A substantial U.S. force presence partnered with local units is necessary.

Indigenous local police forces and militias could create a change in the overall balance of forces. They must, however, be handled differently in Afghanistan compared to Iraq. Three key changes are necessary.

Any local forces that are raised should be based upon established districts, not tribes and villages. The general population must be tied to the government in a self-defense partnership. This simultaneously increases security while increasing the writ of the state.

Militias should not be raised in the absence of foreign and Afghan forces but in augmentation to them. After U.S. and Afghan forces clear an area, militias can then hold the area. It is unclear to Afghanistan's general population who will win, and so placing the militias on their own is unlikely to yield effective results when the bulk of the population is simply biding its time to wait and see who the winner is so they will know with whom to side.

When U.S. troops or Afghan forces cannot be dispatched to clear an area, and it is deemed that that area cannot wait for U.S. or national government forces to arrive, then U.S. Special Forces should be dispatched. They must work in concert with indigenous populations, as is their mantra.[16] Their use as shock troops should be done sparingly.

As a precursor to reducing the number of insurgent factions, regional consensus among prominent state actors must be developed. As noted above, the United States must preclude Pakistan's double game by engaging Pakistani-Indian issues. The United States must also make Afghanistan and Al Qaeda a filter for its policy toward Iran, which is engaging in its own double game of playing both the Afghan government and insurgency against one another. The interests of Russia, China, India, and Saudi Arabia, as well as corresponding U.S. policy, must also be brought into the fold.

Focusing its efforts to co-opt insurgent factions, the United States should attempt to flip the Afghan Taliban. While the Haqqani network may be particularly violent, the Afghan Taliban is the insurgency's center of gravity. They have not only the will but also the necessary demographic and geographic sway to help govern Afghanistan, which has historically been ruled by southern Pashtuns. Both Hekmatyar and the Haqqani network lack demographic sway, geographic coverage, distance from Al Qaeda, and an ability to govern.

The bulk of U.S. forces should be concentrated against the Taliban in order to jeopardize their military position. Akin to Iraq's Sunnis, they need to be placed in a position of needing U.S. and central government assistance. Only then will they likely become independent of Pakistan or turn on any of the other militant groups. As of 2010, three to five years of hard fighting will likely be necessary, at a minimum, to break insurgent momentum through purely military means.

At the same time, the United States itself should open channels to the Taliban, as well as other factions not intimately interwoven with Al Qaeda. Press reports note that the United States assesses that the Afghan Taliban are tired from the fighting, and cracks in insurgent unity are surfacing. The opportunity for direct negotiations, which do not equate to U.S. capitulation, could magnify and exacerbate those fissures.

Having a channel in place will be a crucial first step for when the time is ripe for negotiations, but these negotiations are unlikely to proceed similar to past U.S. conflicts. It is unlikely that any immediate results will be obtained until the fighting has crested and one side has begun to waver, an action which could take three to five years, so expectations must be acclimated. While the Taliban high command will almost certainly ultimately have to be engaged and brought on board, the decentralized nature of the Taliban means that negotiations can, and should, proceed on a piecemeal basis to whittle away locally oriented enemy forces.[17]

No matter what, two levels of buy-in must be obtained. Internal to Afghanistan, the United States must develop a common understanding with the Karzai government and execute in lockstep, with a single voice, so that the insurgents have a clear message, identified interlocutors, and a measure of trust in the process. External to Afghanistan, the United States must broker a new regional security arrangement that takes into account the interests of key regional powers—India, Iran, Russia, and China—in a manner conducive to U.S. interests.

Pakistan, however, plays the most crucial role. Because of its sway over the Taliban, the Haqqani network, Hezb-e-Islami/Gulbuddin, and other associated militant groups, it has the potential to play the role of a spoiler, a role that Pakistan showed it is willing to play when it arrested Mullah Berader. Any outreach to the Taliban must be done in conjunction with negotiations with Pakistan. Any attempt to negotiate independent of Pakistan is highly unlikely to be successful, both because Pakistan is likely to sabotage it and because the Pakistan-based Afghan militants will lack sufficient strength to stand on their own and speak credibly.

Afghan nationalism must be harnessed. The Afghan public generally draws a distinction between foreigners—both foreign fighters from around the world and Pakistani Taliban—and natives. The Taliban are viewed as fellow Afghans. They are perceived to have a rightful place at the political table.

Crucially, Afghanistan's historic power structure—the tribes—must be reinvigorated. The Taliban primarily come from the lowest social and economic classes. "Mohammad Omar has never enjoyed the full support of Pashtuns. He is a lowly figure in tribal terms, and he is blamed by many of them for the calamity that has befallen Afghanistan. Reaching out to tribal leaders is what will move negotiations."[18]

It will be necessary for the United States to accede to Afghanistan's political self-determination. The purpose of negotiations should be to bring the Taliban into a U.S.-backed political order. The United States must be willing to allow a more substantial political presence for the southern Pashtuns, which necessarily implies an increased role for Taliban and related insurgent interests as well.

The United States must remove the stigma of international terrorism from the Taliban to enable negotiations. No Afghan attacked the United States on September 11, and many an Afghan fought the Soviets. Al Qaeda is the enemy that attacked on 9/11 and seeks to again, not the Afghans.

At the same time, the United States must actively back the emerging government structure vice cutting it loose to fend for itself once created. The current fighting is now a de facto continuation and internationalized edition of Afghanistan's long-running, low-grade civil war that existed prior to the U.S. invasion. The idea of peace talks conjures fears of a return of the deposed Taliban regime in many of Afghanistan's formerly Taliban-repressed minorities, the most potent of whom constitute members of the U.S.-aligned former Northern Alliance, and ethnic tension is likely to enliven.[19] The United States must be willing to offer both pressure and inducements to key ethnic factions, notably the Tajiks. More broadly, the United States must offer political, economic, and military aid and guarantees to the emerging Afghan state so that the various Afghan factions have an incentive to sign on to a new and better opportunity.

Simultaneously, Hamid Karzai, and his successor, must be embraced and supported rather than criticized and left to fend for themselves. The Obama administration's public shunning and castigation only forces Afghanistan's president into alliances with warlords inside Afghanistan and with regional states with interests of dubious value to the United States, such as Iran and Pakistan, outside Afghanistan. Setting benchmarks that will benefit Afghanistan's core constituencies and providing assistance to reach those benchmarks, akin to Bush's Iraq benchmarks, will both strengthen Karzai and help build legitimacy for the national government.

Amid political chaos and military uncertainty, President Karzai, who leads a very weak state, is looking out for his family, his clan, his tribe, his ethnic group, and his nation—often in that order. President Karzai's failure to build a political party or to engage in more substantial institution-building only ensures that graft will remain a fundamental adhesive for his personality-based system of government in Afghanistan's highly fractured society. This dynamic must be embraced, built upon, and manipulated, because fighting it is a losing prospect.

Disputes over corruption must be mitigated delicately, selectively, and behind the scenes. Privately, in such a crony-based system devoid of strong political and government institutions, the threat to Karzai's power structure from anticorruption efforts is significant. Publicly, Afghanistan is a culture where "face" and "honor" are crucial.

The issue of graft must also be parsed. Negative corruption drives apart key centers of gravity and precludes the functioning of the state. This must be combated. Positive corruption pulls key centers of gravity together and lubricates state machinery to achieve desired outcomes. In the short term, this must be tolerated.

At the same time, the United States must look to reduce the ease with which corruption occurs, and this means reforming the international contracting processes. The U.S.-led international presence pumps billions of dollars into the contracting process. Injecting such large quantities of cash into a country devoid of a solid legal structure, reliable financial system, and weak enforcement of whatever few laws do exist, in the context of such extreme poverty and political upheaval, is only asking for trouble.

American efforts at improving Afghan governance must also be modified. U.S. efforts in Afghanistan to date have been centered on building a strong, centralized state. A strong, unitary state, however, is counter to Afghanistan's historical and cultural predisposition. In a largely road-less country where only 20 percent of those roads that do exist are paved, where a national electronic communications infrastructure does not exist, where the national government has few to no resources, and where there is only a 30 percent literacy rate at best, the Kabul-based national government isolated in the Hindu Kush mountains cannot provide the necessary services in an effective, efficient, or timely manner to Afghanistan's thirty-four provinces, which possess numerous ethnic groups, languages, and a challenging topography.

U.S. efforts must be redirected toward increasing the political and economic capacity of the local and provincial levels, which serve as the thin line between the insurgent militants and the general populace. While U.S. and foreign efforts have been devoted to building a strong national government, the Taliban have been increasing control at the local level in rural areas, which is where 90 percent of the Afghan population lives. The central government should focus on providing services national in scope such as military and police forces, electricity, roads, postal services, and so forth. Actual governance, however, must occur at the district and provincial levels and be the result of a melding of Afghanistan's traditional tribal, religious, and social structures and customs.[20]

Counterinsurgency is fundamentally an exercise in competitive governance between the state and the insurgents. The provincial and local governments, not Kabul, should focus directly on providing immediate public services, whose absence creates the window within which insurgents operate. The central government would then serve as an overseeing check on local power to counter corruption and ensure overall loyalty by serving as a reserve force to politically, economically, and militarily back these frontline local governments with national-level resources. Any increase in security is only temporary at best unless the Afghan government claims the economic and political space that forms the civic life that insurgents are attempting to dominate.

American assistance must consist of both expertise and financial assistance, but the manner in which it is applied must also change. As happened at the 2010 Kabul conference, the U.S.-led foreign presence must commit to channeling resources through the central government, not undercutting it, in order to empower it and permit it to play its proper role in supporting the provinces.[21] Derived from Kabul-provided funds, locally and provincially administered micro-loans and micro-grants, which are far less susceptible to the corruption that is endemic to massive quantities of money given to ill-managed bureaucracies with poor accountability, will be much more likely to yield high-impact, highly visible results.

A serious hiring program for development personnel on the part of the U.S. government will be necessary to properly administer and implement any new assistance. Afghanistan is a long-term U.S. interest. The United States must begin to build institutional capacity.

Concurrently, the Provincial Reconstruction Team (PRT) program will have to change. Not only will the number of teams have to increase since there is not even one team per province, much less multiple teams per province to account for poor accessibility to many areas, but their composition will also have to change. These teams are overwhelmingly military. The quantity and quality of civilian expertise will have to dramatically increase. It will also be necessary for the number of PRTs to channel their largesse through the provincial and local governments vice serving as independent power centers in the outlying regions that, in practice, undermine the central government by becoming a rival power center with more resources.

It will be necessary to take high-profile acts against negative government corruption at the national and provincial levels. The average Afghan spends approximately one-fifth of his annual income on bribes.[22] The post-2009 national election winner Hamid Karzai must take highly visible steps, both symbolic and substantive. The most corrupt cabinet ministers, provincial governors, and district governors—all of whom are appointed by and respond to Kabul—must be perpetually evaluated, and fired and prosecuted if necessary, with the predisposition that assistance in combating the Taliban and Al Qaeda does not constitute permission to engage in negative corruption. This was exemplified by Mohammad Ibrahim Adel, the minister of mines who took a $30 million bribe to award a contract to a Chinese firm.[23]

Afghanistan's past, and the grievances it has spurred, must be acknowledged. The post–Soviet civil war warlords, who committed mass atrocities and now live openly in Kabul and the provinces, should be subject to a South African–style truth commission. This will afford a measure of justice for the victims while taming and co-opting, but not directly confronting and combating, the competing power structures that these leaders represent.

Afghanistan's opium production must also be addressed. U.S. efforts in Afghanistan to date have largely called for eliminating Afghanistan's poppy crop. This, however, is a situation counter to Afghanistan's socioeconomic dynamics and to achieving the desired politico-military dynamics for counterinsurgency.

Roughly 80 percent of the general populace supports itself through agriculture. Poppies can be found throughout the country, and especially in the regions where the insurgency is strongest. Directly attacking either the crop itself or the crop's immediate producers will only drive the population into the arms of the insurgents by depriving people of their livelihood. Using U.S. forces to stamp out opium poppy is also an ineffective use of limited troops.

Insurgent attacks are very inexpensive. In a relative sense, they are minuscule in cost compared to what it takes to sustain the foreign presence. The insurgency derives sufficient funding from donations—from within Afghanistan and Pakistan as well as from overseas, crime, and other means—to remain viable.

The long-term solution is to build up the state and slowly interpose it, and the opportunities that it brings, between the people and narcotics production, off of which the insurgents leach. This must be accomplished through incentives, such as alternative crop assistance, vice punishment. Poppy production thus becomes a yardstick by which governance and development can be measured.

Afghanistan's political evolution will most likely unfold at a different, almost certainly slower, pace than its security evolution born of the U.S.-led military effort, which will itself take considerable time. When security is expanded, governance and economic development efforts must be ready to rapidly fill the void. Reform at the national and provincial levels, therefore, must proceed concurrently with the expanded military effort and not as a precondition to it.[24]

### Al Qaeda's Global Presence

The United States must continue to engage Al Qaeda's diffuse global presence. Afghanistan and Pakistan make up the core region for the presence of Al Qaeda and its associated militant allies. Al Qaeda, however, maintains a presence in nearly sixty countries, and Islamist insurgencies exist in nearly twenty.

Whenever possible, the United States must seek local surrogates, as with the governments of Somalia and Yemen. This approach conserves U.S. resources. It also keeps the fight local. The local conditions driving Islamic militancy with a potential for global reach can then be addressed, thus undercutting the local group.

The United States must continue to unilaterally attack Al Qaeda operatives and communications around the world where their presence is less substantial but still threatening, in order to preempt attacks. These steps, however, must be done in a reformed manner consistent with traditional U.S. political values. The absence of a domestic political consensus behind any one approach means that enduring, viable policies will not be established because each U.S. administration will seek to implement its own vision in response to the political reaction received by its predecessor. Counterterrorism will become politicized. Policy success against the problem set intended to further the national interest will suffer.

Most fundamentally, and largely in contrast to the Bush administration, the Obama administration must work with Congress to build a legal framework reflecting a political consensus on how to capture, detain, interrogate, adjudicate, and then imprison Al Qaeda suspects. This must be done in a manner consistent with the U.S. constitution, established U.S. jurisprudence, established U.S. political values, and public sentiment. Only then will there be meaningful, long-term alternatives to torturing Al Qaeda detainees, kidnapping and extraditing suspects abroad for torturous interrogation, indefinite detainment without trial, judicial commissions deviating from U.S. standards of justice, warrantless wiretapping, and killing U.S. citizens without trial. Only then will Al Qaeda's critique of U.S. hypocrisy be undercut and its operational capacity diminished. Only then will the political values that define the American national character be ensured and terrorism's domestic political traction stunted.

## CONCLUSION

The U.S.-Al Qaeda struggle is likely to be a long-term one. The political agendas of the United States and Al Qaeda are almost entirely mutually exclusive. Each actor has an enduring nature. And given that Al Qaeda draws upon the world's Muslim community for support, a population of over 1 billion people, the United States is highly unlikely to ever kill or capture all of Al Qaeda's operatives or cut off all of its sources of support. The United States, therefore, must manage this conflict instead of seeking Al Qaeda's elimination.

Hard power is necessary. Terrorism's security threat enables its political potency. Hard power alone can dismantle Al Qaeda's organizational capacity for violence.

A macro U.S. approach favoring hard power, however, is likely to fail. Terrorism's operational dynamics favor Al Qaeda, not the United States. Voluminous resources will be inefficiently expended. In that type of a long-term fight, Al Qaeda will be more likely to win the contest of wills.

A purely hard-power approach also ignores the political core of the U.S.-Al Qaeda struggle that both frames and drives the conflict. At best, U.S. hard-power efforts might hold Al Qaeda in check. At worst, short-term tactical gain is achieved at long-term strategic expense by further aggravating the political base of the conflict through politically offensive means of implementation, such as using force in contravention of international law, as in Iraq, or abandoning human rights when detaining terrorist operatives, as with the U.S. rendition program.

Any hard-power efforts must be executed in tandem with attention to the political context that frames, and thus empowers, their application. These steps give U.S. leadership global legitimacy. This is crucial for U.S. efforts to combat a non-state adversary wherein the actions and attitudes of the general population, which are beyond the purview of the host-state's coercive power, are crucial factors. Due to a long history of a gap between U.S. words and actions in the eyes of Al Qaeda's actual and potential supporters, however, the United States must speak with actions, not words. The United States can then wield its standing to national advantage.

External to Al Qaeda, U.S. efforts can narrow Al Qaeda's room for political maneuver. Employing soft power, U.S. adherence to traditional U.S. political values—the rule of law, a participatory political system emphasizing the importance of international institutions, and democratic values, such as human rights—in the formation and execution of grander U.S. foreign policy, such as not attempting to spread democracy by force and embracing international institutions, will increase domestic and international perceptions of the legitimacy of global U.S. leadership. The stronger this perception, the less likely potential supporters among the disenfranchised, angry, and otherwise disaffected Muslim populace will be willing to actively or passively materially aid Al Qaeda. Employing hard power, the United States can undertake efforts to reduce Al Qaeda's potential access to weapons of mass destruction, deprive Al Qaeda of a venue to engage the United States by withdrawing from Iraq, establish a more positive modus vivendi with Iran, ramp up in Afghanistan, secure a new regional security order for Pakistan to close Al Qaeda's strategic geographic envelope, and pressure Al Qaeda's diffuse global presence, most notably in Yemen and Somalia.

Internal to Al Qaeda, U.S. efforts can play upon Al Qaeda's inherent internal weaknesses, primarily the conflicting nationalisms and endemic localized concerns of Al Qaeda's international polyglot membership. This will help to weaken the political glue that holds a diverse multinational organization with multiple competing centers of gravity together in a unified network directed at the United States. Specifically, the United States can undertake policies that do not serve as a global rallying point against it, such as working to resolve the plight of the Palestinians, reducing the U.S. presence in Iraq, and adhering to traditional U.S. political values and foreign policy emphases.

The political sentiments upon which Al Qaeda capitalizes will always exist. Making Al Qaeda the primary U.S. security policy evaluative prism for political issues salient to Islamic militancy, however, can lessen Al Qaeda's threat to the United States by reducing it to a series of localized national movements, thus eliminating its unified global nature. American political, economic, and military resources will be conserved, and other key foreign and domestic policy issues can then be more meaningfully addressed.

# Notes

**INTRODUCTION**

1. "Brutal Reality: The War is Fueling Global Jihad," *New York Daily News*, 21 February 2007, http://www.intelcenter.com/audio-video/qaeda.html.
2. Shibley Telhami, *The Stakes: America and the Middle East* (Cambridge, MA: Westview, 2002), 5–6.
3. President George W. Bush's address to the nation, 20 September 2001.
4. Stephen M. Walt, "Taming American Power," *Foreign Affairs*, September/October 2005, http://www.foreignaffairs.com/articles/61025/stephen-m-walt/taming-american-power?page=2.
5. "U.S. Recruits a Rough Ally to Be a Jailer," *New York Times*, 1 May 2005; "Terror Detainees Sent to Egypt," *Washington Times*, 16 May 2005; "Ending Torture Outsourcing," *Washington Times*, 11 April 2005; "2 Yemenis Allege Secret U.S. Detention," *Philadelphia Inquirer*, 4 August 2005; Craig S. Smith and Souad Mekhennet, "Algerian Tells of Dark Odyssey in U.S. Hands," *New York Times*, 7 July 2006, http://www.nytimes.com/2006/07/07/world/africa/07algeria.html.
6. See also Thomas Pickering, Carla Hills, and Morton Abramowitz, "The Answer in Pakistan," *Washington Post*, 13 November 2007; Rashid Khalidi, "Yankee Go Home: In the Mideast, America Casts an Imperial Shadow," *Washington Post*, 11 November 2007; Robert Staloff, "How to Win the War of Ideas," *Washington Post*, 10 November 2007.
7. Steven Kull, "America's Image in the World," Testimony before House Committee on Foreign Affairs, Subcommittee on International Organizations, Human Rights, and Oversight, 6 March 2007, http://www.worldpublicopinion.org/pipa/articles/views_on_countriesregions_bt/326.php?nid=&id=&pnt=326&lb=btvoc; Program on International Policy Attitudes, "Large and Growing Numbers of Muslims Reject Terrorism, Bin Laden," 6 March 2007, http://www.worldpublicopinion.org/pipa/articles/international_security_bt/221.php.
8. Fareed Zakaria, "We're Safer than We Think," *Washington Post*, 13 September 2010.

## CHAPTER 1. THE FRAMEWORK OF THE U.S.-AL QAEDA STRUGGLE

1. Graham Allison and Philip Zelikow, *Essence of Decision: Explaining the Cuban Missile Crisis* (New York: Longman, 1999), 16–17; Herbert Simon, "Human Nature in Politics: The Dialogue of Psychology with Political Science," *American Political Science Review* 79 (1985): 293–304. Rationality is defined as "behavior that is appropriate to specified goals in the context of a given situation."

2. Both the United States and Osama bin Laden's Al Qaeda central have a marked disparity in power and presence between themselves and their respective allies. While not insignificant, these lesser allies clearly play a supporting role to their respective power centers. Due to these parallel circumstances, which will be explained in greater detail in the forthcoming chapters, and for the sake of simplicity and clarity, however, this book will refer to the antagonists as Al Qaeda and the United States.

3. Craig Whitlock, "The New Al Qaeda Central: Far from Declining, the Network Has Rebuilt, with Fresh Faces and a Vigorous Media Arm," *Washington Post*, 9 September 2007. A network, by definition, can survive the loss of any of its semiautonomous nodes and continue to function, as each node is imbued with the organization's practical goals, motivating ideology, and operational capabilities. By contrast, the opposite of a network would be a centralized, military-style, hierarchical command-and-control structure, with authority parsimoniously dispersed throughout, that is immobilized when leadership nodes are lost.

4. For more on the origins of Al Qaeda, see John Esposito, *Unholy War: Terror in the Name of Islam* (Oxford: Oxford University Press, 2002).

5. Bard O'Neil, *Insurgency and Terrorism: From Revolution to Apocalypse*, 2nd ed. (Dulles, VA: Potomac Books, 2005), 15.

6. Hamid Mir, "September 28: Interview in *Ummat*," in *JIHAD: Bin Laden in His Own Words, Declarations, Interviews, and Speeches,* ed. Brad K. Berner (Charleston, SC: Booksurge, 2006), 99; "Recorded Audio Message by Ayman al-Zawahiri," Al Jazeera Television, 10 September 2003, and "Exposing the New Crusader War," Usama Bin Ladin, 23 May 2002, both cited in Anonymous, *Imperial Hubris: Why the West Is Losing the War on Terror* (Washington, DC: Brassey's Inc., 2004), 131.

7. Bernard Lewis, "Time for Toppling," *Wall Street Journal*, 27 September 2002; "Now the War Has Begun," in Anonymous, *Imperial Hubris*, 13; Iqbal al-Sibai, "Interview with Al Azhar Grand Imam Shaykh Mohammad Sayyid Tantawi," cited in Anonymous, *Imperial Hubris*, 11. An attack upon the Muslim people is exemplified by U.S. support for "apostate" Islamic governments in Kuwait, the UAE, Egypt, Jordan, Saudi Arabia, and elsewhere. The corrupt, oppressive regimes are viewed as being approved of

and protected by U.S. democracy. An attack upon Muslim lands is exemplified by how "America now occupies and effectively rules the Muslim states of Afghanistan, Iraq, and the states of the Arabian Peninsula, the Prophet Mohammad's birthplace."An attack upon Islam is exemplified by U.S. demands that "Muslim educational authorities alter their curricula to teach a brand of Islam more in keeping with modernity and, not coincidentally, U.S. interests."

8. Anonymous, *Imperial Hubris*, 7.

9. James Turner Johnson, "Jihad and Just War," *First Things: A Journal of Religion and Public Life* (June–July 2002): 12; Bernard Lewis, "Deconstructing Osama," *Wall Street Journal*, 23 August 2002. As noted by Bernard Lewis, "Bin Laden is not a ruler, and therefore not tainted with tyranny and corruption. . . . Even more striking is the contrast demonstrated in his personal life between himself and the present-day rulers of most of the Arab lands. . . . Osama bin Laden presents the inspiring spectacle of one who, by his own free choice, has forsaken a life of riches and comfort for one of hardship and danger." See also Mohsin Iqbal, "Exclusive Interview with Taleban Supreme Leader Mullah Mohammad Omar," 29 April 2002, cited in Anonymous, *Imperial Hubris*, 125.

10. Anonymous, *Imperial Hubris*, 8.

11. Berner, *JIHAD*, 189.

12. Questions can certainly be raised about how genuinely bin Laden feels for these causes and whether or not he is merely exploiting situations for political gain. The bottom line, however, is that he has routinely articulated these grievances as his main foci since the September 11 attacks. These points are what the public sees and evaluates. This information, therefore, is presented at face value without delving into possible ulterior motives because Al Qaeda has established these objectives as a data point in the political dimension of the U.S.-Al Qaeda terrorism struggle.

13. Bruce Lawrence, ed., and James Howarth, trans., *Messages to the World: The Statements of Osama bin Laden* (New York: Verso, 2005), 226.

14. Hamid Mir, "*Ausaf*, 10 November 2001," in Lawrence and Howarth, *Messages to the World*, 139.

15. Malise Ruthven, "Fury for God: The Islamist Attack on America," in *Imperial Hubris*, 158.

16. Statement by Al Qaeda in Saudi Arabia, 3 September 2003, in Brad K. Berner, *The World According to Al Qaeda* (New Delhi: Atlantic Publishers and Distributors, 2007), 251.

17. Anonymous, *Imperial Hubris*, 153.

18. Lawrence and Howarth, *Messages to the World*, 47–48.

19. Anonymous, *Imperial Hubris*, 153.

20. Mir, "*Ausaf*, 10 November 2001," in Lawrence and Howarth's *Messages to the World*, 151.

21. Anonymous, *Imperial Hubris*, 153.

22. For more see Stephen Walt, *Taming American Power* (Corning, NY: Cornell University Press, 2005), 29. As of 2003, U.S. defense spending equaled the next thirteen countries combined, which includes a sevenfold advantage over China. For more, see Richard Cooper, "Is 'Economic Power' a Useful and Operational Concept?" working paper, World Development Indicators Database (Weatherhead Center for International Affairs, Harvard University, 2003). See also *MIT Technology Review*, "The Technology Review Patent Scorecard 2004," http://www.technologyreview/scorecards/2004, cited in Walt, *Taming American Power*, 32. The United States has held steady at 25 to 30 percent of world production from 1960 to the present and possesses an economy 60 percent larger than its closest rival, Japan. China is cited as the rising "peer competitor" power, but it is decades behind.

23. Telhami, *The Stakes*, 134–136.

24. The following works were instrumental in concluding this definition: Alex P. Schmid and Albert J. Jongman, *Political Terrorism: A New Guide to Actors, Authors, Concepts, Databases, Theories, and Literature* (Amsterdam: North-Holland Publishing Company, 1988); Harry Eckstein, ed., *Internal War: Problems and Approaches* (Toronto: MacMillan Publishing Company, 1964); Martha Crenshaw, *Terrorism, Legitimacy, and Power: The Consequences of Political Violence* (Middletown, CT: Wesleyan University Press, 1983); Paul Wilkinson, *Terrorism and the Liberal State* (London: MacMillan, 1973); Harold Vetter and Gary Perlstein, *Perspectives on Terrorism* (Belmont, CA: Wadsworth, 1991); Special Issue: Terrorism and Political Violence, *Peace Review* 7, no. 3/4 (1995).

25. T. Thornton, quoted in Eckstein, *Internal War*; Robert A. Pape, *Dying to Win: The Strategic Logic of Suicide Terrorism* (New York: Random House, 2005).

26. The possible exception to this statement is terrorist employment of a sophisticated weapon of mass destruction. A brief summary of the issue is that while the potential magnitude of devastation from such an attack is high and the social and political impact could be extreme, the likelihood of such an attack is low. As such, this point is acknowledged but not belabored in this book. For further information on this topic see Jessica Stern, *The Ultimate Terrorists* (Boston: Harvard University Press, 1991).

27. David Rappoport, *Politics of Atrocity* (New York: John Jay Press, 1977), 47.

28. Henry Schuster, "Al-Zawahiri Letter under Scrutiny," CNN.com, 19 October 2005, http://www.cnn.com/2005/WORLD/meast/10/19/take.letter/index.html.

29. Eric Schmitt and Mark Mazzetti, "Secret Order Lets U.S. Raid Al Qaeda in Many Countries," *New York Times*, 10 November 2008.

30. Lawrence and Howarth, *Messages to the World*, 112. "On October 10, 2001, the White House announced that it had asked the five major U.S. television networks, ABC, CBS, CNN, Fox, and NBC, to censor al-Qaeda footage, 'which meant in practical terms material from al-Jazeera, since it was the only network in a position to deliver it.' In a 30-minute conference call, National Security Adviser Condoleezza Rice 'urged all the American network chiefs not to screen videos of bin Laden.' All five networks agreed they would vet all their clips from the war in Afghanistan and would not use al-Jazeera's footage live. On October 11, White House press secretary Ari Fleischer 'asked America's newspaper editors not to publish full transcripts of bin Laden's or al-Qaeda's statements.'"

31. Berner, *The World According to Al Qaeda*, 61.

32. Lawrence and Howarth, *Messages to the World*, 126–127; Trudy Rubin, "Al Qaeda Remains the Crux of the Problem," *Philadelphia Inquirer*, 7 September 2008. U.S. efforts to restrict the presence of Al Qaeda in the public debate were not only futile, but they reflected a lack of understanding about Al Qaeda's sophistication and the nature of the U.S. enemy. As bin Laden noted, "The Americans have made laughable claims. They said that there are hidden messages intended for terrorists in bin Laden's statements. It is as if we are living in a time of carrier pigeons, without the existence of telephones, without travelers, without the Internet, without regular mail, without faxes, without email. This is just farcical; words which belittle people's intellects."

33. Al Qaeda's media wing has increased its video production quantity fourfold over 2006. Quality has increased to the point where videos now include subtitles in multiple languages with a 24-hour turnaround capability to exploit current events as they happen. All the while, videos are securely uploaded to the internet such that there is a virtually untraceable chain back to the originators. Whitlock, "The New Al Qaeda Central," sec. A.

34. James Gordon Meek, "Tighten the Net on Evil," *New York Daily News*, 15 March 2009, p. 27.

35. Whitlock, "The New Al Qaeda Central"; J. Aijaz Mangi, "Usama Is Not Caught Despite Exhaustive Efforts," *Ibrat*, 10 March 2003; Meek, "Tighten the Net on Evil."

36. Robert Block, "Al Qaeda or Not? U.S., U.K. Differ on Its Likely Role: Gap Reveals Basic Questions about the Group's Strength and Its Possible Evolution," *Wall Street Journal*, 12 August 2006.

37. David Kilcullen, as quoted in James Fallows, "Declaring Victory," *The Atlantic* 298, no. 2 (2006): 62.

38. Schuster, "Al-Zawahiri Letter under Scrutiny."

## CHAPTER 2. A GAME OF TWISTER:
## AL QAEDA STRATEGY VERSUS BUSH ADMINISTRATION STRATEGY

1. Anonymous, *Imperial Hubris*, 139.
2. Daniel Benjamin and Simon Steven, *The Age of Sacred Terror* (New York: Random House, 2002), 119.
3. Najm, "The Destruction of the Base," in Anonymous, ed., *Through Our Enemies' Eyes: Osama Bin Laden, Radical Islam, and the Future of America* (Washington, DC: Brassey's Inc., 2002), 172. After a trip to Afghanistan to interview Osama, an *Al Quds Al Arabi* journalist in a 1999 Al Jazeera interview explained that Osama "does not want to fight the regimes. . . . He wants to fight the Americans, who are protecting the regimes."
4. Thomas E. Ricks and Bob Woodward, "Marines Enter South Afghanistan: Force to Set Up Base Near Kandahar, Track Members of Al Qaeda," *Washington Post*, 26 November 2001; Bradley Graham, "100 GIs Have Entered Afghanistan," *Washington Post*, 29 November 2001.
5. Marc Kaufman, "U.S. Meeting Envisions Rebuilding Afghanistan," *Washington Post*, 21 November 2001; Keith B. Richburg and Colum Lynch, "Afghan Victors Agree to Talks in Berlin," *Washington Post*, 21 November 2001; Peter Baker, "Uphill Battle Looms on Path to New Kabul," *Washington Post*, 2 December 2001; Karen DeYoung and Marc Kaufman, "Afghan Rebuilding Will Be Costly," *Washington Post*, 10 December 2001.
6. Walter Pincus and Dana Milbank, "Al Qaeda-Hussein Link Is Dismissed," *Washington Post*, 17 June 2004; Keith B. Richburg, "Karzai Officially Declared Winner," *Washington Post*, 4 November 2004.
7. Editorial, "NATO's Afghan Test: U.S., British and Canadian Troops Are Leading a Fierce Fight against the Taliban. They Need More Help from Their Allies," *Washington Post*, 15 September 2006; Pamela Constable, "Afghan City's Rebound Cut Short: Battles between NATO Forces, Resurgent Taliban Make Ghost Town of Kandahar," *Washington Post*, 19 August 2006, http://pqash.pqarchiver.com/washingtonpost/access/1097224541.html; Reuters, "U.S. to Give Afghans $2 Billion in Additional Military Equipment," *Washington Post*, 4 July 2006; Thomas E. Ricks, "U.S. Airstrikes Rise in Afghanistan as Fighting Intensifies: In Response to More Aggressive Taliban, Attacks Are Double Those in Iraq War," *Washington Post*, 18 June 2006.
8. F. Michael Maloof, "Nuclear Know-How Trail," *Washington Times*, 18 July 2006; Bill Powell and Tim McGirk, "The Merchant of Menace: How A. Q. Khan Became the World's Most Dangerous Nuclear Trafficker," *Time*, 14 February 2005, http://www.time.com/time/magazine/article/0,9171,1025193,00.html; Editorial, "Pakistan's Separate Peace,"

*Washington Post*, 13 September 2006. F. Michael Maloof, a former senior security policy analyst in the Office of the Secretary of Defense, claims that this relationship, though publicly unmasked in the 2004–2005 winter, was known to the United States well before the October 2003 incident, when Italian authorities seized a German ship carrying one thousand centrifuges destined for Libya. He alleges that previously turning a blind eye to Dr. Khan's activities due to a confluence of U.S. and Pakistani interests while being able to monitor Dr. Khan finally proved to no longer be worth the cost when the United States needed to both press and reward Pakistan for other issues.

9. Seymour Hersh, "Annals of National Security: The Deal," *New Yorker*, 8 March 2004, http://www.newyorker.com/archive/2004/03/08.

10. Griff Witte and Kamran Khan, "Pakistan Officials Applaud Fighting in Tribal Region," *Washington Post*, 23 March 2007; Editorial, "A Problem of Passivity: Once Again the United States Stands by while Al Qaeda Operates in a Safe Haven," *Washington Post*, 21 February 2007; Peter Bergen, "The Long Hunt for Osama," *Atlantic Monthly*, October 2004, http://www.theatlantic.com/magazine/archive/2004/10/the-long-hunt-for-osama/3508/; "Fatalities in Terrorist Violence in Pakistan 2003–2010," South Asia Terrorism Portal, 3 October 2010, http://www.satp.org/satporgtp/countries/pakistan/database/casualties.htm; Hersh, "Annals of National Security."

11. Bill Roggio, "Pakistan Attempts to Revive Waziristan Accord," *Long War Journal*, 16 July 2007, http://www.longwarjournal.org/archives/2007/07/pakistan_attempts_to.php; Griff Witte, "Pakistani Government Seeks to Salvage Peace Deal," *Washington Post*, 17 July 2007.

12. Editorial, "A Problem of Passivity."

13. Ibid.

14. Witte, "Pakistani Government Seeks to Salvage Peace Deal." Pakistan's State Information Minister Tariq Azim Khan noted, "I don't think our long-term strategy has changed."

15. Alfred Stepan and Aqil Shah, "Pakistan's Real Bulwark," *Washington Post*, 5 May 2004; Editorial, "The General under Siege: Pakistan's Pervez Musharraf Is Running Out of Supporters—Except in Washington," *Washington Post*, 9 July 2007; Benazir Bhutto, "A False Choice for Pakistan," *Washington Post*, 12 March 2007; Fareed Zakaria, "The Real Problem with Pakistan," *Washington Post*, 18 June 2007.

16. N. C. Aizeman, "Musharraf's Contradictory Crackdown on Radicals: Pakistani Groups Increase Power Despite a Ban," *Washington Post*, 5 August 2005. Pakistan makes much political hay out of having handed over seven hundred Al Qaeda operatives to the United States since 11 September 2001.

By contrast, only a single major Taliban figure, Mullah Obeidullah Akhund, has been captured, and he was released three days after the departure of a U.S. delegation to Pakistan that had traveled to Islamabad to press Musharraf for greater cooperation against the Taliban.

17. Kamran Khan and John Lancaster, "Top Al Qaeda Figure Is Held in Pakistan," *Washington Post*, 5 May 2005.

18. "Pakistan: Ally or Adversary?" *Atlantic Monthly*, December 2006, http://www.theatlantic.com/magazine/archive/2006/12/pakistan-ally-or-adversary/5410/.

19. Bhutto, "A False Choice for Pakistan."

20. Mark Mazzetti, "One Bullet Away from What?" *New York Times*, 11 March 2007.

21. Selig Harrison, "Face Down Pakistani Army," *USA Today*, 1 April 2009 (Government Accountability Office [GAO] estimates were even higher at $12.3 billion); Reuters, "U.S. Lacks Anti-Terror Plan, Report Says," *USA Today*, 24 February 2009; Bhutto, "A False Choice for Pakistan."

22. Mazzetti, "One Bullet Away from What?"

23. Program on International Policy Attitudes, "Muslims Believe U.S. Seeks to Undermine Islam," 24 April 2007, http://www.worldpublicopinion.org/pipa/articles/brmiddleeastnafricara/346.php; Glenn Kessler, "The President Asserted Progress on Security and Political Issues. Recent Reports Weren't Often So Upbeat," *Washington Post*, 14 September 2007; Mark Mazzetti "Spy Agencies Say Iraq War Worsens Terror Threat," *New York Times*, 24 September 2006; Peter Bergen and Paul Cruickshank, "Brutal Reality: The War Is Fueling Global Jihad," *New York Daily News*, 21 February 2007. For further details on the perspective of Al Qaeda and that of its actual and potential adherents and supporters as the post-9/11 U.S. military juggernaut unfolded, see Al Qurashi and Abu Ubayd, "Why Did Baghdad Fall?" in Anonymous, *Imperial Hubris*, 15.

24. Program on International Policy Attitudes, "Misperceptions, the Media, and the Iraq War," 2 October 2003, http://www.worldpublicopinion.org/pipa/articles/international_security_bt/102.php?nid=&id=&pnt=102.

25. Secretary of State Colin Powell, address to the United Nations Security Council, "Iraq: Denial and Deception," 5 February 2003, http://www.whitehouse.gov/news/releases/2003/02/20030205-1.html.

26. The Pew Research Center for the People & the Press, "Powell Reversed the Trend but not the Tenor of Public Opinion," 14 February 2003, http://people-press.org/commentary/?analysisid=62.

27. Andrew J. Bacevich, "He Told Us to Go Shopping. Now the Bill Is Due," *Washington Post*, 5 October 2008.

28. On 18 September 2001, at a Pentagon press conference, Secretary of Defense Rumsfeld stated, "We have a choice, either to change the way we live, which is unacceptable, or to change the way that they live, and we choose the latter", Bacevich, "He Told Us to Go Shopping."

29. PBS's *NewsHour*, "Online NewsHour Update: U.S., Allies Won't Seek New UN Vote on Iraq," 17 March 2003, http://www.pbs.org/newshour/updates/diplomacyend_03-17-03.html; CNN.com, "Bush: Join 'Coalition of the Willing,'" 20 November 2002, http://edition.cnn.com/2002/WORLD/europe/11/20/prague.bush.nato/.

30. CBS News, "Text of Bush Speech: President Declares End to Major Combat," 1 May 2003, http://www.cbsnews.com/stories/2003/05/01/iraq/main551946.shtml; Terence Neilan, "Postwar Deaths of U.S. Troops Exceed Combat Toll," *New York Times*, 26 August 2003, http://www.nytimes.com/2003/08/26/international/worldspecial/26CND-IRAQ.html; Scott Peterson, "U.S. Decides to Pay Iraqi Soldiers and Form New Army," *Christian Science Monitor*, 24 June 2003, http://www.csmonitor.com/2003/0624/p01s04-woiq.html; Steven Kull, "America's Image in the World," Testimony before House Committee on Foreign Affairs, Subcommittee on International Organizations, Human Rights, and Oversight, 6 March 2007, http://www.worldpublicopinion.org/pipa/articles/views_on_countriesregions_bt/326.php?nid=&id=&pnt=326; Program on International Policy Attitudes, "World View of U.S. Role Goes from Bad to Worse," 22 January 2007, http://www.worldpublicopinion.org/pipa/articles/international_security_bt/306.php?nid=&id=&pnt=306.

31. Bradley Graham, "U.S. Bolsters Philippine Force: Marines to Join Attack on Militant Group," *Washington Post*, 21 February 2003.

32. Mark Mazzetti, "One Bullet Away from What?" *New York Times*, 11 March 2007.

33. Bradley Graham, "Shortfalls of Special Operations Command Are Cited," *Washington Post*, 17 November 2005.

34. Ibid.

35. Eric Schmitt and Mark Mazzetti, "Secret Order Lets U.S. Raid Al Qaeda in Many Countries," *New York Times*, 10 November 2008.

36. Dana Priest, "Foreign Network at Front of CIA's Terror Fight," *Washington Post*, 18 November 2005. See also Dana Priest, "Help from France Key in Covert Operations," 3 July 2005, and Ken Silverstein, "Official Pariah Sudan Valuable to America's War on Terrorism," *Los Angeles Times*, 29 April 2005.

37. Priest, "Foreign Network at Front of CIA's Terror Fight." "'The vast majority of our successes involved our CTICs,' one former counterterrorism official said. 'The boot that went through the door was foreign.'"

38. Schmitt and Mazzetti, "Secret Order Lets U.S. Raid Al Qaeda."

39. Ibid.

40. Jim Hoagland, "Pricey Rendition," *Washington Post*, 3 July 2005; Don Van Natta Jr., "U.S. Recruits a Rough Ally to Be a Jailer," *New York Times*, 1 May 2005; Shaun Waterman, "Terror Detainees Sent to Egypt; Official, U.S. Deny Torture Is Condoned," *Washington Times*, 16 May 2005; Nat Hentoff, "Ending Torture Outsourcing; House, Senate Efforts Combat CIA Renditions," *Washington Times*, 11 April 2005.

41. The following articles exemplify this point: Dana Priest, "CIA's Assurances on Transferred Suspects Doubted," *Washington Post*, 17 March 2005; "2 Yemenis Allege Secret U.S. Detention," *Philadelphia Inquirer*, 4 August 2005; Smith and Mekhennet, "Algerian Tells of Dark Odyssey in U.S. Hands." A "U.S. government official who visited several foreign prisons where suspects were rendered by the CIA after the attacks of Sept. 11, 2001, said: 'It's beyond that. It's widely understood that interrogation practices that would be illegal in the U.S. are being used.'"

42. Vernon Loeb and Susan Schmidt, "U.S. Wants Enemy Leaders Turned Over If Captured: Interrogation, Trials Planned for Al Qaeda, Taliban Chiefs," *Washington Post*, 2 December 2001; Dana Priest, "Covert CIA Program Withstands New Furor: Anti-Terror Effort Continues to Grow," *Washington Post*, 30 December 2005; Dana Priest, "CIA Holds Terror Suspects in Secret Prisons: Debate Is Growing within Agency about Legality and Morality of Overseas System Set Up after 9/11," *Washington Post*, 2 November 2005.

43. Hentoff, "Ending Torture Outsourcing"; Douglas Jehl, "White House Has Tightly Restricted Oversight of CIA Detentions," *New York Times*, 6 April 2005; Dan Eggen, "Congress Seeks Secret Memos on Interrogation," *Washington Post*, 5 October 2007; Michael Abramowitz, "Bush Defends U.S. Interrogation Methods," *Washington Post*, 6 October 2007.

44. "Omaha Gets Terror War Think Tank," *Omaha World Herald*, 10 April 2005. "'Given the growing understanding of how terrorists "exploit these global processes to do their bidding," it's important for military leaders to partner with the private sector to strengthen the nation's defenses,' said Col. Thomas K. Andersen, STRATCOM's director of intelligence. PTDT's roots go back to the weeks after 9/11, when a retired Marine Corps general working for credit-card giant MBNA contacted defense officials. At the same time, military officials in the terror fight were increasingly looking for information on operation of the transportation, banking, and communications industries."

45. National Commission on Terrorist Attacks Upon the United States, *Monograph on Terrorist Financing: Staff Report to the Commission*, Chapter 4, as

found in "Special Recommendations on Terrorist Financing," 24 April, 2002, http://www.oecd.org/fatf/pdf/GuidFIT01_en/pdf.

46. Ibid; Rohan Gunaratna, *Inside Al Qaeda: Global Network of Terror* (New York: Columbia University Press, 2002), 88–89.

47. Gunaratna, *Inside Al Qaeda*, 88–89.

48. National Commission on Terrorist Attacks Upon the United States, *Monograph on Terrorist Financing: Staff Report to the Commission*, Chapters 2–4.

49. National Commission on Terrorist Attacks Upon the United States, *Monograph on Terrorist Financing: Staff Report to the Commission*, Chapter 4; Jaime Caruana and Claes Norgren, "Wipe Out the Treasuries of Terror," *Financial Times*, 7 April 2004.

50. "UN Expands Sanctions," *Los Angeles Times*, 30 July 2005; National Commission on Terrorist Attacks Upon the United States, *Monograph on Terrorist Financing: Staff Report to the Commission*, Chapter 4. For more information on the Financial Action Task Force, see: http://www.fatf-gafi.org/pages/0,3 417,en_32250379_32236836_1_1_1_1_1,00.html.

51. National Commission on Terrorist Attacks Upon the United States, *Monograph on Terrorist Financing: Staff Report to the Commission*, Chapters 3 and 4. Though there are many United Nations Security Council Resolutions pertaining to terrorism, please pay particular note to the following resolutions reference counterterrorism and financial matters: S/RES1368 (2001), S/RES/1456 (2003), S/RES/1455 (2003), S/RES/1535 (2004), S/RES/1526 (2004), S/RES/1617 (2005), S/RES/1735 (2006); http://www.state.gov/s/ct/intl/c4353.htm.

52. Ibid.

53. National Commission on Terrorist Attacks Upon the United States, *Monograph on Terrorist Financing: Staff Report to the Commission*, Chapter 3. "Policymakers . . . were sometimes surprised to find that intelligence assessments were often supported by information far less reliable than they had presumed."

54. National Commission on Terrorist Attacks Upon the United States, *Monograph on Terrorist Financing: Staff Report to the Commission*, Chapters 2 and 3.

55. Pamela Hess, "World Loses Grip on Terror Funding, Report Says," *Washington Times*, 9 November 2008.

56. National Commission on Terrorist Attacks Upon the United States, *Monograph on Terrorist Financing: Staff Report to the Commission*, Chapters 3 and 4.

57. Ibid.

58. Steve Coll, "Attacks Bear Earmarks of Evolving Al Qaeda: Targets, Timing Both Familiar," *Washington Post*, 8 July 2005; Editorial, "A Problem of

Passivity"; John Ward Anderson and Karen DeYoung, "Plot to Bomb U.S.-Bound Jets Is Foiled: Britain Arrests 24 Suspected Conspirators," *Washington Post*, 11 August 2006.

59. Anonymous, *Imperial Hubris*, 15.

60. Ibid.

61. Anonymous, *Imperial Hubris*, 15–16.

62. Shibley Telhami, "Understanding the Challenge," *The Middle East Journal* 56, no. 1 (2002): 9.

63. Benjamin and Simon, *The Age of Sacred Terror*, 134.

64. Rohan Gunaratna, "Confronting the West: Al Qaeda's Strategy After 11 September," *Jane's Intelligence Review* 14, no. 7 (July 2002): 9–27; Stephen Schwartz, *The Two Faces of Islam: The House of Sa'ud from Tradition to Terror* (New York: Doubleday, 2002), 28. "The early period of the *ummah* remains alive to all Muslims, because it represents a sacred drama, and in this sense Islamic history has never been drained of its holy significance. Muslims feel that they participate collectively and individually in the consequences of past events in a way largely absent from Christianity (but more present in Judaism)."

65. Schuster, "Al-Zawahiri Letter under Scrutiny."

66. Anonymous, *Imperial Hubris*, 169. French citizens were killed in Karachi, Pakistan, in May 2002 and off the coast of Aden, Yemen, in October 2002. German citizens were struck in Djerba, in Tunisia, in April 2002, in Mashera, Pakistan, in July 2002, and in Kabul, Afghanistan, in June 2003. Apart from British troops killed in Afghanistan, British citizens in the financial sector were killed in Istanbul in November 2003. Two hundred Australians, along with some British citizens, were killed in Bali, Indonesia, in October 2002.

67. M. Ignatieff, "Why Are We in Iraq? (And Liberia? And Afghanistan?)," *New York Times*, 7 September 2003.

68. Sudarsan Raghavan, "Iran Giving Arms to Iraq's Sunnis, U.S. Military Says," *Washington Post*, 12 April 2007; Jonathan Finer, "Iraq Plans to Pursue Insurgents' Allies," *Washington Post*, 18 May 2005; Megan Greenwell, "Iran Trains Militiamen inside Iraq, U.S. Says," *Washington Post*, 20 August 2007; Dafna Linzer and Walter Pincus, "Intelligence Chiefs Pessimistic in Assessing Worldwide Threats," *Washington Post*, 12 January 2007; Michael Fletcher, "Al Qaeda in Iraq Is Part of Network, Bush Says," *Washington Post*, 25 July 2007; Editorial, "Iraq's Terrorist Haven," *Washington Post*, 9 September 2004; Peter Baker and Josh White, "Bush Calls Iraq Moral Equivalent of Allies' WWII Fight against the Axis," *Washington Post*, 31 August 2005.

69. Ellen Knickmeyer, "Gulf States Buy Arms with Wary Eye on Iran," *Washington Post*, 4 August 2007; Jeffrey H. Birnbaum, "Democrats' Victory Is

Felt on K Street," *Washington Post*, 23 November 2006, http://www.usip. org/isg/iraq_study_group_report/report/1206/index.html; Walter Pincus, "Negroponte Orders an Update on Terrorism's Influence in Iraq," *Washington Post*, 5 August 2006. The following scholars and articles informed the author's thinking: Ray Takeyh, "Time for Détente with Iran," *Foreign Affairs*, March/April 2007; James D. Fearon, "Iraq's Civil War," *Foreign Affairs*, March/April 2007; Vali Nasr, "When the Shiites Rise," *Foreign Affairs*, July/August 2006.

70. Robin Wright, "Arabs Pressure Rice on U.S. Peace Efforts," *Washington Post*, 4 October 2006; Glen Kessler, "Rice Looks Back for a Way Forward on Mideast Peace," *Washington Post*, 21 February 2007; Scott Wilson, "Hamas Sweeps Palestinian Elections, Complicating Peace Efforts in Mideast," *Washington Post*, 27 January 2006; Scott Wilson, "Palestinian Battles Raise Fears of Coup and Civil War," *Washington Post*, 13 June 2007; Scott Wilson, "Factional Fighting Flares in Gaza Strip," *Washington Post*, 12 June 2007; Scott Wilson, "Routed Fatah Begins to Reorganize in Gaza: Party Launches Protests, Rebuilds Its Armed Wing," *Washington Post*, 9 September 2007.

71. Editorial, "A Palestinian Pact," *Washington Post*, 10 February 2007; Scott Wilson, "Palestinians Reach Deal on a Government," *Washington Post*, 9 February 2007. In fact, the Saudis brokered the accord in Mecca in February 2007 that united Hamas and Fatah, the feuding Palestinian factions that were engaged in a de facto civil war. That this accord was brokered on the eve of Secretary of State Condoleezza Rice's trip to the Middle East and ran counter to the philosophical distinction of "extremists" and "moderates" that she had previously laid out is evidence of the looseness of this understanding and the conflicting and varying aims of the multiple actors who are bound together in a state of mutual dependency (Glenn Kessler, "Rice to Seek Support for Mideast Effort," *Washington Post*, 2 February 2007). The Saudis, and other Sunni Gulf States, need U.S. power to deal with Iran. The United States needs these same states to help implement its policies.

72. Scott Wilson, "Abbas Appoints Crisis Cabinet," *Washington Post*, 18 June 2007; Robin Wright, "U.S. vs. Iran: Cold War, Too," *Washington Post*, 29 July 2007; Kessler, "Rice to Seek Support for Mideast Effort."

73. Program on International Policy Attitudes, "Q&A: Nabil Kukali, Palestinian Center for Public Opinion," 20 August 2007, http://www. worldpublicopinion.org/pipa/articles/brmiddleeastnafricara/384. php?nid=&id=&pnt=384; Program on International Policy Attitudes, "Negative Attitudes Toward the United States in the Muslim World: Do They Matter?" 17 May 2007, http://www.worldpublicopinion.org/pipa/articles/brmiddleeastnafricara; Shibley Telhami, "Arab Attitudes Toward Political and Social Issues, Foreign Policy and the Media," October 2005, http://www.bsos.umd.edu/SADAT/PUB/Arab-attitudes-2005.

74. Peter Baker, "Bush Renews Mideast Efforts," *Washington Post*, 17 July 2007; Robin Wright, "Another Tour Ends without Solid Plans on Mideast Peace," *Washington Post*, 3 August 2007.

75. Seymour M. Hersh, "The Redirection: Is the Administration's New Policy Benefiting Our Enemies in the War on Terrorism?" *The New Yorker*, March 2007, http://www.newyorker.com/reporting/2007/03/05/070305fa_fact_hersh.

76. Hersh, "The Redirection." In January 2007, shortly before leaving his post as DNI (director of National Intelligence) to become the deputy secretary of state, John Negroponte testified to the Senate Select Committee for Intelligence that Hezbollah lay "at the center of Iran's terrorist strategy. . . . It could decide to conduct attacks against U.S. interests in the event it feels its survival or that of Iran is threatened. . . . Lebanese Hezbollah sees itself as Tehran's partner."

77. Hersh, "The Redirection."

78. Hersh, "The Redirection." As noted by Robert Baer, a former CIA operative with long residence in Beirut, "the dog that didn't bark [that] summer [was] Shiite terrorism." There was no wave of terror attacks on U.S. or Israel targets around the world. Nasrallah "could have pulled the trigger, but he did not."

79. Ibid.

80. Schuster, "Al-Zawahiri Letter under Scrutiny."

81. Hersh, "The Redirection." Per a ranking U.S. government consultant, "It's not that we don't want the Salafis to throw bombs; it's who they throw them at—Hezbollah, Moqtada al-Sadr, Iran, and at the Syrians, if they continue to work with Hezbollah and Iran."

82. Hersh, "The Redirection."

83. Robin Wright, "Iraq Considers Sadr Amnesty," *Washington Post*, 5 July 2004; Joshua Partlow, "An Uphill Battle to Stop Fighters at Border," *Washington Post*, 5 May 2007; Karen DeYoung, "Fewer Foreigners Crossing into Iraq from Syria to Fight," *Washington Post*, 16 September 2007; Editorial, "Buildup in Lebanon: Heavy Weapons Flow Freely Across the Border from Syria, the UN Security Council Is Told," *Washington Post*, 5 July 2007; Anthony Shadid, "As Crises Build, Lebanese Fearful of a Failed State," *Washington Post*, 5 June 2007; Peter Baker and Robin Wright, "Bush Appears Cool to Key Points of Report on Iraq," *Washington Post*, 8 December 2006.

84. Hersh, "The Redirection."

85. Hersh, "The Redirection"; James Glanz, "U.S. Presents Evidence of Iranian Weapons in Iraq," *New York Times*, 11 February 2007, http://www.nytimes.com/2007/02/11/world/middleeast/11cnd-weapons.html?_

r=1&scp=2&sq=february%202007%20and%20iraq%20and%20iran%20 and%20weapon&st=cse.

86. Hersh, "The Redirection."

87. "Same Country, Different Views, Poll: Concern in Iraq Peaks among Its Sunni Arabs," ABC News, 17 March 2004, http://abcnews.go.com/sections/ world/WorldNewsTonight/iraq_poll.

88. Anne Gearan, "Rice: Iraq Missed Political Deadlines," *Washington Post*, 30 January 2007; Michael Abramowitz, "Pentagon Chief Talks of Further Iraq Troop Cuts: Gates Expresses Hope Despite New U.S. Report on Unmet Goals," *Washington Post*, 15 September 2007; Michael Abramowitz, "Bush to Endorse Petraeus Plan: Democrats, Some Republicans Seek a Faster Withdrawal," *Washington Post*, 12 September 2007.

89. Dahr Jamail, "Shiite Unity Challenges U.S. Plan in Iraq," *New Standard*, 19 January 2004, http://newstandardnews.net/content/index; Edward Wong, John H. Cushman Jr., and Susan Sachs, "The Struggle for Iraq: Political Process; U.S. Tries to Give Moderates an Edge in Iraqi Elections," *New York Times*, 18 January 2004; BBC News, "Sadr Group Pulls Out of Iraq's Ruling Shiite Bloc," 15 September 2007, and "Iraq Poll September 2007: In Graphics," 10 September 2007, http://news.bbc.co.uk/2/hi/middle_east/; Ali al-Fadhil, "Iran Ties Weaken Iraqi Government Further," Antiwar.com, 14 August 2007, http://www.antiwar.com/ips/fadhily; Dahr Jamail, "A Nail in Maliki Government's Coffin?" Inter Press Service, 3 August 2007, http:// www.dahrjamailiraq.com/hard_news/archives/iraq/.

90. Karen DeYoung, "Analysis: Al-Maliki Weathering Crisis," *Washington Post*, 25 September 2007; STRATFOR, "Iraq: The Sectarian Tables Turn," 4 October 2007, http://www.stratfor.com/memberships/103157/analysis/ iraq_sectarian_tables_turn.

91. Associated Press, "GAO: Iraq Meets Only 5 of 18 Goals Set by Bush," MSNBC, 29 August 2007, http://www.msnbc.msn.com/id/20502905/.

92. The Iraq Study Group Report can be downloaded from the United States Institute of Peace Web site at: http://www.usip.org/isg/iraq_study_group_ report/report/1206/index.html.

93. PBS's *NewsHour*, "President Bush Links War in Iraq to War on Terrorism," 24 May 2007, http://www.pbs.org/newshour/bb/white_house/jan-june07/ terrorism_05-24.html; Pincus and Milbank, "Al Qaeda-Hussein Link Is Dismissed."

94. Megan Greenwell, "U.S. Revises Timetable for Iraq Security," *Washington Post*, 24 July 2007; Reuters, "Pentagon Makes Contingency Plans for Iraq Pullout," *Washington Post*, 26 July 2007.

95. Associated Press, "Saudis Reportedly Funding Iraqi Sunni Insurgents," *USA Today*, 8 December 2006, http://www.usatoday.com/news/world/iraq/2006-

12-08-saudis-sunnis; Hugh Naylor, "Syria Is Said to Be Strengthening Ties to Opponents of Iraq's Government," *New York Times*, 7 October 2007.

96. Program on International Policy Attitudes, "All Iraqi Ethnic Groups Overwhelmingly Reject al Qaeda," 27 September 2006, http://www.worldpublicopinion.org/pipa/articles/brmiddleeastnafricara/248.php?lb=brme&pnt=248&nid=&id=. A 2006 WorldPublicOpinion.org survey found that 94 percent of Iraqis had an unfavorable view of Al Qaeda and 82 percent had a very unfavorable view.

97. Greg Miller, "U.S. Missile Strikes Said to Take Heavy Toll on Al Qaeda," *Los Angeles Times*, 22 March 2009.

98. Ibid.; Jane Perlez, "Pakistan Rehearses Its Two-Step on Airstrikes," *New York Times*, 16 April 2009.

99. Perlez, "Pakistan Rehearses"; Jeremy Page, "Google Earth Reveals Secret History of U.S. Base in Pakistan," *Times* (London), 19 February 2009; Tom Coghlan, Jeremy Page, and Zahid Hussain, "Secrecy and Denial as Pakistan Lets CIA Use Airbase to Strike Militants," *Times* (London), 18 February 2009.

100. Christina Lamb, "Playing with Firepower," *Sunday Times* (London), 14 September 2008.

101. Mark Mazzetti, "CIA Chief Says Qaeda Is Extending Its Reach," *New York Times*, 14 November 2008.

102. Jason Straziuso and Mohamed Olad Hassan, "Somalia's Al Shabab Emulates the Taliban," *Philadelphia Inquirer*, 22 August 2010; "U.S. Asked to Fund Troops to Somalia," *Washington Times*, 2 September 2010.

103. Mazzetti, "CIA Chief Says Qaeda Is Extending Its Reach"; Lolita C. Baldor, "U.S. Terror Training in Yemen Reflects Wider Program," *Washington Times*, 8 September 2010, http://www.washingtontimes.com/news/2010/sep/8/us-terror-training-yemen-reflects-wider-program/; Eric Schmitt and Scott Shane, "Aid to Counter Al Qaeda in Yemen Divides U.S. Officials," *New York Times*, 16 September 2010; Adam Entous, Siobhan Gorman, and Julian E. Barnes, "U.S. Funding Boost Is Sought for Yemen Forces," *Wall Street Journal*, 2 September 2010; Ahmed Al-Haj, "Thousands of Yemenis Flee Battle with Al Qaeda," *Philadelphia Inquirer*, 21 September 2010.

104. Marc A. Thiessen, "Watch Out for Al Qaeda," *Los Angeles Times*, 15 February 2009.

105. For more see Al Qurashi and Abu Ubayd, "A Lesson in War," *Al Ansar* Web site, 19 December 2002, as cited in Anonymous, *Imperial Hubris*, 101. A copy of the translated document can be found at: http://www.au.af.mil/au/awc/awcgate/ssi/mil_strat_global_jihad.pdf; Thiessen, "Watch Out for Al Qaeda"; Al Jazeera Television, "Statement of Usama Bin Ladin," 2002, cited in Anonymous, *Imperial Hubris*, 154.

106. Al Qurashi and Abu Ubayd, "A Lesson in War"; Thiessen, "Watch Out for Al Qaeda"; Craig Whitlock, "Al Qaeda Masters Terrorism on the Cheap," *Washington Post*, 24 August 2008.

107. Whitlock, "Al Qaeda Masters Terrorism."

108. Jeff Leys, "Iraq and Afghanistan Supplemental Spending 2008," Voices For Creative Nonviolence, 17 May 2008, http://vcnv.org/iraq-and-afghanistan-supplemental-spending-2008.

109. Steve Luxenberg, "Book Details Internal Struggle over Afghan Plan," *Washington Post*, 22 September 2010.

110. Ruth Marcus, "Bush's Deficit Spinning," *Washington Post*, 17 November 2010.

111. Joseph E. Stiglitz and Linda J. Bilmes, "A War More Costly than We Thought," *Washington Post*, 5 September 2010.

112. Bacevich, "He Told Us to Go Shopping."

113. J. T. Young, "Hidden behind Defense," *Washington Times*, 8 October 2008.

114. Thiessen, "Watch Out for Al Qaeda." "Bin Laden cites the 9/11 attacks as proof that this [economic] strategy can succeed. In a November 2004 videotape broadcast on Al Jazeera, he boasted that Al Qaeda spent $500,000 on the event, while America lost, 'according to the lowest estimate, $500 billion . . . meaning that every dollar of Al Qaeda defeated a million dollars [of America] . . . besides the huge number of jobs [lost].' . . . These statements tell us something important about the enemy: Although Bin Laden has many skilled bomb-makers and propagandists working for him, he lacks a single competent economist. Yes, the 9/11 attacks did cost America billions of dollars—but our resilient free-market economy replaced every lost job within a few years. We would similarly recover from any attack Al Qaeda might pull off. But the terrorists don't have to be right to be emboldened."

115. Joshua Partlow, "180,000 Private Contractors Flood Iraq," *Washington Post*, 19 September 2007; Editorial, "Among Top Officials, 'Surge' Has Sparked Dissent, Infighting," *Washington Post*, 9 September 2007.

## CHAPTER 3. HERDING CATS: AL QAEDA POST-9/11 MODUS OPERANDI

1. Gunaratna, *Inside Al Qaeda*, 8, 95.

2. UPI, "Saudis Battling Terror," *Washington Times*, 9 April 2005.

3. Phil Hirschkorn and Rohan Gunaratna, "Blowback," *Jane's Intelligence Review*, July 2001, 42–45.

4. John Arquilla, David Ronfeldt, and Michele Zanini, "Networks, Netwar, and Information-Age Terrorism," in *Countering the New Terrorism*, ed. Ian O. Lesser et al. (Washington, D.C.: Rand Corporation, 1999), 39.

5. "Al Qaeda Remains Threat, Officials Warn," *Washington Times*, 14 June 2006; Gunaratna, *Inside Al Qaeda*, 57.

6. Craig Whitlock, "The New Al Qaeda Central: Far from Declining, the Network Has Rebuilt, with Fresh Faces and a Vigorous Media Arm," *Washington Post*, 9 September 2007; Susan Schmidt and Douglas Farah, "Al Qaeda's New Leaders: Six Militants Emerge from Ranks to Fill Void," *Washington Post*, 29 October 2002, http://pqasb.pqarchiver.com/washingtonpost/access/225810991.html.

7. Gunaratna, *Inside Al Qaeda*, 58; Whitlock, "The New Al Qaeda Central"; Editorial, "A Problem of Passivity."

8. Coll, "Attacks Bear Earmarks of Evolving Al Qaeda"; UPI, "Saudis Battling Terror," *Washington Times*, 9 April 2005.

9. Josh Meyer, "Terror Camps Scatter, Persist," *Los Angeles Times*, 20 June 2005.

10. Editorial, "A Problem of Passivity"; "UN Report Says U.S. Breaking Qaeda," *New York Daily News*, 28 September 2006 (for more information on UN terrorism strategy and assessments, please see http://www.un.org/terrorism); Craig Whitlock, "Terrorists Proving Harder to Profile," *Washington Post*, 12 March 2007; Craig Whitlock, "Al Qaeda Leaders Seen in Control: Experts Say Radicals in London, Egypt May Have Followed Orders," *Washington Post*, 24 July 2005; Karen DeYoung, "Al Qaeda's Gains Keep U.S. at Risk, Report Says: Safe Haven in Pakistan Is Seen as Challenging Counterterrorism Efforts," *Washington Post*, 18 July 2007.

11. Yonah Alexander and Michael S. Swetnam, *Usama bin Laden's Al Qaida: Profile of a Terrorist Network* (Ardsley, NY: Transnational Publishers, 2001).

12. Peter Ford, "Al Qaeda's Veil Begins to Lift," *Christian Science Monitor*, 20 December 2001, http://www.csmonitor.com/2001/1220/p6s1-wogi.html; Anthony Shadid and Michael Kranish, "Gains Slow in Global Probe of Al Qaeda," *Boston Globe*, 2 December 2001.

13. Walter Pincus, "Ex-Counterterrorism Chief Cites Rise in Attacks," *Washington Post*, 31 August 2005; Carol Huang, "Al Qaeda 2006: Fighting in Iraq, Regrouping in Afghanistan, Enlisting in Europe: An Assessment of Some of Last Year's Most Significant Gains and Losses for the Terrorist Organization," *Christian Science Monitor*, 1 February 2007; Whitlock, "Al Qaeda Leaders Seen in Control."

14. Craig Whitlock, "Al Qaeda's Far-Reaching New Partner: Salafist Group Finds Limited Appeal in Its Native Algeria," *Washington Post*, 5 October 2006.

15. Ibid.

16. Steve Simon and Jonathan Stevenson, "Al Qaeda Takes It to the Streets," *Washington Post*, 10 October 2010; Sami Yousafzai and Christopher Dickey, "The Coming Terror War," *Newsweek*, 29 September 2010, http://www.newsweek.com/2010/09/29/terrorists-appear-to-be-planning-a-big-attack.html; Bill Gertz, "Inside the Ring," *Washington Times*, 26 August 2010.

17. Simon and Stevenson, "Al Qaeda Takes It to the Streets"; Peter Finn, "Al Qaeda Likely to Try Small-Scale Attacks on U.S., Officials Say," *Washington Post*, 23 September 2010.
18. Simon and Stevenson, "Al Qaeda Takes It to the Streets"; Finn, "Al Qaeda Likely to Try Small-Scale Attacks on U.S., Officials Say."
19. Simon and Stevenson, "Al Qaeda Takes It to the Streets."
20. Finn, "Al Qaeda Likely to Try Small-Scale Attacks on U.S., Officials Say."
21. Ibid.
22. Michael Slackman and Souad Mekhennet, "A New Group that Seems to Share Al Qaeda's Agenda," *New York Times*, 8 July 2006, http://query.nytimes.com/gst/fullpage.html?res=9E03E2DD1030F93BA35754C0A96 09C8B63. "'It is the first time we see a pure Islamic resistance and not a nationalist movement involved in the Israeli resistance,' said Mr. Shahadeh, [a Jordanian researcher] 'with long-established contacts among jihadist adherents. . . . The logo, for example, is a symbol of a globe, a sword, and a Koran. There is nothing about Palestine.'"
23. Bryan Bender, "Specter Surfaces of World of Local Qaeda Offshoots," *Boston Globe*, 8 July 2005; "The New Al Qaeda: Local Franchises," *Christian Science Monitor*, 11 July 2005.
24. Brynjar Lia and Thomas Hegghammer, "Jihadi Strategic Studies—The Alleged al-Qaida Policy Study Preceding the Madrid Bombings," *Studies in Conflict and Terrorism* 27, no. 5 (2004); Craig Whitlock, "Architect of New War on the West: Writings Lay Out Post-9/11 Strategy of Isolated Cells Joined in Jihad," *Washington Post*, 23 May 2006, http://www.nupi.no/IPS/filestore/Lia2006_The_Al-Qaida_strate_76568a.pdf.
25. Coll, "Attacks Bear Earmarks of Evolving Al Qaeda."
26. Steve Coll and Susan B. Glasser, "Terrorists Turn to the Web as a Base of Operations," *Washington Post*, 7 August 2005.
27. Susan B. Glasser and Steve Coll, "The Web as Weapon: Zarqawi Intertwines Acts on Ground in Iraq With Propaganda Campaign on Internet," *Washington Post,* 9 August 2005.
28. Coll and Glasser, "Terrorists Turn to the Web as a Base of Operations."
29. Coll and Glasser, "Terrorists Turn to the Web as a Base of Operations"; Glasser and Coll, "The Web as Weapon."
30. Coll and Glasser, "Terrorists Turn to the Web as a Base of Operations"; Glasser and Coll, "The Web as Weapon."
31. Craig Whitlock, "Keeping Al Qaeda in His Grip: Al-Zawahiri Presses Ideology, Deepens Rifts among Islamic Radicals," *Washington Post*, 16 April 2006. "With groundbreaking elections taking place in Iraq, Egypt, the Palestinian territories and even Saudi Arabia, al-Zawahiri and his ideological allies fear that popular sentiment in the Middle East could be turning against

their goal of establishing a united caliphate to rule over the world's entire Muslim population, many Al Qaeda experts contend. The Arab world has witnessed change over the last year or two that is almost equivalent to the amount of change that occurred over the previous two decades. He can't remain isolated from these changes. He has to respond to them."

32. Mark Mazzetti, "Qaeda Leaders Losing Sway over Militants, Study Finds," *New York Times*, 15 November 2006.

33. "National Security Report Card," *Washington Post*, 9 December 2005. The National Commission on Terrorist Attacks Upon the United States, more informally known as the 9/11 Commission, has been very critical of the U.S. government's counterterrorism policy and its implementation to date, yet it has rated the government's efforts against terrorist financing with the sole "A" (actually an "A-") in its report card evaluating how well the federal government has responded to commission recommendations to better secure the United States. Documented evidence shows that in excess of $100 million has been seized.

34. Schuster, "Al Zawahiri Letter under Scrutiny."

35. For more information, see National Commission on Terrorist Attacks Upon the United States, *Monograph on Terrorist Financing: Staff Report to the Commission*, Chapter 2.

36. Ibid. Only after NSC-initiated interagency trips to Saudi Arabia in 1999 and 2000, and after interviews of bin Laden's family members in the United States, was the family fortune myth discredited.

37. Ibid.; Gunaratna, *Inside Al Qaeda*, Chapter 2.

38. National Commission on Terrorist Attacks Upon the United States, *Monograph on Terrorist Financing: Staff Report to the Commission*, Chapter 2.

39. Gunaratna, *Inside Al Qaeda*, 84.

40. Ibid., 83.

41. National Commission on Terrorist Attacks Upon the United States, *Monograph on Terrorist Financing: Staff Report to the Commission*, Chapter 2.

42. John Diamond, "Flow of Terror Funds Being Choked, U.S. Says: Intelligence Analysts Track Smuggled Cash," *USA Today*, 19 June 2006; National Commission on Terrorist Attacks Upon the United States, *Monograph on Terrorist Financing: Staff Report to the Commission*, Chapter 2.

43. National Commission on Terrorist Attacks Upon the United States, *Monograph on Terrorist Financing: Staff Report to the Commission*, Chapter 2.

44. Ibid.

45. Ibid.; Diamond, "Flow of Terror Funds Being Choked."

46. Craig Whitlock, "From Iraq to Algeria, Al Qaeda's Long Reach," *Washington Post*, 30 May 2007; Schuster, "Al Zawahiri Letter under Scrutiny"; National Commission on Terrorist Attacks Upon the United States,

*Monograph on Terrorist Financing: Staff Report to the Commission*, Chapters 2 and 3.

47. Thomas Harding, "Al Qaeda Using Gambling Websites to Launder Money, Says Terror Expert," *Daily Telegraph* (London), 2 January 2009.

48. *The* Al Qaeda *Manual*, "UK/BM-1 Translation," http://www.justice.gov/ag/manualpart1_1.pdf.

49. Gunaratna, *Inside Al Qaeda*, Chapter 2, and p. 86; National Commission on Terrorist Attacks Upon the United States, *Monograph on Terrorist Financing: Staff Report to the Commission*, Chapters 2 and 3. Islamic banks are based upon religious law, which prohibits usury. They each have a board of religious monitors to ensure compliance. Iran, Pakistan, and Sudan, in fact, have converted their entire banking system to Islamic dictates. As a result, Islamic banks derive their income and provide money to customers via different methods. These consist of: (1) profits and losses are shared between the bank and the loan recipient from the venture for which the loaned money was spent, (2) a no-interest loan is simply given to a needy person, (3) the lending bank becomes a shareholder in the receiving institution, (4) the bank effectively buys the receiving institution for a price that includes the cost of the loan and then resells that institution at a mark-up, and (5) the bank essentially buys the receiving institution and leases it back to the loan recipient, who slowly pays off the loan. Three types of accounts exist: (1) a current account that bears no interest that the depositor controls and can close at any time, (2) a limited investment account that the bank controls and uses to invest, and both the bank and the depositor share any gains or losses, and (3) a limited investment account where the bank uses it to invest only in concurrence with the depositor and any profits or losses are shared.

50. This information on the *hawala* financial system and Al Qaeda financing comes from: National Commission on Terrorist Attacks Upon the United States, *Monograph on Terrorist Financing: Staff Report to the Commission*, Chapters 2 and 3.

51. Gunaratna, *Inside Al Qaeda*, 84 (the official banking system processed roughly $1 billion, whereas the *hawala* networks processed an estimated $2.5–3 billion); William F. Wechsler, "Strangling the Hydra: Targeting Al Qaeda's Finances," Chapter 1 in *How Did This Happen? Terrorism and the New War*, eds. James F. Hoge and Gideon Rose (Westview Press, 2001); Douglas Frantz, "Secretive Money Moving System Scrutinized for Bin Laden Funds," *International Herald Tribune*, 3 October 2001.

52. Gunaratna, *Inside Al Qaeda*, 84; Wechsler, "Strangling the Hydra"; Frantz, "Secretive Money Moving System Scrutinized for Bin Laden Funds."

53. This information on the *hawala* financial system and Al Qaeda financing comes from: National Commission on Terrorist Attacks Upon the United

States, *Monograph on Terrorist Financing: Staff Report to the Commission*, Chapters 2 and 3.

54. Diamond, "Flow of Terror Funds Being Choked"; National Commission on Terrorist Attacks Upon the United States, *Monograph on Terrorist Financing: Staff Report to the Commission*, Chapters 2 and 3. Stuart Levey, the Department of the Treasury's undersecretary for terrorism and financial intelligence, has stated, for example, that Al Qaeda financed bombings in Indonesia in 2002 and 2003 by smuggling $30,000 in cash for each attack to allied terrorists in Asia.

55. Rohan Gunaratna, "The Lifeblood of Terrorist Organizations: Evolving Terrorist Financing Strategies," Chapter 2 in *Countering Terrorism through International Cooperation*, ed. Alex Schmid (Rome: International Scientific and Professional Advisory of the UN and the UN Terrorism Prevention Branch, 2001); National Commission on Terrorist Attacks Upon the United States, *Monograph on Terrorist Financing: Staff Report to the Commission*, Chapters 2 and 3. There is not, however, total agreement on this number. Some retroactive estimates post-2001 place annual operating costs at slightly less than $50 million.

56. National Commission on Terrorist Attacks Upon the United States, *Monograph on Terrorist Financing: Staff Report to the Commission*, Chapter 2. Other than bin Laden, the person with the most important role in Al Qaeda financing was reportedly Sheikh Qari Sa'id. Sa'id, a trained accountant, had worked with bin Laden in the late 1980s when they fought together in Afghanistan. He subsequently worked for one of bin Laden's companies in Sudan in the early to mid-1990s. Sa'id was apparently notoriously tightfisted with Al Qaeda's money. He reportedly vetoed a $1,500 expense for travel to Saudi Arabia to get visas for the 9/11 attacks until bin Laden overruled him (although there is no reason to believe that Sa'id knew the reason for the travel at that time). Due to this extreme frugality, operational leaders may have occasionally bypassed Sa'id and the Finance Committee and requested funds directly from bin Laden. For a detailed discussion of specific examples, also see Gunaratna, *Inside Al Qaeda*, 86–87.

57. Whitlock, "The New Al Qaeda Central."

58. Gunaratna, *Inside Al Qaeda*, 86–87.

## CHAPTER 4. THE HEART OF THE CONFLICT:
## THE U.S.-AL QAEDA STRUGGLE'S POLITICAL DIMENSION

1. Coll, "Attacks Bear Earmarks of Evolving Al Qaeda."

2. The 2006 Zogby poll asked: "When you think about Al Qaeda, what aspect of the organization, if any, do you sympathize with most?" Al Qaeda's primary goal of creating a Talibanesque, pan-Islamic state received only

single-digit support (Lebanon 2 percent, Egypt 7 percent, Jordan 9 percent, Morocco 6 percent, UAE 1 percent, Saudi Arabia 9 percent), http://www. zogby.com/soundbites/ReadClips.cfm?ID=12357.

3. Gallup Poll Editorial Staff, "Blame for September 11 Attacks Unclear for Many in Islamic World," 1 March 2002, http://www.gallup.com/poll/5404/ Blame-Sept-Attacks-Unclear-Many-Islamic-World.aspx. The poll results showed Lebanon at 3 percent support, Egypt at 13 percent support, Jordan at 5 percent support, Morocco at 8 percent support, the UAE at 1 percent support, and Saudi Arabia at 13 percent support, http://www.zogby.com/ soundbites/ReadClips.cfm?ID=12357; Program on International Policy Attitudes, "Large and Growing Numbers of Muslims Reject Terrorism, Bin Laden," 6 March 2007, http://www.worldpublicopinion.org/pipa/articles/ international_security_bt/221.php?nid=&id=&pnt=221; Steven Kull, "How Muslims and Americans View Each Other," 18 February 2007, http://www. worldpublicopinion.org/pipa/articles/views_on_countriesregions_bt/330. php?nid=&id=&pnt=330.

4. Ralph Peters, "Killing Muslims: America Needs to Publicize Al Qaeda's Main 'Achievement,'" *New York Post*, 23 January 2010. The information noted in this article came from a 2009-released report by West Point's Combating Terrorism Center, "Deadly Vanguards: A Study of Al Qaeda's Violence against Muslims," which drew exclusively from Arabic-language media reports and included only incidents for which Al Qaeda directly claimed responsibility.

5. Program on International Policy Attitudes, "Large and Growing Numbers of Muslims Reject Terrorism, Bin Laden."

6. Program on International Policy Attitudes, "Muslim Publics Oppose Al Qaeda's Terrorism, but Agree with Its Goal of Driving U.S. Forces Out," 24 February 2009, http://www.worldpublicopinion.org/pipa/articles/ brmiddleeastnafricara/591.php?nid=&id=&pnt=591.

7. Ibid.

8. Pew Global Attitudes Project, "The Great Divide: How Westerners and Muslims View Each Other," 22 June 2006, http://pewglobal.org/reports/ display.php?ReportID=253.

9. Program on International Policy Attitudes, "Large and Growing Numbers of Muslims Reject Terrorism, Bin Laden"; for the Zogby poll, see http:// www.zogby.com/soundbites/ReadClips.cfm?ID=12357.

10. Program on International Policy Attitudes, "Muslims Believe U.S. Seeks to Undermine Islam," 24 April 2007, http://www.worldpublicopinion.org/ pipa/articles/brmiddleeastnafricara/346.php; see also Robert Fisk, "He Is Alive. There Can Be No Doubt About It. But the Questions Remain: Where on Earth Is He, and Why Has He Resurfaced Now?" *Independent* (London), 14 November 2002 as cited in Anonymous, *Imperial Hubris*, 7.

11. Stephen M. Walt, "Taming American Power," *Foreign Affairs*, September/ October 2005, http://www.foreignaffairs.com/articles/61025/stephen-m-walt/taming-american-power?page=2.

12. Telhami, "Understanding the Challenge"; Program on International Policy Attitudes, "Global Poll Finds That Religion and Culture Are Not to Blame for Tensions between Islam and the West," 16 February 2007, http://www.worldpublicopinion.org/pipa/articles/international_security_bt/317.php?nid=&id=&pnt=317; Program on International Policy Attitudes, "Muslim Publics Oppose Al Qaeda's Terrorism, but Agree with Its Goal of Driving U.S. Forces Out"; Pew Global Attitudes Project, "Confidence in Usama bin Laden," http://pewglobal.org/database/?indicator=20; Gallup, "Voice of the People, 2003," January 2004, http://www.icpsr.umich.edu/icpsrweb/ICPSR/studies/24482; Pew Global Attitudes Project, "The Great Divide: How Westerners and Muslims View Each Other"; Program on International Policy Attitudes, "Muslim Publics Oppose Al Qaeda's Terrorism, but Agree with Its Goal of Driving U.S. Forces Out."

13. Program on International Policy Attitudes, "Global Poll Finds that Religion and Culture Are Not to Blame"; Pew Research Center for People and the Press, "America Admired, yet Its New Vulnerability Seen as Good Thing, Say Opinion Leaders: Little Support for Expanding War on Terrorism," 19 December 2001, http://people-press.org/report/145/.

14. Kull, "America's Image in the World."

15. Chicago Council on Global Affairs, "World Publics Reject U.S. Role as the World Leader," 17 April 2007, http://www.worldpublicopinion.org/pipa/articles/views_on_countriesregions_bt/345.php?nid=&id=&pnt=345; Program on International Policy Attitudes, "World View of U.S. Role Goes from Bad to Worse," 22 January 2007, http://www.worldpublicopinion.org/pipa/articles/international_security_bt/306.php?nid=&id=&pnt=306.

16. Heather Mason Kiefer, "Poll of Islamic World: Favorability toward U.S., Britain," 26 February 2002, http://www.gallup.com/poll/5722/Poll-Islamic-World-Favorability-Toward-U.S.-Britain.aspx; Pew Global Attitudes Project, "American Public Diplomacy in the Islamic World," 27 February 2003, http://people-press.org/commentary/?analysisid=63.

17. Program on International Policy Attitudes, "Global Views of United States Improve While Other Countries Decline," April 18 2010, http://www.worldpublicopinion.org/pipa/articles/views_on_countriesregions_bt/660.php?nid=&id=&pnt=660&lb=.

18. Pew Global Attitudes Project, "Confidence in Obama Lifts U.S. Image around the World: Most Muslim Publics Not So Easily Moved," 23 July 2009.

19. Program on International Policy Attitudes, "Global Views of United States Improve While Other Countries Decline."

20. Program on International Policy Attitudes, "World Publics See European Union as a 'Positive Influence,'" 21 March 2007, http://www.worldpublicopinion.org/pipa/articles/views_on_countriesregions_bt/335.php?nid=&id=&pnt=335; Program on International Policy Attitudes, "Global Views of United States Improve While Other Countries Decline."

21. Pew Research Center, "America Admired"; Telhami, *The Stakes*, 41, or Telhami, "Understanding the Challenge"; Program on International Policy Attitudes, "Global Poll Finds That Religion and Culture Are Not to Blame."

22. Telhami, *The Stakes*, 43.

23. Pew Research Center, "America Admired"; Telhami, *The Stakes*, 98–99.

24. This poll conducted personal interviews in Egypt, France, Indonesia, Iran, Kuwait, Lebanon, Pakistan, Saudi Arabia, the United Arab Emirates, and Venezuela between March 4 and April 3, 2002.

25. Kull, "America's Image in the World."

26. These numbers are drawn from the terrorism database maintained by the RAND Corporation and the Oklahoma City National Memorial Institute for the Prevention of Terrorism. See also Peter Bergen and Paul Cruickshank, "Brutal Reality: The War Is Fueling Global Jihad," *New York Daily News*, 21 February 2007.

27. The representative countries were Kuwait, Pakistan, Morocco, Iran, Indonesia, Lebanon, and Turkey. For more on Islamic opposition to the U.S. invasion of Afghanistan see Gallup Poll Editorial Staff, "Many in Islamic World Question Motives for U.S. Military Campaign," 1 March 2002, http://www.gallup.com/poll/5407/Many-Islamic-World-Question-Motives-U.S.-Military-Campaign.aspx. For more on opposition from Latin American countries see Telhami, *The Stakes*, 42.

28. Kull, "America's Image in the World."

29. The statistics for this and the preceding three paragraphs come from Program on International Policy Attitudes, "Global Poll Finds That Religion and Culture Are Not to Blame for Tensions between Islam and the West."

30. WorldPublicOpinion.org, "Muslims Believe U.S. Seeks to Undermine Islam."

31. Ibid.

32. Ibid.

33. Program on International Policy Attitudes, "Muslims Believe U.S. Seeks to Undermine Islam" and "Muslim Publics Oppose Al Qaeda's Terrorism, but Agree with Its Goal of Driving U.S. Forces Out."

34. Program on International Policy Attitudes, "Muslims Believe U.S. Seeks to Undermine Islam" and "Muslim Publics Oppose Al Qaeda's Terrorism, but Agree with Its Goal of Driving U.S. Forces Out."

35. Program on International Policy Attitudes, "Muslims Believe U.S. Seeks to Undermine Islam" and "Muslim Publics Oppose Al Qaeda's Terrorism, but Agree with Its Goal of Driving U.S. Forces Out."

36. Samuel P. Huntington, "The Clash of Civilizations?" *Foreign Affairs*, Summer 1993, http://www.foreignaffairs.com/articles/48950/samuel-p-hunt ington/the-clash-of-civilizations.

## CHAPTER 5. A QUESTION OF IMPORTANCE:
## THE OBAMA ADMINISTRATION AND IRAQ

1. Rick Atkinson, "Left of Boom: The Struggle to Defeat Roadside Bombs, Part I," *Washington Post*, 30 September 2007; "Crocker: Iraqi Government 'Dysfunctional,'" *Washington Post*, 11 September 2007; Michael Abramowitz and Jonathan Weisman, "Senators Take Petraeus, Crocker to Task," *Washington Post*, 11 September 2007; William Branigin, "Petraeus, Crocker Expected to Ask for More Time in Iraq," *Washington Post*, 10 September 2007.

2. Karen DeYoung, "Al Qaeda in Iraq May Not Be Threat Here: Intelligence Experts Say Group Is Busy on Its Home Front," *Washington Post*, 18 March 2007; Paul Krugman, "The Arithmetic of Failure," *New York Times*, 27 October 2006; "Brutal Reality: The War Is Fueling Global Jihad"; Mark Mazzetti, "Spy Agencies Say Iraq War Worsens Terror Threat," *New York Times*, 24 September 2006.

3. Niles Lathem, "Saudis Are Becoming Top Threat to Our GIs," *New York Post*, 29 June 2005; Josh Meyer and Mark Mazzetti, "In a Battle of Wits, Iraq's Insurgency Mastermind Stays a Step Ahead of U.S.," *Los Angeles Times*, 16 November 2005.

4. "Al Zarqawi's Network Bigger, Stronger," *Houston Chronicle*, 23 October 2005; Michael Slackman and Scott Shane, "Terrorists Trained by Zarqawi Went Abroad, Jordan Says," *New York Times*, 11 June 2006.

5. Bruce Crumely, "Notebook: The New Bin Laden?" *Time*, 5 September 2005, Richard Beeston, Catherine Philip, and Michael Theodoulou, "Bin Laden's Ruthless Rival Spreads Tentacles of Jihad across Region," *Times* (London), 18 November 2005.

6. Anton La Guardia, "Foreign Fighters Only a Tiny Part of the Rebellion," *Daily Telegraph* (London), 30 June 2005.

7. Richard Beeston and James Hider, "Following the Trail of Death: How Foreigners Flock to Join Holy War," *Times* (London), 25 June 2005.

8. Rod Nordland and Michael Hirsh, "Fighting Zarqawi's Legacy," *Newsweek*, June 2006, 32.

9. Peter Mansoor, "How the Surge Worked," *Washington Post*, 10 August 2008.

10. Joshua Partlow, "For U.S. Unit in Baghdad, an Alliance of Last Resort,"

*Washington Post*, 9 June 2007; David W. Brannan, "We Didn't Kill Al Qaeda," *Los Angeles Times*, 9 June 2006.

11. Nordland and Hirsh, "Fighting Zarqawi's Legacy"; Brannan, "We Didn't Kill Al Qaeda."

12. Joshua Partlow, "Zarqawi Group Vows to Press Attacks," *Washington Post*, 12 June 2006; DeYoung, "Al Qaeda in Iraq May Not Be Threat Here"; Thomas E. Ricks, "Shrine Bombing as War's Turning Point Debated," *Washington Post*, 13 March 2007.

13. DeYoung, "Al Qaeda in Iraq May Not Be Threat Here."

14. Fawaz Gerges, "Al Qaeda's Hydra Head in Iraq," *Christian Science Monitor*, 22 June 2006; La Guardia, "Foreign Fighters Only a Tiny Part of the Rebellion"; Nordland and Hirsh, "Fighting Zarqawi's Legacy"; DeYoung, "Al Qaeda in Iraq May Not Be Threat Here."

15. Scott Shane, "The Grisly Jihadist Network That He Inspired Is Busy Promoting Zarqawi's Militant Views," *New York Times*, 9 June 2006; Nordland and Hirsh, "Fighting Zarqawi's Legacy."

16. Sebastian Rotella and Josh Meyer, "Zarqawi May Have Spawned an Army of Admirers," *Los Angeles Times*, 10 June 2006. "'It's the media emphasis that really made him a global phenomenon,' a senior Italian counterterrorism official said. 'And his videos are more popular because he is pure action. Bin Laden is more boring.'"

17. Ibid.; Abramowitz, "Bush to Endorse Petraeus Plan."

18. Liz Sly, "Iraq to Need U.S. Troops for Years, Official Says," *Los Angeles Times*, 9 September 2010.

19. Jason Campbell, Michael O'Hanlon, and Amy Unikewicz, "The State of Iraq: An Update," *New York Times*, 4 September 2007; Rod Nordland and Alissa J. Rubin, "Sunni Fighters Say Iraq Didn't Keep Job Promises," *New York Times*, 24 March 2009; Timothy Williams and Duraid Adnan, "Sunnis in Iraq Allied with U.S. Quitting to Rejoin Rebels," *New York Times*, 17 October 2010.

20. Campbell, O'Hanlon, and Unikewicz "The State of Iraq: An Update"; Nordland and Rubin, "Sunni Fighters Say Iraq Didn't Keep Job Promises"; Williams and Adnan, "Sunnis in Iraq Allied with U.S. Quitting to Rejoin Rebels"; Leila Fadel, "Sunni Awakening Officers Are Kicked Off Police Force in Iraq," *Washington Post*, 27 September 2010.

21. Lara Jakes, "Looking at Lessons That Can Be Learned from Iraq," *Washington Post*, 27 August 2010; Williams and Adnan, "Sunnis in Iraq Allied with U.S. Quitting to Rejoin Rebels."

22. Mowaffak al-Rubaie, "Federalism, Not Partition," *Washington Post*, 18 January 2008, http://www.washingtonpost.com/wp-dyn/content/article/2008/01/17/AR2008011702240.html; Associated Press, "Kurds Warn-

ing of War with Iraqi Government," *Arizona Daily Star*, 15 February 2009; Leila Fadel, "Census Postponed Again amid Ethnic Disputes," *Washington Post*, 4 October 2010.

23. Liz Sly, "Iraq's Maliki: Strongman or Merely Strong?" *Washington Post*, 22 December 2010.

24. Ibid.

25. Lara Jakes and Qassim Abdul-Zahra, "Iraqi Leaders Not Following U.S. Advice on Gov't," Associated Press on AOL News, 21 October 2010, http://www.aolnews.com/story/iraqi-leaders-not-following-us-advice-on/806553.

26. Rebecca Santana, "Sunnis' Hand Is Weak in Iraq," *Philadelphia Inquirer*, 13 November 2010.

27. Chelsea J. Carter, "U.S. General Says Key Province Lacks Support by Iraq," *Boston Globe*, 8 January 2009.

28. Kenneth Katzman, "Iraq: Politics, Elections, and Benchmarks," Congressional Research Service, 3 March 2010, http://www.fas.org/sgp/crs/mideast/RS21968.pdf; "Iraq Benchmark Report Card: One Year after the Surge," Center for American Progress, 24 January 2008, http://www.americanprogress.org/issues/2008/01/benchmark.html; Lionel Beehner and Greg Bruno, "What Are Iraq's Benchmarks?" Council on Foreign Relations Backgrounder, 11 March 2008, http://www.cfr.org/publication/13333/; Nancy A. Youssef, "Iraq, U.S. See the Future Differently," *Houston Chronicle*, 19 March 2009.

29. Anne Gearan, "An Antiterror Role for Holdover Troops," *Philadelphia Inquirer*, 26 February 2009; Chelsea J. Carter, "Broad Contours of Iraq Exit Are Taking Shape," *Arizona Daily Star*, 1 March 2009.

30. Peter Baker and Elisabeth Brumiller, "Obama Favoring Mid-2010 Pullout in Iraq, Aides Say," *New York Times*, 25 February 2009; Youssef, "Iraq, U.S. See the Future Differently"; Max Boot, "Maliki's Actions, and Obama's Inaction, Threaten an Iraq Democracy," *Los Angeles Times*, 9 May 2010.

31. Boot, "Maliki's Actions, and Obama's Inaction, Threaten an Iraq Democracy"; Ernesto Londono and Craig Whitlock, "U.S. Drawdown Comes at Time of High Risk In Iraq," *Washington Post*, 14 May 2010; Lara Jakes, "Looking at Lessons that Can Be Learned from Iraq," *Washington Post*, 27 August 2010; Derrick Z. Jackson, "End of Combat Yields Surge of Contractors," *Boston Globe*, 4 September 2010.

32. Carter, "Broad Contours of Iraq Exit Are Taking Shape."

33. Steven Lee Myers, "Iraq Recount Mired in a New Dispute," *New York Times*, 4 May 2010; Anthony Shadid, "Iraqi Deal to End De-Ba'athification," *New York Times*, 12 May 2010; Steven Lee Meyers, "Iraqi Politicians Break Bread, but Not the Standoff," *New York Times*, 21 May 2010; Boot, "Maliki's Actions, and Obama's Inaction, Threaten an Iraq Democracy"; Sam Dagher,

"Election Victories Help Kurds in Iraq Push for More Sovereignty," *New York Times*, 3 May 2010; Sam Dagher, "Iraq Wants the U.S. Out," *Wall Street Journal*, 28 December 2010; John Leland and Jack Healy, "After Months, Iraqi Lawmakers Approve a Government," *New York Times*, 22 December 2010; Leila Fadel, "Still Struggling to Form Government, Iraq Breaks a World Record," *Washington Post*, 1 October 2010.

34. Leland and Healy, "After Months, Iraqi Lawmakers Approve a Government"; Dagher, "Iraq Wants the U.S. Out"; Sly, "Iraq's Maliki: Strongman or Merely Strong?"; Myers, "Iraq Recount Mired in a New Dispute"; Shadid, "Iraqi Deal to End De-Ba'athification"; Meyers, "Iraqi Politicians Break Bread, but Not the Standoff"; Boot, "Maliki's Actions, and Obama's Inaction, Threaten an Iraq Democracy."

35. Steven Lee Myers, "Iraq's Fissures Only Deepen," *New York Times*, 4 October 2010; Anthony Shadid, "Iraqi Leaders Fear for Future after Their Past Missteps," *New York Times*, 17 August 2010; Dana Hedgpeth, "U.S. Rebuilding in Iraq Is Missing Key Goals, Report Finds: Production of Oil, Electricity Falls Short," *Washington Post*, 30 April 2007; Editorial, "Iraqi Oil Sector Feeble, GAO Finds," *Washington Post*, 3 August 2007; Reuters, "Problems for the Iraqi Oil Industry," *Washington Post*, 2 July 2007. See also Nina Shea, "Iraq's Endangered Minorities," *Washington Post*, 27 August 2007; David Gavlak, "Jordan Appeals for Help in Dealing with Iraqi Refugees: 750,000 Have Crossed Border, Costing Kingdom $1 Billion a Year, International Aid Conference Is Told," *Washington Post*, 27 July 2007; Megan Greenwell, "A Dismal Picture of Life in Iraq: Nearly a Third of Population Needs Emergency Aid, Report Says," *Washington Post*, 31 July 2007; Sudarsan Raghavan, "UN Decries Neglect of Iraqi Refugees," *Washington Post*, 7 July 2007; and "Ignoring Iraqi Opinion in the Name of Democracy," Fairness & Accuracy in Reporting press release, 2 June 2004, http://www.fair.org/index.php?page=1833.ear.

36. Leland and Healy, "After Months, Iraqi Lawmakers Approve a Government."

37. Ibid.

38. Anthony Shadid and John Leland, "Anti-U.S. Cleric Returns to Iraq, and to Power," *New York Times*, 6 January 2011; Anthony Shadid, "Sadrists Project Confidence," *New York Times*, 7 January 2011; Aaron C. Davis, "Sadr Foments Resistance by Iraqis," *Washington Post*, 9 January 2011.

39. Ned Parker, "Al Qaeda in Iraq Rises from the Ashes," *Los Angeles Times*, 13 September 2010.

40. Associated Press, "More Foreign Fighters Seen Slipping Back into Iraq," 5 December 2010, http://www.google.com/hostednews/ap/article/ALeqM5iPUXvyVD9cVX2Ql3-kvpvSBLV6KQ?docId=6688ea51d95642a8a8790298fd14d078.

41. Associated Press, "Al Qaida Stronghold of Mosul Is Proving a Security Nightmare," *Arizona Daily Star*, 10 March 2009; Rebecca Santana, "Iraqis Back in the Grip of a Familiar Unease," *Philadelphia Inquirer*, 15 May 2010; Borzou Daragahi, "Ready to Give Up on Iraq," *Los Angeles Times*, 20 May 2010; Steven Lee Myers, "Coordinated Attacks in Iraqi Cities Kill More Than 100," *New York Times*, 11 May 2010; Sinan Slaheddin, "Dragnet after the Devastation," *Washington Times*, 12 May 2010; WSJ News Roundup, "Iraq Blasts Kill 25 after Game of Soccer," *Wall Street Journal*, 15 May 2010; Borzou Daragahi, "Scores Are Killed in Iraqi Violence," *Los Angeles Times*, 11 May 2010; Leland and Healy, "After Months, Iraqi Lawmakers Approve a Government."

42. Parker, "Al Qaeda in Iraq Rises from the Ashes"; Timothy Williams, "Insurgent Group in Iraq, Declared Tamed, Roars," *New York Times*, 28 September 2010; Anthony Shadid, "Coordinated Attacks Strike 13 Iraqi Cities," *New York Times*, 26 August 2010.

43. Parker, "Al Qaeda in Iraq Rises from the Ashes"; Williams, "Insurgent Group in Iraq, Declared Tamed, Roars"; Shadid, "Coordinated Attacks Strike 13 Iraqi Cities."

44. Ernesto Londono, "Sunni Insurgent Groups Gather to Plan Comeback," *Washington Post*, 1 June 2010.

45. United Press International (UPI), "Special Reports: Sadr Reforms Mehdi Army amid Iraqi Crisis," 20 May 2010, http://www.upi.com/Top_News/Special/2010/05/20/Sadr-reforms-Mehdi-Army-amid-Iraqi-crisis/UPI-84961274385757/.

46. Steven Lee Myers, "Attacks on Baghdad Green Zone Surge," *New York Times*, 30 September 2010.

47. Ibid.; Baker and Brumiller, "Obama Favoring Mid-2010 Pullout in Iraq."

48. John J. Kruzel, "Special Operations Forces in Iraq to Remain through Drawdown," American Forces Press Service, 1 April 2010, http://www.defense.gov/news/newsarticle.aspx?id=58579.

49. Thomas E. Ricks, "The War in Iraq Isn't Over, The Main Events May Not Even Have Happened Yet," *Washington Post*, 15 February 2009; Ernesto Londono and Aziz Al Wan, "Two Blasts Kill More Than 80 in Iraq: Bombings Add to Fears That Insurgency Will Grow as U.S. Departs," *Washington Post*, 24 April 2009.

50. "Osama Just Bin Given a Big Break," *New York Daily News*, 10 June 2006.

51. Ibid.; Schuster, "Al-Zawahiri Letter under Scrutiny." "Zarqawi was both a leader of and a problem for Al Qaeda in Iraq. Al Qaeda's international leadership—Egyptian-born Ayman al-Zawahiri and Saudi native Osama bin Laden—wanted to rein in Zarqawi's vicious and savage attacks, including the videotaped beheadings of some of his victims. Zarqawi was truly ter-

rorizing—but even the Al Qaeda leadership felt his brutality against fellow Muslims was counterproductive to their goal of defeating the West."

52. Editorial, "A Good Year in Iraq," *Washington Post*, 23 December 2010.

53. Kenneth M. Pollack, "Five Myths About Leaving Iraq," *Washington Post*, 22 August 2010.

## CHAPTER 6. A QUESTION OF PRIORITIES:
## THE OBAMA ADMINISTRATION AND IRAN

1. Gerald F. Seib, "Message to Iran Shows Strategy Shift," *Wall Street Journal*, 24 March 2009.

2. Eli Lake, "Seeking Leverage, U.S. Puts Pressure on Iran," *Washington Times*, 31 March 2009.

3. Peter Finn, "Al Qaeda Deputies Harbored by Iran: Pair Are Plotting Attacks, Sources Say," *Washington Post*, 28 August 2002; Peter Finn, "Iran Is Said to Give Up Al Qaeda Members," *Washington Post*, 11 August 2002; Pamela Constable, "In Kabul, Iranian Blasts U.S. Shift to 'Angry Policy,'" *Washington Post*, 14 August 2002.

4. Steven Mufson and Marc Kaufman, "Longtime Foes U.S., Iran Explore Improved Relations," *Washington Post*, 29 October 2001.

5. Glen Kessler, "In 2003, U.S. Spurned Iran's Offer of Dialogue," *Washington Post*, 18 June 2006.

6. Editorial, "Iranian Abandons Push to Improve U.S. Ties," *Washington Post*, 30 May 2002.

7. Joshua Partlow, "Tehran's Influence Grows as Iraqis See Advantages," *Washington Post*, 26 January 2007.

8. Robert Haddick, "Are the Ayatollahs Using COIN?" This Week at War, *Small Wars Journal*, 12 February 2010, http://smallwarsjournal.com/blog/2010/02/this-week-at-war-are-the-ayato/.

9. David E. Sanger, "U.S. May Drop Key Condition for Talks with Iran," *New York Times*, 14 April 2009.

10. Reuters, "Iran Nuclear Weapon Is 1–3 Years Away: U.S.'s Gates," http://reuters.com/, 11 June 2010; Adam Entous, "U.S. Officials See Iran Nuclear Bomb Probable in 3–5 Years," http://reuters.com/, 13 April 2010; David E. Sanger, "Officials Say Iran Could Make Bomb Fuel in a Year," *New York Times*, 15 April 2010; Agence France-Presse (AFP), "No Iran Nuclear Weapons Capacity for at Least a Year: Gates," http://www.yahoo.com/, 13 April 2010.

11. Reuters, "Iran Nuclear Weapon Is 1–3 Years Away: U.S.'s Gates"; Entous, "U.S. Officials See Iran Nuclear Bomb Probable in 3–5 Years"; Sanger, "Officials Say Iran Could Make Bomb Fuel in a Year"; AFP, "No Iran Nuclear Weapons Capacity for at Least a Year: Gates."

12. Phil Stewart and Adam Entous, "Iranian Missile May Be Able to Hit U.S. by 2015," 19 April 2010, http://www.reuters.com/article/idUSTRE63J04H20100420; Ali Sheikholeslami, "Iran Says No Plan for Missile Able to Reach U.S." Bloomberg BusinessWeek, 21 April 2010, http://www.businessweek.com/news/2010-04-21/iran-says-no-plan-for-missile-capable-of-hitting-u-s-update1-.html.

13. David Ignatius, "Buying Time With Iran," *Washington Post*, 9 January 2011.

14. Daniel Dombey, "U.S. May Cede to Iran's Nuclear Ambition," *Financial Times*, 4 April 2009.

15. Borzou Daragahi, "Iran Signs $3.2 Billion Natural Gas Deal with China," *Los Angeles Times*, 15 March 2009.

16. Christopher Boucek and David Donadio, "A Nation on the Brink," *The Atlantic*, April 2010, 52.

17. Adam Goldman and Matt Apuzzo, "Iran Quietly Frees Al Qaeda Prisoners," *Jerusalem Post*, 14 May 2010.

18. Thomas Joscelyn, "Sweet Home Iran," *Weekly Standard*, 24 May 2010.

19. Ibid. Most disturbingly, former CIA director George Tenet claimed in his 2007 book *At the Center of the Storm* (New York: Harper Collins, 2007) that Al Qaeda operatives inside Iran attempted to purchase Russian nuclear devices.

20. Goldman and Apuzzo, "Iran Quietly Frees Al Qaeda Prisoners."

21. Hersh, "The Redirection."

22. Charles Krauthammer, "The Myth of Iran's 'Isolation'," *Washington Post*, 11 June 2010; Jay Solomon, "Panetta Warns of Iran Threat," *Wall Street Journal*, 28 June 2010.

23. Doyle McManus, "Obama's Iran Strategy," *Los Angeles Times*, 22 February 2009; Lawrence J. Korb and Laura Conley, "The Contributions of Iran," *Boston Globe*, 24 October 2008.

24. McManus, "Obama's Iran Strategy"; Korb and Conley, "The Contributions of Iran."

25. Seib, "Message to Iran Shows Strategy Shift."

26. Sanger, "U.S. May Drop Key Condition for Talks with Iran."

27. Ibid.; Jay Solomon, "U.S. Seeks to Assure Arabs on Iran," *Wall Street Journal*, 27 April 2009.

28. Dombey, "U.S. May Cede to Iran's Nuclear Ambition."

29. McManus, "Obama's Iran Strategy."

30. For more on these aspects of the U.S. relationship with Iran, see Paul Richter, "Iran Has Interest in a Stable Afghanistan, Clinton Says," *Los Angeles Times*, 31 March 2009, and David E. Sanger, "Obama Takes Several Gambles in Bid to Defuse Nuclear Standoff with Iran," *New York Times*, 11 February 2010.

31. Richter, "Iran Has Interest in a Stable Afghanistan"; Sanger, "Obama Takes Several Gambles in Bid to Defuse Nuclear Standoff with Iran."

32. For more on these aspects of the U.S. relationship with Iran, see Richter, "Iran Has Interest in a Stable Afghanistan," and Sanger, "Obama Takes Several Gambles in Bid to Defuse Nuclear Standoff with Iran."

33. Eli Lake and Nicholas Kralev, "U.S. Alters Course on Syria," *Washington Times*, 7 April 2009.

34. Sanger, "Obama Takes Several Gambles in Bid to Defuse Nuclear Standoff with Iran."

35. Lake, "Seeking Leverage."

36. Ray Takeyh, "What Iran Wants," *Washington Post*, 29 December 2008.

37. McManus, "Obama's Iran Strategy."

38. Amir Taheri, "Iran Has Started a Mideast Arms Race," *Wall Street Journal*, 23 March 2009.

39. William J. Broad and David E. Sanger, "U.S. Is Pushing to Deter a Mideast Nuclear Race," *New York Times*, 3 May 2010.

40. Roula Khalaf and James Drummond, "Gulf in $123 Bn U.S. Arms Spree," *Financial Times*, 21 September 2010; Anna Mulrine, "Blockbuster U.S. Arms Sale to Saudi Arabia: Will It Deter Iran?" *Christian Science Monitor*, 21 September 2010.

41. Paul Richter, "Iran Sanctions: U.S. and Allies May Narrow Their Approach," *Los Angeles Times*, 29 December 2009.

42. Reuters, "Iran: Leader Dismisses Deadline for Deal on Shipping Nuclear Fuel," *New York Times*, 23 December 2009.

43. William J. Broad, "Small Step in Iran's Nuclear Effort Suggests Ambitions for a Weapon, Experts Say," *New York Times*, 10 February 2010.

44. Combined Dispatches, "Iran Starts Work on New Nuclear Plant," *China Daily*, 20 April 2010.

45. Joby Warrick, "Iran's New Centrifuge Raises Concerns about Nuclear Arms," *Washington Post*, 2 May 2010.

46. Julia Damianova and Borzou Daragahi, "Iran Step Could Boost Ability to Enrich Uranium, Diplomats Say," *Los Angeles Times*, 15 May 2010.

47. Associated Press, "Iran's Nuclear Plant May Be Ready by Aug.," *Boston Globe*, 21 May 2010; Broad and Sanger, "U.S. Is Pushing to Deter a Mideast Nuclear Race"; Associated Press, "Tehran to Start Loading Fuel in Nuclear Reactor," *Wall Street Journal*, 1 October 2010.

48. David E. Sanger and William J. Broad, "Iran Remains Defiant, Nuclear Agency Says," *New York Times*, 7 September 2010.

49. Lake, "Seeking Leverage."

50. Ibid.; Solomon, "U.S. Seeks to Assure Arabs on Iran."

51. McManus, "Obama's Iran Strategy."

52. James Hider, "Iran Comes out on Top in Secret Simulated War Games," *Times* (London), 3 December 2009.

53. Reuters, "Scenarios: Global Impact if Israel Strikes Iran," 29 March 2010, http://www.reuters.com/article/idU.S.LDE62N1CX.

54. Miles Amoore, "Iran Pays Taliban to Kill U.S. Soldiers," *Sunday Times* (London), 5 September 2010; Jeff Stein, "New Intelligence on Iran Antiaircraft Missiles in Afghanistan," SpyTalk, *Washington Post*, 12 August 2010, http://blog.washingtonpost.com/spy-talk/2010/08/intelligence_report_iranian_an.html.

55. Amoore, "Iran Pays Taliban to Kill U.S. Soldiers"; Stein, "New Intelligence on Iran Antiaircraft Missiles in Afghanistan."

56. Amoore, "Iran Pays Taliban to Kill U.S. Soldiers"; Stein, "New Intelligence on Iran Antiaircraft Missiles in Afghanistan."

57. David E. Sanger, "Three Faces of the New China," *New York Times*, 26 September 2010.

58. Ibid.

59. Sanger, "Three Faces of the New China"; Anne Applebaum, "China's Quiet Path to Power," *Washington Post*, 28 September 2010.

60. Arthur Herman, "America's Looming China Challenge," *New York Post*, January 26, 2010.

61. Fred Hiatt, "Does Russia Get It," *Washington Post*, 4 October 2009.

62. Ibid.

63. Solomon, "U.S. Seeks to Assure Arabs on Iran."

64. John Pomfret, "Oil, Ideology Keep China from Joining Push against Iran," *Washington Post*, 30 September 2009.

65. Mark Helprin, "Farewell to America's China Station," *Wall Street Journal*, 17 May 2010.

66. Ibid.

67. Robert Kagan, "The Russia 'Reset' Fraud," *Washington Post*, 25 May 2010.

68. Alexei Barrionuevo and Ginger Thompson, "Brazil's Diplomacy Worries U.S. Officials," *New York Times*, 15 May 2010; Thomas Erdbrink, "Brazil and Turkey Seek Nuclear Deal with Iran," *Washington Post*, 16 May 2010; David Sanger and Mark Landler, "Major Powers Have Deal on Sanctions for Iran," *New York Times*, 19 May 2010; Marc Champion, "In Risky Deal, Ankara Seeks Security, Trade," *Wall Street Journal*, 18 May 2010; David Sanger and Michael Slackman, "U.S. Is Skeptical on Iranian Deal for Nuclear Fuel," *New York Times*, 18 May 2010.

69. Sanger and Landler, "Major Powers Have Deal on Sanctions for Iran."

70. Tarek El-Tablawy, "New Iran Sanctions Could Strengthen Revolutionary Guard," *Washington Post*, 10 October 2009.

71. Bill Gertz and Eli Lake, "Russia Can Send Missiles to Iran," *Washington Times*, 21 May 2010.

72. Glen Kessler and Colum Lynch, "Major Powers Agree to Sanction Iran," *Washington Post*, 19 May 2010.

73. Pomfret, "Oil, Ideology Keep China from Joining Push against Iran."

74. Thomas Erdbrink and Colum Lynch, "Iran Is Prepared for Fuel Sanctions," *Washington Post*, 24 June 2010.

75. Peter Baker, "Obama Signs into Law Tighter Sanctions on Iran," *New York Times*, 2 July 2010.

76. Sara Carter, "Iran Army Officer Defied Islamic Officials," *Washington Examiner*, 14 April 2010.

77. Program on International Policy Attitudes, "Analysis of Multiple Polls Finds Little Evidence Iranian Public Sees Government as Illegitimate," 3 February 2010, http://www.worldpublicopinion.org/pipa/articles/brmid dleeastnafricara/652.php?nid=&id=&pnt=652&lb=brme.

78. Ibid.

79. Alvin Richman, "Post-Election Poll in Iran Shows Little Change in Anti-Regime Minority," 18 February 2010, http://www.worldpublicopinion.org/pipa/articles/brmiddleeastnafricara/653.php?nid=&id=&pnt=653&lb=brme.

80. Fareed Zakaria, "The Fantasy of an Iranian Revolution," *Washington Post*, 21 June 2010.

81. Jay Solomon, "U.S. Shifts Its Strategy toward Iran's Dissidents," *Wall Street Journal*, 11 June 2010.

82. Carter, "Iran Army Officer Defied Islamic Officials."

83. Bill Gertz, "Military in Iran Seen as Taking Control," *Washington Times*, 21 June 2010.

84. The American-Israel Public Affairs Committee (AIPAC), "IRGC Designation Key Step in Preventing Nuclear Iran," MEMO, 26 October 2007, http://www.aipac.org/Publications/AIPACAnalysesMemos/AIPAC_Memo_-_IRGC_Designation_Key_Step_in_Preventing_Nuclear_Iran__3_.pdf.

85. El-Tablawy, "New Iran Sanctions Could Strengthen Revolutionary Guard."

86. Ibid.

87. Sanger, "Obama Takes Several Gambles in Bid to Defuse Nuclear Standoff With Iran."

88. Kimberly Dozier, "Mullen: Iran Will Continue to Strive for Nukes," *Washington Post*, 29 June 2010.

89. Ibid.

90. Thomas Erdbrink, "Iranian President Answers Sanctions," *Washington Post*, 29 June 2010; Thomas Erdbrink and Joby Warrick, "Iran Derides Sanctions, Talks of Reducing Cooperation with Inspectors," *Washington Post*, 11 June 2010; David E. Sanger, "Iran Bars Nuclear Inspectors in Response to Sanctions," *New York Times*, 22 June 2010.

91. Robert Haddick, "What Iran Learned from Saddam," *Small Wars Journal*, 18 June 2010, http://smallwarsjournal.com/blog/2010/06/this-week-at-war-what-iran-lea/.

92. David Ignatius, "Who Loses the Iran Game?" *Washington Post*, 6 December 2009.

93. Associated Press, "Israel Says It Is Capable of Striking Iran," *Boston Globe*, 11 May 2010.

94. Solomon, "U.S. Seeks to Assure Arabs on Iran."

95. Hugh Tomlinson, "Saudi Arabia Gives Israel Clear Skies to Attack Iranian Nuclear Sites," *Times* (London), 12 June 2010.

96. Glenn Kessler and Greg Miller, "Israel: Syria Giving Scuds to Hezbollah," *Washington Post*, 14 April 2010; Eli Lake, "Hezbollah May Have Scud-Type Missiles," *Washington Times*, 22 April 2010.

97. Reuters, "U.S., Israel Say Syria Arming Hezbollah with Missiles," http://www.reuters.com/, 27 April 2010.

98. McManus, "Obama's Iran Strategy."

99. Doyle McManus, "U.S. in a Foreign Policy Corner on Iran," *Los Angeles Times*, 13 June 2010; David E. Sanger, "Beyond Iran Sanctions That Probably Won't Work, Plans B, C, D . . . ," *New York Times*, 11 June 2010.

100. McManus, "U.S. in a Foreign Policy Corner on Iran"; Sanger, "Beyond Iran Sanctions That Probably Won't Work, Plans B, C, D. . . ."

**CHAPTER 7. A QUESTION OF LEVERAGE:**
**THE OBAMA ADMINISTRATION AND PAKISTAN**

1. Scott Shane, "The War in Pashtunistan," *New York Times*, 6 December 2009.

2. Karen DeYoung, "Obama Outlines Regional Afghan Strategy," *Washington Post*, 28 March 2009.

3. Editorial, "Pakistan's Separate Peace," *Washington Post*, 13 September 2006.

4. April Witt, "Afghan, Pakistani Forces Intensify Fighting along Contested Borders," *Washington Post*, 20 July 2003, http://pqasb.pqarchiver.com/washingtonpost/access/371879251.html; John Lancaster and Kamran Khan, "Pakistan to Step Up Border Operations," *Washington Post*, 23 February 2004; Pamela Constable, "Battle Ends in Pakistani Tribal Lands: Militants Release 14 Hostages, Criticism of Government Operation Widens," *Washington Post*, 29 March 2004; John Lancaster, "Pakistani Forces Take Back Town from Tribesmen: Thousands Flee as Deadly Battle Subsides," *Washington Post*, 6 March 2006; Griff Witte, "Violence Kills More than 60 in Northwest Pakistan," *Washington Post*, 14 September 2007.

5. Witt, "Afghan, Pakistani Forces Intensify Fighting along Contested Borders"; Lancaster and Khan, "Pakistan to Step Up Border Operations"; Constable, "Battle Ends in Pakistani Tribal Lands"; Lancaster, "Pakistani Forces

Take Back Town from Tribesmen"; Witte, "Violence Kills More than 60 in Northwest Pakistan."

6. Griff Witte, "Pakistan Truce Appears Defunct: Insurgents Strike Police, Troops," *Washington Post*, 16 July 2007; Griff Witte, "Taliban Fighters Void Second Truce in Pakistan," *Washington Post*, 20 August 2007; Pamela Constable, "In Tribal Pakistan, an Uneasy Quiet: Pact Fails to Deter Backing for Taliban," *Washington Post*, 28 September 2006; Editorial, "Al Qaeda's Sanctuary: Pakistan's Tribal Areas Look a Lot Like Afghanistan in 2001—And the Bush Administration Is Tolerating It," *Washington Post*, 21 December 2006; Editorial, "A Problem of Passivity"; Griff Witte, "Pakistani Government Seeks to Salvage Peace Deal," *Washington Post*, 17 July 2007. Pakistan's state information minister, Tariq Azim Khan, noted, "I don't think our long-term strategy has changed."

7. Griff Witte, "Musharraf, Bhutto Reach Tentative Deal to Let Her Return with Amnesty: Pakistan Supreme Court Rules That Scheduled Election Can Proceed," *Washington Post*, 5 October 2007; Griff Witte, "Musharraf Names Ex-Spy Chief to Lead Army: Charges against Bhutto May Be Dropped," *Washington Post*, 3 October 2007.

8. Witte, "Musharraf Names Ex-Spy Chief to Lead Army."

9. Dexter Filkins, "Right at the Edge," *New York Times Magazine*, 7 September 2008, MM52; Dexter Filkins, "The Long Road to Chaos in Pakistan," *New York Times Magazine*, 28 September 2008, WK3.

10. Mark Mazzetti and Eric Schmitt, "Afghan Strikes by Taliban Get Pakistan Help, U.S. Aides Say," *New York Times*, 26 March 2009.

11. Ibid.

12. Eli Lake, "Pakistan Seen Restricting Data Obtained from Mullah," *Washington Times*, 18 May 2010; Adam Entous, "Taliban No. 2 Interrogations Yield Useful Intel: U.S.," http://www.reuters.com/, 20 April 2010; Eric Schmitt, "Captured Leader Offers Insight into the Taliban," *New York Times*, 6 May 2010.

13. Lake, "Pakistan Seen Restricting Data Obtained from Mullah."

14. Ibid.; Dexter Filkins, "Pakistanis Say Taliban Arrest Was Meant to Hurt Peace Bid," *New York Times*, 23 August 2010.

15. Greg Miller, "Pakistan Released Insurgents, Officials Say," *Washington Post*, 11 April 2010; Filkins, "Pakistanis Say Taliban Arrest Was Meant to Hurt Peace Bid."

16. Filkins, "Pakistanis Say Taliban Arrest Was Meant to Hurt Peace Bid."

17. Ibid.

18. Trudy Rubin, "Danger on Remote Pakistan Border," *Philadelphia Inquirer*, 5 October 2008.

19. Trudy Rubin, "Karachi's Powder Keg," *Philadelphia Inquirer*, 3 May 2009.

20. For more on the Haqqani network, Hekmatyar, and issues with Pakistan, see Filkins, "The Long Road to Chaos in Pakistan."

21. Tavernise and Masood, "Pakistan Weighs Changes to Revise Constitution."

22. Mark Hosenball, "Mehsud's Pals in High Places," *Newsweek*, 13 April 2009.

23. Filkins, "The Long Road to Chaos in Pakistan"; Simon Cameron-Moore, "Militancy Spirals as Court Keeps Musharraf in Limbo," Reuters, 1 November 2007, http://www.reuters.com/article/idUSISL163591; Riaz Khan, "Pakistani Troops Surrender," *Ground Report*, 2 November 2007, http://www.groundreport.com/World/Pakistani-troops-surrender-to-Taliban-fighters/2837390; Kathy Gannon, "Militants Gaining Ground in Pakistan," *USA Today*, 1 November 2007, http://www.usatoday.com/news/topstories/2007-11-01-3588894876_x.htm; Filkins, "Right at the Edge."

24. Carlotta Gall and Sabrina Tavernise, "Pakistani Taliban Are Said to Expand Alliances," *New York Times*, 7 May 2010.

25. Kathy Gannon, "Pakistan Losing Fight against Militants," *Arizona Daily Star*, 5 December 2008; Isambard Wilkinson and Dean Nelson, "Lahore Attack Heralds Spread of Taliban-Trained Groups to Pakistani Heartlands," *Sunday Telegraph* (London), 8 March 2009.

26. Shahan Mufti, "Suicide Attacks a Growing Threat in Pakistan," *Christian Science Monitor*, 10 October 2008; Mark Landler and Elisabeth Bumiller, "Now, U.S. Sees Pakistan as a Cause Distinct from Afghanistan," *New York Times*, 1 May 2009; Anwar Shakir, "Pakistan Seizes Second Tribal Zone in Anti-Taliban Offensive," *BusinessWeek*, 15 April 2010, http://www.businessweek.com/news/2010-04-14/pakistan-seizes-second-tribal-region-in-anti-taliban-fight.html; Tom Wright, "Militants Overtake India as Top Threat, Says Pakistan's ISI," *Wall Street Journal*, 17 August 2010.

27. "Qaeda to Pakistan: Set Up Islamic State," *Boston Globe*, 5 October 2008.

28. Raza Khan, "Taliban Patrols Peshawar," *Washington Times*, 26 March 2009.

29. Sabrina Tavernise, Richard A. Oppel Jr., and Eric Schmitt, "Insurgents Make Inroads in Key Pakistan Province," *New York Times*, 14 April 2009; Wilkinson and Nelson, "Lahore Attack Heralds Spread of Taliban-Trained Groups to Pakistani Heartlands."

30. Tavernise, Oppel Jr., and Schmitt, "Insurgents Make Inroads."

31. Ibid.

32. Ibid.; Karin Brulliard and Pamela Constable, "Pakistani Militants Spreading Roots," *Washington Post*, 10 May 2010.

33. Jane Perlez, "Official Admits Militancy Has Deep Roots in Pakistan," *New York Times*, 3 June 2010.

34. David Sanger, "Pakistan Strife Raises U.S. Doubts on Nuclear Arms," *New York Times*, 4 May 2009; Bryan Bender, "Pakistan, U.S. in Talks on Nuclear Security," *Boston Globe*, 5 May 2009; Tom Wright, "Pakistan Looks for U.S.

Deal," *Wall Street Journal*, 16 October 2010; Press Trust of India, "Pakistan Has More Nukes and Fissile Materials Than India: Report," *Daily News & Analysis*, 2 August 2010, http://www.dnaindia.com/world/report_pakistan-has-more-nukes-and-fissile-materials-than-india-report_1417821.

35. Praveen Swami, "Pakistan's Nuclear Arms Push Angers America," *Daily Telegraph* (London), 11 October 2010; Wright, "Pakistan Looks for U.S. Deal."

36. Swami, "Pakistan's Nuclear Arms Push Angers America"; Wright, "Pakistan Looks for U.S. Deal."

37. David Sanger, "Pakistan Strife Raises U.S. Doubts on Nuclear Arms," *New York Times*, 4 May 2009; Bryan Bender, "Pakistan, U.S. in Talks on Nuclear Security," *Boston Globe*, 5 May 2009; Wright, "Pakistan Looks for U.S. Deal."

38. Sanger, "Pakistan Strife Raises U.S. Doubts on Nuclear Arms"; Bryan Bender, "Pakistan, U.S. in Talks on Nuclear Security," *Boston Globe*, 5 May 2009; Wright, "Pakistan Looks for U.S. Deal."

39. Ibid.; Alex Rodriguez, "Pakistani Militant Groups Out in the Open," *Los Angeles Times*, 8 May 2010; Brulliard and Constable, "Pakistani Militants Spreading Roots."

40. Brulliard and Constable, "Pakistani Militants Spreading Roots"; Jane Perlez and Pir Zubair Shah, "In Violent Karachi, Pakistani Insurgency Finds a Haven and a Forge," *New York Times*, 22 May 2010.

41. Zahid Hussain, "Pakistani Ex-Spy Is Killed," *Wall Street Journal*, 1 May 2010; Karin Brulliard, "A Death amid Blurred Allegiances," *Washington Post*, 3 May 2010; Alex Rodriguez, "A Complex Target Confronts Pakistan," *Los Angeles Times*, 24 May 2010; Munir Ahmed and Ishtiaq Mahsud, "Intel: Pakistan Taliban Chief Now Believed Alive," *Washington Post*, 29 April 2010.

42. Sabrina Tavernise, Richard A. Oppel Jr., and Eric Schmitt, "United Militants Threaten Pakistan's Populous Heart," *New York Times*, 13 April 2009.

43. Saeed Shah, "Pakistani Tribesmen Organize to Fight Taliban Insurgents," *Miami Herald*, 27 September 2008; Trudy Rubin, "Pakistan Turns Taliban Tide," *Philadelphia Inquirer*, 15 April 2010; Sabrina Tavernise and Pir Zubair Shah, "Killings Rattle Pakistan's Swat Valley," *New York Times*, 22 April 2010.

44. Richard Oppel Jr., "Radio Spreads Taliban's Terror in Pakistani Region," *New York Times*, 25 January 2009.

45. Saeed Shah, "Pakistani Tribesmen Organize to Fight Taliban Insurgents," *Miami Herald*, 27 September 2008; Trudy Rubin, "Pakistan Turns Taliban Tide," *Philadelphia Inquirer*, 15 April 2010; Sabrina Tavernise and Pir Zubair Shah, "Killings Rattle Pakistan's Swat Valley," *New York Times*, 22 April 2010.

46. Jane Perlez and Pir Zubair Shah, "Confronting the Taliban, Pakistan Finds Itself at War," *New York Times*, 3 October 2008; Anwar Shakir, "Pakistan Seizes Second Tribal Zone in Anti-Taliban Offensive," *BusinessWeek*, 15 April 2010, http://www.businessweek.com/news/2010-04-14/pakistan-seizes-second-tribal-region-in-anti-taliban-fight.html; Ron Moreau and Sami Yousafzai, "A Surge of Their Own," *Newsweek*, 3 May 2010; Adam Entous, "Pentagon: Pakistan to Decide North Waziristan Timing," Reuters, 20 May 2010. http://www.reuters.com/article/idUSTRE64J6F520100520.

47. Amanda Hodge, "Pakistan Army Sure It Has Upper Hand in Tribal Areas," *The Weekend Australian*, 17 April 2010; Carlotta Gall and Sabrina Tavernise, "Pakistani Taliban Are Said to Expand Alliances," *New York Times*, 7 May 2010; Editorial, "Training in Waziristan," *Washington Post*, 6 May 2010; Ahmed Rashid, "North Waziristan: Terrorism's New Hub?" *Washington Post*, 5 May 2010.

48. Moreau and Yousafzai, "A Surge of Their Own."

49. Tom Wright, "Militants Overtake India as Top Threat, Says Pakistan's ISI," *Wall Street Journal*, 17 August 2010; Jane Perlez, "U.S. Urges Action in Pakistan after Failed Bombing," *New York Times*, 9 May 2010.

50. Ralph Peters, "The Pak Civil War," *New York Post*, 1 May 2009; Rashid, "Terrorism's New Hub in Pakistan"; Wright, "Militants Overtake India as Top Threat."

51. Wright, "Militants Overtake India as Top Threat."

52. Ibid.; Raza Khan, "Taliban Leader Seeks to Prevent Offensive," *Washington Times*, 9 June 2010.

53. Saeed Shah, "Tribe Trying to Keep Out Al Qaeda Allies," *Miami Herald*, 25 December 2010.

54. Editorial, "Pakistan Hesitates Again," *New York Times*, 23 January 2010; Rashid, "Terrorism's New Hub in Pakistan."

55. Jane Perlez and Helene Cooper, "Signaling Tensions, Pakistan Shuts NATO Route," *New York Times*, 1 October 2010; Reuters, "NATO Tankers Torched in New Attack," *New York Times*, 9 October 2010; Chris Brummitt and Kimberly Dozier, "Pakistan Threatens to Stop Protecting NATO Supply Lines," *Washington Post*, 29 September 2010.

56. Pakistan Floods 2010: Latest Facts, News, Photos & Maps, http://mceer.buffalo.edu/infoservice/disasters/Pakistan-Floods-2010.asp.

57. Rubin, "Pakistan Turns Taliban Tide."

58. Hodge, "Pakistan Army Sure It Has Upper Hand in Tribal Areas"; David Ignatius, "Pakistan's Untamed Frontier," *Washington Post*, 3 October 2010; Gannon, "Pakistan Losing Fight against Militants."

59. Wright, "Militants Overtake India as Top Threat."

60. Ibid.

61. Reuters, "Pakistan: UN Report Finds High Level of Displacement," *New York Times*, 18 May 2010.

62. "Wary of South Waziristan," *St. Louis Post-Dispatch*, 30 April 2010.

63. Hodge, "Pakistan Army Sure It Has Upper Hand in Tribal Areas."

64. Jane Perlez and Pir Zubair Shah, "Pakistan Uses Tribal Militias in Taliban War," *New York Times*, 24 October 2008.

65. Ibid.

66. Ibid.

67. Ibid.

68. Ibid.

69. Ayesha Nasir, "Pakistani Vigilantes Take on Taliban," *Christian Science Monitor*, 4 March 2009; Filkins, "Right at the Edge."

70. Filkins, "Right at the Edge."

71. Ibid.

72. Michael Rubin, "Sixty Miles from the Capital," *Weekly Standard*, 11 May 2009.

73. Ibid.

74. Zahid Hussain and Matthew Rosenberg, "Pakistani Peace Deal Gives New Clout to Taliban Rebels," *Wall Street Journal*, 14 April 2009; Rubin, "Sixty Miles from the Capital."

75. Karin Brulliard, "Pakistan Launches Full-Scale Offensive: 30,000 Troops Deploy in Militant Stronghold," *Washington Post*, 18 October 2009.

76. Sabrina Tavernise, "Pakistan: President Gives Up Expanded Powers," *New York Times*, 20 April 2010; Sabrina Tavernise and Salman Masood, "Pakistan Weighs Changes to Revise Constitution," *New York Times*, 7 April 2010.

77. Sadanand Dhume, "Why Pakistan Produces Jihadists," *Wall Street Journal*, 5 May 2010; Tavernise and Masood, "Pakistan Weighs Changes to Revise Constitution."

78. Mosharraf Zaidi, "Pakistan Is Fighting Terror," *Wall Street Journal*, 7 May 2010; Selig Harrison, "Face Down Pakistani Army," *USA Today*, 1 April 2009.

79. Isambard Wilkinson, "U.S. Imperils Pakistan's Battle against Bankruptcy by Withholding $1 Billion," *Daily Telegraph* (London), 15 November 2008.

80. Ibid.; Matthew Rosenberg and Zahid Hussain, "Pakistan's Leader Stirs Fresh Turmoil," *Wall Street Journal*, 26 February 2009; Ai Yang, "Early U.S. Pullout from Afghanistan Could Be a Problem for Pakistan," *China Daily*, April 8, 2010.

81. Anwar Shakir, "Pakistan Seizes Second Tribal Zone in Anti-Taliban Offensive," http://www.bloomberg.com/, 15 April 2010; Zaidi, "Pakistan Is Fighting Terror."

82. Paul Wiseman, "Pakistan's Slump Creates Opening for Terrorists," *USA Today*, 24 February 2009.

83. Ibid.; Jane Perlez, "Generals in Pakistan Push for Shake-Up of Government," *New York Times*, 29 September 2010.
84. Karin Brulliard and Karen DeYoung, "U.S., Pakistan Chiefs of Intelligence Meet," *Washington Post*, 30 November 2010.
85. Perlez, "Generals in Pakistan Push for Shake-Up of Government."
86. Ibid.
87. Perlez, "Official Admits Militancy Has Deep Roots in Pakistan."
88. Ibid.
89. Griff Witte and Karen DeYoung, "Pakistan Detains Many Indefinitely," *Washington Post*, 22 April 2010.
90. Eric Schmitt, "Disappearances with Reported Ties to Pakistan Worry U.S.," *New York Times*, 30 December 2010.
91. Griff Witte and Karen DeYoung, "Pakistan Detains Many Indefinitely," *Washington Post*, 22 April 2010; Schmitt, "Disappearances with Reported Ties to Pakistan Worry U.S."
92. Declan Walsh, "Taliban Rules over 4M Pakistanis," *Guardian* (London), 11 June 2010.
93. Jane Perlez and Pir Zubair Shah, "Taliban Exploit Class Rifts to Gain Ground in Pakistan," *New York Times*, 17 April 2009.
94. Ibid.; Jane Perlez and Pir Zubair Shah, "Pakistan Regains Control of Remote Area, for Now," *New York Times*, 9 March 2009.
95. Jonathan S. Landay, "Crumbling Pakistan Signals Danger," *Arizona Republic*, 17 April 2009.
96. Pamela Constable, "Insurgent Threat Shifts in Pakistan," *Washington Post*, 31 March 2009.
97. Brulliard and DeYoung, "U.S., Pakistan Chiefs of Intelligence Meet"; Perlez, "Generals in Pakistan Push for Shake-Up of Government"; Declan Walsh, "Army Chief Gives List of 'Corrupt Ministers,'" *Guardian* (London), 2 October 2010.
98. Brulliard and DeYoung, "U.S., Pakistan Chiefs of Intelligence Meet"; Perlez, "Generals in Pakistan Push for Shake-Up of Government"; Walsh, "Army Chief Gives List of 'Corrupt Ministers.'"
99. Karin Brulliard and Karen DeYoung, "U.S. Courts Pakistan's Top General, with Little Result," *Washington Post*, 1 January 2011.
100. Brulliard and DeYoung, "U.S., Pakistan Chiefs of Intelligence Meet."
101. Landler and Bumiller, "Now, U.S. Sees Pakistan as a Cause Distinct from Afghanistan"; Doyle McManus, "Fear and Loathing in Pakistan," *Los Angeles Times*, 8 March 2009.
102. Ralph Peters, "Just Walk Away," *New York Post*, 4 May 2009.
103. Ibid.
104. Reuters, "Pakistan: Donors Commit $5 Billion More in Aid," *New York*

*Times*, 18 April 2009; Ken Dilanian, "U.S. to Boost Development Aid to Pakistan," *USA Today*, 27 March 2009.

105. Bryan Bender, "Pakistan, U.S. in Talks on Nuclear Security," *Boston Globe*, 5 May 2009.

106. Ibid.

107. Ibid.

108. Jane Perlez, "U.S. Urges Action in Pakistan after Failed Bombing," *New York Times*, 9 May 2010.

109. Karen DeYoung, "U.S., Pakistan Tread Delicately toward More Cooperation," *Washington Post*, 29 April 2010; Adam Entous, "U.S. Says Wants More from Pakistan, Could Boost Aid," Reuters, 7 May 2010, http://www.reuters.com/article/idUSN07225897; Landler and Bumiller, "Now, U.S. Sees Pakistan as a Cause Distinct from Afghanistan."

110. Jeremy Page, "British Forces Train Pakistan's Frontier Corps to Fight Al-Qaeda," *Times* (London), 21 March 2009; Eric Schmitt and Jane Perlez, "Secret U.S. Unit Trains Commandos in Pakistan," *New York Times*, 23 February 2009; Adam Entous and Julian E. Barnes, "U.S. Plans Increased Military Aid for Pakistan," *Wall Street Journal*, 20 October 2010.

111. Peters, "The Pak Civil War"; Eric Schmitt, "Officer Leads Old Corps in New Role in Pakistan," *New York Times*, 7 March 2009.

112. Page, "British Forces Train Pakistan's Frontier Corps to Fight Al Qaeda."

113. Greg Miller, "Options Studied for a Possible Pakistan Strike," *Washington Post*, 29 May 2010.

114. Ibid.

115. David S. Cloud, "CIA Drones Have Broader List of Targets," *Los Angeles Times*, 6 May 2010.

116. Adam Entous, "Special Report: How the White House Learned to Love the Drone," Reuters, 18 May 2010, http://www.reuters.com/article/idUSTRE64H5SL20100518; Cloud, "CIA Drones Have Broader List of Targets"; Miller, "Options Studied for a Possible Pakistan Strike."

117. Doyle McManus, "U.S. Drone Attacks in Pakistan 'Backfiring,' Congress Told," *Los Angeles Times*, 3 May 2009; Alex Rodriguez and David Zucchino, "U.S. Drone Attacks in Pakistan Get Mixed Response," *Los Angeles Times*, 2 May 2010; Entous, "Special Report: How the White House Learned to Love the Drone."

118. Ken Dilanian, "Pakistan Steps Up Anti-Taliban Efforts," *USA Today*, 5 March 2010.

119. McManus, "U.S. Drone Attacks in Pakistan 'Backfiring'"; Editorial, "Drones Take Toll on Al Qaeda Leaders," *USA Today*, 3 June 2010; Cloud, "CIA Drones Have Broader List of Targets"; Entous, "Special Report: How the White House Learned to Love the Drone."

120. Entous, "Special Report: How the White House Learned to Love the Drone."

121. Ibid.

122. Craig Whitlock and Greg Miller, "Al Qaeda Likely to Replace Leader," *Washington Post*, 2 June 2010; Editorial, "Another Terror War Success," *Wall Street Journal*, 2 June 2010; Greg Miller and Craig Whitlock, "Al Qaeda's Third Ranking Leader Is Reported Dead," *Washington Post*, 1 June 2010; Khan, "Taliban Leader Seeks to Prevent Offensive."

123. Bill Roggio, "Evidence Presented of U.S. Involvement in 2009 Airstrike in Yemen," *Long War Journal*, 7 June 2010, http://www.longwarjournal. org/archives/2010/06/evidence_presented_o.php; Bill Roggio, "Pakistani Taliban Claim Credit for Failed NYC Times Square Car Bombing," *Long War Journal*, 2 May 2010, http://www.longwarjournal.org/archives/2010/05/ pakistani_taliban_cl.php.

124. Mark Mazzetti and Scott Shane, "Evidence Mounts for Taliban Role in Car Bomb Plot," *New York Times*, 6 May 2010.

125. David S. Cloud, "U.S. Analyst Faults U.S. Drone Use," *Los Angeles Times*, 3 June 2010; Charlie Savage, "UN Official Set to Ask U.S. to End CIA Drone Strikes," *New York Times*, 28 May 2010.

126. Alexander Mayer, "U.S. Acknowledgement of Predator Program Unlikely to Alter Pakistani Perceptions," Threat Matrix, *Long War Journal*, 4 June 2010, http://www.longwarjournal.org/threat-matrix/archives/2010/06/al_ jazeeras_gregg_carlstrom_ha.php

127. Rodriguez and Zucchino, "U.S. Drone Attacks in Pakistan Get Mixed Response."

128. Spencer Ackerman, "New Poll: Pakistanis Hate the Drones, Back Suicide Attacks on U.S. Troops," Danger Room, *Wired*, 30 September 2010, http://www.wired.com/dangerroom/2010/09/new-poll-pakistanis-hate-the- drones-back-suicide-attacks-on-u-s-troops/.

129. Mayer, "U.S. Acknowledgement of Predator Program Unlikely to Alter Pakistani Perceptions."

130. Adam Entous, Julian E. Barnes, and Tom Wright, "U.S. Warns Pakistan: Fight Taliban or Lose Funding," *Wall Street Journal*, 2 October 2010; Entous and Barnes, "U.S. Plans Increased Military Aid for Pakistan"; Jane Perlez and Helene Cooper, "Signaling Tensions, Pakistan Shuts NATO Route," *New York Times*, 1 October 2010.

131. Bob Herbert, "The Afghan Quagmire," *New York Times*, 6 January 2009; Mark Mazzetti and Eric Schmitt, "Shaky Pakistan Is Seen as a Target of Plots by Al Qaeda," *New York Times*, 11 May 2009.

132. Sebastian Abbot, "U.S. Lacks Good Options for Responding to Successful Terrorist Attack Linked to Pakistan," *Los Angeles Times*, 2 June

2010, http://discussions.latimes.com/20/sns-ap-as-pakistan-us-few-options/ 10?sort=desc.

133. Asif Shahzad, "Pakistan, China Reach Deals," *Philadelphia Inquirer*, 19 December 2010.

134. Glenn Kessler, "Questionable China-Pakistan Deal Draws Little Comment from U.S.," *Washington Post*, 20 May 2010; Ashish Kumar Sen, "Chinese Deal with Pakistan Hems Obama," *Washington Times*, 13 May 2010.

135. Glenn Kessler, "Questionable China-Pakistan Deal Draws Little Comment from U.S.," *Washington Post*, 20 May 2010; Ashish Kumar Sen, "Chinese Deal with Pakistan Hems Obama," *Washington Times*, 13 May 2010; Tony Blankley, "Without Preparation or Response," *Washington Times*, 5 May 2009, http://www.washingtontimes.com/news/2009/may/05/without-preparation-or-response/.

136. Walsh, "Taliban Rules over 4M Pakistanis."

## CHAPTER 8. A QUESTION OF WILLPOWER:
## THE OBAMA ADMINISTRATION AND AFGHANISTAN

1. Richard Norton-Taylor, "NATO Divided over Troops and Money to Tackle Deepening Crisis," *Guardian* (London), 19 February 2009.

2. Jackson Diehl, "An 'Afpak' About-Face for Obama," *Washington Post*, 10 May 2009.

3. Karen DeYoung, "War Review Cites Strides, Is Less Confident on Afghan Governance," *Washington Post*, 15 December 2010.

4. Graham Allison and John Deutch, "The Real Afghan Issue Is Pakistan," *Wall Street Journal*, 30 March 2009.

5. Ibid.

6. Ahmed Rashid, "In Afghanistan, Let's Keep It Simple," *Washington Post*, 6 September 2009.

7. Ibid.

8. M. Ashraf Haidari, "Progress amid Violence," *Washington Times*, 13 September 2010; Joseph L. Galloway, "General: More Troops Aren't the Answer," *Miami Herald*, 10 August 2008.

9. Galloway, "General: More Troops Aren't the Answer"; Ann Marlowe, "Fighting a Smarter War in Afghanistan," *Wall Street Journal*, 21 December 2009.

10. Matthew Rosenberg, "Corruption Suspected in Airlift of Billions of Cash from Kabul," *Wall Street Journal*, 25 June 2010, http://online.wsj.com/article/SB10001424052748704638504575318850772872776.html#articleTabs=article.

11. Colum Lynch, "Afghan Opium Trade Hits New Peak: UN Report Describes a Scale of Narcotics Production Not Seen in Two Centuries," *Washington Post*, 28 August 2007.

12. Ibid.

13. Walter Pincus, "Pentagon Hopes to Expand Aid Program: Legislation Would Help Fund Foreign Governments' Military, Security Forces," *Washington Post*, 13 May 2007; Molly Moore, "Rice Presses Allies to Boost Afghan Aid: NATO, Europe Urged to Join U.S. in Increasing Commitments of Money and Manpower," *Washington Post*, 27 January 2007; The World Bank, "Economic Growth Is Creating 'Political Space' for Deeper Reforms in South Asia: World Bank Report," 15 September 2006, http://www.world bank.org.af/wbsite/external/countries/southasiaext/afghanistan; New Strategic Security Initiative, "Afghanistan Policy Page," Development Issues, 26 January 2010, http://newstrategicsecurityinitiative.org/wp-content/uploads/2010/01/Policy-Page-06-Development-Issues-download-PDF4.pdf; Donald Rumsfeld, "Afghanistan: Five Years Later," *Washington Post*, 7 October 2006.

14. Jon Boone, "Afghan Donations Fall Billions Short," *Financial Times*, 19 February 2009.

15. Ernesto Londono, "Afghan Government Awards Oil Contract in First Phase of Revenue-Generation Plan," *Washington Post*, 13 December 2010, http://www.washingtonpost.com/wp-dyn/content/article/2010/12/13/AR2010121302851.html?sid=ST2010121305143; Johnathan S. Landay, "China's Thirst for Copper Could Hold Key to Afghanistan's Future," McClatchy Newspapers, 8 March 2009, http://www.mcclatchydc.com/2009/03/08/63452/chinas-thirst-for-copper-could.html; American Public lic Media, "Afghanistan Copper, Lithium Worth $1 Trillion," *Marketplace*, 14 June 2010, http://marketplace.publicradio.org/display/web/2010/06/14/am-afghanistan-copper-lithium-worth-1-trillion/.

16. Susan B. Glasser, "Projects to Rebuild Afghan Roads Going Nowhere, Despite Promises," *Washington Post*, 7 August 2002; Griff Witte, "Afghans See Marked Decline since 2005," *Washington Post*, 24 February 2007; Ann Scott Tyson, "General Warns of Perils in Afghanistan," *Washington Post*, 14 February 2007.

17. "5 Killed in Afghan Governor's Compound," *Washington Times*, 26 April 2009.

18. Mark Mazzetti and Eric Schmitt, "U.S. Study Is Said to Warn of Crisis in Afghanistan," *New York Times*, 9 October 2008; Sayed Salahuddin, "Corruption's Tentacles Reaching across Afghanistan," Reuters, 10 July 2010, http://blogs.reuters.com/afghanistan/2010/07/10/corruptions-tentacles-reaching-across-afghanistan/; William Easterly, "How Not to Win Hearts and Minds," *Wall Street Journal*, 16 August 2010.

19. Mazzetti and Schmitt, "U.S. Study Is Said to Warn of Crisis in Afghanistan"; Salahuddin, "Corruption's Tentacles Reaching across Afghanistan";

Easterly, "How Not to Win Hearts and Minds"; Craig Whitlock, "Pentagon Sees Afghan Instability Leveling Off," *Washington Post*, 29 April 2010; Reuters, "UN Report Finds Corruption Rife in Afghanistan," 19 January 2010, http://www.reuters.com/article/idU.S.LDE60I00F._CH_.2400; Salahuddin, "Corruption's Tentacles Reaching across Afghanistan"; Alissa J. Rubin and Adam B. Ellick, "More Trouble Ahead for Kabul Bank," *New York Times*, 15 September 2010; Michael O'Hanlon, "New Reasons for Hope in Afghanistan," Politico.com, 28 September 2010, http://www.politico.com/news/stories/0910/42781.html.

20. Deb Reichmann, "UN Chief: Security in Afghanistan Has Not Improved," *AOL News*, 19 June 2010, http://www.aolnews.com/story/un-chief-security-in-afghanistan-has-not/801358; Julian E. Barnes, "Afghan Taliban Seen as Making Gains," *Los Angeles Times*, 29 April 2010; Sig Christenson, "Official: Taliban Confident of Afghan Victory," *San Antonio Express News*, 28 December 2009; Miles Amoore, "Taliban Win 1,600 Bounty for Each NATO Soldier Killed," *Sunday Times* (London), 23 May 2010; Alissa J. Rubin, "Expanding Control, Taliban Refresh Stamp on Afghan Justice," *New York Times*, 8 October 2010; Jerome Starkey, "Under Taleban Rule: How Insurgents Run Shadow Government In Helmand," *Times* (London), 4 October 2010.

21. "In Afghanistan, the Civil 'Surge' That Isn't," *Morning Edition*, National Public Radio (NPR), 7 September 2010; Joshua Partlow, "Taliban Targeting U.S. Contractors," *Washington Post*, 17 April 2010; Noor Khan and Tim Sullivan, "Attacks Against Contractors Surging in Afghanistan," *Independent* (London), 24 April 2010.

22. "In Afghanistan, the Civil 'Surge' That Isn't," *Morning Edition*; Partlow, "Taliban Targeting U.S. Contractors"; Khan and Sullivan, "Attacks Against Contractors Surging in Afghanistan."

23. Rashid, "In Afghanistan, Let's Keep It Simple."

24. Stephen Grey, "Taliban's Supreme Leader Signals Willingness to Talk Peace," *Sunday Times* (London), 18 April 2010.

25. Barnes, "Afghan Taliban Seen as Making Gains"; Reichmann, "UN Chief: Security in Afghanistan Has Not Improved"; Christenson, "Official: Taliban Confident of Afghan Victory"; Amoore, "Taliban Win 1,600 Bounty for Each NATO Soldier Killed."

26. Reichmann, "UN Chief: Security in Afghanistan Has Not Improved"; Barnes, "Afghan Taliban Seen as Making Gains"; Christenson, "Official: Taliban Confident of Afghan Victory"; Amoore, "Taliban Win 1,600 Bounty for Each NATO Soldier Killed"; Rubin, "Expanding Control, Taliban Refresh Stamp On Afghan Justice"; Starkey, "Under Taleban Rule: How Insurgents Run Shadow Government In Helmand."

27. Maria Abi-Habib, "Afghans See Karzai, Iran Hands in Poll," *Wall Street Journal*, 5 November 2010.
28. Ibid.
29. Heidi Vogt, "Afghanistan to Void a Quarter of Ballots," *Boston Globe*, 20 October 2010; Editorial, "The Next Afghan Election," *New York Times*, 6 September 2010.
30. Abi-Habib, "Afghans See Karzai, Iran Hands in Poll."
31. Peter Baker and Karen DeYoung, "Bush Promises Strong Effort to Counter Resurgent Taliban: U.S. to Extend Troop Increase in Afghanistan, Take Fight to Enemy Forces before Their Spring Offensive," *Washington Post*, 16 February 2007; John Ward Anderson, "Afghan General Cautious on Peace Talks," *Washington Post*, 21 September 2007; Craig Whitlock, "Pentagon Sees Afghan Instability Leveling Off," *Washington Post*, 29 April 2010; Anne Gearan, "Pentagon 'Cautiously Optimistic' on Afghan War," Associated Press, http://dailynews.yahoo.com/, 5 May 2010; Barnes, "Afghan Taliban Seen as Making Gains"; Michael Cohen, "The Grim Reality in Afghanistan," *New York Daily News*, 3 May 2010; Peter Spiegel, "Pentagon Reports Taliban Gains and Strains," *Wall Street Journal*, 29 April 2010; Rahim Faiez, "Taliban Overrun District in Eastern Afghanistan," *Atlanta-Journal Constitution*, 1 November 2010; Statoids, "Districts of Afghanistan," 2009, http://www.statoids.com/yaf.html.
32. Bill Theobald, "101st Commander Says Insurgent Push Halted in Eastern Afghanistan," *Nashville Tennessean*, 14 October 2010; Moreau and Yousafzai, "A Surge of Their Own."
33. Associated Press, "Taliban Chief: Insurgents' Strategy Is War of Attrition," *USA Today*, 16 November 2010.
34. Yaroslav Trofimov, "Taliban Influence Grows in North," *Wall Street Journal*, 19 October 2010.
35. Geoff Ziezulewicz, "Recent Attacks Roil Largely Peaceful Western Afghanistan," *Stars and Stripes*, 1 November 2010.
36. Tom Shanker, "Insurgents Set Aside Rivalries on Afghan Border," *New York Times*, 29 December 2010.
37. O'Hanlon, "New Reasons for Hope in Afghanistan"; Moreau and Yousafzai, "A Surge of Their Own."
38. Mark Landler, "U.S. Tries to End Flow of Bomb Item to Afghanistan," *New York Times*, 15 November 2010; Christenson, "Official: Taliban Confident of Afghan Victory"; Peter Spiegel, "Pentagon Reports Taliban Gains and Strains," *Wall Street Journal*, 29 April 2010; Phil Stewart, "Threat Rising from Homemade Afghan Bombs: U.S. Army Chief," Reuters, 6 May 2010; Tom Coghlan, "Mysterious 'White Taleban' Strike Fear in Village Hearts," *Times* (London), 14 May 2010; Alex Rodriguez, "Pakistani Smugglers Sup-

plying Afghan Bombmakers," *Los Angeles Times*, 1 May 2010; Gretel C. Kovach, "International Force Seizes Explosive, Weapons in Afghanistan," *San Diego Union-Tribune*, 2 November 2010.

39. Julius Cavendish, "Taliban Fighters Hone a Tactic," *Christian Science Monitor*, 14 June 2010; Reichmann, "UN Chief: Security in Afghanistan Has Not Improved"; Landler, "U.S. Tries to End Flow of Bomb Item to Afghanistan."

40. Reichmann, "UN Chief: Security in Afghanistan Has Not Improved."

41. George F. Will, "Waiting Games in Afghanistan," *Washington Post*, 17 June 2010; Ben Farmer and Alex Spillus, "U.S. Toll in Afghanistan War Reaches 1,000," *Daily Telegraph* (London), 23 February 2010, http://www.telegraph.co.uk/news/worldnews/asia/afghanistan/7300536/U.S.-toll-in-Afghanistan-war-reaches-1000.html; Chris Lawrence, "More Than 1,000 U.S. Troops Killed In Afghanistan," CNN, 8 June 2010, http://www.cnn.com/2010/U.S./06/08/afghanistan.deaths/index.html; Heidi Vogt, "Afghanistan to Void a Quarter of Ballots," *Boston Globe*, 20 October 2010; Reuters, "Afghan Foreign Troops Death Toll Hits 500 for 2010," 5 September 2010, http://www.reuters.com/article/idUSTRE6850LL20100906; Karim Talbi, "600 Foreign Troops Killed in Afghanistan in 2010," http://www.yahoo.com/, 25 October 2010.

42. Deborah Haynes, "Special Forces Are Taking Out up to Six Taleban Targets a Day, Says U.S. Chief," *Washington Times*, 23 September 2010; Kimberly Dozier, "Petraeus Highlights Special Ops Successes in Afghanistan," *Fayetteville Observer*, 4 September 2010; Spencer Ackerman, "Drones Surge, Special Ops Strike in Petraeus Campaign Plan," Danger Room, *Wired*, 18 August 2010, http://www.wired.com/dangerroom/2010/08/petraeus-campaign-plan/; Thom Shanker, Elisabeth Bumiller, and Rod Nordland, "Despite Gains, Night Raids Split U.S. and Karzai," *New York Times*, 16 November 2010.

43. David Ignatius, "Diplomacy with a Punch," *Washington Post*, 19 October 2010; Greg Jaffe, "U.S. and Afghan Forces Launch Major Assault in Eastern Province of Konar," *Washington Post*, 29 June 2010; Rajiv Chandrasekaran, "U.S. Sending Tanks to Hit Harder at Taliban," *Washington Post*, 19 November 2010.

44. Greg Miller, "Taliban Unscathed by U.S. Strikes," *Washington Post*, 27 October, 2010.

45. Ernesto Londono, "Afghan Civilian Casualties Up Sharply, UN Reports," *Washington Post*, 25 December 2010.

46. David S. Cloud, "Afghan Civilian Deaths Rise," *Los Angeles Times*, 2 November 2010.

47. Londono, "Afghan Civilian Casualties Up Sharply, UN Reports."

48. John Ward Anderson, "Emboldened Taliban Reflected in More Attacks, Greater Reach," *Washington Post*, 25 September 2007; Editorial, "Insurgent Attacks Kill More Afghan Civilians," *Washington Post*, 17 April 2007; Galloway, "General: More Troops Aren't the Answer"; and David Wood, "Taliban Cause Most Civilian Deaths, but U.S. Gets the Blame," *Politics Daily*, 15 January 2010, http://www.politicsdaily.com/2010/01/15/taliban-cause-most-civilian-deaths-but-u-s-gets-the-blame/. See also "Afghan Deaths Threaten Support for U.S. Offensive," *Morning Edition*, NPR, 23 April 2010, http://www.npr.org/templates/story/story.php?storyId=126195738; Cloud, "Afghan Civilian Deaths Rise."

49. Wood, "Taliban Cause Most Civilian Deaths."

50. Londono, "Afghan Civilian Casualties Up Sharply, UN Reports."

51. Reuters, "Afghan Violence in 2010 Kills Thousands: Government," 3 January 2011, http://www.reuters.com/article/idUSTRE7020YU20110103.

52. Cloud, "Afghan Civilian Deaths Rise"; Noah Shachtman, "Bombs Away: Afghan Air War Peaks with 1,000 Strikes in October," Danger Room, *Wired*, 10 November 2010.

53. Cloud, "Afghan Civilian Deaths Rise."

54. Robert Haddick, "The Biden Plan Returns," This Week at War, *Small Wars Journal*, 22 October 2010, http://smallwarsjournal.com/blog/2010/10/print/this-week-at-war-the-biden-pla/; David Martin, "U.S. Trying to 'Kill Its Way Out' of Afghan War," *World Watch*, CBS News, 18 October 2010, http://www.cbsnews.com/8301-503543_162-20019917-503543.html.

55. Cloud, "Afghan Civilian Deaths Rise"; Shachtman, "Bombs Away."

56. Jackson Diehl, "For Obama, Three Afghanistan Tests," *Washington Post*, 29 March 2009; Spiegel, "Pentagon Reports Taliban Gains and Strains"; Wood, "Taliban Cause Most Civilian Deaths"; Whitlock, "Pentagon Sees Afghan Instability Leveling Off"; Don Nissenbaum, "Battling 'Insurgent Math' in Afghanistan," Checkpoint Kabul, McClatchy Newspapers, http://blogs.mcclatchydc.com/kabul/2010/04/battling-insurgent-math-in-afghanistan.html, David Ignatius, "How to Win Over the Afghans," *Washington Post*, 21 November 2010.

57. Diehl, "For Obama, Three Afghanistan Tests"; Spiegel, "Pentagon Reports Taliban Gains and Strains"; Wood, "Taliban Cause Most Civilian Deaths"; Whitlock, "Pentagon Sees Afghan Instability Leveling Off"; Nissenbaum, "Battling 'Insurgent Math' in Afghanistan"; Ignatius, "How to Win Over the Afghans."

58. Ignatius, "How to Win Over the Afghans."

59. Diehl, "For Obama, Three Afghanistan Tests"; Spiegel, "Pentagon Reports Taliban Gains and Strains"; Wood, "Taliban Cause Most Civilian Deaths";

Whitlock, "Pentagon Sees Afghan Instability Leveling Off"; Ignatius, "How to Win Over the Afghans."

60. Slobodan Lekic, "Taliban Numbers Unaffected by Allied Troop Surge," *Boston Globe*, 7 January 2011.

61. James T. Quinlivan, "Force Requirements in Stability Operations," *Parameters* 25 (Winter 1995–1996), http://carlisle-www.army.mil/usawc/parameters/1995/quinliv.htm. This article examined the number of troops that peacekeeping forces have historically needed to maintain order and cope with insurgencies. Mr. Quinlivan's comparisons suggested that even small countries might need large occupying forces. Specifically, Mr. Quinlivan did a historical survey of insurgencies and devised troop-to-population ratios. In his estimation, more peaceful situations necessitated from four to ten troops per one thousand inhabitants. More restive situations, such as the British campaign against communist guerillas in Malaya and the fight against the Irish Republican Army in Northern Ireland, however, necessitated twenty troops per one thousand inhabitants. "The implication was clear: 'Many countries are simply too big to be plausible candidates for stabilization by external forces.'"

62. David Wood, "Allegation: Some Contractors in Afghanistan Paying Protection Money to Taliban," *Politics Daily*, 21 December 2009, http://www.politicsdaily.com/2009/12/21/allegation-contractors-in-afghanistan-paying-protection-money-t/; Hamid Shalizi, "Afghan Firms 'Pay Off Taliban with Foreign Cash,'" Reuters, 13 October 2010, http://www.reuters.com/article/idUSTRE69C1GZ20101013; Paul Richter, "Audit: U.S. Funds Went to Taliban," *Los Angeles Times*, 1 October 2010; Rajiv Chandrasekaran, "Security Ruling Prompts Firms to Shutter Major Afghan Projects," *Washington Post*, 22 October 2010; Joshua Partlow, "U.S. Asks Karzai for Assurance on Aid Workers," *Washington Post*, 14 October 2010.

63. Heidi Vogt and Rahim Faiez, "Karzai: Security Firms Have 4 Months To Disband," *Washington Times*, 16 August 2010; Katherine Houreld, "Afghan Security Companies Agree to Disband in Stages," *Philadelphia Inquirer*, 11 November 2010; Robert Haddick, "War Is Hell. COIN Is Worse," This Week At War, *Small Wars Journal*, 20 August 2010, http://smallwarsjournal.com/blog/2010/08/this-week-at-war-war-is-hell-c/; Houreld, "Afghan Security Companies Agree to Disband in Stages."

64. Rajiv Chandrasekaran, "Security Ruling Prompts Firms to Shutter Major Afghan Projects," *Washington Post*, 22 October 2010.

65. Haddick, "War Is Hell. COIN Is Worse"; Ahmed Rashid, "Why a Forlorn Karzai Is Breaking with the West," *Financial Times*, 19 November 2010; Robert Haddick, "Karzai Speeds Up the End-Game," This Week At War, *Small Wars Journal*, 30 October 2010.

66. Associated Press, "Petraeus: Taliban Footprint Growing," *USA Today*, 1 September 2010; Anna Mulrine, "Heading Deeper into Afghanistan," *U.S. News & World Report*, 13 October 2008; Spiegel, "Pentagon Reports Taliban Gains and Strains"; Editorial, "Afghanistan Today," *New York Times*, 22 October 2010.

67. Nirmala Ganapathy, "Regional Powers Jostle for Role in Afghanistan," *Singapore Straits Times*, 28 August 2010.

68. Bill Gertz, "Inside the Ring: Tehran-Taliban Links," *Washington Times*, 11 November 2010.

69. Ibid.; Sara A. Carter, "Iran Seen Providing More Training, Weapons to Afghan Insurgents," *Washington Examiner*, 28 December 2010.

70. April Witt, "As U.S. Retreats, Iran Puts Its Money into Afghan Province," *Washington Post*, 17 June 2003; Larry Thompson and Michelle Brown, "The Next Afghan Crisis," *Washington Post*, 12 June 2002; "Official: 1.9 Million Afghan Refugees in Iran Now," Payvand News of Iran, 15 January 2003, http://www.payvand.com/news/03/jan/1079.html; UN Refugee Agency, "UNHCR Global Appeal 2007—Islamic Republic of Iran," 1 December 2006, http://www.unhcr.org/home/PUBL; Dexter Filkins, "Iran Is Said to Give Top Karzai Aide Cash by the Bagful," *New York Times*, 24 October 2010; Dexter Filkins and Alissa J. Rubin, "Afghan Leader Admits His Office Gets Cash from Iran," *New York Times*, 26 October 2010.

71. Maria Abi-Habib, "Afghans Say Tehran Is Blocking Fuel Flows," *Wall Street Journal*, 22 December 2010; Michael Kamber and Taimoor Shah, "Iran Stops Fuel Delivery, Afghanistan Says, and Prices Are Rising," *New York Times*, 23 December 2010; Associated Press, "Iran Blocks Fuel Trucks' Passage to Afghanistan," *Boston Globe*, 5 January 2011; Associated Press, "Afghans Protest Iran Fuel Truck Ban," *Arizona Daily Star*, 7 January 2011.

72. Pamela Constable, "Iranians, Afghans Attempt Diplomacy," *Washington Post*, 12 February 2002; Pamela Constable, "The General in His Labyrinth," *Washington Post*, 15 October 2006; Editorial, "Too Slow on Nukes," *Washington Post*, 11 June 2004; "Pakistan against IAEA Quizzing A. Q. Khan," *Washington Post*, 26 September 2007.

73. Gertz, "Inside the Ring: Tehran-Taliban Links."

74. Emily Wax, "Kabul Attack May Intensify India-Pakistan Proxy Battle," *Washington Post*, 11 October 2009.

75. Ibid.

76. Kathy Lally, "Russia Wonders Why U.S. Would Turn Away from Treaty," *Washington Post*, 19 November 2010; Times Wire Reports, "Militants Hit NATO Supplies," *Los Angeles Times*, 2 December 2008; Ann Scott Tyson, "Afghan Supply Chain a Weak Point," *Washington Post*, 6 March 2009; Clifford J. Levy, "Poker-Faced, Russia Flaunts Its Afghan Card," *New York*

*Times*, 22 February 2009; Tom Shanker and Richard A. Oppel Jr., "U.S. to Widen Supply Routes in Afghan War," *New York Times*, 31 December 2008; Associated Press, "Uzbekistan: New U.S. Supply Line," *New York Times*, 4 April 2009; Sabrina Tavernise, "Avoiding Pakistan, New Supply Route to Afghanistan Opens," *New York Times*, 4 March 2009.

77. "Report: Afghanistan War Effort Failing," *Washington Times*, 11 November 2010; Edward Cody, "Europeans Reluctant to Follow Obama on Afghan Initiative," *Washington Post*, 3 April 2009; David Brunnstorm and David Morgan, "NATO Allies Offer Limp Response to U.S. Afghan Call," Reuters, 19 February 2009, http://www.reuters.com/article/idU.S.LJ818937; Steven Erlanger, "Europe's Revolving Door in Afghanistan," At War, *New York Times* blog, 21 December 2009, http://atwar.blogs.nytimes.com/2010/05/20/a-quiet-tense-night-for-a-first-patrol/?scp=1&sq=%22Europe%27s%20revolving%20door%22&st=cse); "Italy to Withdraw Afghan Troops," *Daily Telegraph* (London), 13 October 2010; Reuters, "British Schedule for Pullout Confirmed," *Chicago Tribune*, 1 September 2010; Ian Austen, "Canada to End Combat Role in Afghanistan at End of 2010," *New York Times*, 17 November 2010; Roland Watson, "Troops Will Leave Afghanistan by 2015 Even if Violence Carries On," *Times* (London), 16 November 2010.

78. Leo Cendrowicz, "Can NATO Modernize Before It Becomes Obsolete?" *Time*, 18 November 2010.

79. Ganapathy, "Regional Powers Jostle for Role in Afghanistan."

80. Editorial, "Plan B for Afghanistan," *Washington Post*, 8 October 2009.

81. Christenson, "Official: Taliban Confident of Afghan Victory."

82. Cody, "Europeans Reluctant to Follow Obama"; Shane, "The War in Pashtunistan"; Frederick Kagan and Kimberly Kagan, "How Not to Defeat Al Qaeda," *The Weekly Standard*, 5 October 2009.

83. "Jones: Afghanistan Strategy a 'Three-Legged Stool,'" *Morning Edition*, NPR, 31 March 2009.

84. Nathaniel Fick and Vikram Singh, "Winning the Battle, Losing the Faith," *New York Times*, 5 October 2008; Christina Lamb, "War on Taliban Cannot Be Won, Says Army Chief," *Sunday Times* (London), 5 October 2008.

85. Christina Lamb, "Quiet Crawl to Peace on the Afghan Shuttle," *Sunday Times* (London), 15 March 2009.

86. Seth G. Jones, "Going the Distance," *Washington Post*, 15 February 2009.

87. Diehl, "For Obama, Three Afghanistan Tests."

88. Ann Scott Tyson, "'Sustained' Push Seen in Afghanistan," *Washington Post*, 19 February 2009.

89. Helene Cooper, "Putting Stamp on Afghan War, Obama Will Send 17,000 Troops," *New York Times*, 18 February 2009; Richard Sisk, "Make It 33,000 Troops—Gates," *New York Daily News*, 4 December 2009; "The Afghanistan Strategy," *Los Angeles Times*, 2 December 2009.

90. Karen DeYoung, "U.S., NATO to Announce 'Transition' Strategy in Afghanistan War," *Washington Post*, 14 November 2010; "'Fraction' of Forces in Afghanistan to Stay Past 2014: Gates," http://www.yahoo.com/, 20 November 2010; Peter Baker and Rod Nordland, "U.S. Plan Offers Path to Ending Afghan Combat," *New York Times*, 15 November 2010; Nancy A. Youssef, "Under New Plan, U.S. Troops Will Stay in Afghanistan Till 2014," McClatchy Newspapers, 16 November 2010; Nancy A. Youssef, "U.S. Puts Brake On Afghan Pullback," *Miami Herald*, 10 November 2010; Anna Mulrine, "Afghanistan: Is 2014 the New 2011 for Pentagon War Planners?" *Christian Science Monitor*, 16 November 2010.

91. Greg Miller, "Taliban Unscathed by U.S. Strikes," *Washington Post*, 27 October 2010.

92. Mary Beth Sheridan, "NATO Allies Pledge 7,000 More Troops for Afghanistan Mission," *Washington Post*, 5 December 2009.

93. Christopher Duquette, "Myths and Troop Surges," *Washington Times*, 21 December 2009.

94. Yochi J. Dreazen, "U.S. Strategy in Afghan War Hinges on Far-Flung Outposts," *Wall Street Journal*, 4 March 2009.

95. Robert Kaplan, "Man versus Afghanistan," *Atlantic Monthly*, April 2010, 64.

96. Ibid., 71.

97. Kevin Spak, "Taliban Money Men Outwit U.S.," *Newser*, 19 October 2009, http://www.newser.com/story/72010/taliban-money-men-outwit-us.html; Peter Kenyon, "Exploring the Taliban's Complex, Shadowy Finances," *Morning Edition*, NPR, 23 June 2010, http://www.npr.org/templates/story/story.php?storyId=124821049.

98. Rod Nordland, "NATO Drive on Kandahar Begins, with Mixed Results," *New York Times*, 9 September 2010.

99. O'Hanlon, "New Reasons for Hope in Afghanistan"; Kevin Sieff, "Afghan Troops Overrated, Audit to Show," *Financial Times*, 7 June 2010; O'Hanlon, "How to Win in Afghanistan."

100. O'Hanlon, "How to Win in Afghanistan"; Tom Coghlan, "'Immense' Challenges as Afghan Police Training Programmes Continue," *Times* (London), 15 May 2010; Adam Entous, "Hundreds More Trainers in Afghanistan May Be Needed," Reuters, 17 May 2010.

101. C. J. Chivers, "Gains in Afghan Training, but Struggles in War," *New York Times*, 13 October 2010.

102. Ignatius, "How to Win Over the Afghans."

103. Chivers, "Gains in Afghan Training, but Struggles in War"; O'Hanlon, "How to Win in Afghanistan."

104. Chivers, "Gains in Afghan Training, but Struggles in War."

105. "Clueless and Stoned: How U.S. Forces See Their Local Comrades," *Times*

(London), 5 October 2010; Shaun Waterman, "Training Afghans a Daunting Task," *Washington Times*, 7 September 2010; Yochi Dreazen, "U.S. Says Afghan Forces Growing Faster Than Expected," *National Journal*, 25 October 2010.

106. Dreazen, "U.S. Says Afghan Forces Growing Faster Than Expected."

107. Desmond Butler, "U.S. Likely to Spend Billions in Afghanistan for Years," *Washington Times*, 9 September 2010.

108. Chivers, "Gains in Afghan Training, but Struggles in War"; M. Ashraf Haidari, "Afghanistan's Need for Security Force Trainers," *New York Times*, 7 May 2010.

109. Dreazen, "U.S. Says Afghan Forces Growing Faster Than Expected"; Butler, "U.S. Likely to Spend Billions in Afghanistan for Years"; Associated Press, "Afghanistan Tab: $6B a Year after Planned Drawdown," *USA Today*, 7 September 2010.

110. Sieff, "Afghan Troops Overrated, Audit to Show"; Walter Pincus, "Gauging the Price Tag for Afghanistan's Security," *Washington Post*, 21 December 2010; Butler, "U.S. Likely to Spend Billions in Afghanistan for Years"; Associated Press, "Afghanistan Tab: $6B a Year after Planned Drawdown," *USA Today*, 7 September 2010.

111. Eltaf Najafizada and James Rupert, "Afghan Police's Lack of Guns and Gas Shows U.S. Exit Plan Flaw," Bloomberg, 31 August 2010, http://www.bloomberg.com/news/2010-08-31/afghan-police-unit-s-lack-of-guns-and-gas-shows-flaw-in-u-s-exit-strategy.html; Quinlivan, "Force Requirements in Stability Operations."

112. Michael Gordon, "Afghan Strategy Poses Stiff Challenge for Obama," *New York Times*, 2 December 2008.

113. Rahim Faiez, "Afghan Official Says U.S. Numbers Too Low," *Boston Globe*, 2 December 2009.

114. Alistair MacDonald and Maria Abi-Habib, "Afghans, U.S. to Boost Local Security," *Wall Street Journal*, 7 January 2011.

115. David S. Cloud, "Afghans to Set Up Village Police Units by March," *Los Angeles Times*, 20 October 2010; Yochi Dreazen, "Going Native," *National Journal*, 13 November, 2010.

116. Cloud, "Afghans to Set Up Village Police Units by March"; Dreazen, "Going Native."

117. Dexter Filkins, "In Recruiting an Afghan Militia, U.S. Faces a Test," *New York Times*, 15 April 2009; Michael M. Phillips, "U.S. Takes Afghan Strategy to Villages," *Wall Street Journal*, 15 April 2009; Tom Coghlan, "U.S. Pins Its Hopes on 'Dad's Army' to Turn Tide in Fight for Local Loyalties," *Times* (London), 27 April 2009; Dreazen, "Going Native."

118. Cloud, "Afghans to Set Up Village Police Units by March."

119. Filkins, "In Recruiting an Afghan Militia, U.S. Faces a Test"; Phillips, "U.S. Takes Afghan Strategy to Villages"; Coghlan, "U.S. Pins Its Hopes on 'Dad's Army'."

120. Heidi Vogt and Noor Khan, "Taliban Vow to Step Up Attacks in Afghanistan," *Boston Globe*, 30 April 2009.

121. Julian Barnes, "Efforts to Recruit Pashtuns in Afghan South Falter," *Wall Street Journal*, 13 September 2010.

122. Dreazen, "Going Native"; Sara A. Carter, "U.S. Troops Now Working with Local Militia Groups," *Washington Examiner*, 5 October 2010.

123. Georgie Anne Geyer, "Afghanistan Abstracts," *Washington Times*, 5 March 2009.

124. David Jackson and Tom Vanden Brook, "Obama Signals Afghanistan War Shift," *USA Today*, 27 March 2009.

125. Joshua Partlow, "Afghan President to Push for Peace Deals with Rebels," *Washington Post*, 3 May 2010.

126. Ibid.

127. Spencer Ackerman, "A Year in, Amnesty Deal Lures Only Three Percent of Taliban," Danger Room, *Wired*, 3 January 2011, http://www.wired.com/dangerroom/2011/01/a-year-in-amnesty-deal-lures-only-3-percent-of-taliban/

128. Grey, "Taliban's Supreme Leader Signals Willingness to Talk Peace"; Seth G. Jones, "Going the Distance," *Washington Post*, 15 February 2009.

129. Anand Gopal, "Key Afghan Insurgents Open Door to Talks," *Christian Science Monitor*, 19 March 2009.

130. Ibid.

131. Steve Coll, "War by Other Means," *New Yorker*, 24 May 2010, 24.

132. James Blitz, "Gates Says U.S. Talks with Taliban Conceivable," *Financial Times*, 10 October 2008.

133. Greg Miller, "Growth in Al Qaeda's Presence Seen," *Los Angeles Times*, 11 March 2009; Bill Roggio, "Analysis: Al Qaeda Maintains an Extensive Network in Afghanistan," *Long War Journal*, 29 July 2010, http://www.longwarjournal.org/archives/2010/07/analysis_al_qaeda_ma.php.

134. Bill Roggio, "Coalition, Afghan Forces Strike at Al Qaeda-Linked Cells in North and East," *Long War Journal*, 27 August 2010, http://www.longwarjournal.org/archives/2010/08/coaltion_afghan_forc.php; Sami Yousafzai and Ron Moreau, "Inside Al Qaeda," *Newsweek*, 4 September 2010, http://www.newsweek.com/2010/09/04/inside-al-qaeda.html; Rowan Scarborough, "Low Al Qaeda Count Stirs New Debate on War," *Washington Times*, 16 August 2010; Yochi J. Dreazen, "Al Qaida Returning to Afghanistan for New Attacks," *National Journal*, 18 October 2010, http://www.nationaljournal.com/njonline/no_20101018_2792.php; Craig Whitlock, "Al Qaeda

Presence Limited in War," *Washington Post*, 23 August 2010; Kathy Gannon, "Foreigners Boost Insurgency in Afghanistan's East," *Washington Times*, 20 August 2010; Bill Roggio, "Taliban Leader Linked to Pakistan-Based Lashkar-E-Islam Captured in Afghan East," *Long War Journal*, 18 December 2010, http://www.longwarjournal.org/archives/2010/12/taliban_leader_linke.php.

135. Roggio, "Coalition, Afghan Forces Strike"; Yousafzai and Moreau, "Inside Al Qaeda"; Scarborough, "Low Al Qaeda Count Stirs Debate on War"; Dreazen, "Al Qaida Returning to Afghanistan for New Attacks"; Gannon, "Foreigners Boost Insurgency in Afghanistan's East"; Thomas L. Day and Jonathan S. Landay, "Allies Warned Time Is Running Out," McClatchy Newspapers, 28 December 2009.

136. Roggio, "Coalition, Afghan Forces Strike"; Yousafzai and Moreau, "Inside Al Qaeda"; Scarborough, "Low Al Qaeda Count Stirs Debate on War"; Dreazen, "Al Qaida Returning to Afghanistan for New Attacks"; Gannon, "Foreigners Boost Insurgency in Afghanistan's East"; Day and Landay, "Allies Warned Time Is Running Out."

137. Ignatius, "How to Win Over the Afghans."

138. Karin Brulliard and Karen DeYoung, "New Turn in Afghan, Pakistani Relations," *Washington Post*, 19 June 2010; Ron Moreau, "Ta-Ta Taliban?" *Newsweek*, 19 June 2010; Eric Schmitt, "Taliban Fighters Appear Quieted in Afghanistan," *New York Times*, 27 December 2010.

139. Brulliard and DeYoung, "New Turn in Afghan, Pakistani Relations"; Moreau, "Ta-Ta Taliban?"

140. Brulliard and DeYoung, "New Turn in Afghan, Pakistani Relations"; Moreau, "Ta-Ta Taliban?"

141. Syed Saleem Shahzad, "Holbrooke Reaches Out to Hekmatyar," *Asia Times Online*, 10 April 2009, http://www.atimes.com/atimes/Middle_East/KD10Ak04.html; Reuters, "Hekmatyar's Men Supplying Taliban Intelligence to NATO: Officials," *Dawn* (Karachi), 9 July 2010, http://www.dawn.com/wps/wcm/connect/dawn-content-library/dawn/the-newspaper/front-page/hekmatyars-men-supplying-taliban-intelligence-to-nato-officials-970; Tim McGirk, "A Civil War among Afghanistan's Insurgents," *Time*, 8 March 2010, http://www.time.com/time/world/article/0,8599,1970474,00.html; Institute for the Study of War, "Hezb-i-Islami," Themes, http://www.understandingwar.org/themenode/hezb-e-islami-gulbuddin-hig; Bill Roggio, "Taliban, HiG Infighting Leads to Split in Afghan Insurgency in the North," *Long War Journal*, 8 March 2010, http://www.longwarjournal.org/archives/2010/03/taliban_hig_infighti.php.

142. Joshua Partlow, "Afghan Leaders Are Cutting Ties with Karzai," *Washington Post*, 23 July 2010; Laura King, "An Afghan Taliban Commander Feels NATO's Heat, but It Could Backfire," *Los Angeles Times*, 24 October 2010.

143. Partlow, "Afghan Leaders Are Cutting Ties with Karzai"; King, "An Afghan Taliban Commander Feels NATO's Heat, but It Could Backfire."

144. O'Hanlon, "New Reasons for Hope in Afghanistan"; Sean D. Naylor, "The Deadliest Insurgents," *Army Times*, September 2010; David S. Cloud and Ken Dilanian, "U.S. Intensifies Attacks on Militants in Pakistan," *Los Angeles Times*, 29 September 2010.

145. Jon Boone, "Afghan President 'Has Lost Faith' in U.S. Ability to Defeat Taliban," *Guardian* (London), 10 June 2010; Dexter Filkins, "Karzai Is Said to Doubt West Can Defeat Taliban," *New York Times*, 12 June 2010.

146. Jonathan S. Landay and Nancy A. Youssef, "Experts: U.S. Has No Long Term Political Strategy for Afghanistan," McClatchy Newspapers, 16 June 2010, http://www.mcclatchydc.com/2010/06/16/96019/experts-us-has-no-long-term-political.html; Peter Nicholas and Paul Richter, "Obama Weighs Outreach to Taliban," *Los Angeles Times*, 13 May 2010.

147. Sami Yousafzai and Ron Moreau, "Not Your Father's Taliban," *Newsweek*, 17 May 2010; Christina Lamb, "Slaughter of Commanders Drives Taliban to the Table," *Sunday Times* (London), 14 November 2010.

148. Yousafzai and Moreau, "Not Your Father's Taliban."

149. Scott Atran, "Turning the Taliban Against Al Qaeda," *New York Times*, 27 October 2010.

150. Lamb, "Slaughter of Commanders Drives Taliban to the Table."

151. Yousafzai and Moreau, "Not Your Father's Taliban"; Jon Boone, "Taliban Claims Success Against NATO Night Raids," *Guardian* (London), 1 November 2010; Brulliard and DeYoung, "New Turn in Afghan, Pakistani Relations."

152. Steve Coll, "War by Other Means," *New Yorker*, 24 May 2010, 24.

153. Helene Cooper, "Dreaming of Splitting the Taliban," *New York Times*, 8 March 2009.

154. Diehl, "For Obama, Three Afghanistan Tests"; Greg Jaffe and Karen DeYoung, "Karzai to Urge Caution as U.S. Pushes to Empower Local Leaders," *Washington Post*, 12 May 2010

155. Sue Pleming, "Building Up Afghan Capacity Seen as Key Challenge," Reuters, 22 April 2010.

156. Jaffe and DeYoung, "Karzai to Urge Caution as U.S. Pushes to Empower Local Leaders."

157. Anne Kornblut and Scott Wilson, "Obama Focuses on Civilian Effort in Afghanistan Strategy Review," *Washington Post*, 15 October 2009.

158. Matthew Green, "Confidence in Kandahar Campaign Wanes," *Financial Times*, 28 May 2010.

159. Karen DeYoung and Craig Whitlock, "Kandahar Offensive Not on Schedule," *Washington Post*, 11 June 2010; Green, "Confidence in Kandahar Cam-

paign Wanes"; Rod Nordland, "Afghanistan Strategy Shifts to Focus on Civilian Effort," *New York Times*, 9 June 2010.

160. Karen DeYoung, "Afghan Aid Spent with Little Local Input, Audit Finds," *Washington Post*, 27 October 2010.

161. Ibid.

162. Galloway, "General: More Troops Aren't the Answer"; Diehl, "For Obama, Three Afghanistan Tests."

163. Michael O'Hanlon and Hassina Sherjan, "The Tide May Be Turning in Afghanistan," *USA Today*, 16 February 2010.

164. Tom Vanden Brook, "Afghan War Hits Peak of Disfavor," *USA Today*, 17 March 2009.

165. Thomas Harding, "Public Will Demand Afghan Progress, Says Gates," *Daily Telegraph* (London), 10 June 2010; Anne Gearan, "Gates: Progress in Afghan War Must Come This Year," *Washington Post*, 9 June 2010; *Washington Post*/ABC News Poll, "Slumping Support for Afghan War," *Washington Post*, 16 December 2010.

166. Karen DeYoung, "Obama Outlines Afghan Strategy," *Washington Post*, 28 March 2009.

## CONCLUSION: THE OBAMA ADMINISTRATION AND THE WAY FORWARD

1. Peter Bergen, "Al Qaeda at 20," *Washington Post*, 17 August 2008.

2. Jack A. Goldstone, *Understanding September 11th* (Hartford: Yale Press, 2002).

3. Walt, *Taming American Power*.

4. Thucydides, *History of the Peloponnesian War*, trans. Rex Warner (431 BC; reprint, London: Penguin Books, 1972).

5. AFP, "Rogue WMDs Major Threat to U.S.: Pentagon Official," 10 June 2010, http://dir.groups.yahoo.com/group/osint/message/124507.

6. For a more in-depth discussion, please see Graham Allison, *Nuclear Terrorism: The Ultimate Preventable Catastrophe* (New York: Henry Holt, 2004); Matthew Bunn, Anthony Weir, and John Holdren, *Controlling Nuclear Warheads and Materials: A Report Card and Action Plan* (Cambridge, MA: Project on Managing the Atom, Belfer Center for Science and International Affairs, 2004); Matthew Bunn, *The Next Wave: Urgently Needed New Steps to Control Warheads and Fissile Material* (Cambridge, MA: Project on Managing the Atom, Belfer Center for Science and International Affairs, 2000); and Matthew Bunn and Anthony Wier, "The Seven Myths of Nuclear Terrorism," *Current History*, April 2005, http://www.bcsia.ksg.harvard.edu.

7. Zalmay Khalilzad, "How to Outmaneuver Iran in Iraq," *Wall Street Journal*, 10 November 2010, http://online.wsj.com/article/SB10001424052748703514 904575602341835694642.html.

8. Karen DeYoung,"War Review Cites Strides, Is Less Confident on Afghan Governance," *Washington Post*, 15 December 2010, http://www. washingtonpost.com/wp-dyn/content/article/2010/12/14/ AR2010121407714.html

9. Karin Bruilliard and Karen DeYoung, "U.S. Courts Pakistan's Top General, with Little Result," *Washington Post*, 1 January 2001.

10. Arnaud De Borchgrave, "Geopolitical Psychiatry," *Washington Times*, 23 March 2009.

11. Ibid.

12. Walter Pincus, "Gauging the Price Tag for Afghanistan's Security," *Washington Post*, 21 December 2010.

13. C. Christine Fair, "A Better Bargain for Aid to Pakistan," *Washington Post*, 30 May 2009.

14. Yochi J. Dreazen, "Pakistan: The Wavering Ally," *National Journal,* 16 October 2010.

15. Trudy Rubin, "Signs of Hope in Obama's Afghan Plan," *Philadelphia Inquirer*, 29 March 2009; Matthew B. Stannard, "Applying Iraq's Broader Lessons in Afghanistan," *San Francisco Chronicle*, 24 February 2009.

16. Trudy Rubin, "Afghanistan Is No Iraq, Except It Requires a Calculated Strategy," *Philadelphia Inquirer*, 22 February 2009.

17. Ahmed Rashid, "Time for America to Talk Turkey with the Taliban," *Financial Times*, 3 November 2010.

18. Turki Al Faisal, "A To-Do List for Afghanistan," *Washington Post*, 9 October 2009.

19. Ben Farmer, "Warlords Re-arm as Taliban Join in Peace Talks," *Sunday Telegraph* (London), 24 October 2010.

20. Fick and Singh, "Winning the Battle, Losing the Faith"; Eric T. Olson, "Rethink the Afghanistan Surge," *Christian Science Monitor*, 17 March 2009.

21. M. Ashraf Haidari, "Progress amid Violence," *Washington Times*, 13 September 2010.

22. Fick and Singh, "Winning the Battle, Losing the Faith."

23. Joshua Partlow, "Afghan Minister Accused of Taking USD30 Million Bribe," RAWA News, 18 November 2009, http://www.rawa.org/temp/ runews/2009/11/18/afghan-minister-accused-of-taking-30-million-bribe. html.

24. Henry A. Kissinger, "A Strategy for Afghanistan," *Washington Post*, 26 February 2009.

# Index

Afghanistan: airstrikes in, 185, 186; casualties and combat fatalities in, 182, 183, 184–85, 186; civil war in, 205, 249; combatant factions, 205–7; corruption in, 114, 179, 186, 200, 218, 222, 246–48; cost of war in, 59–62; cost to create state to counter Taliban, 177; counterinsurgency strategy in, 176–77, 194–220, 222, 247–48; counterterrorism strategy in, 191–94, 221–22; cross-border attacks, 35–36, 137, 195–96; elections in, 34, 181; enemy-centric efforts, 183–84; as focus of U.S. strategy, 23, 24; governance and economic issues in, 177–81, 194, 204, 217–19, 221, 222, 245–49; hard-power approach to, 243–49; Helmand province, 76, 198–99; India, relationship with, 189; indigenous forces in, 199–205, 243–44; insurgency in, 181–88, 203–4, 212–17, 239–40; insurgent groups, co-opting of, 207–17, 244–45; international aid to, 178, 180, 188–90, 219, 221; invasion of, 32, 34, 62, 114; Iran, relationship with, 188–89; Iran and U.S. position in, 124; loss of for Al Qaeda, 49; military in, 34–35, 199–205, 220, 243–44; nationalism in, 245; occupation of, 16–17, 254–55n7; opium production, 178, 179, 198–99, 219, 238, 249; Pakistan, interaction between Afghan militants and, 137–43, 175, 289n6; Pakistan, relationship with, 37, 189–90, 221; Pakistan and U.S. operations in, 172, 173; political future of, 214–15, 249; political will in, 219–20; population distribution in, 197–98; private security forces in, 186–87; public opinions in, 185–86, 219–20; Al Qaeda, safe haven in, 177, 223; Al Qaeda activities in, 23, 57, 209–10; security in, 181–88, 194, 195–217, 222, 243, 249; stable state in, 63; success in, 220, 223; surge of resources for, 222; Taliban, negotiations with, 140, 195, 208–9, 214–15, 216, 245–46; Taliban control in, 60, 195, 221, 223, 244–45; terrorist attacks in, 264n66; troop distribution in, 198–99; troop drawdown in, 197; troop levels in, 186, 243, 303n61; troop surge in, 186, 196–99, 202, 222, 243; troops in, attacks on, 92; troops in, training and transition roles of, 200, 201–2, 243–44; U.S. failure in, 113, 193–94; war in, opinions about, 89, 223, 277n27; war in, verge of collapse of, 221; withdrawal from, 190, 208, 209, 214, 220

Africa: Afghanistan war, opposition to, 89; embassy bombings in, 34, 78, 79, 116; North Africa, 6, 68, 97; Al Qaeda in, 70, 97; training camps in, 68

Ahmadinejad, Mahmoud, 114, 129–30

Al Qaeda. *See* Qaeda, Al

Arabian Peninsula, occupation of states of, 16, 18, 20, 254–55n7

Assad, Bashar al-, 3, 53

axis of evil, 3–4, 35, 114, 229

Azerbaijan, 83, 84, 85, 91, 92

Baluchistan, 135, 136, 137, 142, 149, 159, 162, 175, 196, 239

banks, 77, 78, 128, 273n49

Banna, Hassan al-, 12–13

Berader, Mullah, 139–40, 245

bin Laden, Osama: appeal to U.S. public, 18; blending of with Saddam Hussein, 41; duty of, 14; followers of, number of, 6; jihad, call for by, 14; leadership role of, 14, 66, 72, 110, 111, 255n9; leadership role of, challenge to, 97, 100, 279n16; messages from, 257n30, 257n32; opinions about in Middle East, 84, 90, 110; Pakistani policy toward, 38; Al Qaeda financing and, 274n56; surrender of, 192; U.S. as target of attacks, 33, 258n3; on U.S. economy, 58, 269n114; videos of, 28; wealth of, 72–73,

48, 59; Islamic militancy in, 71; London transit system attack, 29, 59, 69, 83; public opinions in, 83, 90; terrorist plots against, 69; UN sanctions, enforcement of, 46

Green Movement, 114, 120, 124, 129–32, 133

Guantánamo Bay prison, 43, 89–90

Hamas, 51, 114, 123, 265n71

Haqqani network, 139, 149, 150, 168, 175, 182, 183, 189, 191, 210–11, 214, 239–40, 245

hawala system, 77–78, 80

Hezb-e-Islami/Gulbuddin (HiG), 139, 149, 175, 182, 191, 211–12, 239–40, 245

Hezbollah: bombing of, 266n81; Iran and, 52, 132, 266n76; Israel, threat to from, 123; Israel-Hezbollah war, 89, 92, 124, 132; struggle against in Lebanon, 52, 53; Syrian support for, 53; terrorism attacks by, 52, 266n78; U.S. interests and, 114

human rights violations, 4, 89–90

Hussein, Saddam, 40, 41, 62

Ibn Taymiyya, Taqi al-Din Ahmad, 11–12, 13

improvised explosive device bombings (IEDs), 182–83, 184, 188, 210

India: Afghanistan, relationship with, 189; China, relationship with, 172; Muslims in, treatment of, 16; nuclear activities of, 145; Pakistan, relationship with, 37, 141, 149, 150, 172, 175, 189, 221, 238–39; terrorist attacks in, 69, 145, 147; U.S., relationship with, 238–39; U.S.-Indian nuclear deal, 37

Indonesia: aid to from U.S., 42; Bali, terrorist attack in, 79, 83, 264n66, 274n54; democracy, support for, 85, 91; Obama family ties to, 87; Palestinian conflict, importance to, 88–89, 277n24; public opinions in, 83, 84, 92, 277n27; U.S. war against Islam, 91

insurgency: in Afghanistan, 181–88, 203–4, 212–17, 239–40; amnesty for former insurgents, 103, 208; cost of attacks, 249; counterinsurgency strategy, 176–77, 194–220, 222, 247–48; global insurgency and terrorism, 30; insurgent groups, co-opting of, 207–17, 244–45; troop levels to combat, 186, 303n61

Internet and technology, 71–72, 75, 100, 279n16

Inter-Services Intelligence Directorate (ISI), 138–43, 147, 149, 189, 211–13

Iran: Afghanistan, relationship with, 188–89; Afghanistan and U.S. operations in, 206; Afghanistan war, assistance offer for, 114; arms embargo against, 128; arms purchases by, 121; axis of evil membership, 3–4, 114; China, relationship with, 125–28; clerical regime in, 114, 120, 122, 124, 129–30, 131–32, 233–34; containment approach to, 124–32, 134; conventional warfare, prohibition of, 232–33; double game approach, 188–89; elections in, 129–30; energy sector, investment in, 128–29; hard-power approach to, 232–35; Hezbollah and, 52, 132, 266n76; hostile posture toward, 4–5, 32, 63; Iraqi insurgents, aid to, 50; Iraqi security and, 109; military strikes against, 117, 122–23, 132, 133–34; nuclear program of, 35, 54, 89, 114–15, 118, 119, 120–23, 132, 134, 189, 233, 234–35, 284n16; oil in, 125–26, 127, 128–29; Pakistan, relationship with, 37, 189; Palestine, political leverage in, 63; Palestinian conflict, importance to, 277n24; public opinions in, 83, 277n27; Al Qaeda, influence over, 115–17, 235, 284n16; regime change in, 117–18, 120, 124, 129–32, 233–34; sanctions against, 115, 116, 125–32, 172–73, 234; Saudi Arabia and, 20; Sunni-Shiite relations in, 51, 52; support for U.S. following 9/11 attacks, 3; Syria and Iranian behavior and, 119; terrorism, support for by, 53–54, 113–14, 233; U.S., relationship with, 133–34, 234; Yemen, influence in, 115–16

Iranian Revolutionary Guard Corps (IRGC), 114, 118–19, 128, 129, 131

Iraq: anti-American public opinion in, 41, 49; civil war in, 109, 110, 111–12; cost of war in, 59–62; de-Ba'athification laws, 103–4; as focus of U.S. strategy, 23; governance and economic issues in, 96, 102–5, 106–9, 111; hard-power approach to, 235–36; insurgency in, 204–5, 206;

about in, 82–84, 274–75n2; terrorism financing from, 47; U.S. support for governments in, 254–55n7

United Nations (UN): Afghanistan activities and, 4; blacklists from, 46; casualties statistics from Afghanistan, 184; drone strategy, response to, 168–69; Iran, sanctions against, 115, 116, 125–32, 172–73; Iraq invasion and, 4, 40; opinions about, 85; Powell's presentation to, 40; sanctions, enforcement of, 46; terrorism financing, resolutions on, 44–45, 46, 263n51

United States (U.S.): allies of, 9, 254n2; anti-American attitudes, 41, 48–49, 70, 86–87, 93, 95, 170–71; appeal to U.S. public by bin Laden, 18; attempted terrorist attacks in, 2, 68; cohesiveness and viability as political entity, 10–11; defeat of Al Qaeda, U.S. policy for, 1, 5, 31, 231; drone missile strategy, 56–57, 63, 150, 155, 166–71, 172, 242–43; economy of, 18, 58–62, 63–64, 226, 256n22, 269n114; energy needs of, 18–20; financing terrorism, policy on, 43–47, 272n33; foreign policy, public pressure to change, 22; India, relationship with, 238–39; intelligence sharing with Pakistan, 165–66; Iran, relationship with, 133–34, 234; Islam, war against, 91–92; Israel, support for, 41, 88–89, 228; long-term strategy of, 7; military threat to, 225; Muslim public perceptions of, 84–90; 9/11 attacks, responsibility for, 92–93; Pakistan, influence in, 173; Pakistan, policy toward, 35–40, 56–57, 140–43, 162–71, 174–75, 259n8; Pakistan, relationship with, 237–39; path to victory, 23–24, 257n30; political and economic values, Muslims' opinions about, 85–90, 91, 92, 94–95; political values, foreign policy, and strategic decision-making, 5, 7, 27–28, 227, 229–31; preemptive focus of foreign policy, 4; public opinions in, 220; radicalization of American citizens, 70; Russia, policy toward, 36–37; Saudi-funded schools and mosques in, 74; structure and political traditions of, 9–10, 11; supply lines through Pakistan, 150–51,

163, 190; supply lines through Russia, 190; support for following 9/11 attacks, 2–3; terrorism, response to, 70; as terrorism cause, 17; terrorism policy, criticism of, 28; as terrorist target, 7, 33–34, 50, 70, 168, 258n3; threat to from Al Qaeda, 7, 9, 32, 225–27, 252; Times Square bombing attempt, 68, 147, 149, 150, 164, 168; world standing of, 5, 30, 41, 86–90, 226. *See also* 9/11 attacks

U.S.-Al Qaeda struggle: blame for, 17; defensive political objectives, 17; duration of conflict, 24–25; economic implications of, 58–62, 63–64, 269n114; failures and successes of, 62–64; force and coercion, application of, 7; gains in, securing, 50–62; hard power, application of, 7, 9, 24–26, 27, 29, 32, 34, 62–64, 224, 225, 227, 232–49, 250–51; long-term strategy for, 7, 20, 49, 226, 250; martial conflict of, 3; mujahideen-style victory in, 49; outcome of, 30; participants in, 9–15, 254n2, 254–55n7; path to peace, 18; path to victory, 20–24, 30, 32, 257n30; political conflict of, 2, 3, 6, 7, 9, 27–28, 30, 81, 82, 90–94; political efforts of U.S., 26–27, 29–30; soft power, role of in, 7, 32, 34, 63, 227–31, 251; strengths and weaknesses of strategies, 24–29, 257nn32–33, 257n35; tactical advantage of Al Qaeda, 25–26, 28–29, 257n33, 257n35; U.S. disadvantages in, 80–81; U.S. interests in, 18–20; U.S. policy and, 2, 7, 29–30; U.S. withdrawal from Arabian Peninsula and, 18; violent conflict in, 90

USA PATRIOT (Uniting and Strengthening America by Providing Appropriate Tools Required to Intercept and Obstruct Terrorism) Act, 44

Wahhabism, 74–75

war: cost of, 59–62; jihad compared to, 13; terrorism compared to, 21; U.S. fight against terrorism as though fighting war, 30

Waziristan Accord, 35–36, 67, 137

weapons of mass destruction (WMD), 4, 21, 40, 122–23, 232, 233, 235, 256n26

## About the Author

Kevin McGrath is a senior analyst with the MASY Group, a global intelligence and risk management firm in Washington, D.C. He holds a Ph.D. from the University of Maryland.